Christianity as a World Religion

ALSO AVAILABLE FROM BLOOMSBURY

The Study of Religion, George D. Chrissides and Ron Geaves
The Daoist Tradition, Louis Komjathy
The Bloomsbury Reader on Islam in the West, Edward Curtis

Christianity as a World Religion

An Introduction

Second Edition

Sebastian Kim and Kirsteen Kim

Bloomsbury Academic
An imprint of Bloomsbury Publishing Plc

B L O O M S B U R Y
LONDON • OXFORD • NEW YORK • NEW DELHI • SYDNEY

Bloomsbury Academic
An imprint of Bloomsbury Publishing Plc

50 Bedford Square
London
WC1B 3DP
UK

1385 Broadway
New York
NY 10018
USA

www.bloomsbury.com

Bloomsbury is a registered trade mark of Bloomsbury Publishing Plc

First edition published in 2008

This second edition published in 2016
Reprinted 2017 (twice)

British Library Cataloguing-in-Publication Data
A catalogue record for this book is available from the British Library.

ISBN: HB: 978-1-4725-6935-6
PB: 978-1-4725-6934-9
ePub: 978-1-4725-6937-0
ePDF: 978-1-4725-6936-3

Library of Congress Cataloging-in-Publication Data
A catalog record for this book is available from the Library of Congress.

Cover design by Dani Leigh
Cover image © Kazuyoshi Nomachi/Corbis

Typeset by Newgen Knowledge Works (P) Ltd., Chennai, India
Printed and bound in Great Britain

Contents

Preface to the Second Edition

When *Christianity as a World Religion* was first published in 2008 it was one of the first one-volume introductions to the contemporary phenomenon of world Christianity. Since then there has been a great growth of interest in world Christianity which has resulted in deeper reflection and many new publications. In preparation for this new edition, we not only had the benefit of reviews of the first edition but also the constructive suggestions of many colleagues in different parts of the world who had kindly read and commented on the earlier text. Using these new resources and helpful advice, we have been able not only to thoroughly update the text but also to deepen the conceptual understanding of world Christianity and analysis of its diverse manifestations. This new edition also has an increased word count and contains maps and pictures to aid understanding.

With regard to structure, we have reorganized the order of the continents to emphasize the spread of Christianity into Asia and Africa as well as Europe in the first millennium. In addition we have been able to separate out Australia, New Zealand and the Pacific Islands into a new chapter. The gradual de-centring of Europe and the West in world Christianity thus becomes clearer as does the role of local agents in the growth of Christianity worldwide. Within the chapters we have also done some reorganization to draw out more fully key themes in world Christianity such as migration, new religious movements, global Catholicism, plural societies, political engagement and persecution of Christian communities. We have also increased the number of subheadings for easier navigation. Each chapter has a summary, and we have retained the study questions and recommended readings which were a feature of the first edition.

The concluding chapter has been developed to include reflections on the discipline of world Christianity itself. In it we emphasize two important points: first, the plurality of Christianity in each continent – hence the use of 'Christianities' in the heading of each continental chapter; and second, the interconnectedness of the faith across geopolitical regions which has only been increased by recent developments in communications technology and by migration movements. Furthermore, we have used the final chapter as an opportunity to revisit the four perspectives that guided our study of Christianity in different regions. From this we discover that its history is polycentric, its theology cannot be unified, its inter-religious relations are contingent on many local factors, and its socio-political engagement is highly contextual. We point out that these findings have significant implications for Christianity's future and also serious consequences for the way it is taught and studied.

Acknowledgements

The authors wish to acknowledge the people in the following institutions and organizations around the world through whom they have gained insight into Christianity as a world religion:

- All Nations Christian College, UK
- Cambridge Centre for Christianity Worldwide (formerly the Henry Martyn Centre), UK
- Commission for World Mission and Evangelism, World Council of Churches
- Cross-Cultural Missionary Training Institute, South Korea
- Edinburgh 2010 project and the Regnum Edinburgh Centenary Series
- Fuller Theological Seminary, USA
- Global Network for Public Theology
- International Association for Mission Studies
- International Munich-Freising Conference
- Lausanne Theology Working Group
- Leeds Trinity University, Department of Humanities, UK
- Presbyterian University and Theological Seminary, South Korea
- Union Biblical Seminary, India
- United College of the Ascension, Selly Oak, Birmingham, UK
- University of Birmingham, Department of Theology and Religion, UK
- University of Cambridge, Faculty of Divinity, UK
- Yale–Edinburgh Group on the History of the Missionary Movement and World Christianity
- York St John University, Faculty of Education and Theology, UK

For this second edition, we wish to acknowledge the help of the following people who read different parts of the book and offered constructive feedback: Victor Aquilan, Kwabena Asamoah-Gyadu, Richard Baawobr, Rosemary Dewerse, Martha Frederiks, David Hilliard, John Hitchen, Michael Jagessar, Daniel Jeyaraj, Todd Johnson, Jonas Jørgensen, Valentin Kozhuharov, Nelus Niemandt, Tim Noble, Anthony O'Mahony, Lalsangkima Pachuau, Ken Parry, G. Patrick, Peter Phan,

Marie-Hélène Robert, Cathy Ross, John Roxborogh, Fritz Strenger, Yanyan Sun, Agustinus Sutiono, Adriaan van Klinken and Gina Zurlo. Nevertheless, responsibility for the content lies with us.

We also wish to thank Lalle Pursglove, Lucy Carroll and Anna MacDiarmid of Bloomsbury for their initiative and professionalism.

Illustrations

Maps

1

Introduction

Chapter Outline

The term 'world religion' was used in the late nineteenth century to express the confidence of European Christians then that Christianity was the universal religion, unlike other religions of the world, which were local and provisional. Today the sense is more from the language of plurality and diversity: that Christianity is one of a group of transregional religions, all of which can be called 'world religions'. Christianity is regarded as a world religion in that it is deemed by politicians or academics to be worthy of equal respect in the public sphere, along with other world religions such as Islam, Hinduism, Buddhism and Judaism. According to Tomoko Masuzawa (2005), both usages reveal their origins in Western classification of 'the rest'. Moreover, the classification privileges systems of belief that have a literature and recorded history. Not only 'world religion' but even 'religion' is a contested category. Its use during the colonial period to define and categorize 'Hinduism' and 'Buddhism' reflects Christian theological assumptions and colonial agendas (King 1999). Similarly, this ideological designation of Christianity does not reveal much, if anything, about how or where Christianity is expressed on the ground, which is the main interest of this book. In describing Christianity as a world religion, we do not mean either to privilege Christianity above other religions, or necessarily to classify or ally it with other entities called 'religion'. We wish rather to discuss many meaningful senses, other than the ideological, in which Christianity may be described as a

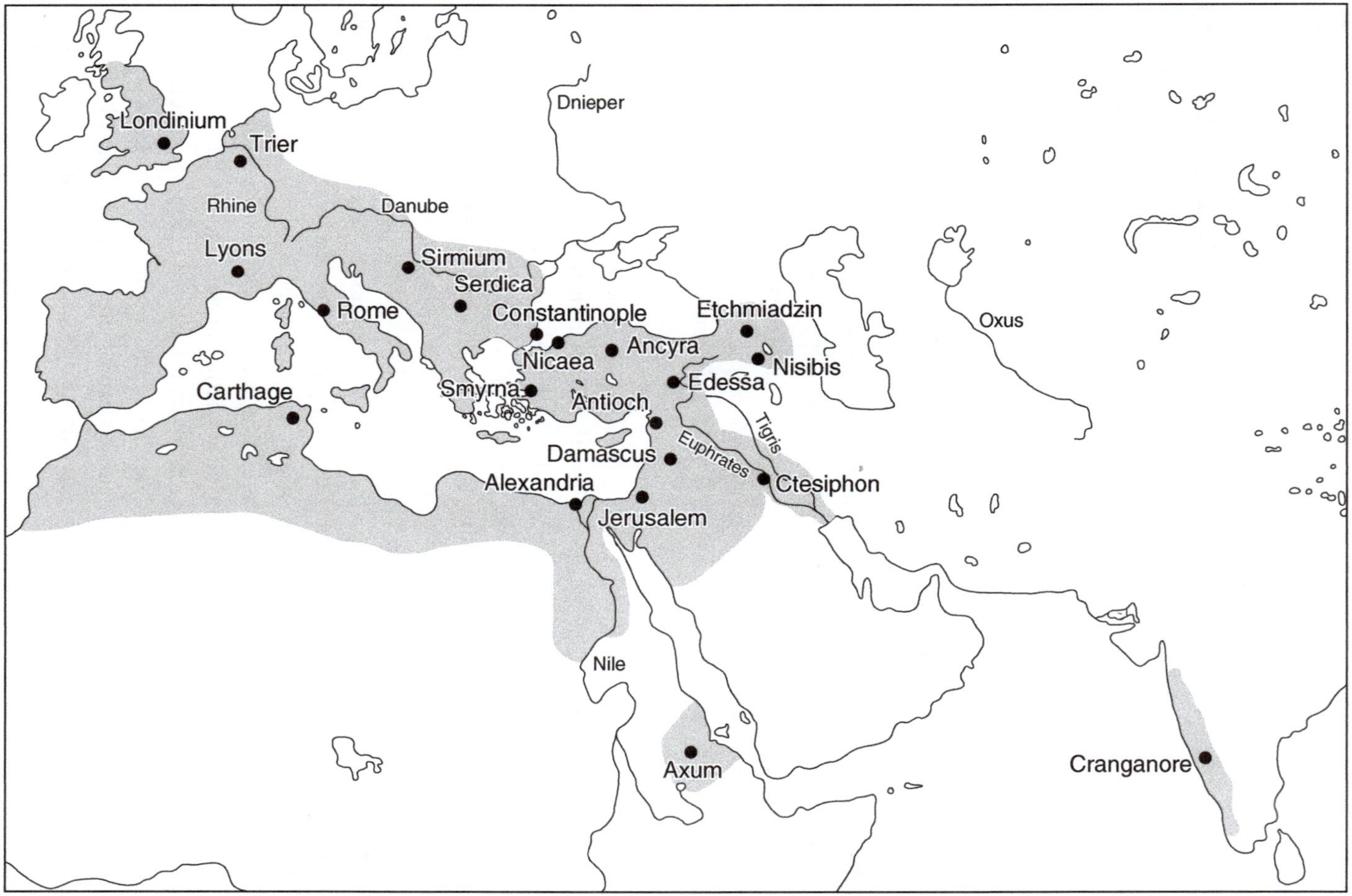
Londinium
Trier
Rhine
Danube
Dnieper
Lyons
Sirmium
Serdica
Rome
Constantinople
Etchmiadzin
Oxus
Ancyra
Nicaea
Nisibis
Edessa
Smyrna
Antioch
Carthage
Tigris
Euphrates
Damascus
Ctesiphon
Alexandria
Jerusalem
Nile
Axum
Cranganore

world religion. These have more to do with the nature of Christianity and its different expressions around the world.

In our view, there are six main ways in which Christianity may be described as a 'world religion': topographically, Christianity is spread across the globe and is not just the religion of one region; theologically, Christianity claims to be universally applicable and locally inclusive; geographically, Christianity has always been widespread and practised locally in different communities across the world; socio-politically, the worldwide presence of Christianity today is not primarily the result of attempts by powerful churches to replicate themselves worldwide but the result of indigenous response and grassroots movements; historically, Christianity does not have one single strand of development, one centre, or a linear history but is diffuse, locally divergent and adapted to different contexts; and structurally, Christianity is transnational, and Christians around the world are connected to one another through many different organizations and networks. In this introductory chapter we will discuss each of these descriptions in dialogue with current literature. Most of this literature is on 'world Christianity', which we consider to be a shorthand for 'Christianity as a world religion'.

As we have said, Christianity justifies its description as a world religion because of its inherently missionary nature and universal claims and also because – both historically and in the present – it is spread worldwide and globally interconnected while being at the same time locally rooted in many different societies and cultures. Because Christianity is – and has been since the first century – polycentric, we cannot tell an overarching historical narrative. Therefore, in order to investigate Christianity as a world religion, we will take a regional approach. In the following six chapters we will look at Christianity in each of the modern continents: Asia, Africa, Europe, Latin America and the Caribbean, North America and Oceania. By entitling the chapters 'European Christianities', 'African Christianities' and so on, we suggest first that Christianity is not merely present within each continent (Christianity in Europe, Christianity in Africa, etc.) but that the religion is manifested in local communities and rooted in cultures there. Christianity is as African as it is European, as Asian as it is North American and so on. Although inevitably much more information is available about those areas of the world where there are large Christian communities, we try to include regions where Christians are few and the experience of Christians who are minorities. Second, by using the plural 'Christianities', we signal that the faith is not defined by territory. Although there are common geopolitical factors that influence the development of Christianity in different regions, there are a variety of expressions of Christian faith in each continent as a result of both historical and ecclesial factors (Phan 2011:1–6).

In this book, 'world Christianity' is not used like 'world music'; that is, to refer only to 'non-Western Christianity'. We include Europe and North America alongside Asia, Africa, Latin America and Oceania for two main reasons: first, on the basis that Christianity in the contemporary West is integral to an interconnected phenomenon of global flows with multiple centres and diverse manifestations. Second, studying European and Western Christianities among the others puts them in world perspective. It is sobering for Europeans and North Americans to realize that they are a minority among the world's Christians and that the most vibrant recent Christian movements have emerged from Africa, Asia, Latin America and Oceania. We have arranged the chapters in the order that Christianity arrived: Asia, Africa, Europe, Latin America and the Caribbean, North America and Oceania. The downside of this is that readers may need to go to the index in order find further information about contemporary denominations and movements in their continents of origin.

Our examination of Christianity in each continent will include four overlapping perspectives that run through each chapter: first, although our focus is on contemporary belief and practice, we set the local Christianities in the historical perspective of their origins and reception. Second, we look at the distinctive forms of worship, church and theologies emerging from particular cultures. Third, we consider the interaction of churches with the other religions in each part of the world. And fourth, we analyse the interaction of the Christian communities with the wider society, its politics and economics. In considering the origin and nature of its local presence and relations and its self-understanding and expression, we will highlight key characteristics of Christianity in particular regions, discuss issues by incorporating contemporary scholarship, and signpost for readers resources and avenues for further research.

Topography: Mapping Christianity

One way of studying 'world Christianity' is by analysis of the statistics of church membership and growth, mapping the territory over which it is spread and analyzing the extent of its presence in different cultures or people groups. David B. Barrett (1982; 2001) pioneered ecumenical work in the field of statistical analysis of Christianity in his *World Christian Encyclopedia*. His work was taken up by Todd M. Johnson at Gordon-Conwell Theological Seminary near Boston who launched the *World Christian Database*. The methodologies for data collection are explained and sources include census and survey results as well as estimates from religious communities and in-country informants. The only question that remains is whether scholars of religion tend to inflate figures to emphasize the importance of the study of religion (Grim et al. 2014:x). The *Atlas of Global Christianity* (Johnson and Ross 2009), which draws on the *Database*, is the source for the statistics in this volume, unless otherwise stated.

Statistics

The label 'Christian' is difficult to define and attach, and therefore numbers of Christians will depend on the criteria used. However, it is estimated that about one-third of the world's population is Christian. This makes Christianity the largest of what are considered world religions. This proportion is roughly what it was a century ago, and it is predicted to remain the same for the foreseeable future. In 2013, Europe, Africa and Latin America (including the Caribbean) had roughly a quarter each of the world's Christians; 15 per cent were in Asia, 12 per cent in North America and 1 per cent in Oceania. These figures represent Christian majorities in Europe, the Americas and Oceania. In Africa roughly half the population is Christian. However, in Asia, which has roughly two-thirds of the world's population, Christians are less than 10 per cent. The statistics by continent disguise a more complex picture at national and local level. In the Americas, Christians are relatively evenly distributed throughout, but the Christian map of Africa is strikingly weighted to the sub-Saharan section of the continent. In Asia, the Christian map is patchy. Armenia, Georgia, Cyprus and the Philippines are predominantly Christian. South Korea has a Christian minority of about a third. However, absolute figures give a different perspective. For example, the Republic of Singapore has about 16 per cent Christians, about 740,000 in all; but the 12 per cent of its huge neighbour Indonesia who call themselves Christian number 29 million people. Although estimated at only 5 per cent and 9 per cent of their populations, respectively, the number of Christians in India is put at 58 million and in China at 115 million. As a result of migration, many Christians of European descent are geographically removed from Europe and found instead in North America, Australia, New Zealand and South Africa. However, the Christian populations of all these countries – and of Europe – are undergoing a 'darkening' (Tiénu 2006:40), as Christianity is increasing among indigenous communities and is also the faith of growing communities of more recent migrants.

The *World Christian Database* categorizes Christians into six groups: Anglican, Independent, Marginal, Orthodox, Protestant and Roman Catholic. We follow the categories of Catholic and Orthodox, recognizing overlaps between them and diversity within each. Because we are more concerned with broad historic movements and a typology of worship (see later), we prefer two further categories of Evangelicalism and Pentecostal–charismatic or Renewal Christianity, which are recognized in the *Atlas of Global Christianity*. Since the Anglican and Marginal categories together amount to only 5 per cent of Christians, we do not always count them separately. While acknowledging the attempt of Anglicanism to include both Reformed and Catholic wings, we nevertheless include Anglicans under the category of Protestant, unless otherwise stated. So Protestantism encompasses all denominations arising historically from within the Protestant Reformation in Europe and some other later groups that attempted to reform them, such as Methodists – although many of the latter overlap with the category of Evangelical below. 'Marginal' refers to groups which are not recognized as Christian by the Catholic or Protestant traditions to which they claim to belong. This is not only because they deviate from core Christian teaching about the Trinity and the divine–human nature of Christ but also because, in most cases, they profess to have additional divine revelation, or privileged access to it. We name marginal groups where relevant, but we do not specify marginal as a category. Evangelical and Pentecostal Christianity are trans-continental movements. These may overlap with each other, and we will discuss each in more detail later. These umbrella terms cut across the other categories and mostly include the category of Independent. Independent churches, according the *Atlas*, are so named because they claim independence from the historic denominations of Europe. The emphasis is on those that have arisen outside the West as a protest against colonialism or neocolonialism but we notice that free churches in the North are also included. By definition, 'Independent' churches are not possible to discuss as a unified category but many have been included among broader definitions of Pentecostal–charismatic (by, e.g., Anderson 2004) or have Evangelical traits. Evangelicals may be Independents or belong to Protestant denominations. Pentecostal–charismatic Christians may be members of (independent) Pentecostal churches or members of any of the charismatic movements within Protestant, Catholic or Orthodox churches.

It is important to realize that Catholics make up half of all Christians and therefore, by this measure, study of the Catholic Church should be central to understanding Christianity as a world religion. Protestants (including Anglicans) are about 22 per cent and Orthodox about 12 per cent. Evangelicals represent between 11 and 31 per cent of the world's Christians depending on how they are defined. Pentecostal–charismatic or Renewalist Christians are estimated to be 26 per cent of all Christians.

What counts as membership of any of these groupings is another difficult question. It may mean, at one end of the spectrum, fulfilling the requirements of baptism and confirmation in the largest of all transnational organizations, the Roman Catholic Church. Or, at the other end, it may mean occasional participation in a local congregation. Furthermore, the relation between the Christian label and Christian belief and practice is also complex. Although they may try by using multiple sources and by measuring levels of religious freedom, statisticians cannot readily distinguish self-designation and assignation to a Christian group. The adjective 'Christian' may be used in many different senses to refer to a kind of morality based on the Sermon on the Mount, certain cultural traits, membership of a particular community, belief in certain doctrines or participation in certain ritual activities (cf. Davie 1994). 'Christian' may or may not indicate regular Christian practice. In some European countries, such as Denmark and Norway, where citizens automatically belong to the national church unless they opt out, levels of baptism and confirmation of children are also high, but regular church attendance may be as low as 3 per cent. In many places in Africa and Asia, being a Christian implies regular attendance at worship and church events, and also a high level of giving – many churches expect a tithe (10 per cent) of income. In some countries, especially under

Islamist, communist and other totalitarian regimes, being known as a Christian carries a high social cost and faith may be in secret or underground and therefore difficult to measure. Where there is a secular constitution and religious freedom, the decision to become or remain a Christian may be a private matter, for example, in North America and South Korea. But elsewhere – in India, for example – religious belonging may be inherited as a marker of ethnic or caste identity and a matter of status in law.

Demographic changes

Despite its limitations, statistical and topographical analysis has helped to create the discipline of 'world Christianity'. Some of its most significant insights come from consideration of demographic changes in Christian populations. In the 1970s and 1980s, Scottish mission historian Andrew Walls (2002a) drew attention to fact that Christianity's recent recession in Europe and its growth in Africa, Latin America, Asia and Oceania is only the most recent example of the way the faith grows by 'serial expansion'. Egypt and Syria were once almost 'axiomatically Christian', and Arabia once had Jewish tribes and Christian towns, while barbarian Europe was synonymous with all that was anti-Christian (29). Until 923, estimates suggest, most Christians lived where the majority of the world's people lived – in Asia and Africa. But by 1500 about 90 per cent of all Christians were to be found in Europe. After this the pendulum began to swing the other way. From about the middle of the twentieth century, Christianity could no longer be described statistically as a 'European religion', and after 1981 the number of Christians in the global South once again exceeded those in the North. By 2013 it was estimated that only a quarter of Christians lived in Europe. Where once Christianity may have appeared to be a trans-Atlantic phenomenon, today the 'Pacific rim', from South Korea to New Zealand and Chile to Alaska, increasingly looks like a 'Christian Arc' (Jenkins 2002:102). The five countries with the highest percentages of Christians (between 99 and 97 per cent) were the relatively small ones of Samoa, Romania, Malta, Guatemala and Kiribati. The five nations with the largest populations of Christians were the United States, Brazil, China, Mexico and Russia (Grim et al. 2014:38). Statistical analysis also reveals the rapid acceleration in recent decades of the depletion of Christian communities in the Islamic world.

Kenneth Scott Latourette (1971[1945]:417–18), the early-twentieth-century scholar of Christianity as a world religion, interpreted the 'expansion' of Christianity in three perspectives: geographical expansion – according to the numbers of Christians and churches; the vigour of Christianity in any given era – measured by the emergence of new movements; and 'Christian-ness' or 'the effect of Christianity upon mankind as a whole'. The first two perspectives are measurable and dominate even in Latourette's own work. The last perspective is more difficult, if not impossible, to assess. However in order to understand Christianity as a world religion, it is necessary to go beyond the surface level of counting, mapping and describing practices and movements. For this reason, in this book, we will analyse contemporary Christianity in each continent not primarily in terms of demographics, but also by considering Christian history, self-understanding, the impact of its local presence and the quality of its relations with others. Counting numbers is a starting point, but it is a very rough guide to the Christian-ness of any region or community.

Theology: Christianity as essentially worldwide

Mark Juergensmeyer (2003:5) points out that (almost) all religions are found in diaspora and that religion 'has always been global, in the sense that religious communities and traditions have always maintained permeable boundaries. They have moved, shifted, and interacted with one another around the globe'. Religion is spread by the movement of people. Whether a religion stays within the diaspora community or spreads beyond it depends on the external circumstances but also – and perhaps more importantly – upon the nature of the religion itself. A key factor is whether it makes a universal appeal and/or a personal invitation. Generally speaking, Christianity is one of those religions to which outsiders can convert, and are invited to convert. Since Christianity claims theological universality and local inclusivity, it is spread by conversion and by missions or sharing the good news (evangelism or evangelization) as well as by migration and globalizing processes.

The missionary nature of Christianity was much discussed in the wake of the colonial period as the extent of the complicity of Christian missionaries with colonial oppression was revealed. However, much less remarked on was the way missions, with popular support at home, challenged and even subverted colonial agendas, defended humanitarian causes and (perhaps unintentionally) stimulated opposition to colonial rule (Porter 2004). Missionaries were, sometimes unfairly, made to carry much of the blame for the cultural aspects of imperialism to the extent that some church leaders among the colonizers and the formerly colonized repudiated mission altogether. Others engaged in rethinking the meaning of mission, and Christian relations with those outside the community in general, by looking again at the Bible, church traditions and the history of missions. The balance of the conclusions, as presented by South African mission theologian David Bosch (2011[1991]), is that Christianity is essentially missionary, but that mission in the way of Jesus Christ is not in power but in weakness (2 Cor. 13:4). It is primarily the multifaceted witness to the nature of God, as revealed in Jesus Christ, which is an integral part of Christian living and inherent in the nature of the church. 'Mission' (derived from the Latin '*mitto*', 'I send') is first and foremost the action of God in sending Jesus Christ into the world in love for its salvation (John 3:16). Jesus's disciples understand themselves to be sent into the world in the same way (John 20:21–23). According to the gospels of Matthew and Mark, the going is in obedience to the command of Christ, sometimes referred to as 'the Great Commission', to make disciples (Matt. 28:18–20) or preach the good news (Mark 16:15–18). In the Lukan narrative, mission is described as 'witness' under the impulse of the Holy Spirit (Luke 24:46–48; Acts 1:8). In the apostle Paul's understanding, the salvation that is proclaimed and demonstrated by the Christian community is available to all and comprehensive of the whole of life (Col. 1:19–20). It unites people of different ethnicity, social status and gender (Gal. 3:23) (see also Bevans and Schroeder 2004; Skreslet 2012).

The instinct of Christians to share their faith was encouraged by some of the conditions in which Christianity arose (Schnelle 2005:138–70) and formalized by certain decisions made by the church. First, at the Jerusalem Council (Acts 15) in about 48 AD, it was resolved that Gentiles (or Greeks) were equally members of the church with the original Jewish members on the basis that they had also received the Holy Spirit. In future only the moral demands of the law of Moses, summed up by Jesus Christ as love of God and neighbour, not the external requirements of circumcision and the food laws, were considered binding (Gonzales 2001). The new community of both Jews and Gentiles called 'Christians' (Acts 11:26) was characterized by a willingness to 'contextualize' or re-express its faith and life in different situations and societies (Dunn 2006:333; cf. 1 Cor. 9:22). The decision of the Council was also an endorsement of the mission of the apostle Paul to the Gentiles. But since fewer Jews responded to the gospel, the church took on an increasingly Gentile nature. Second, although the first Christians worshipped at the temple in Jerusalem, which continued to have great significance for them, this was no longer possible for Christians, or Jews, after the desecration and destruction of the Temple by the Romans in 70 AD. Instead Rome, and later Constantinople, became the premier centres for Christianity. Distance from Jerusalem was no longer a limitation on the spread of the faith; its centres multiplied and became ever more far-flung. Third, the public criterion for inclusion in the Christian community became baptism in the name of God, the Father, Son and Holy Spirit. It signified (among other things) a participation in the dying and rising of Jesus Christ to a new life of obedience made possible in the Holy Spirit. Unlike the Jewish initiation rite of circumcision, baptism was a simple act, inclusive of women, who played a prominent role in the church, and inexpensive for a community which included many poor people. Although not always confirmed in practice, in these and other ways Christianity was affirmed as unlimited by ethnicity, geography or socio-economic status, and therefore had the potential to spread through all communities worldwide. World Christianity recognizes this Christian pluralism (Sanneh 2008) and internationalism, which encourages indigeneity (Robert 2008).

Geography: Christianity as globally widespread and locally rooted

Christianity has always been geographically widespread and practised locally in different communities across the world. In the second volume of his work, which we know as the Acts of the Apostles, the gospel writer Luke, presents a vision of the church spreading outwards from Jerusalem to Judaea and 'the ends of the earth' (Acts 1:8). This sense of a universal faith is balanced by Luke's emphasis on the diversity of communities which had received the gospel, even in the first century. The Pentecost narrative (Acts 2) lists the places from which the Jews gathered in Jerusalem for the festival had come. They range from Pontus in the north of Asia Minor (modern Turkey) south to Egypt; from Rome in the west to Elam, east of Arabia. Luke stresses the many different languages they spoke. In the first three centuries, Christianity moved from a Jewish setting in Palestine to a Hellenistic–Roman one, and it also took root among the 'barbarians' beyond the Roman empire in further parts of what we now know as Asia, Africa and Europe. Those who received the message shaped it to their own culture and circumstances. Evidence for the ethnic diversity of early Christianity is found in the records of the ecumenical church councils of the first five centuries (Tanner 2001). There were disputes among Christians from different local churches, for example, Antioch and Alexandria. The varied documents that make up the New Testament are attributed to Christian communities from Syria to Rome, and the fact that they were written in Greek, the lingua franca of the Roman Empire, shows that the Christian community transcended language groups. At no time in its history has Christianity been the religion of one ethnic group or practised uniformly according to identical rites and teaching.

Missionaries, known in the first centuries as 'apostles' (Greek for 'sent one' or 'messenger'), deliberately carried the message to different lands. In the New Testament the application of the word 'apostle' is sometimes to the Twelve, the disciples of Jesus, and sometimes to a wider group. The archetypal apostles are Peter and Paul, who were given authority to preach the gospel by the church. Peter led the church in Jerusalem and Palestine and was martyred in Rome. Paul undertook several journeys around the eastern Mediterranean founding churches. Most Christianized peoples around the world remember the apostle or saint who brought the good news to them, whether this was in the first centuries or more recently. In most cases the apostles travelled to where there were already Jewish or Christian communities in diaspora or to where there was a group who requested missionaries to come and instruct them, as in the case of the 'Macedonian call' (Acts 16:9). However, the Christian message was not spread only by people specially designated for the job. Traders, slaves and migrants took their faith with them and shared it as they moved (or were trafficked) around the Roman Empire and beyond. In many cases the spread of the faith was accidental in that it was sparked by the scattering of a Christian community due to persecution, as, for example, in Acts 8, 11 and 18 (Wedderburn 2004:59–78).

Luke's account gives particular attention to the missionary work of the apostle Paul, whose work he seems to have known at first hand. Paul's travels took him from Jerusalem northward into Syria and westward into Asia Minor (today's Turkey), Greece and Italy, ending in Rome, the centre of the empire. However, we also get glimpses in the New Testament of the spread of the gospel beyond the imperial borders. Within the book of Acts (8:27) we hear how Philip baptized a eunuch from the court of Candace, 'queen of the Ethiopians' and at the beginning of Matthew's (2:1) gospel, we learn that Magi, a Persian word referring to 'wise men' or astrologers, came to worship Jesus. Christianity spread not only to the west but in all directions, so that by the end of the first millennium it had become the faith of people as far south as Ethiopia, as far north as Russia, as far west as Ireland and as far east as China (Irvin and Sunquist 2001).

Sociology: World Christianity as globalization from below

The global spread of Christianity is often explained by the expansion of Europe and the rise of US power. However the relationship of Christianity to processes of globalization is not straightforward. Christianity is not inherently a European religion. Nor is the worldwide presence of Christianity today primarily the result of attempts by powerful churches to replicate themselves worldwide but the result of indigenous response and grassroots movements (Sanneh 2003). Christianity is primarily a people-movement. Although non-personal forms of communication are used in evangelism, the development of world Christianity is largely the result of personal contact, the formation of communities and migration.

Christianity is one example of how the contemporary world is globalized; both in the sense of the extension of one entity across the entire globe and also in the sense of time and space being compressed within a network (cf. Schreiter 1997:8). Christianity, like other world religions, is both an agent of globalization and a product of it. One of the unforeseen consequences of contemporary globalization may be the further spread of Christianity. Globalization is most commonly understood as a top-down homogenizing process determined, from the point of view of the right, by markets or, from the perspective of the left, by political hegemony (Vásquez and Marquardt 2003:2), and it is assumed that world Christianity is the result of Western colonial and neocolonial expansion. But although, sociologically, the spread of Christianity cannot be disconnected from matters of economics and politics, sociologist Roland

Robertson (1992) showed that cultural processes of globalization do not necessarily follow the same global flows as capital and power. There may be many globalization processes going on, arising from multiple centres and interrelating with one another, and these include some popular movements that are not in the service of the dominant global players. Pentecostalism is one example (Berger and Huntington 2002). Furthermore, any globalization, no matter where it started, has knock-on effects that inexorably alter the situation of all (Beyer 1994:9).

Drawing on studies of the Americas, Manuel Vásquez and Marie Marquardt (2003:3) recognize a 'globalization from below', which is not about 'domination and homogenization' but about 'resistance', 'heterogeneity' and 'negotiation' at the grassroots. This is much closer to the pattern for the spread of early Christianity as suggested in the New Testament. Beyer (1994) further draws attention to the fact that religion is not only a culture but also a social system. As a social system, Christianity is the church, or communions of churches, which may be structured institutionally in the public sphere or privately, and may be both locally rooted and transnational. Christianity consists of many movements, which may be elite or popular, and faith is not only a matter of word and thought but also of deed and material acts. It is spread by people, agents whose actions are dependent on events. The globalization of Christianity – as both culture and system – is a fact, and theories of globalization help to analyse the processes involved, but it is 'a complex, historically contingent cluster of processes involving multiple actors, scales, and realms of human activity' (Vásquez and Marquardt 2003:3).

A great deal of attention has been paid to the mission history of the intentional spreading of Christianity from centres of power in the West during the last five centuries. However, missionary plans and expectations have frequently been confounded. The delegates at the World Missionary Conference in Edinburgh in 1910, which drew Protestant (and Anglo-Catholic) missionaries from all over the world, presumed that Christianity was being spread by their activities (Stanley 2009:16). Many of them worked with governments to train a local elite whom they hoped would be the foundation of the new churches. The succeeding century has shown that the work of the missionaries who originally carried the message is only the catalyst for the local activity of its reception, dissemination and transformation in a new cultural and social context. This reception is often by the poor rather than the elite of those nations. In 1910, it was expected that Japan and India, which were regarded as the most civilized of the non-Western nations, would soon become majority Christian. In fact the percentage of Christians in those nations has risen little in a century. The greatest growth in East Asia has occurred in Korea, which the Japanese annexed that year as part of their imperial expansion across the Asia-Pacific region. In India, Christian growth has been mainly among the outcastes or Dalits rather than among the higher castes, and the greatest church growth of all has been in what the leaders of 1910 regarded as the 'darkest' and most heathen continent – sub-Saharan Africa (Kerr and Ross 2009). Now it is apparent that, despite the harshest communist oppression, the church in

China put down roots and is today growing rapidly. Reflecting on the postcolonial period, Dana Robert (2000) points to the 'irony' that, historians and sociologists who saw world Christianity as an arm of European imperialism failed to notice that the most rapid growth of churches in Asia, Africa and Latin America has been since colonial independence and not before. Because Christianity is more a people's movement than a political one, 'growth among the grass roots did not mirror the criticisms of the intellectual elites' (53). In this book we prefer to concentrate on 'the indigenous discovery of Christianity rather than the Christian discovery of indigenous societies' (Sanneh 2003:10). We focus on the way the faith has been received and how in different geopolitical, social and cultural contexts believers have made it their own.

Figure 1.1 'Vision of Abraham' (2012) by Jyoti Sahi, Indian artist and theologian of inculturation.

History: Christianity as translatable and contextual

Historically, because of its open invitation and universal appeal, Christianity did not remain a religion in diaspora or the faith of enthusiastic missionaries, but instead over two thousand years the Christian faith was received by many new peoples who made it their own. Christianity does not have one single strand of development, one centre or a single history, but Christian history is diffuse, complex and polycentric. The faith has had multiple centres from the time of Jesus, when the focus was divided between Jerusalem and Galilee. It later developed in different patriarchates – Rome, Constantinople, Antioch, Alexandria and Constantinople – and other cities beyond the Roman Empire such as Nisibis in Persia, Cranganore in India, Axum in Ethiopia and Xi'an in China. Christianity today is also polycentric, although theologians from Africa, Asia and Latin America complain that their colleagues in the West have yet to appreciate this (e.g. Tiénu 2006). As well as Rome, Athens and Chicago, major Christian hubs today include Lagos, Seoul, Bengaluru and São Paulo. Furthermore, Christianity has exhibited a remarkable ability to become at home in many different global settings far from its original homeland. It has changed internally as a result of encounters with different cultures so that 'the largest world religion is in fact the ultimate local religion' (Robert 2000:56).

As a result of this diversity, one of the early ecumenical Christian debates was about the canon of Scripture, or what should be included in (or rather excluded from) the Bible. For the Christian church the compilation of the Bible was a secondary activity, an 'accident' rather than the 'substance' of apostolic witness, which was to the 'living Word', Jesus Christ (H. Chadwick 2002:34). Nevertheless, with more than thirty gospels alone in circulation by the end of the second century, there were disputes about which were authoritative, and church leaders found it necessary to list those that they believed were traceable to the early apostles and whose contents were in keeping with the teaching of the contemporary church. The New Testament documents were circulated in Greek, but it was also decided to include books of the Jewish canon, according to its Greek translation (the Septuagint). Therefore the Christian Bible represents within itself two broad linguistic–cultural perspectives: Hebrew and Greek. Over the first five centuries ecumenical agreement was reached that the four gospels attributed to Matthew, Mark, Luke and John were authoritative, together with thirteen letters attributed to Paul, the Acts of the Apostles, the first letter of Peter and the first letter of John. The status of the Epistle to Hebrews, James, 2 John, 3 John, 2 Peter, Jude and Revelation continued to be debated and different sections of the church operated with slightly different canons. It is of deep significance for Christianity as a world religion that the churches accepted four parallel accounts of Jesus's life and ministry and set them side by side. These cover the same ground of

Jesus's life, death and resurrection but vary in the traditions they include, present the material differently and do not always agree on historical detail, or even sometimes on theological meaning. The gospels are attributed to different disciples and plainly represent the views of churches in different geopolitical and cultural contexts. Despite evidence within the text of attempts to reconcile conflicts between these accounts, a plurality of Christian theologies was retained within the one Bible (Dunn 2006).

On the basis of its spread across Africa, Lamin Sanneh (1989) argues that Christianity exhibits 'translatability', that is, Christians have always translated religious texts and developed vernacular expressions of the faith, including local names for God. The New Testament itself is a translated text because Jesus preached in Aramaic not Greek, and so Christianity does not have a sacred language. Sanneh regards translation, both linguistic and cultural, as a pattern in the spread of Christianity worldwide ever since Hellenistic Jews and Greek received the gospel. The whole Bible and liturgy were translated into Latin in North Africa and into Syriac by the fourth century. In the first millennium the Christian scriptures were also translated into Coptic in Egypt, Ge'ez in Ethiopia, into Armenian and Slavonic and at least portions into Chinese. Although the Roman Catholic Church maintained Latin as the language of scripture and worship as a sign of the universality of the church into the twentieth century, such resistance to translation was a precipitating factor in the Protestant Reformation of the sixteenth century.

The expectation of translation is not only about language but all dimensions of what is necessary if a religion is to be owned by people of a different culture, including spirituality, theology, inter-religious relations and forms of social engagement. When Martin Luther (1520) complained about the 'Babylonian captivity' of the church of his day, he was referring to matters of doctrine and social justice. Similarly, from the perspective of many theologians from other regions, the Western churches, even the Protestant ones, have not overcome their 'Latin captivity' (Boyd 2014), or the captivity of their doctrine to the categories of Greek thought in which it was first formulated (Samartha 1991), or the Western garb in which it was promulgated (Mbiti 1971), or the context of power and privilege in which it has been developed (Segundo 1976). When Christianity takes root in a new cultural context, it is not only the outward form of the faith which is affected but also its content that is challenged and reshaped in that setting.

Furthermore, not only is Christianity adapted to the new context, but there is a deeper-level and long-term interaction between the faith and its new cultural surroundings that results in fresh expressions of the Christian gospel (Bediako 1992) or even reinvention of the faith (Parratt 1995). In this respect, 'translation' does not fully capture what takes place. Christianity may be imported as a package and translated but the local people encounter the person of Jesus Christ for themselves and respond according to their own cultural patterns and thought forms (Koyama 1974). The analogy often used is that of a seed planted in a new soil, which takes from the soil as well as bringing something new (Coe 1976).

Figure 1.2 Patriarch Bartholomew I of Constantinople attends an Orthodox service in honour of Saints Cyril and Methodius in Mikulcice, Czech Republic, 25 May 2013. Image: iStock.

Stephen Bevans (2002) has classified the processes by which the church thought about 'inculturation' or 'contextualization' in diverse cultures. Most recognize this as a two-way process in which Christianity changes culture and context reshapes Christian faith and understanding. That this mutual interaction does indeed represent what is happening is shown on the one hand by the influence worldwide of Christian values, often mediated through Westernization, and on the other hand by the tensions within transnational and transcultural church bodies caused by resistance to Western norms by churches in other parts of the world, for example, around economic issues and questions of sexuality. In summary, Christianity is mobile because it allows for a plurality of beliefs and practices. Although change is sometimes resisted, Christianity has shown a great propensity to be 'translated' and re-expressed in different contexts.

Structure: Transnational forms of Christianity

'Religious communities are among the oldest of transnationals', and they are vigorous creators of transnational civil society (Rudolph 1997:1). Christianity is locally expressed but it is also connected together through many organizations and networks. Throughout this book we will be referring to five main steams of Christianity: Orthodox, Catholic, Protestant and the transdenominational categories of Evangelical and Pentecostal–charismatic. These may be distinguished in terms of historical origin and contemporary worship practices.

Five streams of world Christianity: historical origins

The Orthodox churches and the Roman Catholic Church each claim an unbroken historical, theological, liturgical and organizational development from the apostles: the Roman Church to Peter and the Orthodox churches to Paul (Greek or Eastern), Philip (Ethiopian), Mark (Coptic) and Thomas (Syrian). The first churches were offshoots of Jewish synagogues or group meetings in homes or sometimes in secret places for fear of the authorities. They might be loosely linked through the ministry activities of their apostle (e.g. the Pauline churches of the New Testament). Gradually larger churches with dedicated buildings emerged in cities led by bishops, supported by elders or presbyters, who were in contact with one another. By the late second century, bishops in a province might meet as a synod. Where Christianity became a public religion, the churches took on modified forms derived from imperial cults. These are reflected in the priestly forms of the liturgy, the costumes or vestments worn, the art and musical instruments used, and also in the fact that the priests became exclusively male. As the church spread across two empires – the Roman and the Persian – by the third century, dioceses emerged under one bishop who was responsible for several churches. In the fourth century, rugged monastic life flourished in the deserts of Syria and Egypt before spreading to Rome, Constantinople, Armenia, Cappadocia and across the Christian world. The patterns of monasticism presented an alternative and also a complement to the diocesan structures. In the early fourth century, the semi-independent kingdom of Armenia became the first Christian kingdom. About the same time, Christianity became an official religion of the Roman Empire under Constantine and gradually its structures, scriptures, worship, morality, buildings, theology and so on became regularized within imperial jurisdiction. Roman emperors called councils of the whole church – that is, ecumenical councils, including some bishops from beyond the empire. At the Councils of Nicaea (325) and Constantinople (381), the 'fathers' of the church formulated the doctrine of the Trinity in what is now called the Nicene Creed.

However, it became difficult for the church to hold together. The political situation made it hard for the Persian Christians and others outside the Roman Empire – today referred to as Oriental Orthodox – to receive the Christological definition of the council of Chalcedon (451). Eastern Orthodoxy is derived from churches in the eastern part of the Roman Empire which comprised the ancient patriarchates of Constantinople, Jerusalem, Antioch and Alexandria. Although the two Orthodoxies – Eastern and Oriental – are not in communion with each other, they have been in official dialogue since the 1980s. Both Roman Catholic and Orthodox churches claim apostolic succession – that is, bishops are consecrated by other bishops in an unbroken line to the first disciples. Catholics and Eastern Orthodox both affirm the Council of Chalcedon. However, the two churches drifted apart after the fall of the western Roman Empire and the rise of Islamic empires which dominated Orthodox lands. They have been formally divided since 1054. The differences between them have to do both with the exercise of primacy (or the role of the Pope) and also doctrine: Eastern Orthodox theology begins with the creed agreed at the Councils of Nicaea (325) and Constantinople (381), whereas the theology of Augustine of Hippo has been the starting point for most Catholic theology. While the Orthodox churches were mostly under the dominance of Islam, the medieval Catholic Church grew in alliance with European states and the Pope or bishop of Rome proclaimed as universal teachings that had not been ecumenically agreed.

'Protestant', in our usage, applies to all the churches that split away from the Roman Catholic Church as a result of the Reformation in Europe in the sixteenth century and some developments of those. These are fragmented into different 'denominations' or families of churches with a shared historical origin: Lutheran, Anglican, Reformed, Calvinist or Presbyterian, Methodist, Baptist and others (see Chapter 4). 'Evangelical' refers primarily to a movement, originating in trans-Atlantic Protestant revivals in the eighteenth, nineteenth and twentieth centuries (see Chapter 6). Evangelicalism is expressed in particular churches or denominations and also by movements within Protestant churches, particularly within Anglicanism. However, the term 'Evangelical' has a wide variety of other meanings. First, it may simply refer to any Christian with a special concern to convey the 'good news' (euangellion in Greek). Second, it may be a general term for Protestants, which avoids the negative connotation of 'protest'. This is the usual meaning in continental Europe. In Britain and North America and countries influenced by modernity in Africa and Asia, 'Evangelical' often has a third, more restricted meaning referring to groups, churches and organizations that are related historically and/or theologically to the Pietist and Methodist revivals of the eighteenth century and subsequent revivals or 'awakenings'. During the late-nineteenth and early-twentieth-century debates between liberals and fundamentalists, Evangelicalism came to be more doctrinally defined. In this sense it does not necessarily correspond with particular denominations – although some denominations, notably Methodists and Baptists, are more inclined to Evangelicalism than others – but it may be a badge of doctrinal orthodoxy within other denominations, such as Anglicanism. It may also be a label for independent local congregations. Sometimes the term 'Evangelical' is confused with 'fundamentalist', but the latter term is best reserved for a particular twentieth-century movement that arose within

Evangelicalism (Marty and Appleby 1992). There are some Evangelicals who reject charismatic styles of worship, but in many cases Pentecostal–charismatics adopt an Evangelical theology. So, fifth, 'Evangelical' may be a term for 'Pentecostal'. In Latin America, Evangélicos is a general name for Protestant, but most of the Christians referred to by the term are Pentecostals.

The newest and most difficult term to define is 'Pentecostal–charismatic', which is an umbrella term for many different movements with a common emphasis on the experience of the Holy Spirit. Pentecostalism is the fastest growing form of Christianity today. Its spread has been facilitated not only by its inherent missionary impulse (Anderson 2007) but also because of its strong links with migration movements (Dempster, Klaus and Petersen 1999). It may be regarded as exemplifying 'globalization from below' (Martin 2002:5–6) or even be seen as an Africanization of Christianity because of its 'black root' in African-American spirituality at Azusa Street (Hollenweger 1997). It has further been suggested that it will determine the shape of Christianity in the twenty-first century (Cox 1996). Because of various 'revivals' and 'charismatic movements', Pentecostal–charismatic-type Christianity may also be found among Christians who are otherwise Protestant, Catholic or Orthodox. In Africa the indigenous churches of the 'spirit type' and also the 'prosperity type' may be called 'Pentecostal' (see Chapter 3). The term therefore refers to any one or all of three 'branches': denominations named 'Pentecostal', charismatic renewal movements and indigenous churches in Africa, Asia and Latin America that show Pentecostal-type features. This usage is problematic (see Anderson 2004:166–83). Other churches, particularly indigenous churches in Africa but also some in Asia, are co-opted under the umbrella of 'Pentecostalism' because of phenomenological similarities alone. They do not have any historical or contemporary affiliation with Pentecostal denominations. It is a case of 'categories originating from the North being used to explain and somehow take credit for what is going on in the South' (Robert 2000:57). Therefore we shall qualify the term and distinguish the three branches where possible.

Five streams of world Christianity: Patterns of worship

Another way of distinguishing the five transcontinental forms of Christian church is by observable differences in patterns of worship between them today. These fall into three categories (cf. White 2001). In the Catholic Church and Orthodox churches, priority is given to the sacraments or mysteries. For Catholics there are seven such 'visible signs of divine power manifested to humanity': baptism, confirmation, the Eucharist, penance or reconciliation, anointing the sick, matrimony and holy orders (Cunningham 2009:101). The Orthodox churches are more flexible about what is included in what they prefer to call the 'mysteries', 'the continuing signs that Pentecost is still occurring within the heart of Christ's Church' (McGuckin 2008:278). For both, the central act of worship is the Eucharist or thanksgiving: the ritual re-enactment by the priest and people of the last supper of Jesus with his disciples before his sacrificial death and resurrection to life. Salvation is imparted through the reverent partaking of bread and wine consecrated by the Holy Spirit. The Eucharist restores communion with God and fellow worshippers and furthers cosmic reconciliation. Often referred to by Catholics as the 'mass', as long as there is a priest, the Eucharist is celebrated daily and in the context of a liturgy which also includes the preaching of the Word. Although there may be services of worship without the Eucharist, the obligation of believers is to partake whenever possible of the 'Real Presence' of Christ in the elements of bread and wine. The Orthodox Eucharistic liturgy conveys the same sense of bodily encounter with the Divine and extends this pattern to the whole of life. The world is offered up to God and, through Christ and the power of his resurrection, renewed and transformed. For both Catholic and Orthodox, the Eucharist is performed within a specially constructed sacred space and participation in it involves not only intellect but all the senses: smell, taste, touch, sound and sight. Both traditions are distinguished from the other streams of Christianity by the reverence shown to visual symbols in worship: icons or sacred pictures in Orthodox churches and statues in Catholic ones. Moreover, both single out certain individuals after death for holy status as saints, and both give special veneration to the Virgin Mary. Roman Catholic liturgy underwent significant development in Europe after the rise of Protestantism and most recently through the Second Vatican Council (1962–65). As a result of dialogue with Orthodox tradition, some aspects of its public worship were brought closer to Orthodox patterns (e.g. in the inclusion of the *epiclesis* or invocation of the Holy Spirit) but in other ways, the Council created further differences (e.g. in the stress on community which reduces the barriers between priest and people in worship) (Bradshaw 2009).

The vast majority of Protestant churches also celebrate the Eucharist regularly, although they may refer to it as 'Holy Communion' or (especially in Evangelical churches) 'the Lord's Supper'. Although the Eucharist is a sign of unity in Christ, the Roman Catholic and Orthodox churches are not in communion with one another today (in the sense of being able to celebrate the Eucharist together and recognizing one another's rites), or with Protestant churches, and some of the latter do not 'communicate' either. This is source of distress for many Christians since the church is the body of Christ, and it is unthinkable that Christ can be divided (1 Cor. 1:13). Overcoming division is a key goal of the ecumenical movement, or movement for Christian unity. However, in Protestantism equal or greater importance is given to the 'preaching of the Word', usually by means of a sermon. The relative significance is indicated in the church architecture. Where Catholic and Orthodox buildings have a consecrated 'altar' – preferably of stone, Protestants may prefer a 'communion table' and give relatively more prominence to the pulpit (ambo or lectern). Some Protestant churches maintain the traditional pattern of daily Eucharist, but most celebrate it less frequently – some only twice a year, or not at all in the case of the Quakers. Where Orthodox and Catholic clergy remain male, it is increasingly common in the West for Protestant clergy to be female. The Eucharist carries a range of meanings across the Protestant denominations from Anglicans' continued acceptance of Catholic doctrine of the 'real presence' of Christ in the consecrated elements of bread and wine to Lutherans' 'sacramental union', Calvin's 'pneumatic presence' and Zwingli's teaching that they are merely a memorial of Christ's work. This spectrum of meanings roughly corresponds to the level of sacredness attributed to the elements of bread and wine and to the restrictions on who may preside at the table. Following the Reformers, Protestants generally accept only two sacraments or, in some denominations, 'ordinances': communion and baptism. Although the Protestant Reformation proclaimed *sola scriptura*, or Scripture alone, the historic Protestant churches today generally strive for a balance between attention to 'Word' and 'Sacrament' in worship.

Following the worship taxonomy, we roughly define Evangelical churches as Protestant churches in which the sermon, rather than Holy Communion, is the climax of worship. This is generally accompanied by a more conservative faith. In churches affected by the Pentecostal–charismatic movement, the emphasis is not on partaking of the Eucharist, or even hearing the Word, but on experiencing the Holy Spirit. When they meet, Pentecostal worshippers anticipate 'the immediate presence of God' by the power of the Spirit. Although there is usually a leader at the service, his (or possibly her) role is to excite the congregation and call for a response. Because it is 'immediate', every member of the congregation is open to receiving 'gifts of the Spirit' (charismata) to contribute to the worship service (Anderson 2004:9). And because the presence and work of the Spirit cannot be controlled, the events of the service are (or appear to be) spontaneous and the constituent parts of the worship (the hymns, prayers, sermon) are not written down but are performed according to a more flexible oral tradition. Bodily movements of various forms – such as swaying, dancing and clapping – may be expected, prayer may be very loud and simultaneous and ecstatic behaviour occurs in many cases. Manifestations of the Spirit in the congregation, such as dreams and visions, are taken seriously. Tangible results of prayer are expected in personal life, including bodily healing and prosperity, as the result of prayer (Hollenweger 1997:18–19). In parts of the world where there is a strong awareness of a world of spirits, exorcism and prayer for victory over evil spirits may be an important part of the worship. Altogether, Pentecostalism is 'a potent mixture of the premodern and the postmodern, of the preliterate and the postliterate, of the fiesta and the encounter group' (Cox 1996:110). Such striking differences, especially from the worship practices of the churches that developed in Europe, have caused tensions and splits with the older traditions.

Study questions and further readings

- In what senses is Christianity a world religion?
- How does the changing demography of the Christian population worldwide influence the dynamics of world Christianity?
- How does the spread of Christianity relate to other globalizing processes?
- In understanding world Christianity, what is contextualization and why is it important?
- Summarize the distinguishing features of Catholic, Orthodox and Protestant churches and Evangelical and Pentecostal–charismatic Christianities, respectively.

Anderson, A. H. (2004), *An Introduction to Pentecostalism*. Cambridge: Cambridge University.

Bevans, S. B. and R. P. Schroeder (2004), *Constants in Context*. Maryknoll, NY: Orbis.

Irvin, D. T. and S. W. Sunquist (2001), *History of the World Christian Movement*. Vol. I. Maryknoll, NY: Orbis.

Robert, D. L. (2009), *Christian Mission*. Chichester: Wiley-Blackwell.

Walls, A. F. (2002), *The Cross-Cultural Process in Christian History*. Maryknoll, NY: Orbis.

2

Asian Christianities

Chapter Outline

The name 'Asia' refers to nearly one-third of the world's land from Suez and the Ural Mountains in the west to the Pacific in the east. The adjective 'Asian' defines nearly two-thirds of the world's people from Turkish to Japanese, from Siberian to Indonesian. 'Asian' does not refer to a shared cultural or historical identity. The diversity of the continent is illustrated by the fact that all the 'world religions' originated in Asia, including Christianity. The peoples of Asia have interacted with one another for centuries, and many aspects of their religions have been shared across boundaries. On the ground there is 'multiple religious belonging' of various kinds, or rather Asians have 'complex religio-cultural identities' (Laksana 2014). But from an aerial point of view, the major religions are spread like a patchwork across Asia. Christianity is found around the eastern and southern edges of the Asian continent: in Northeast Asia, Southeast Asia and the tip of South Asia. There is a 'Muslim band' across Asia from Turkey through the Levant and the Gulf to Pakistan and Bangladesh, then across the Bay of Bengal to southern Thailand, Malaysia, Indonesia and the southwestern part of the Philippines. It stretches northwards also into Central Asia and Northwest China. Hinduism predominates in India and Nepal. Buddhism is scattered across Sri Lanka and Southeast Asia in its Theravada form and in Japan and other parts of East Asia as Mahayana. Confucianism and Taoism are influential across East Asian cultures and Zoroastrianism similarly in West Asia but their organized expression is small. The proportion of Christians, less than 10 per cent, is

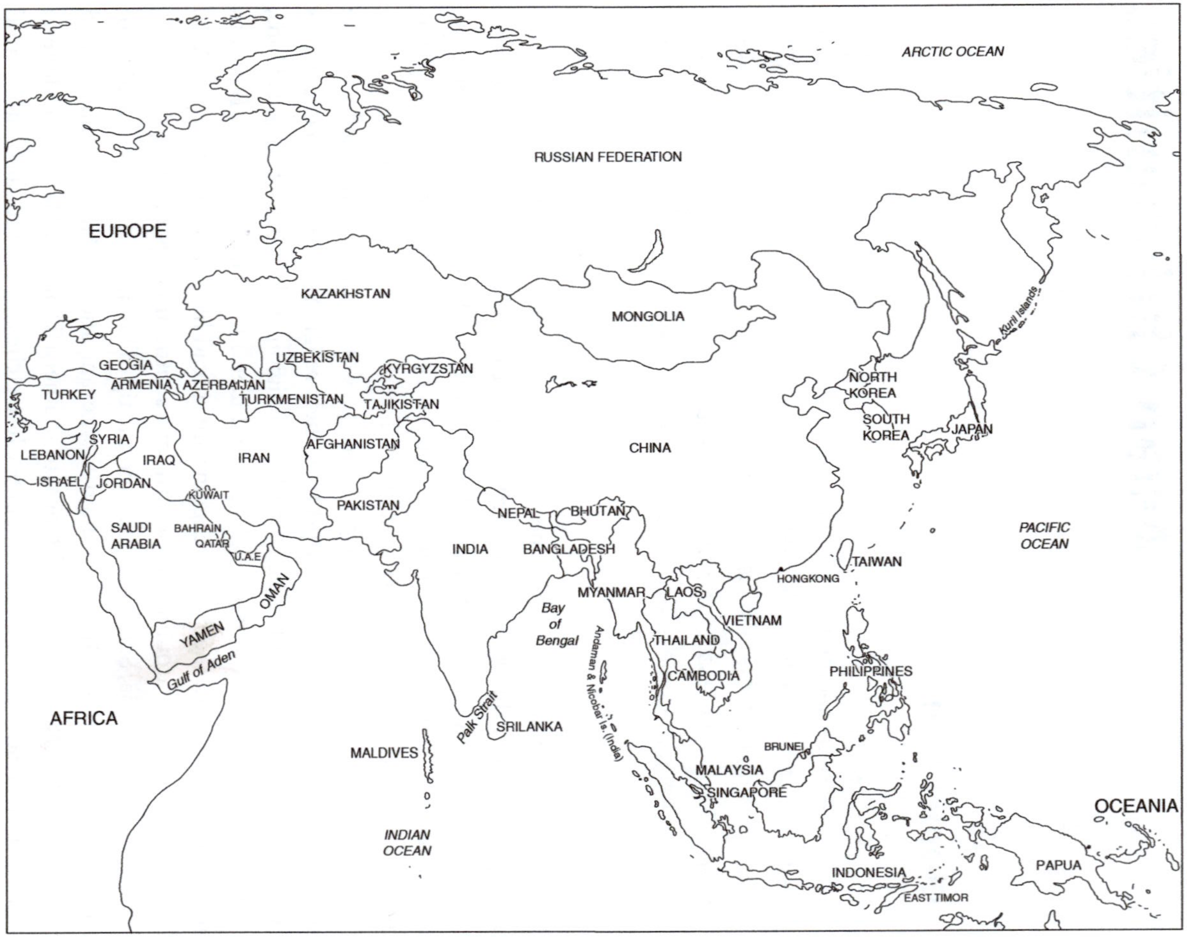
ARCTIC OCEAN
RUSSIAN FEDERATION
EUROPE
KAZAKHSTAN
MONGOLIA
Kuril Islands
GEOGIA
ARMENIA
AZERBAIJAN
UZBEKISTAN
KYRGYZSTAN
TURKEY
TURKMENISTAN
TAJIKISTAN
NORTH KOREA
SOUTH KOREA
JAPAN
SYRIA
LEBANON
IRAQ
IRAN
AFGHANISTAN
CHINA
ISRAEL
JORDAN
KUWAIT
PAKISTAN
NEPAL
BHUTAN
SAUDI ARABIA
BAHRAIN
QATAR
U.A.E
INDIA
BANGLADESH
PACIFIC OCEAN
TAIWAN
HONGKONG
OMAN
MYANMAR
LAOS
VIETNAM
Bay of Bengal
YAMEN
THAILAND
Andaman & Nicobar Is. (India)
CAMBODIA
PHILIPPINES
Gulf of Aden
AFRICA
Palk Strait
SRILANKA
MALDIVES
BRUNEI
MALAYSIA
SINGAPORE
OCEANIA
INDIAN OCEAN
PAPUA
INDONESIA
EAST TIMOR

much lower than on any other continent. Nevertheless, in absolute numbers there are estimated to be more Christians in Asia than in North America, although relatively small changes in calculation of the proportion of Christians in China and India – as the world's most populous nations – affect the figures considerably. The point is that most Asian Christians live as minorities among people of other faiths. In Asia, the religio-cultural context particularly shapes Christianity in each country, so it is this that we shall use as the main frame of our analysis.

Syriac Christianity

Syriac Christianity is a Semitic from of the faith that expanded across Asia to Persia, India and China in the first millennium. Its spread was associated particularly with the apostle Thomas and facilitated by the Jewish diaspora. The local language of the Roman province of Judaea where Jesus was born was Aramaic, although the language of trade was Greek. Aramaic was related to biblical Hebrew. It was also spoken in the province of Syria to the north and, skirting the deserts of Arabia, eastward into Mesopotamia (Iraq) and Persia (Iran). After the church was established in Jerusalem, the gospel spread first to the Syrian cities of Damascus (Acts 9:1–6) and Antioch (11:19–26). By the second century, the city and kingdom of Edessa in the upper Euphrates had become its main centre. The story of Edessa's evangelization is told in the third-century *Acts of Thecla*. In Edessa Christianity could be practised publically and was even adopted briefly by the king. Syriac – the Aramaic dialect of Edessa – developed as the language of this eastern branch of the church. A synthesis of the gospels in Syriac (the *Diatessaron*) was circulated by the late second century, and there was a complete Syriac Bible (the *Peshitta*) by the end of the fourth century. Other ancient Syriac documents include a manual for leaders of local churches known as the *Didache*, which shows that Christianity was rural as well as urban and took a distinctively Semitic form which was relatively egalitarian and charismatic (Irvin and Sunquist 2001:63–5). Syriac Christianity developed a distinctive theological expression that was more literary than philosophical. The Edessan Christian philosopher Bardaisan looked both westward to Greek or Hellenistic culture and east to Persia, India and China, and he held his Syriac Christianity together with a belief in astrology and fate (Moffett 1998:64–9). Gnostic Christianity, or a spiritualized faith, was also prevalent in Syria and Persia, and opposed by third century catholic and orthodox theologians from the region like Justin Martyr, who was born in Samaria, and Irenaeus of Lyons, who came from Smyrna. Related to Gnosticism was the ascetic form of Christianity that developed in the desert and led to the formation of monasteries. Some of the remaining Syrian monasteries today have operated more or less continuously from the early centuries (Brock 2010a). The Syriac language and literature, which are still used there, have only come to

Western attention in the modern period when they have challenged assumptions about the earliest church and revealed its diversity.

Edessa was situated at the crossroads of the 'Silk Road', the main trade route east to China, and a north–south trade route between Armenia and Arabia and on to India. Bardaisan reported in the second century that there were Christians as far east as modern Pakistan. Before the fourth century, Nisibis in Persia became a further centre for Syriac Christianity. However, when Christianity became the religion of the Roman Empire, the Sassanid rulers of Persia, who promoted Zoroastrianism, did not appreciate the Emperor Constantine's concern for the Christians there. They saw the church as a threat and persecuted Christians in Persia. Some, like the theologian Ephraem the Syrian, moved westwards into Roman territory; others moved, or were transported, further east. Nevertheless, the Syriac church continued to grow and spread. In this period the rural monastic communities, which were centres of education and evangelism, were safe havens and took on greater importance for the church. Aphrahat was head of a monastic community near Mosul on the River Tigris in the fourth century. He became one of the most important exponents of Christianity and engaged in dialogue with local Jewish leaders in a way that was largely independent of the debates within the Graeco-Roman Empire (Moffett 1998:125–30).

After 409 AD, Christianity was tolerated by the authorities, and a synod was called in Seleucia-Ctesiphon, the Persian capital (just south of modern Baghdad), to re-establish the church. It was attended by bishops from as far east as Samarkand in Central Asia. On the recommendation of the patriarch of Antioch and the bishop of Edessa, the Persian church adopted the faith of Nicaea and the polity and calendar agreed there. In 424, at the synod of Dadyeshu, which included bishops from modern Afghanistan, the catholicos, or patriarch, of all the churches of Persia was declared to hold equal authority to the existing patriarchates of Rome, Alexandria and Constantinople. However, Persian Christians were soon suffering under new imperial persecutions. They were marginalized under a system called *melet* and were forbidden to evangelize Zoroastrians. For political and cultural reasons, the Persians rejected the Chalcedonian definition and followed Theodore of Mopsuestia.

The Christians already in India and Central Asia were not involved in the dispute about the two natures of Christ between the theologians of Antioch in Syria and Alexandria in Egypt, which formed the background to the councils of Ephesus and Chalcedon (both in modern Turkey) in 431 and 451. These councils rejected two extremes: the view of Eutyches of Constantinople that the two natures were combined into one at the incarnation and the teaching attributed to Nestorius of Antioch that the two natures were separate. By the sixth century, in Syria and Egypt, which were under Roman rule and Greek influence, nationalists resented the 'Melkites', or pro-Greeks. The view of Cyril of Alexandria that Jesus Christ had one incarnate nature persisted and was increasingly adopted by Syrian Christians as well. They found support from the Theodora – co-emperor with Justinian – who sponsored Syriac missions to the east and south. The mission led by Jacob Baradeus, who was based in Edessa, promoted this 'monophysite' theology as a rival to Greek Orthodoxy and revived the Syrian churches (hence the name 'Jacobite' is sometimes applied to them).

The situation of the first Christians in Asia Minor (roughly modern Turkey) is revealed in the mid-first-century letters of the apostle Paul (himself born in the region). The book of Acts also describes how his missions were received (and sometimes not received) by a religiously and ethnically mixed but largely Hellenized population with close links to the region of Achaea in Greece. Wherever he travelled, Paul generally began by preaching in the synagogues of the Jews, but it was overwhelmingly Gentiles who responded to the message. The Gentile Christians struggled with Judaizers who insisted Christians should be circumcised and live according to the Jewish law (see Galatians). The tension between Jewish and Gentile Christians in the region was played out on a world stage in the second century when the teaching of Marcion, from the Black Sea coast, that the creator God of Jewish teaching was evil and not the Father of Jesus Christ was countered by Irenaeus from Smyrna, who had become bishop of Lyons in Gaul (modern France) (Irvin and Sunquist 2001:71–2).

The letters in the book of Revelation (The Apocalypse) were addressed to the churches in Asia Minor. They show how Christians in this largely pagan context faced basic but difficult moral questions like whether they could eat meat sold in the marketplace that had been offered to idols as part of the slaughter ritual, whether they could intermarry with non-Christians and what kind of sexual behaviour and dress was appropriate for believers. Church leaders attempted to resolve these issues by recourse to the tradition they had received, consideration of best practice among the pagans and the wisdom of their elected bishops, such as Polycarp, who was bishop of Smyrna and reputed to have been a disciple of the apostle John. They also received advice from church leaders in other parts of the world, such as Ignatius of Antioch, who passed through Asia Minor on his way to execution in Rome. The struggles of the Christians of Asia Minor with Paganism erupted into violence in the early third century when leaders of Pagan cults, whose income was threatened by the growth of Christianity (cf. Acts 19), destroyed churches, and Christians retaliated by attacking temples.

The book of Revelation appears to have been written during a time of persecution either under the emperor Domitian (81–96) or possibly under Vespasian (69–79). These and later persecutions contributed to apocalyptic expectation and prophetic visions of the future, together with subversive attitudes to Roman authority, which recur in this region. In 112 Pliny the Younger, governor of Bithynia, sought advice from the emperor on how to deal with Christians. His practice was to offer them the chance to worship the Roman gods and curse Christ. If they refused to do so, they were put to death. Polycarp was martyred in this way in 156. Prophecy was a strength of the church in Asia Minor. Montanism or the 'New Prophesy' erupted in the second half of the second century led by Priscilla, Maximilla (both women) and Montanus, who claimed direct inspiration by the Holy Spirit. This was a charismatic movement that did not recognize the constraints on ministry that were being established in the catholic or orthodox churches at the time and in which other spiritual gifts, including 'speaking in tongues' and wonder-working, were widely practised. The 'New Prophesy' was suppressed in the fourth century, after which charismatic phenomena tended to be regarded with suspicion by the established church (Trevett 2002).

Growth and persecution in West Asia

West Asia – or from a European perspective the 'Middle East' – was the cradle of Christianity. It was the birthplace of Jesus and the first disciples and the heartland of Christianity in the first four centuries. Indeed, considering the origins of the participants and the leading theologians – such as the Cappadocian fathers – in the early councils, it could be said that the faith of Nicaea is Asian (Tanner 2002). For the most part, the Asian churches have been marginal in the Zoroastrian, Confucian, Hindu, Buddhist, Muslim and other regimes of the continent. In many cases they were actively suppressed. Consequently, their history has been largely 'lost' (Jenkins 2008), but the churches have not entirely disappeared. Most still exist in the continent or in diaspora elsewhere in the world. Others have joined the Catholic Church through processes which in most cases preserved their ancient rites. In the modern period, as Christianity grows again in many parts of Asia, their histories are being recovered and are being used to support the paradigm of 'world Christianity' as diverse and polycentric.

The apostle Paul claimed to have preached the gospel in Arabia (Gal. 1:17), although he does not afterwards refer to any churches there. However, in the early centuries, Christian ascetics established themselves in the northern deserts of the peninsula and there were Christian traders among its many ports. Several Arab border kingdoms had Christians among the ruling families by the sixth century: the Ghassanid kingdom near Persia called Jacob Baradeus to evangelize them; Lakhmid near Syria had Christians among the ruling family in Hira; and Himyar, the southwest of modern Yemen, had a bishop in Najran and was sending out evangelists to Arabia. However, trouble between Jews and Christians and invasion from Ethiopia in 519 led to the martyrdom of Christians in Najran. A later Ethiopian general Abrahah built a cathedral in his new capital San'a and in 570 launched an unsuccessful military campaign, with elephants, against Mecca, a rival pilgrimage site where the Kab'ah also reputedly housed icons of Jesus and Mary. Two years after the death of the Prophet Muhammad (632), Jews and Christians were expelled from Arabia. The Christians of Najran were deported to southern Mesopotamia (Irvin and Sunquist 2001:260–4). Within forty years, under the Rashidun Caliphate, Arab armies had swept into the Persian Empire, through North Africa as far as Libya and into parts of what was now the Byzantine Empire in West Asia, although Asia Minor was spared until the arrival of the Seljuk Turks in the eleventh century.

Christian communities under Muslim rule

The effect on the Christians within the areas conquered by Muslim armies was varied. Arab Christians were required to become Muslim on pain of death. Other Christians were encouraged to convert to Islam but otherwise allowed to practise their faith under certain conditions: they must surrender their weapons, pay a poll tax, refrain from criticizing the prophet Muhammad and the Qur'an, and make no public display of their religion. Although the Arab conquerors protected Christians through the system of *dhimmi* and relied on Christians as local administrators, accountants and educators for several centuries, and although some Christian continued to thrive as merchants and physicians, they were not allowed to take up military or political roles. The system marginalized Christians and marked them out as subordinate. Islam was enforced as the final religion: Muslims who converted to Christianity risked being killed; Christian men could not marry Muslim women and children of Christian wives were counted as Muslim; no new churches could be built and churches which became mosques could not be changed back again. Gradually, over the next few centuries the pressures on Christians increased, and the majority of Christians under Islamic rule emigrated, converted or were absorbed by marriage (Irvin and Sunquist 2001:269–78). Nevertheless by the middle ages substantial Christian communities had remained under a succession of Muslim empires. When European treatment of minorities in medieval times is considered, it could be argued that 'it was generally better to be a Christian or a Jew in an Islamic society than a Jew or Muslim in a Christian society' (Armour 2002:29).

Under pressure from Muslim rulers, Christians in the region looked for support from their fellow Christians in the West in various ways. In 1095 Byzantine emperor Alexios II called for help against the Turks threatening Constantinople and Pope Urban II launched the Crusades (see Chapter 4). Parts of the Syriac churches at various points united with Rome, partly for protection. The Maronite Church, which has its origins in a distinct community in Syria long oriented to Rome, had formally joined the Catholic Church in 1203. Others joined later during the Ottoman Empire which, from 1300, grew from a base in Asia Minor. Under the Ottomans, Franciscans and Carmelites worked in Palestine and Dominicans and Capuchins in Mesopotamia and Persia. In the nineteenth century, when France was dominant in the region, their work was revitalized by several French women's congregations. The Chaldean Catholic Church is the part of the Assyrian Church of the East or Persian Church that has joined itself to Rome. The Oriental Orthodox churches – Armenian, Syrian and Coptic – all have Catholic counterparts. There is also a (Melkite) Greek Catholic

Church. Finally, there is a Latin Patriarchate of Jerusalem, which was re-established in 1847 and now includes a Hebrew Catholic Church in Israel (O'Mahony 2010a).

Some Orthodox Christians responded to various Protestant missions that entered from the early nineteenth century, at a time of rising British involvement in the region. As well as converting Muslims and promoting Christianity among the Jews, these aimed to 'revive' or reform the Orthodox churches. Anglican mission began from a Church Missionary Society (CMS) base established on Malta in 1815 and spread to Egypt and Turkey. From the 1820s, the Basel Mission introduced Reformed Protestantism to the Russian Caucasus and Persia, the American Board of Commissioners for Foreign Missions brought Congregationalism (and later Presbyterianism) to Lebanon, Turkey and Iran. However, from the 1840s the Orthodox churches excommunicated Protestant sympathizers, leading to the setting up of separate Protestant churches (Moffett 2005:376–402). Russian Orthodox missions to strengthen Orthodox churches began in the 1890s and led to the absorption of some communities into the Russian Church. Lutheran churches also appeared (Murre-van den Berg 2006). The remaining Eastern or Greek Orthodox churches are divided between the ancient patriarchates: Jerusalem, Antioch, Alexandria and Constantinople. However Antioch accounts for the vast majority. Today most Syriac churches use Arabic for all but the most sacred parts of the liturgy.

The crisis facing Christians in West Asia today has been building up over the last century but it is particularly in the past 20 years that suffering and emigration have reached appalling new levels. It has been precipitated by several developments in which Christians have been caught up. First, although also aimed at Muslims, it was primarily Christian communities that benefited from the educational, medical and other services provided by the colonial missions. As these communities revived, they tended to use nationalism to address their grievances against Ottoman rule. Nationalist movements by Christian communities (Greece, Serbia and Bulgaria) contributed to the break-up of the Ottoman Empire during the First World War and this is now resented. Second, the creation of the state of Israel in 1948 and subsequent defeats of Arab forces with Western support caused great anger across the Muslim world and showed no regard for the interests of the Christians in the region. Third, partly as a reaction against the West, three Arab movements arose, all of which are opposed to each other: secular Arab nationalism and two Islamic movements – Sunni Islamism (Salafism), sponsored by Saudi Arabia, and Shi'ite Islamism supported by Iran. The latter two especially are anti-Christian. Fourth, Christians are seen as complicit in Western interventions to pursue the 'war on terror' in Afghanistan, Iraq and now against Islamic State in Syria and other countries. The scale of the crisis calls into question the survival of Christianity in its ancient heartlands (Josua 2015). As a bloc of Islamic nations has emerged that is hostile to the West and Christianity, Christians have been made to bear the blame for Western military interventions and even – in the age of the internet – perceived offences toward Islam in the West such as the Danish cartoons depicting the prophet Muhammad in 2005 and Pope Benedict's Regensburg address in 2006.

The crisis for Christians in West Asia today

In the remainder of this section, we will consider the current situation of Christian communities in the nations of Western Asia, using especially the work of Anthony O'Mahony (O'Mahony and John Flannery 2010; O'Mahony and Loosley 2010). Armenia is one of three countries within the Caucasus between the Black and Caspian Seas – the others being Georgia and Azerbaijan. It became the first permanent Christian kingdom anywhere when King Tiridates III was baptized at the end of the third century and the national church elected its own patriarch or *catholicos*. Within a century or so, the scriptures had been translated into the Armenian language. Its neighbour Georgia was Christianized from Greece in the fourth century and maintained the Chalcedonian orthodoxy, but the Armenian Church adopted an Alexandrian position. Under Catherine the Great in the late eighteenth century, the Russian Church helped revive the church in Georgia, which had been distinguished for its literature and church architecture in the eleventh and twelfth centuries but fragmented by Mongol invasion. In the nineteenth century it underwent a process of Russification, including the submission of its leadership to the Russian patriarch. Resistance was led by the church, but although autocephaly was restored in 1943, under Soviet rule the church had little freedom until the 1980s. The church grew rapidly in the post-Soviet era when the president and former communist leader Eduard Shevardnadze was baptized and today includes most of the population. The Udin Christians of Azerbaijan, who first believed in the third century, were left largely undisturbed in a remote part of the country by Muslim invaders. A few thousand remain today and are reviving their language and faith in a context of Islamic resurgence with the help of the Russian Church. It was not until the eleventh century that Armenia came under Muslim dominance (the Seljuk Turks). When in the late nineteenth century, the Armenian people sought independence from the Ottoman Empire through a nationalist movement supported by wealthy compatriots in Russia, they were persecuted. This culminated in 1915–17 in what many nations have condemned as genocide. By the end of the First World War, the Armenians in Turkish territory had been annihilated. Today the Catholicos of All Armenians, in Etchmiadzin, Armenia, exercises responsibility not only over the three million Orthodox in Armenia but also over an estimated diaspora of twice that number in the region and also in Europe, North America, Australia and elsewhere.

Aramaic-speaking Syrian Christians in Turkey were also massacred during the First World War. The reply of an elderly man in Aleppo when asked how they had endured after being forced from their homes gives an indication of the way in which faith, identity and community are intertwined for the Syrian churches: 'To remain faithful we must be conscious of ourselves; love and help each other; encourage the youth to obey and serve the church; and study the tradition. In this way we can keep our identity' (Chaillot 1998:149). In 1910, Asia Minor was still more than 20 per cent Christian, including large numbers of Syrian and Armenian Christians in the east of the country, Greek Orthodox in the west, Catholics of various rites and Protestant churches planted within the past century. Although the resistance leader Mustafa Kemal (Atatürk) created a modern secular state in what was left after the defeat of the Ottomans by Western forces, Turkishness was closely identified with Islam and Christians were associated with the West. Greeks were massacred in 1922, but a solution was found when Greece and Turkey exchanged their Christian and Muslim populations, leaving two neighbouring states of almost completely different religious allegiance. Syrian Christians were also killed during the Kurdish uprising of 1925–26, when most fled into French-occupied Syria. Further brutality in the 1970s encouraged many to move to Germany or Sweden as guest workers. When Pope Benedict visited Turkey in 2006, he reminded Turks of their Christian roots, and on his visit in 2014 Pope Francis controversially referred to the fate of the Armenians as genocide.

Many Christians were among those Palestinians displaced by the creation of the state of Israel in Palestine in 1948, and again in the 1967 war by the Israeli annexation of East Jerusalem, Gaza and the West Bank. Since then Israeli settlements have relentlessly encroached on Palestinian territory, and many Palestinians have emigrated or are living in the refugee camps in Palestine and in neighbouring countries. Within Israel-Palestine, Christians – mainly Arab – are now no more than 2 per cent and are concentrated in Galilee and in the Occupied Territories. In political discussions about a solution to the crisis in Israel-Palestine, the presence of Christians is often ignored and all Arabs are (wrongly) assumed to be Muslim. Palestinian Christians often feel hurt that the Christian tourists who visit the holy places rarely encounter the local Christian communities, most of who are effectively imprisoned by Israeli occupation. Religious rights are not upheld for Christians or Muslims in either the West Bank under the Palestinian administration or the Gaza Strip under Hamas (Sered and Ben-David 2015). Nevertheless, all the churches in the world trace their origins to Jerusalem and most wish to maintain a presence there: the Catholic Church is the largest single body; the Greek Orthodox, which claims precedence as the direct successor of James, leader of the very first church, is the second largest. The holy places in Jerusalem and Bethlehem are managed internationally by centuries-old agreements between various Orthodox churches and the Catholic Church. Several Protestant churches also have a long-standing presence: the oldest Protestant church being the Anglican Christ Church in Jerusalem, consecrated in 1849 (Ward 2006:191–7). Anglican membership has dwindled to a few thousand like most of the other Protestant groups. 'Messianic Judaism', a movement of Christians from a Jewish background that began in the United States in the 1970s, is similarly small in number in Israel but it is growing.

Figure 2.1 Icon of the Virgin Mary on the separation wall built by the Israeli government around Palestinian territory in the West Bank. Image: iStock.

The Palestinian question and the status of the city of Jerusalem are central to the politics of the whole West Asian region, if not the world. The suffering of the Palestinians is keenly felt by Muslims and is a focus of Muslim anger directed at the West. But Christians are divided on the issue. On the one hand, there are Christians in many parts of the world actively campaigning for the rights of Palestinian Christians. Although the World Council of Churches (in the process of formation) supported the establishment of the state of Israel and helped Jews to emigrate there, it now has a special programme of 'accompaniment' to highlight the plight of the Palestinians. On the other hand, many Evangelical Christians are influenced by Christian Zionism, a movement whose views of the significance of Jerusalem for the end times motivate them to support the security of the state of Israel over the Palestinian cause through such organizations as the International Christian Embassy Jerusalem (Cohn-Sherbok 2006). The Second Vatican Council endorsed Catholic dialogue with both Jews and Muslims and the Catholic Church has also been working to bring unity among the churches. Pope John Paul II had reached doctrinal agreements with the Oriental Churches of the region on Christological differences that had existed since Chalcedon. In 2010, Pope Benedict XVI called a synod for the Middle East to urge unity among the churches and collaboration with other faiths. The Synod, which was held in Arabic, was undoubtedly a further step forward but church leaders from the Middle East also challenged the Catholic Church on the Palestinian question and on its lack of inclusion of their patriarchs in decision-making.

There has been no Arab Christian community in the Arabian Peninsula since the expulsion of the seventh century. The seven countries currently occupying the peninsula do not permit conversion to Christianity or allow clergy into the country so Christian activities have been restricted to social service. Since most of these countries are now exceedingly rich with oil wealth, few Christian charities are now working anywhere except in Yemen. However many Christians live in Arabia; they form around 10 per cent of the population in Kuwait, Bahrain, Qatar and the United Arab Emirates but most are expatriates. The majority are Catholics; many of them are domestic workers from the Philippines and other parts of Asia or workers in the oil industry. While there they usually have to rely on lay leadership, if it is possible for them to meet at all. In Saudi Arabia particularly, Christian meetings, particularly of Asians, may be broken up and their leaders expelled, publically beaten or even executed (Mandryk 2010:728–30). Bahrain is the most relaxed country for Christians; it has an American Mission Hospital and an Arab Christian community. Some Christian agencies encourage Christian evangelists with a mission to Muslims to enter these countries as 'tent-makers' (Acts 18:3), that is, to take secular employment and make use of any opportunities to witness. To do so is exceedingly difficult and dangerous – not least to those local people who may respond to the message. As Muslim communities grow in the West, build mosques funded by Saudi Arabia and demand increasing freedom to practise their religion, Christians feel entitled to ask why Christian minorities in the peninsula are denied these same rights.

The Persian Church of the first millennium spread the Christian gospel across Asia, but there are hardly any ethnic Persian Christians today in modern Iran. In the early nineteenth century, East India Company chaplain Henry Martyn laid a foundation for later Christian communities in Persia when he worked with Indian companions to translate the whole of the New Testament into Urdu, Persian and Judaeo-Persic. But during the (Islamic) Iranian Revolution of 1978–79, and after it, Christians (and other minorities) suffered. For example, the Anglican bishop Hassan Dehqani-Tafti escaped with his life but his son was shot and killed. Most churches had some or all of their properties and institutions (hospitals and schools) confiscated.

The constitution instituted after the Revolution protects minorities in the traditional Islamic way, and allows for their representation in the legislature, but conversion to Christianity can result in a death penalty. Among the less than 1 per cent of the population who are Christian, the Orthodox are Armenian, Assyrian, Russian and Greek; the Roman Catholics worship according to three different rites: Chaldean, Latin and Armenian; Protestants are Anglican, Presbyterian and various independent groups, many of which worship clandestinely and pay a terrible price if discovered (Josua 2015).

Christians have been in Iraq virtually since the inception of Christianity, and several groups of Christians today still use an ancient Syriac liturgy that was indigenous to Mesopotamia: Chaldean Catholics, Assyrian Church of the East, Syrian Catholics and Syrian Orthodox. The first two of these are now in communion with one another following a landmark declaration on Christology by Pope John Paul II and Mar Dinkha IV, catholicos-patriarch, in 1994. There are other Orthodox – Armenian and Greek, small minority communities of Catholics following other rites, and several Protestant groups. The Assyrian community suffered severe persecution and scattering during the break-up of the Ottoman Empire. But under former president Saddam Hussein, the Ba'athist regime protected Christians – 3 per cent of the population – from Islamizers and they had their own community law and schools. Tariq Aziz, Saddam's deputy prime minister, was from the Chaldean community, which after its union with Rome in 1830 benefitted from modern education provided by Dominicans, Carmelites and Jesuits. But among its other devastating effects, the US-led invasion that toppled Saddam's government also unleashed violence against Christians, accelerating migration to Syria, Kurdish-controlled areas and the West (Healey 2010; Rassam 2010). The bombing of Our Lady of Salvation Syrian Chaldean Catholic Church in Baghdad in 2010 caused another mass exodus. Then in 2014 the so-called Islamic State attempted to convert or kill the Christians – mostly Church of the East – and Yasidis living in the Plain of Nineveh and Mosul and destroy their heritage. This may be the final end of the Church of the East in what has been its homeland for nearly two thousand years (Josua 2015).

In the Levant. Jordan is an independent kingdom and Syria and Lebanon are republics that were gradually socially engineered under a French mandate from the First World War in an attempt to promote communal harmony. Christians in Jordan are mainly Greek Orthodox congregations of Palestinian Arabs whose population has dwindled to about 3 per cent. Lebanon has the largest Christian minority of any country in the Middle East and is the most religiously diverse in the region. The relative size of religious communities is a politically sensitive issue and has not been measured in a census since the 1930s when Christians as a whole made up more than 50 per cent of the population. Among Christians, the Maronite Catholic community predominates; Maronites regard the country as their spiritual home and held a privileged political position until the civil war of 1975–90. After the war, the Catholic Church held a special synod for Lebanon in 1991–95 and the Maronite Church, under Patriarch Sfeir, was influential and active in the reconstruction and in voicing community grievances (McCallum 2010). There are large Melkite Catholic and Greek Orthodox groups in Lebanon, plus many other churches and also Christian organizations working with refugees. The communal relations of Lebanon and Jordan have already been tested by influxes of refugees from Palestine, then Iraq, and at the time of writing, from Syria. In 2010, Syria had a remaining Christian population of about 5 per cent – well over a million. The largest single Church was the Catholic Church, following several rites, but Greek and Syrian Orthodox churches were also large. The regime of Bashar al-Assad was supported by most Christians because it offered them protection. Since the 'Arab Spring' of 2011, they and their minority communities have been particularly exposed and experienced great suffering.

Syriac Christians have a unique contribution to make to intra-Christian dialogue because Syriac Christianity is represented in many different churches – covering the whole spectrum of Christological traditions – Catholic/Orthodox (Chalcedon), Oriental Orthodox and the Church of the East (Brock 2010b). The conflict that has engulfed the modern state of Syria is a disaster for the whole nation and region, especially the Christians who are disproportionately represented among the refugees currently fleeing to Europe, and also a loss for world Christianity. The Orthodox churches of the whole West Asia region are now scattered across the world, where many of them are being revived to support diaspora communities. On the one hand this gives Orthodox Christians an opportunity to disseminate their faith and interact with Christians in other regions, from which for many centuries they have been separated. On the other hand, it poses a number of challenges to the displaced Orthodox churches such as ecclesiastic jurisdiction in new territories, competition in a religious marketplace, how to use new freedoms in public life and questions of the limits to the diversification of their communities (Clapsis 2004). While the dispersal of Orthodoxy can be expected to enrich Christianity in other parts of the world, it is a tragedy for those populations and diminishing for the remaining society. Although the possibility of the return of Christianity to its first-millennium heartlands looks remote, some Christians optimistically claim there are statistically significant numbers of Muslims 'turning to Christ' – mostly Evangelicalism or Pentecostalism – in several countries, including in the Arab world (Garrison 2014). Others claim there is a movement of hidden Christian believers who remain 'Muslim' in the sense that they exercise the key characteristic of 'submission'. While these reports are not easily verifiable, churches are growing in the Muslim diaspora, especially among Iranians (Miller 2015).

Religions and caste in South Asia

The Saint Thomas Christians

The first Christian in India may have been Thomas, the doubting disciple of Jesus. In Indian traditions such as the *Thomas Parvam* and in the, possibly second-century, Syriac *Acts of Thomas*, he is said to have gone there in obedience to Christ's command to evangelize all nations and at the invitation of King Gundaphar. The existence in the first century of a king with the name Gundaphar has been proven, and there were trade routes to India both by sea and over land. Thomas is reputed to have been martyred in India, and in 370, Ephraem the Syrian proclaimed the return of his bones to Edessa (Moffett 1998:24–44). Other scholars consider it is more likely that the ancient Orthodox Christians of India, who call themselves 'Saint Thomas' Christians are descended from the church known to have been established by Thomas of Cana (Kinnān), a Persian merchant, who in 345 AD settled in the area of Cranganore (modern Kodungallur in Kerala). He came with a community of settlers, probably fleeing persecution, and a bishop and several priests under the authority of the Persian church (Frykenberg 2008:91–115). The rise of Islam encouraged further migrations of Syrian, Persian and Arabian Christians to ports around India. The Christians became part of Indian society to the extent that they have adopted a high-caste identity and many have held privileged positions in society over many centuries. While the communities gradually adopted the local languages, a branch of the Saint Thomas Christians has maintained the ancient Syriac liturgy, vestments and rituals. But Christianity is not known to have spread beyond that ethnic community.

Christianity in Persian or Syrian form has been part of the religious tapestry of the Indian subcontinent for nearly two thousand years. Arguably, the greatest problem for the Orthodox Church has not been its minority status among Hindus and Muslims, but the actions of other Christians. Although John of Montecorvino baptized some Indians along the Malabar Coast in 1293, Roman Catholicism only became established in South India by the Portuguese, who maintained the territory of Goa as their chief colony on the subcontinent from 1510 until 1961. From this base, Franciscans and other missions expanded. Fishing communities around the southern coast and in nearby Ceylon (Sri Lanka) responded to the Jesuits, led by Francis Xavier. The Paravars, who received Portuguese protection, turned in large numbers to Christianity and laid the foundation of an Indian Catholic Church. Although friendly relations were established by the Franciscans, the growing Latinizing power of the Roman Catholic Church in India, led by the Jesuits, caused the Saint Thomas Christians to experience what some describe as 'suppression and disfigurement' (Moffett 2005:12) and even 'slavery and persecution' (Jacob 2001). Using the power of the Portuguese state and the Inquisition, at the Synod of Diamper in 1599, Catholic

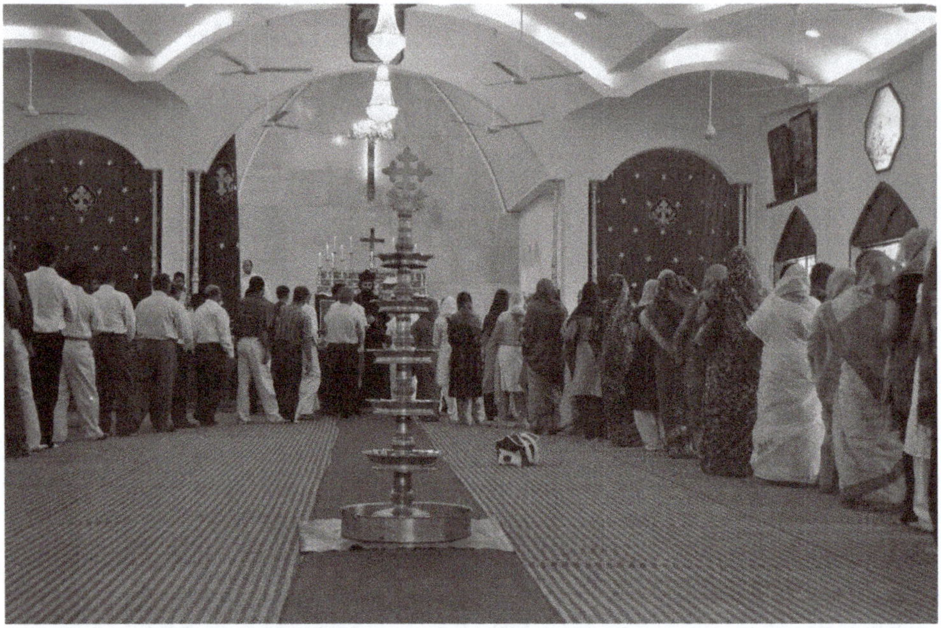

Figure 2.2 Men and women lining up separately to receive communion at St Mary's Jacobite Syrian Orthodox Cathedral, Bengaluru, India. The oil lamp in the foreground is another example of inculturation. Photograph by Jacques Matthey.

Church leaders sought to force the allegiance of all Christians in India to Saint Peter, not Saint Thomas (Moffett 2005:3–19). Most of the Saint Thomas Christians were brought under the Catholic Church but were allowed to keep their Syriac and Chaldean liturgies. However, in 1653 a large number gathered at Koonen Cross near Cochin to reject Catholicism and, cut off by the Portuguese from any patriarch, they installed their own metropolitan (Frykenberg 2008:116–41). With the help of the Dutch, the Indian Orthodox first gained recognition not from the Church of the East but from the patriarchate of Antioch. While the 'Jacobite' church retains this West Syrian connection, the 'Malankara' church has re-established the link with the Church of the East. The Syrian Orthodox split again in the mid-nineteenth century as a result of a reform movement that began under the influence of missionaries of the (Anglican) CMS, who came initially to 'revive' the Orthodox Church and began by translating the Bible into the vernacular language Malayalam (Moffett 2005:415–18). Under pressure, after 1836, some became Anglicans and others, under Abraham Malpān, established the Mar Thoma Syrian Church of Malabar, which is Evangelical Protestant in doctrine while retaining traditional Saint Thomas vestments, church structures and liturgical features (Frykenberg 2008:244–9). Most of the Saint Thomas churches are currently in dialogue with one another. The Malankara Orthodox Syrian Church maintains many social and evangelistic activities and supports smaller denominations; leaders such as Geevarghese Mar Osthathios have been active in the World Council of Churches (WCC). However, after centuries of surviving effectively as a caste community in Hindu society, many Orthodox are resistant to any form of outreach which would dilute their caste identity.

Inculturation

The first Protestant churches in the Indian subcontinent were established from the beginning of the eighteenth century by those who responded to missionaries from Germany (Lutheran and Reformed) and Britain (Baptist, Anglican, Methodist). A highly indigenized church resulted from the work of the German Pietists Bartholomäus Ziegenbalg and Heinrich Plütschau sent by the Danish king to his colony at Tranquebar (in modern Tamil Nadu) in 1706, who worked with the common people and paid close attention to local culture (Hudson 2000). Since the British discouraged mission work, William Carey from England established himself at another Danish Colony – Serampore near Kolkata – in 1793 where a Baptist community grew up. As the British became more involved in India, Anglicans pressed for missions. Some became more closely associated with the British government's colonial rule but Evangelical, Catholic and non-conformist missions, which from the mid-nineteenth century included US American agencies, often annoyed the British authorities who feared conversions would upset inter-religious relations.

Because of the stratified caste structure of Hindu India, from the start both Protestant and Catholic missionaries were faced with the dilemma of whether to aim to win the high castes in the hope of changing society from the top down or whether to preach to the lowest castes, who were most obviously in need of salvation. Of the early Jesuit missionaries, Francis Xavier focused on the latter group and Robert de Nobili chose the former. Some outstanding Indian leaders became Christians in the nineteenth century, especially through dialogue and educational initiatives. Brahmabandab Upadhyay, a Bengali Brahmin who became a Roman Catholic, relaid the foundations of Indian Christian theology on Vedantic Hinduism rather than Greek philosophy (Lipner 1999). Narayan Vaman Tilak was known as the poet-saint of Maharashtra and established a tradition of hymnody in Marathi. Pandita Ramabai challenged the position of women in India and led a revival movement (Hedlund, Kim and Johnson 2011). The attempt to reach the high castes required a deep engagement with Hindu culture, but between the ending of the Rites Controversy and the Second Vatican Council, the Catholic Church in India kept a distinctively Latin identity, despite the many affinities between Catholic and Hindu devotional practices (Ballhatchet 2002:520). When Upadhyay suggested the formation of a religious order of Indian Christian sannyasis (holy men) based around an ashram (hermitage), he was refused permission, but this model was later pioneered by the English Benedictine Bede Griffiths and others, including, from the 1970s, Vandana, formerly leader of the Sisters of the Sacred Heart of Jesus in India (K. Kim 2007). Raymundo Panikkar (1981) followed this Hindu-Christian approach in the realms of systematic theology, comparing the perfect union of Jesus Christ with God the Father to the Hindu aspiration to self-realization. Other pioneers of Indian Christian theology, such as A. J. Appasamy, an Anglican bishop, preferred to use the bhakti tradition of Hindu mysticism in the Bhagavadgita, following Sundar Singh, a Sikh convert, who took up the wandering life of a sadhu (wandering holy man) and offered Indians 'the Water of Life in an Indian cup'.

Indian Protestants did not often separate from the mission churches but one example where they did so was a caste group called the Shanars or Nadars in the Tirunelveli district of South India who in 1857 founded the Hindu-Christian Church of the Lord Jesus. Among the new churches that have emerged as a result of revival movements and the work of indigenous mission organizations, a well-known example is the network of autonomous 'assemblies' founded on the teaching of Bakht Singh in the 1930s and now mainly in Chennai, Hyderabad, Kalimpong (West Bengal) and Mumbai. In order to present a united witness, in 1947, the year of independence, a merger of Congregational, Presbyterian, Methodist and Anglican churches formed the Church of South India, and provided the basis for similar schemes of union of Episcopal and non-Episcopal churches in North India (1970), Pakistan (1970) and Bangladesh (after 1971). In 1978 a joint council was established by the Church of South India, Church of North India and the Mar Thoma Church, exhibiting a high degree of union: intercommunion, doctrinal unity, episcopal polity, mutual recognition of one another's ministry and some joint activities. However, Lutheran and Evangelical churches are outside this framework and so are Pentecostal churches, which were first established in South India around 1911. One of the best known today is the Indian Pentecostal Church of God, founded by Syrian Christians in Kerala in the 1930s. In 2001 it was estimated that 20 per cent of South Indian Protestants are Pentecostals, mostly Dalits, who participate in an indigenous version of Christianity that has strong parallels with traditional Indian popular religion in the areas of miracle healing and exorcism. One of the most influential charismatic evangelists was D. G. S. Dhinakaran, a member of the Church of South India, whose Jesus Calls Ministry offers healing and whose followers have helped establish a university (Bergunder 2008). Such indigenous and self-supporting movements are important in a climate where Christianity is criticized as a Western religion. Even more significant for proving that 'Christianity is Indian' is the recovery of the early history of Syriac Christianity in India (Hedlund 2004).

Since the partition of British India in 1947, Christians in Pakistan and Bangladesh have been separated from their fellow believers in India, where the strength of the church lay, and are living among overwhelming Muslim majorities. Although there were Saint Thomas Christians in Pakistan, the oldest extant Christian community is the Catholic Church, which has more than a million adherents. Protestants, who are mostly brought together in the National Council of Churches, are about 1.5 million. Most converted from the lowest castes from the mid-nineteenth century or during more recent urbanization. Altogether Pakistan has the largest Christian community in a Muslim country except for Indonesia but most Christians are marginalized both by caste and religion and constitute one of the few Christian communities in Asia that rank below the national average socially, economically and educationally (Amjad-Ali 2012). Although the churches run schools and hospitals that are sought after for their high standards, in a context of increasing Islamization, Christians are vulnerable to blasphemy laws and to reprisals for Western aggression elsewhere in the Islamic world. Many middle-class Christians have emigrated and the prominent Catholic politician Shahbaz Bhatti, an outspoken opponent of the blasphemy laws, was murdered by Islamic militants in 2011 (Wilfred 2014:46–47). In Bangladesh, Christians had relatively more freedom to practise their faith until the election of the Nationalist Party in 2001. Although Christians form less than 1 per cent of the population of nearly 160 million, they have a relatively high profile since local and overseas churches run many social development programmes for the wider community. The largest churches are Roman Catholic and Baptist; the latter stemming from the Serampore mission. The Catholic Church whole-heartedly supported the nationalist cause in the war with Pakistan that led to Bangladeshi independence in 1971. Many Bangladeshi Christians are in tribal communities in the hills bordering Northeast India and Myanmar. Or they belong to the Santal community which is also found in India and Nepal and was evangelized by a Norwegian-Danish mission from the mid-nineteenth century. There are also reported to be large numbers who follow Jesus as a Muslim, in the sense of one who surrenders to God, but use the Bible as their source of authority.

To the south, Persian Christians were a powerful minority in Sri Lanka (Ceylon) in the sixth and seventh centuries, but today's Christians are more recent: Catholics since the sixteenth century, who constitute about 90 per cent, and Protestants since the Dutch period. The Dutch expelled the Portuguese priests in 1658 but the Oratorians of Goa, a lay community led by Fr Joseph Vaz, secretly sustained the Catholic community, who were mostly fisherman. Since the 1980s, there has been a charismatic revival and the Assemblies of God, present since 1924, has become the largest non-Catholic church (Somaratna 2012). Comprising about 9 per cent of the population, Christians belong in equal numbers to both the Tamil and Sinhalese communities, and in the recent conflict they acted as peacemakers, especially through Christian–Buddhist dialogue (Schmidt-Leukel 2005).

To the north of India, in the isolated Hindu kingdom of Nepal, after a brief Capuchin mission in the eighteenth century, Christianity was forbidden from 1769 until 1951. Some Nepalis who travelled to India brought back Christian literature and made use of Christian medical and educational facilities just over the border. In 1951 Protestant missions negotiated entry together, under the umbrella now called the

International Nepal Fellowship, solely to undertake charitable activities but churches soon grew, started by Nepali Christians. Christians suffered severe persecution in the 1960s, but Evangelical and Pentecostal churches have increased rapidly, evangelized by the Nepali diaspora as well as by Indians and other foreigners. Christians are estimated to number over 3 per cent today and they are among the groups working to end oppression by the Hindu elite.

In the post-independence nation of India, most Christians live in the South Indian states of Kerala, Tamil Nadu and Andhra Pradesh. There are rural parts of those states where Christians form a local majority. Roman Catholics make up by far the largest single group of Indian Christians and are concentrated among the Malayalam-speaking community. The other major centre of Christian population is in the hill country of Northeast India – the pocket between Bangladesh and Myanmar. Tribal people, some of them head-hunters within the past 100 years, had migrated there from the direction of China. From the mid-nineteenth century, the Naga, Mizo, Garo, Khasis and other tribes in the hills invited English Baptists from Serampore, American Baptists and Welsh Presbyterians, and also spread the gospel among themselves. Conversions increased through a series of revival movements, beginning in 1905–07 in the Khasi Hills. In the state of Nagaland, Christians are more than 90 per cent today. Protestant Christianity in Northeast India is in keeping with local customs and conditions. For example, Mizo Christians celebrate Christmas in large church groups by roasting wild pigs and singing throughout the night. The annual Baptist convention in Meghalaya attracts tens of thousands of people in family and church groups to a tent meeting. Catholic missions began in Assam, Bhutan, Manipur and the Khasi Hills in the late nineteenth century, and the Church has spread across the region. Evangelists from Northeast India work with their kinsfolk across the relatively porous borders into Myanmar, in the isolated Buddhist Kingdom of Bhutan and in Bangladesh. Others work cross-culturally among the majority communities of India through indigenous mission organizations. The tribal peoples of Northeast India have been resisting the incursions of the majority Indian community into their traditional lands and Indian government policy of Sanskritization with the result that access to the region is restricted and the tribal peoples, that is, Christians mostly, suffer human rights abuses (Behera and Biehl 2015).

Liberation

Since Upadhyay, Christian theologians from the Indian subcontinent have dared to challenge the rigidity of Western academic method and embrace new creative forms of theology (Boyd 2014). In the 1960s, the Protestant lay theologian M. M. Thomas, who came from a Mar Thoma family, developed a theology of revolution (1966), which was also in keeping with the socialist model for national development of the time. It was influential in the WCC, of which he was a moderator. In the 1960s and 1970s, Indian Catholics working among the poor or low and outcaste developed theologies of humanization and liberation. The Jesuit activist Samuel Rayan was one of the first to welcome Latin American liberation theology. He adapted it for Indian conditions by challenging its historical and rational framework and developed a spirituality of liberation which drew on indigenous cultural traditions, such as the pre-Aryan shakti tradition of the creative force, which subverts Vedic Hinduism (K. Kim 2007).

Despite the efforts to reach the elite by inculturation, in the late nineteenth and early twentieth centuries all the churches grew rapidly by 'mass conversions' of communities of outcaste and tribal groups (Frykenberg 2008:206–42). These communities make up the overwhelming majority of Christians in the subcontinent today. Outcastes, formerly known as 'untouchables' but who now choose to designate themselves 'dalit' (broken), used conversion as a protest against Hindu caste practices and as a means of improving their socio-economic status. Caste distinctions are being broken down by urbanization, positive discrimination by government and – since 1991 – a market-oriented society. Nevertheless, and especially in rural areas, dalit communities still face harassment, exclusion from water supplies and exploitation by the higher castes. Despite the reputation of Jesus Christ for eating with outcastes and sinners, caste practices were by no means eradicated in the churches. In Orthodox, Catholic and Protestant churches there are many instances of outcastes not being invited to share the same loaf or communion cup (Robinson 2003:69–92). Christian dalits suffer doubly. They are discriminated against in the church and also socially in that they do not qualify for the government benefits intended to counter discrimination. This is on the grounds that Christianity does not (officially) acknowledge caste. Thus the dalit Christian struggle is both with Hindu society but also with the Christian community. Using the tools of postcolonial studies, A. P. Nirmal and other theologians of outcaste groups have developed a theology from below – *of* the dalits rather than *for* them – to counter what V. Devasahayam (1997) has described as their 'pollution, poverty and powerlessness'. Contemporary dalit theology stresses dalit identity and agency and how dalit perspectives challenge other Christians (Rajkumar, Dayan and Asheervadham 2014).

Caste cannot be separated from gender. India is one of the few countries in the world where the number of females is less than the number of males, due to selective abortion, female infanticide, deprivation and abuse. Women face problems such as the dowry system, lack of education, discrimination, ill-treatment and lack of representation (despite government quota systems) and dalit women are 'the *dalits* of the *dalits*' (Manorama 1992). Indian feminist theologians have condemned this situation as sinful and drawn inspiration from the 'alternative' society of Jesus and the Shakti tradition since Shakti is feminine (Kumari 1993).

Hindu-Christian relations

Indian Christian theology is not only concerned with inculturation and liberation but also with dialogue with other faiths and ideologies (Thomas 1997). India has been the laboratory in which theology of religions and inter-religious dialogue has been developed over the past century (1910–2010) (Behera 2011). Indian reflection significantly influenced the positive approach of *Nostra Aetate*, the declaration produced by the Second Vatican Council on the relation of the church to non-Christian religions, which took an inclusive view (Gispert-Sauch 1997:458). Jacques Dupuis, veteran Jesuit missionary in India, offered a development of this which avoided accusations of paternalism (Dupuis 1997). However, since caste is a feature of Hinduism, dialoguing with the high caste and showing solidarity with the low or outcastes are often incompatible. Indian theologians loyal to Vedantic traditions and those supporting dalit causes are often opposed to each other, and Indian Catholics struggle to hold together respect for religions with eradication of poverty, inculturation with liberation. Among Protestants there is a similar struggle to be both 'evangelical and dialogical' (Selvanayagam 2012). After independence, P. D. Devanandan (1964), who founded the Christian Institute for the Study of Religion and Society, redefined Christian mission as actively participating in the struggle for a new society in dialogue with neo-Hindus and secularists. Stanley Samartha (1979) promoted dialogue within the WCC and established its approach of 'commitment with openness'. Samartha, who dialogued with caste Hindus, saw the church as integrated with the wider community but Evangelical theologians, who are mainly relating to lower castes, stress the distinctiveness of the Christian community, the Christian responsibility to evangelize and the mission of conversion (Ramachandra 1996). Nevertheless, many of today's Indian Evangelical missionaries, whether working with international agencies such as Operation Mobilisation and InterServe or indigenous Indian missions, such as the Indian Missionary Society and the Friends Missionary Prayer Band, are deeply committed to social projects and advocacy for the poor.

The Indian independence movement against the British encouraged the growth of Hindu nationalism and an ideology of Hindutva or Hinduization which sees the presence of Muslims and Christians as both a religious and a political threat. Foreign missionaries and funds were restricted from the 1950s. From this perspective both inculturation and liberation came under attack. Attempts to present the Christian gospel in a Hindu way, particularly the ashram movement, arouse the suspicions of Hindus that they are a duplicitous attempt to win more converts. Evangelicals and liberation theologians have also been criticized because of their implied offers of a better life which, from a Hindu point of view, introduces an unworthy or 'ulterior' motive for conversion. In this debate Indian Christians who are the products of mass conversion movements see the motives of their ancestors impugned by both Hindus and Christians, and the stories of their search for liberation and identity remain untold. Conversion, or baptism, has been the most contentious issue between Christian and Hindu communities.

In India conversion took on the meaning of leaving the former religion and joining the Christian community. It is offensive to elite Hindus, who see it as a rejection of Hindu culture, and incomprehensible to those who understand Hinduism to be the inclusive way of life of India. Furthermore, it has become politicized because of the way that under British rule Indian communities were identified with particular religions and also because the main Christian communities are situated at the nation's extremities. In post-colonial India, Hindu objections to conversion have been concretized in three main ways: by the introduction of Hindu 'personal laws', which were disadvantageous for caste Hindus who converted to another religion (1955–56); by the limitation of social benefits for converts from Scheduled Caste backgrounds (1950s); and by the passing of the 'freedom of religion acts' in various states to protect Hindus against proselytization (1960s onwards). Where they operate, these measures effectively block individuals or groups from changing their community allegiance, except by 'home-coming' to Hinduism (S. Kim 2003). The difficulty of officially changing from one community to another is the main reason why, although according to census results Christianity is about 2.3 per cent and declining, the real figure may be nearer 5 per cent. This includes a 'Yesu Darbar' movement in North India of secret believers and unbaptized Christians which avoids legal difficulties. These new followers of Jesus are poor and seek healing and spiritual power. Militant Hinduism reached a new level in 1998 when a Hindu party was elected to central government for the first time. Reports increased of the destruction of churches, rape of nuns, killings of priests and general harassment of Christians. One of the worst episodes was in Kandhamal district in Orissa in 2008. This is far from the only case in which the recent Pentecostal growth and mission among low castes and outcastes has been a factor in violence by Hindu militants against Christians (Bauman 2015). Not only do Christians struggle to find an appropriate response to these threats but the danger is they become even more divided along caste lines about how to witness to Christ in India.

The Sri Lanka Catholic theologian Aloysius Pieris called for a 'double baptism' of Christianity in both 'the Jordan of Asian religions' and 'the Calvary of Asian poverty' (Pieris 1988:45–8). Asia remains deeply religious, however, the Indian model of religious pluralism and inter-religious dialogue is challenged today in India and it is not replicated across Asia. For example, Christians in South Korea think differently about inter-religious relations: they do not feel colonial guilt about their treatment of other religions; the Confucian cultural context values loyalty to a particular religious discipline; and religious conversion is not a political issue because Korean identity is firmly grounded on an ethnic basis (Lee 1999). In Korea, therefore, though the context is arguably more multireligious, the contours of debate are very different (Baker 2008). With regard to poverty, while Asians are rapidly joining the world's elite, both Hinduism and Buddhism promote the ascetic life. Jesus Christ is widely respected as a religious figure, and although Asian portraits of Jesus vary depending on whether he is set alongside Buddha, Krishna, Confucius or Muhammad, there is some common agreement that Jesus's significance lies in his suffering. However, Dalit and feminist theologians reject any valorization of poverty and emphasize the empowering and life-giving powers of Jesus (Orevillo-Montenegro 2006; Kwok 2000). Asians are divided on whether Christ's suffering is an example to follow by self-denial or a once for all sacrifice which means his followers need not suffer. This dilemma is another aspect of the inculturation–liberation debate because it is about whether Christianity should be ascetic, as the elite religious traditions of Asia are, or life-affirming like the local religions of the poor.

Minority and restriction in Central Asia

The Turkic and Mongol peoples of Central Asia mostly followed Shamanistic religious practices but Persians brought Zoroastrianism, and Buddhism spread from India. From the third century Manichaeism also grew in the region. It was a synthesis of Gnostic Christianity and Zoroastrianism which produced a dualistic belief in a cosmic battle between the darkness of the material world and spiritual enlightenment. The Persian, East Syrian, Assyrian church, or Church of the East began to develop independently from the churches of Syria and Mesopotamia and by the end of the sixth century it had appointed its own patriarch. By 600 AD the Persian church already included members of nomadic tribes such as the Huns and Turks, who lived in cities on the Silk Road to China. In the sixth to the tenth centuries, the church maintained a chain of monasteries in what are now Uzbekistan, Kazakhstan and Tajikistan. Despite the rise of Islam in its homelands under the Umayyad Caliphate and Abbasid Caliphates, Persian Christianity continued its spread eastward. By the end of the first millennium, the Uighurs, who had been Manicheans for several centuries, and the Kerait Turks had become Christians. Persian Christianity – still using Syriac – expanded not as an imperial religion but along Persian trade routes. John England (1996:2) claims that 'for centuries the Church of the East included greater numbers over vastly greater distances than the Churches of Rome or Byzantium, and this without colonial or imperial domination'. And he sees this non-aggressive Christian witness as an inspiration for Christianity in Asia today.

When the Mongols arose under Genghis Khan in the thirteenth century and took over most of the hitherto Muslim lands, as well as large parts of China and Europe, they were open to adopting other religions. Persian Christians had been in the area since the seventh century, and they were included at the Mongol court and in Mongol armies. Knowing this, a Franciscan, John of Plano Carpini, made representation from the pope at the Mongol court in Karakorum. A few years later another Catholic, William of Rubruck, was engaged in a dialogue before Möngke Khan with a Muslim and a Buddhist, but most Mongol rulers had become Muslims. Nevertheless, the Dominican Thomas Mancasole established the first Latin diocese in Central Asia in Samarkand in 1329. This was short-lived because the Christian communities in Central Asia were virtually destroyed by the Turko-Mongol conqueror Timur or Tamerlane in the late fourteenth century and erased from popular memory. Just a few ancient Christian communities have survived and preserved their heritage through their faith. Persian Christian church buildings also remain in a few places, especially in Kyrgyzstan.

Today the Central Asian republics of Kazakhstan, Kyrgyzstan, Tajikistan, Turkmenistan and Uzbekistan, which were once part of the Soviet Union, have a combined population of about sixty million of many different ethnic groups but these are mostly Sunni Muslims. The majority of Christians are in Orthodox churches from the Tsarist colonial period and are mostly ethnic Russians, although Christians of different kinds and from other countries under Russian control are also settled there. Some of them were 'Old Believers', who dissented from reforms of the Russian Church in the seventeenth century. Migrations increased in the turbulent years before and after the Bolshevik Revolution and during the Soviet period, bringing large communities of Ukrainians, Byelorussians, Germans, Koreans and others. Kazakhstan and Kyrgyzstan have Christian minorities of 13 and 6 per cent, respectively, but elsewhere Christians are less than 2 per cent. Freedom of religion after the end of Soviet domination saw the revival of Orthodox Christianity and also a great rise in practice of Islam in all these countries. In some places Roman Catholic, Lutheran and other churches serve minority groups originally from Poland, Germany and other parts of Europe, although these populations are rapidly declining. Since 1991, many new Evangelical and Pentecostal churches have sprung up, as a result of missions from the West and other parts of Asia as well as local initiative. Among the newer missions, South Koreans are particularly active among the substantial Korean minorities in Uzbekistan and Kazakhstan. However, the Russian Church declares itself to be non-proselytizing and denounces the 'competition', preferring to build relations with Muslim communities (Peyrouse 2014). Christians generally may experience intolerance from the majority populations. Furthermore, all the republics imposed restrictions on religious freedom at the turn of this century to target Islamic extremism which also further restricted the activities of non-Orthodox Christians and Christians with a Muslim background (Vysotskaya 2015).

Since Timuk, it has been a capital offence for any Afghan to convert to Christianity, and there have hardly been any witnessing communities in that country. Following the suppression of the Taliban, there are believed to be a few thousand Muslim-background believers among the Afghans today. Of the Mongolian people, some live inside modern China and others in the separate nation of Mongolia along China's northern border – the world's most sparsely populated country. Persian Christianity did not survive and the Mongols did not respond to Catholic or Russian Orthodox outreach. Attempts by Protestants to evangelize the people in the eighteenth and nineteenth centuries resulted in the translation of the Bible but few if any converts. The modern Mongolian Protestant church has only officially existed since 1991, following a bloodless transition to democracy which brought an influx of aid workers, including Christians who have also been active in education. Christians are less than 2 per cent of the population but Protestant denominations and Independent churches are growing.

Martyrdom and blessing in Northeast Asia

The nations of Northeast Asia – China, Japan and Korea – share a Confucian and Mahayana Buddhist heritage. In the Confucian way of thinking, China is the 'elder brother' to Korea and Japan, which look westwards for their classical art and literature. The Chinese Confucian model of a strong centralized state has largely determined the pattern of reception of the gospel in all three countries. Religious belief and practice is subject to the favour of the rulers and closely regulated.

China

The presence of Persian Christianity in China had been all but forgotten by 1625, when workmen near the city of Xi'an, the former capital in Northwest China, unearthed a toppled monument. It gave an account in Chinese and Persian of Christianity's arrival in China with A-lo-pen, a Persian bishop, in 635 – a thousand years before. It outlined Christian doctrine and practice in a distinctively Syriac form. It described the religion as 'the Way', a biblical description of Christianity (Acts 9:2), using the Chinese word '*dao*' (as in Taoism). It praised the wisdom of the emperor, who permitted the propagation of this 'Way', and recounted the history of the Christian community, which had flourished until 698 AD when, apparently, Buddhists caused controversy and later violence against Christians. However, it was restored by another emperor in 742, which was the occasion for erecting the monument. There are no Christian communities in China now that are directly descended from that Persian mission. Perhaps the faith was too inculturated – other discoveries of Christian texts at the Mogao Caves, for instance, suggest a syncretized faith. Or maybe Christianity was mainly practised by immigrant communities who later assimilated, voluntarily or by force, or were removed elsewhere (Moffett 1998:287–323). But Persian Christianity continued in China into the Middle Ages. In 1281, King Edward I of

England attended a mass in Bordeaux, France, in which the celebrant used a liturgy that was Syriac in language and ritual. The priest himself, called Sauma, was of Ongut race and from a small monastery near Beijing. He told them that many Mongols were Christians and that they had received the Christian message directly from the apostle Thomas. When Sauma later celebrated the Eucharist in Rome, the conclusion was that 'the language is different, but the rite is one' (433–4).

In 1294, during the Mongol rule of China and Korea, the Franciscan envoy John of Montecorvino came to Beijing, and in the next decade he built a wooden church and conducted mass in Latin. Despite complaints from the Persian Christians that there was already a Christian community in the city, the Franciscan mission lasted until about 1360. It was more than two hundred years before the next Catholic missionaries arrived in Beijing during the Ming Dynasty. They were Jesuits led by the great Matteo Ricci who had won the emperor's favour. By the early seventeenth century a Chinese church was established in Beijing, supported by the three 'pillars': the scholars Paul Xu Guangqi, Michael Yang Tingyun and Leon Li Zhizao. They continued Ricci's method of mediating Christianity through the introduction of Western science and philosophy to the nation. Over the next century the church spread south and east of Beijing, to the lower Yangtze region, Fujian, and Shandong among a wider cross-section of society (Moffett 2005:105–42). However, after the papal condemnation of the Chinese rites in 1715 (see Chapter 4), the threat of Catholicism to the Chinese state was more obvious, and in 1724 the Chinese emperor suppressed Christian mission. During this time, the Chinese Church was largely led by Chinese, including a few who had become priests, and it adapted itself to local culture. Christianity spread to Sichuan province and became a popular movement (Harrison 2013). Unfortunately, its millenialist tendencies and foreign connections alarmed the authorities and episodes of severe persecution against Chinese Christians continued for 120 years (Moffett 2005:120–32).

In the mid-nineteenth century, British, French and North American missionaries took advantage of the establishment of 'treaty ports' and other privileges won for foreigners by the Opium Wars, but their efforts to establish Protestantism were naturally hampered by their political affiliations. However, their translations of the Bible and the work of the Chinese evangelists who spread and taught it began to influence Chinese society, for example, in the Taiping Rebellion (1851–64), which exhibited a 'syncretic' form of Protestantism (Tiedemann 1999). After 1860, with its government greatly weakened by Western and later Japanese incursions, China became the largest mission field in the world – especially for the United States. Catholic missions returned in force aiming to rescue and protect their flock. But their efforts to bring the indigenous church back into line with Roman practice caused tensions with the Chinese leadership. The missions of the older Protestant denominations prioritized programmes of education, medicine and famine relief. Converts therefore had a variety of motives for joining the Christian faith and attracted the label 'rice Christians'.

Missionary education – including of women – encouraged the development of a Christian middle class which was progressive and pro-modernization. Except through the Catholic Church and Hudson Taylor's China Inland Mission (CIM), the mass of Chinese in the interior, not to mention minority groups in China, had little encounter with Christianity. Converts, both Catholic – now protected by France – and Protestant lived in Christian villages isolated from other Chinese and were frequently in danger from anti-Christian violence. The worst was the Boxer Rebellion of 1900 when over 30,000 Chinese Christians were killed as well as 250 foreign missionaries, for which there were fierce reprisals by British and French troops. During the unstable years of the early twentieth century, Christian fortunes fluctuated: they were either favoured by modernists as 'anti-traditional' or persecuted by communists as 'cultural imperialists' but on the whole Christianity, especially Protestantism, flourished (Bays 2012).

From a Chinese point of view, the social gospellers of the large Protestant denominations Westernized and then Christianized while the independent Faith Missions – now including Pentecostals – Christianized and then Westernized but the net result was the same (Leung 2001:142). The first type of mission established institutional churches closely related to Western structures, which were dominated by missionaries. However, after the baptism of the nationalist leader Chiang Kai-shek in 1930, and in the context of growing instability and reduced funding for missions from the West, a more indigenous church emerged, following the 'three-self' paradigm (see chapter 4). The second type, especially the work of the CIM, resulted in local fellowships on a house–church pattern. From about 1900 revivalists, both Western and Chinese, including a notable woman Dora Yu (Yu Cidu) and later the combative John Sung (Song Shangjie), stimulated the formation of Chinese-founded churches (Bays 2012:121–41). Since these were active in evangelism, networks of independent churches soon emerged. These included: the Little Flock led by Watchman Nee (Ni Tosheng), who emphasized spiritual life as the key to bodily holiness in what he saw as the end times; the Jesus Family of Jing Dianying who, with his wife, set up a cooperative or commune, which was then replicated across northern and northwestern China; the True Jesus Church, a Pentecostal group; and the Christian Church in Christ of Wang Ming-Dao, who exercised a strictly moral and prophetic ministry that had no time for the social gospel or enthusiasm for indigenization of missionary Christianity (Xi 2010). Wang was imprisoned for 23 years by the communist regime for his criticism of the later patriotic church and, in the post-communist period, he was regarded by many as the unofficial leader of the underground churches. At the grassroots in all the churches were women, who were attracted particularly by the more feminized, compassionate Jesus of nineteenth-century Holiness movements. At the same time they learned to read, experienced liberation from foot-binding and other oppressive customs and engaged in movements for social change (Kwok 1992).

The War of Resistance against Japan (1937–45), followed by the Civil War (1947–49), was a time of turmoil for all Chinese, and the activities of the mission churches especially came under tight control by both Chinese and Japanese authorities, although the independent Chinese churches mostly flourished and some attempted to evangelize western China (Bays 2012:141–9). After the Chinese Communist Party won the power struggle with the nationalists in 1949 and established the People's Republic of China (PRC), Christian churches – Protestant and Catholic – were under pressure to show their allegiance to the Party. The Christian Manifesto (1950), drafted by Y. T. Wu (Wu Yaozong), an activist in the YMCA, was signed by half of China's Protestants. It pre-empted government action against the churches by pledging support for anti-imperialism, anti-feudalism and anti-bureaucratic capitalism and the building of a 'New China'. Capitalizing on an earlier expression of unity, the National Christian Council (founded 1922), in 1952 Wu established the (Protestant) Three Self Patriotic Movement (TSPM), which became a state organization. Subverting the missionary mantra of 'three-self', the aims of the TSPM were to remove foreign influence and demonstrate Protestant church support for PRC. Although most of the mission churches joined, many Chinese-initiated churches refused to join TSPM and went underground (Wickeri 1988; Bays 2012:158–68).

The establishment of the Catholic Patriotic Association (CPA) in 1957 was the result of a more protracted struggle. By this time the Chinese Church had about three million adherents – three or four times that of the Protestant mission churches. It was deeply rooted but dominated by foreign priests. Globally, in 1949 the Catholic Church had directed Catholics not to cooperate with communists on pain of excommunication. The Chinese Church was predominantly rural but had a strong base in Shanghai where the papal nuncio Antonio Riberi used the Legion of Mary and other devotional organizations to protest and Bishop Gong Pinmei led the clergy resistance to the inevitable (Bays 2012:169–75). The authorities forbade the CPA to have any contact with the Vatican; this led to the Chinese Church appointing its own leaders and clergy being required to reject the authority of the pope and any further teaching from the magisterium.

At the beginning of the Great Leap Forward in 1958, most churches were forcibly closed, clergy were forced onto the land, and a generic form of worship was imposed. At the outbreak of the Cultural Revolution in 1966, all religious activity – except the quasi-religious Maoism – was regarded as superstitious and anti-revolutionary. Bibles were burned and priests and pastors were imprisoned and often tortured. From 1966 until Deng Xiaoping's open-door policy in 1979, Christianity survived in only a deinstitutionalized and declericalized form in the prison camps or in underground or 'house-churches'. In rural areas Protestant house-churches grew strongly despite the rigours of communist oppression and they overtook Catholic numbers (Bays 2012:176–87).

Despite the severity of the repression, after permission was given for religious activity and the legitimacy of Protestantism and (Chinese) Catholicism was recognized in the context of the economic liberalization of 1979, China experienced what even the authorities called 'Christian fever'. Thousands of churches (re)opened among the Han Chinese, especially in Henan and the provinces along the east coast. In addition, Korean Chinese were active in starting churches, especially in Shandong Province. Furthermore, some minority groups, such as the Lisu in Yunnan who had been reached by CIM missionary James O. Fraser and the Karen evangelist Ba Taw before 1949, even claimed Christianity as a mark of their ethnic identity. Protestant churches were encouraged to join the China Christian Council (CCC), controlled by the TSPM, which describes itself as 'post-denominational'. Bishop K. H. (Kuang-hsun) Ting, originally an Anglican and a committed communist who held government posts, led the TSPM and the CCC from 1980 to 1997. His 'theological reconstruction' seemed to some as a one-sided adaptation to socialist society in its emphasis on Christian social service, and he kept a tight rein on church activities. Nevertheless, he created space for the church, protected it and raised Christianity to a higher profile than at any time in its history in China (Wickeri 2007:370–9). However, many congregations, suspicious of the CCC as a government organization, have chosen to remain 'unregistered', and the religious enthusiasm has generated many new groups, some of which are radically sectarian. The Holy See is treading a delicate path between the CPA, which it has never declared heretical, and the underground Catholic Church that emerged after the Cultural Revolution led by those who had refused to join the CPA and asserted their loyalty to Rome. Rural Protestant and Catholic churches show signs of being syncretized with folk religion, which makes both church and government authorities uneasy (Bays 2012:187–99). There is religious freedom in China for churches that stay within the limits set by government, which preclude interfering with government policies, proselytizing, baptizing or teaching religion to children, or contacting foreign organizations without permission (Chan 2015). Churches that contravene these rules, or do not register, risk censure by the authorities and are at the mercy of local officials.

Although the distinction between official and underground or unregistered Protestant churches is now breaking down at a local level, there is continuing tension between them and the CCC/TSPM. Accounts of the church from these different situations can yield widely varying views. The house-churches – some of which may now have their own buildings – tend to regard the official churches with suspicion, and many have chosen not to register; consequently estimates of the numbers of Christians vary widely. A Chinese and a US-based survey in 2010 came up with figures for the total number of Protestants of 23 million and 30 million, respectively, or between 1.8 and 2.3 per cent of the population, which were much lower than predicted after the initial post-communist enthusiasm (Huang 2015). However, for the same year, the *Atlas of Global Christianity* (Johnson and Ross 2009) gave a figure of

Figure 2.3 The entrance to the new building at Nanjing Union Theological Seminary, China, which is the major seminary of the China Christian Council. Bishop K. H. Ting was the principal here until his death in 2012.

115 million or 8.6 per cent for the total number of Christians and the Catholic-run Faith Institute for Cultural Studies gave a figure of 6 million Catholics, not including the underground church (Jin and Qui 2011:119). Clearly caution should be exercised with respect to the figures, but there is no doubt that Christian belief and practice has become widespread in China. Moreover, since the 1990s it has become more of an urban and middle-class phenomenon.

Christianity has also taken a cultural form disconnected from the churches. Centres for the study of Christianity have opened in university departments of religion, which not only introduce Western theology to China but also engage in Sino-theology (Choong 2008). This is stimulating the emergence of an intellectual Christianity with a distinctive theology of modernization that sees Christianity as having 'positive effects', including social service and social care, 'theological thought-building' toward a moral and ethical contribution to society, and the promotion of overseas exchange (Huang 2015). Although Christians may be respected for their high moral standards, religious faith is officially incompatible with membership of the Chinese Communist Party, and therefore with social advancement. Nevertheless today there are party members willing to declare themselves Christian. The Chinese government has gone from attempting to co-opt (1949–57), suppress (1958–66) and even eradicate (1966–79) the faith to a policy of recognizing it but weakening it by promoting more ancient Chinese religions or merely containing it by regulation (1979–2010; Yang 2012:65–84). The long-term impact on Chinese society of the Christian revival is too early to call. But whatever happens, the numbers involved and the status of China ensures it will have great significance for world Christianity.

The Chinese Communist Party could not halt the spread of Christianity in the Chinese diaspora, or in the neighbouring territories of Taiwan, Macao and Hong Kong, which it did not control. By the twentieth century Catholic and Presbyterian Christianity were already established on Taiwan, the largest territory, among the indigenous people and the Chinese settlers. With the migration of nationalist Chinese to Taiwan after the communist victory on the Chinese mainland, came not only the other mission churches from China but also most of the indigenous churches such as the True Jesus Church and the Little Flock. More recently the latter have been growing fast and are re-evangelizing China from a Taiwanese base (Tang 2011:402–4). In the 1970s, leaders of the Presbyterian Church, which drew its main support from among the majority population who lived in Taiwan before 1949, campaigned vigorously – and at the cost of imprisonment – for the rights of the Taiwanese against the Nationalist-Chinese government of the Mainlanders, who ruled Taiwan as a one-party state from 1949 to 2000 (Lo 2011). From the experience of their island, claimed by China and occupied by Japan from 1895 to 1945, Taiwanese Presbyterians have been leaders in the discussion as to how theology should be done in Asia. Shoki Coe advocated a theology of 'contextualization' of the gospel by the local people with regard to social as well as cultural concerns instead of missionary 'indigenization' (Coe 1976). C. S. (Choan-seng) Song (1988), former president of Tainan Theological Seminary, developed an influential 'theology from the womb of Asia' which weaves together biblical and Asian stories.

By the terms under which Macao was returned to China in 1999, the Roman Catholic Church is permitted to maintain the presence it has had since 1553 and its links to Rome. For centuries the Christian gateway to China, the churches, also including Anglican and Presbyterian, include about 5 per cent of the half-million residents now. During the communist era they supported many illegal migrants from China but today they struggle against the prevailing ethos of gambling (Lo 2011).

Hong Kong was a British colony for 150 years and an Anglican diocese from 1849. However, ministry to the Chinese was left to a catechist Lo Sam-Yuen. Yuen, who had worked among his fellow South Chinese in the Australian goldfields and was ordained in Hong Kong in 1863, was supported by the CMS but his work was only brought together with the diocese from the 1930s by Bishop Ronald Hall. It was also Hall who controversially ordained the first woman Anglican priest, Hong Kong-born Li Tim-Oi, to serve Macao in the emergency situation of 1944 when there were no other priests (Ward 2006:256–9). When Hong Kong was overwhelmed by an influx of refugees from China in the late 1940s, the Anglicans pioneered new housing schemes. Today, Christians – Protestants of all varieties and Catholics – form about 10 per cent of the seven-million population despite the relatively high emigration of Christians before the handover to China in 1997. Large numbers of these Christians are now found in Canada, Australia and the United States. Despite the fears of some, there is continued religious freedom, and Protestant denominations play an active role in society by running educational institutions, including three universities and seven hospitals dating from the colonial period. The territory also continues its role as a hub for mission in China and ministry in the Chinese diaspora, which partly explains the large number of Christian publishing houses and broadcasting activities (Lo 2011). Christians played an active role in negotiations for the return of the territory to China and so leaders who chose to remain in Hong Kong after 1997 feel a responsibility to work for reconciliation. At the political level this means overcoming the suspicion that exists between the Hong Kong Chinese brought up in the Western system and the Chinese Communist Party. Evangelical Lutheran theologian Lap Yan Kung suggests that trust between the two depends on a revision of the Confucian filial piety analogy in which the relationship is often couched. While traditional Confucianism expects unconditional love of child for parent, the Christian gospel highlights the love of the parent for the child (John 3:16) (Kung 2005:185).

Japan

The first Japanese to respond to the Christian message was a fugitive named Anjirō, who met the Jesuit missionary Francis Xavier in Malacca and persuaded him to come to Japan. Xavier was well received in 1549 at the court of the daimyo, or feudal lord, Ōuchi Yoshitaka, who traded with the Portuguese through the port of Nagasaki. The mission's success was partly due to the fact that the Jesuits set up schools, hospitals and homes for the elderly and children. These were run by lay catechists, including a women's society led by Naitō Julia, which was not allowed elsewhere in the world (Ward 2012). During the following 'Christian century', a faith adapted to Japan was adopted by other daimyos and their people. It spread to the capital city Kyoto, and by 1614 there was probably a larger proportion of Christians in Japan than the 2.3 per cent there are estimated to be now, although they were concentrated in the lands of sympathetic feudal lords. However, the Tokygawa Shogunate, which unified Japan in 1600, persecuted Christians: all churches were closed, all Christian practice, in public or in secret, was prohibited and Christians were tortured to produce apostasy, often by treading on an image of Christ. According to one estimate, about half of the Catholics in Japan today are descendants of Kakure Kirishitan or lay communities, especially around Nagasaki, who hid their faith for the next two centuries (Moffett 2005:93). Ironically, the second atomic bomb dropped on Japan in 1945 destroyed Saint Mary's Cathedral, which had been built on the site where early Catholics had been forced to apostatize.

In 1859, after Japan was forced by Western powers to open selected ports to foreign settlement, Catholic missionaries re-entered the country and some 'hidden Christians' revealed themselves and rejoined the Roman Catholic Church. But a much larger proportion, mainly islanders, chose to keep attending the Buddhist temples and maintaining the distinct practices they had evolved in secret. The first Protestant churches, founded mostly by North American missionaries, were Episcopal, Presbyterian, (Dutch) Reformed, Methodist and Baptist. Since anti-Christian edicts were in place until 1873, very few converted, although a Russian Orthodox mission begun in 1861 made better progress and by 1875 there were already two Japanese priests. However, there are now more than three times as many Protestants as Catholics in Japan and even fewer Orthodox. Protestant educational work and the formation of student Christian 'bands' helped to produce some outstanding leaders including Jo Niishima, who founded Doshisha University. The first converts were from among the samurai and were active politically. These progressive thinkers understood Christianity to be the secret of the West's success. But the enthusiasm for Christianity cooled in the last decade of the nineteenth century with the rise of Japanese nationalism (Moffett 2005:502–20). As Japan built up its military power and expanded its empire across East Asia, Christians occasionally resisted but more often accommodated the growing militarization and imperial conquest. Most missionaries had to leave and so the churches became independent of foreign control. The Japanese churches sent missionaries to help Christians in the other countries of East and Southeast Asia that were occupied by the growing Japanese Empire. Catholics and virtually all Protestants eventually complied with the requirements for State Shinto rituals and observance of the emperor cult, even making theological justification for the practice (Mullins 1998:20). From as early as 1877, some of the mission churches had united in an ecumenical spirit, but it was the threat of organizational extinction by the government, as war threatened and the regulations on churches tightened, that resulted in almost all the Protestant churches joining together in 1941 to make a single United Church of Christ in Japan. Today the church retains the core of that union – Reformed, Methodist and Congregational – and remains the largest single denomination. After the end of the Pacific War, several thousand foreign missionaries entered the country, leading to a proliferation of smaller churches, but not to significant long-term increase in the proportion of Christians.

The Protestant churches in Japan have spawned many indigenous groups (Mullins 1998). The earliest was the 'nonchurch' movement founded by Uchimura Kanzō in 1901. It was primarily a prophetic reaction against the foisting of foreign denominational divisions and extra-biblical practices on Japanese Christians. The founders of

The Way (1907) and Christ Heart Church (1927) rebelled against the institutionalism of Western religion and its exclusivism, insisting that the scriptures of various Asian religions were also vehicles of revelation and adopting traditional Japanese religious practices. Later indigenous churches have been more oriented to popular religiosity and more Pentecostal or charismatic in nature, such as the restorationist-style Spirit of Jesus Church (1941). This church and some others have evolved ways of relating to the world of the dead, which is the function of traditional ancestor veneration. Japan has its share of neo-Pentecostal movements; some of these are among the substantial Korean minority or the result of missions from South Korea itself. Along with the general population, the churches are aging but the Catholic Church at least is being revitalized by migrant workers from Southeast Asia.

Although Japanese Christians are in a small minority, they have contributed disproportionately to education and social welfare. Christians have campaigned for the rights of minorities such as the indigenous Ainu people in Hokkaido. Kagawa Toyohiko was influential internationally for his ministry to the poor (Mullins 2014). Tetsu Katayama became Japan's first socialist (and Christian) prime minister in 1947 and, as a Christian pacifist, he effectively put a stop to the remilitarization desired by the Americans and some other Japanese (Phillips 1981). In the aftermath of Japan's defeat and the dropping of the atom bombs, Lutheran theologian Kazoh Kitamori wrote his groundbreaking work *Theology of the Pain of God* (ET 1965). The book influenced the German theologian Jürgen Moltmann's wrestling with similar issues in the 1960s in *The Crucified God* (ET 1973). However, Kitamori did not address the issue of Japanese complicity in their own suffering and in the suffering they caused other Asian nations during their imperial rule. In contrast, the Catholic doctor Nagi Takashi from Nagasaki controversially saw the victims of the bombing as pure lambs sacrificed to God and encouraged those left behind to reflect on why they were not worthy to join them (Miyamoto 2011:111–41). The churches worked for peace and in 1967 the Kyodan and other churches began to admit their wartime collaboration, but they have yet to succeed in persuading the wider society to deal with the militarist past to the satisfaction of neighbouring countries (Miyahira 2008).

Korea

Until the late nineteenth century, the rugged Korean peninsula was tightly controlled by a Confucian state. It was difficult for foreign missionaries to penetrate and it was not high on their agenda. In both the Protestant and the Catholic cases, it was Koreans who took the initiative to bring Christianity to their homeland (Kim and Kim 2015). A group of Korean intellectuals studying the Chinese works of Ricci on science and philosophy became interested in the Christian faith itself and sent one of their number, Yi Seung-hun, to Beijing where in 1784 he was baptized by a Jesuit priest. Returning home, he baptized his fellows and that lay community, existing before any mission or hierarchy, is considered the foundation of today's Catholic Church. After the end of the Rites Controversy, Korean converts were instructed to stop their traditions of ancestor worship. This set them at odds with their rulers and Catholics were subjected to several waves of persecution, culminating in 1866 in the deaths of eight thousand or half of the Catholic population. As a result, Korea has a strong martyr cult and one of the highest number of saints of any country in the world. The first priest to celebrate mass in Korea was a Chinese, James Zhou Wen-mo, in 1795. He was hidden from the authorities by Columba Kang Wan-suk, a remarkable woman who led a community of women who defied Confucian convention by remaining celibate (Ledyard 2006). The Catholic community survived in Christian villages in remote islands and mountains. These challenged the Confucian class system, gave women a greater role and showed particular compassion to children. French priests were smuggled in from 1836. As French control over the Church increased after the forced open of the peninsula to Japan and the West in 1876, the tradition of virgin women was suppressed. Nevertheless, Korean Catholics had laid the foundations of religious freedom, mass literacy, even democracy and provided direct links to the world beyond China (Yu 1996).

Almost one hundred years after Yi's baptism, a Protestant convert Suh Sang-ryun risked his life to carry copies of a Korean translation of Luke's Gospel into Korea. The translation was initiated by Scottish Presbyterian John Ross across the border

Figure 2.4 An early morning prayer meeting at Myungsung Church, Seoul, South Korea, the largest Presbyterian church in the world.

in China. In this highly Confucian culture, the new book was read avidly and Ross's Korean disciples founded Protestant lay communities. A year or so later in 1885, under pressure from foreign powers, the government permitted the first Protestant missionaries – a Presbyterian and a Methodist from the USA – to enter. They baptized the Koreans and connected the Korean church with global Christianity. The 'three-self' missionary policy shared by all the main missions from the 1890s was taken equally seriously by Korean Christians, who started local congregations, schools and hospitals across the country. Much of the pioneer work was done by 'Bible women' – lay women evangelists (Choi 2009:65–77).

In a turbulent period when Korea was fought over by Chinese, Russian and Japanese forces, the Protestants fostered nationalist hope through new communities, education, access to modern business and links with the apparently benevolent United States. In 1907 a revival broke out in Pyongyang, now capital of North Korea, and an indigenous Christianity was born. A chief characteristic of Korean Christianity was attention to the Bible and its employment of Confucian methods of repeated reading and memorization to study it. Christian converts saw parallels between their situation of subjection to Japan, which was actualized in annexation in 1910, and the experience of the Israelites. Protestant and Catholic Christians resisted through emigration, armed resistance and assassination attempts on Japanese figures of authority. In 1919, revival leader Kil Son-Ju and other Protestant pastors worked with other religious leaders to mount the peaceful March 1 independence movement. The movement was crushed but it sealed the Protestant churches' association with nationalism. During the period of Japanese occupation (1910–45) the churches kept the millennial hope of liberation alive in several ways. Yun Chi-ho inspired a self-strengthening movement to prepare the nation for independence; Ahn Chang-ho and others built up the diaspora in China, Manchuria, Siberia and the United States and worked internationally to free Korea (Wells 1990); and Lee Yong-do and others led revival movements which defied the Japanese authorities and sustained the churches in Korea. Protestants mounted the only organized resistance to the imposition of Shinto shrine worship, believing it contravened the first commandment; at least 50 were killed and others imprisoned. Nevertheless, churches that remained public were forced to comply. Ironically, the Catholic Church, which had earlier in China resisted Confucian ancestor veneration at such cost, made a concordat with Japan in 1936 which permitted participation in Shinto ceremonies which were seen as civil not religious rituals (Park Chang-won 2011:149–60). After the liberation in 1945, the first of many splits within the dominant Presbyterian Church was over issues of collaboration with the Japanese.

In the partitioned peninsula from 1945, many Christians were attracted by the social ideals of the communists but, despite the fact that he had come from a Protestant family, when the revolutionary leader Kim Il-Sung took control of the north under Soviet occupation, he suppressed all religious activity. Today little is known for certain about the state of Christianity in North Korea. Although there are a handful of official Protestant, Catholic and Orthodox churches with relations with South Korean churches and international networks, religion remains tightly controlled. Most believers are relegated to the lowest class of society and many are in prison.

In South Korea Christianity grew rapidly until, in the 2005 census, nearly 30 per cent of Koreans declared themselves Christians, eclipsing the other main organized religion, Buddhism. This growth is unparalleled in Asia in regions where other world religions are already established. The growth of Christianity in the 1950s–1980s is explained in several ways. The first is the construction of South Korea in contradistinction to the atheistic communist North as a religiously free but strongly Christian-influenced nation. The stronghold of Protestantism was in the Pyongyang region and Christians there were better educated and more modernized than others. Many fled south between 1945 and 1953 and founded new churches among the displaced; these were anti-communist and had a vision for a Christian nation. The pre-eminent example is Presbyterian pastor Han Kyung-Chik who founded Youngnak Church in Seoul which ministered to other refugees by aid, pastoral care, education and help with businesses. Han was awarded the Templeton Prize for his work in 1992. Today the Church has programmes to help a new wave of North Korean refugees to integrate into South Korea and since famine struck the North in the 1990s it has had active aid and development work there.

The Catholic Church and international Protestant bodies supported the establishment of an independent South Korea as a bulwark against the tide of communism in Asia. During and after the Korean War (1950–53), Catholic agencies were the largest non-government source of aid to South Korea. Missionaries of all kinds poured in under the US-oriented administration of Rhee Syng-man, a Methodist, and further diversified the religious landscape. Church leaders committed themselves to evangelistic work and supported the undemocratic and military-backed governments of the 1950s, 1960s and 1970s. This was partly because of their shared fear of communism but also because of their drives for modernization for the national good. Christians were well placed to take advantage of the situation in the Western-oriented South and played a significant role in the development of South Korea as a world-leading economy. However, from the 1970s, their uncritical support for military governments was denounced by other progressive Christians, influenced by theologies of humanization and liberation, and looking back to the Christian role in the independence movement. Although imprisoned and tortured for their political activities, Ahn Byung-mu, Suh Nam Dong and other Protestant 'minjung theologians' took the side of poor people and oppressed workers (minjung) (Christian Conference of Asia 1981). Roman Catholic priests and intellectuals, such as the poet Kim Chi-ha, were also active in the minjung movement and the support of Korea's first cardinal,

Stephen Kim Sou-hwan, was pivotal in the eventual achievement of democratic government in South Korea from 1988 (S. C. H. Kim 2015).

Korean church growth was partly the result of systematic evangelistic campaigns which had a nationalist and anti-communist flavour (T. Lee 2010). Durkheimian sociologists look to the role of churches in offering networks for pastoral support and mutual help during rapid urbanization in the 1960s–1980s to explain it. Others favour a supply-side theory that the growth resulted from competition in the religious marketplace created by religious freedom and urbanization. Korea became famous for its 'mega-churches', particularly Yoido Full Gospel Church, founded by Paul, later David, Cho Yonggi, which now claims more than three-quarters of a million members. Cho developed techniques of prayer and evangelism that would guarantee health, well-being and prosperity. This 'prosperity theology' was criticized for resembling some of the practices of the ancient shamanistic religion of the Korean people and the 'positive thinking' of late capitalism but equally it was in continuity with the tradition of revivalism during Japanese colonial rule (Ig-jin Kim 2003). The legacy of Korean indigenous religion is among the cultural affinities suggested to explain church growth. This is especially prevalent among women and contributes to a strong charismatic stream across the churches. However, charismatic Christianity is under the control of the (overwhelmingly) male leadership and their preferred Confucian style of operating, which is ordered and disciplined. Korean churches thus combine two complementary faces which meet both elite and popular religious needs. This is comprehensible in the context of belief in the yin–yang balance between female and male principles which is ubiquitous in East Asia. But yin–yang is experienced by many women as oppressive, so Korean feminists have sought an alternative framework of traditional religion for their theologizing (Choi 2005).

That the growth of Protestantism was closely linked to modernization is shown by the way post-war Korean churches were built in modern styles and made use of the latest technology to convey a future-oriented message of good news. However, as Korea moves rapidly from modernity into post-modernity, the mainstream Protestant churches have been losing ground. By 2005, 40 per cent of all Christians were Catholics and this proportion is rising. Catholicism has been growing since the 1950s but in a more gradual and consolidated way. It was only in 1962 that the Catholic Church of Korea was established in its own right. The Church has a more rigorous selection process and exercises greater controls on theological training than Protestants. Tastes in spirituality have become more traditional and this makes Catholicism more attractive. But the main reasons for the growth of Catholicism and the decline of Protestantism are the prominent role of the Catholic Church for human rights and democratization; the commitment of the Church to deliver much of the government's social care; and the ability of the Catholic Church to remain above the allegations of corruption and scandal that have damaged some Protestant leaders. Much of the recent Catholic growth is by transfer from Protestantism.

Korean Christians regard the growth of the church and the economic miracle of twentieth-century Korea both as blessings from God – and see a close connection between the two (K. Kim 2015). The overseas missionary movement from South Korea, which ranks among the largest in the world, stems from this confidence coupled with a sense of responsibility to repay the debt of the gospel, compassion for those less fortunate and the emergence of South Korea on the world stage. The widespread Korean diaspora, especially, in the United States (R. Kim 2015), China, Russia and parts of Central Asia, Japan and Brazil, is another vehicle of evangelism and offers bases for missionary work. Korean missionaries also pioneer beyond these communities and some work in countries inhospitable to Christianity, for example, by working for Korean businesses in Muslim countries. Missionaries not only bring their religious practices but also their education, business and practical skills, especially in medicine – both Western-style and acupuncture. In this way, the Korean gospel is being deliberately exported across the globe (Kim and Ma 2011). Furthermore, since the 2002 football World Cup was played in Korea, a Korean or 'Hallyu' wave of cultural influence has spread across Asia, and particularly China. In this low-key way also Christian values are being spread from Korea.

Diversity and struggle in Southeast Asia

Although there are claims that relics of Persian Christianity have been found in Burma (Myanmar), Siam (modern Thailand), Annam (North Vietnam), Malaya (Malaysia and Singapore), and Java and Sumatra (in modern Indonesia), this is not conclusive (Moffett 1998:459–62). There does not seem to be any continuity between earlier forms of Christianity and the first Catholic missions of the sixteenth century. Today in each of the countries of Southeast Asia, different Christianities have each evolved their own responses to their religious and social contexts. As in many other parts of Asia, Christianity in this region is divided by government policies into Catholic and Protestant for administrative and census purposes. This is not so surprising considering that their respective missions entered in different centuries, came from different Western nations, spoke different languages, referred to different sources of authority, worshipped in very different ways and, more often than not, were in competition with each other. However, the situation militates against ecumenical cooperation and Orthodox churches' struggle to gain legitimacy, as in the case of the Russian Orthodox Church in China (Ying 2011:159–61).

Vietnam, Cambodia, Laos, Burma/Myanmar and Thailand

Despite the Confucian centralized state control of religion in Vietnam, the Catholic Church has been well established in parts of the country since the early-seventeenth-century work of Jesuits, including the famous Alexandre de Rhodes who set up an organization of lay catechists and a French hierarchy and reduced the Vietnamese language to writing. As in other parts of Confucian Asia, the church experienced periodic persecution. This was repeated after the country was partitioned in 1954 by the communist regime in the North, from which many Christians fled south. The Vietnamese bishops lobbied for independence from France in 1945 and the Vietnamese Church was established in its own right in 1960. During the Vietnam War, Western missionaries in the South also worked among the tribal peoples, joining the Christian and Missionary Alliance, which had been doing this since 1911. After the end of the Vietnam War in 1975, the Vietnamese fleeing poverty and the communists included relatively more Christians – especially Catholics, many of whom are settled today in the United States, Australia and Europe. Religion was strictly controlled in the socialist republic but since 1988 religions have enjoyed more freedoms. Marian devotion, focused around Our Lady of La Vang, is strong and so is a cult of the martyrs, many of whom were canonized in 1988 (Phan 2011). Despite communism and the predominant Buddhism, Vietnamese Catholic theologian Peter Phan argues that Confucian norms dominate Vietnamese lives today and influence the way Jesus Christ is understood. Jesus, he points out, was the epitome of filial piety: he upheld the commandment 'to honour father and mother' (Matt. 19:18; Luke 2:51–2). Phan goes on to show that the biblical traditions can be interpreted to mean that Jesus has become the pre-eminent ancestor in a way analogous to Vietnamese tradition (Phan 2003a:126–43). Today Christianity, mainly Catholic, is a minority of about 8 or 9 per cent of the population but is growing rapidly. Phan considers the greatest threat to the Church is not the so-called communist system but the indifference to religion due to the relentless pursuit of wealth. The same could be said for many other parts of East Asia.

In several other countries of Southeast Asia – Cambodia, Laos, Burma/Myanmar and Thailand – Christians are part of much smaller minorities among majority Theravada Buddhist societies. Despite Catholic missions since the sixteenth century and Protestant missions since the early nineteenth century, the people have resisted evangelization, partly because in none of these countries has Christianity ever been associated with nationalism (Tiedemann 1999:408). Christians (and Buddhists) were almost annihilated by the xenophobic Khmer Rouge in Cambodia in the 1970s. Late-twentieth-century missions by US American and diaspora Christians have resulted in the growth of independent churches, the largest of which is a Pentecostal body, the New Apostolic Church. Laos also experienced repression under communists but today has growing Catholic and Evangelical communities.

Successive Catholic missions have attempted to evangelize the majority Burmese population of Myanmar over six centuries but Christians, who may make up 8 per cent of the population, are mainly Baptists and from tribal groups. The Karen people saw the coming of the US American missionary couple Adoniram and Ann Judson in 1813 as the fulfilment of their own beliefs and prophecy. The Karen later shared their faith with the Kachin while other missionaries reached the Chin. However, the assertion of a distinctive Christian identity by these minority groups was seen as a threat to the Burmese, who have used Buddhism to create a national identity and oppressed other religions by policies of disinformation, discrimination and violent persecution. Government actions have been condemned internationally but armed conflict continues in the Karen region (Storaker 2015). In Thailand too most of the Christians (who form less than 2 per cent of the population) are not of Thai descent but are Chinese, Vietnamese or from tribal minorities. Christians are perceived as foreign in this nation which has the distinction of being the only nation in southern Asia that has never submitted to colonial rule and is defined by an identity in which ethnicity is synonymous with being Buddhist. As Thailand becomes more urban and more cosmopolitan, Christianity is growing and Korean missionaries have been particularly influential on Thai Christianity. It is the view of the Federation of Asian Bishops' Conferences (Catholic) that until the people decide that they need Christianity, the church should content itself with working with followers of other religions for justice and peace (Phan 2011:144–5).

Malaysia and Singapore

In Malaysia and Indonesia, Christians live mainly in the context of Islam, which has been dominant in the Malay Peninsula since the fifteenth century. The constitution of independent Malaysia was set up in 1957 to favour the majority – but economically poor – Malay community, who are identified by it as Muslim. Today there is increasing Islamization, including Shari'a law, and proselytization of Malays is forbidden. Christians are from the other major communities: Chinese, who are financially powerful; Indians, mostly among the Tamils who came (or were brought) to work for the British in colonial Malaya; Eurasians, descended from colonizers; and indigenous peoples, a tiny minority in Peninsular (West) Malaysia but a two-thirds of East Malaysia – a separate territory on the island of Borneo. Together Christians form about 9 per cent of the total population of Malaysia. Although denominations fall along ethnic and language lines, all come together in the Christian Federation for political purposes, especially to oppose the more radical Islamic reforms and to promote peace in a nation that has witnessed many ethnic tensions, which were fuelled by British and Japanese colonial policies.

Syriac Christian traders were active in the Malay Peninsula in the seventh century or earlier, and in the fifteenth century Persian and Armenian communities settled there. From the early sixteenth century, Roman Catholic missionaries, including Francis Xavier, based themselves in Malacca, from which the Portuguese traded. The later Dutch merchants set up their own Reformed church but did not evangelize the locals and suppressed the earlier forms of Christianity. So the earliest Malaysian Protestant church was begun by the London Missionary Society in the early nineteenth century; today it is Presbyterian and mainly Chinese. Methodists – Chinese, and Tamil – are the largest group among the Protestants in peninsular Malaysia and there are also many Anglicans. In East Malaysia the Evangelical Church of Borneo, started by Australian missionaries in the 1960s, saw mass conversions of tribal people and rapid growth to become the largest single denomination. Catholicism in the peninsula was revived by the Paris Foreign Mission in the late eighteenth century and in Borneo by the Mill Hill Missionaries a century later. It now constitutes about half of the Christian population. Since the end of the Second World War many more Evangelical and Pentecostal groups have grown up in different parts of the nation. These have been introduced by missionaries from the West, from other parts of Asia – including immigrants from mainland China who brought the True Jesus Church, and by Malaysians themselves, especially Chinese. However, the indigenous people – Orang Asli and others, who make up two-thirds of Malaysia's Christians, are hardly represented in church leadership (Chia 2011).

Despite vibrant church activity, Methodist bishop Hwa Yung memorably complained that Malaysian theology was dominated by issues from the West. He wrote that it was more like a banana – yellow on the outside but white inside – than a juicy mango (Hwa 1997). However, attempts to inculturate Christianity in Malay language and culture have run into difficulties because laws have been enacted to protect Malays from proselytization. These forbid, for example, a Malay translation of the Bible, Christian use of the word 'Allah' for God, and Christian hosting of Muslims at religious events. Christians have found moves toward Islamization frightening but theologians like Albert Sundararaj Walters caution against reactionism and advocate a proactive approach of deep engagement with Islamic thought by theologians and lay people (Walters 2002). Christians may be prevented from persuading Muslims toward Christianity but they 'are not prohibited from reflecting afresh on their understanding of Islam' and working with Muslims for the good of Malaysia (Ong 1998:176).

Singapore, which separated from the rest of the Malay Peninsula in 1965, is dominated by the Chinese community. The government of Singapore has been strongly anti-communist and also very conservative in a Confucian way. In Singapore and among the Chinese diaspora across Southeast Asia, Evangelicalism and Roman Catholicism were strengthened by their anti-communist stance (Tiedemann 1999:408). The flip-side of this is that radical and progressive Christianity were suppressed. In 1987,

Catholic activists were rounded up, held without trial and accused of Marxist conspiracy, and the WCC-related Christian Conference of Asia, which was also promoting human rights, was expelled. Today there is greater opportunity for theological reflection, but Singaporean culture and politics continue to discourage Christian involvement in social matters. However, Evangelical and Pentecostal worship and evangelism flourish. Over 16 per cent of Singaporeans are Christians (including some from the Tamil and other communities). There are many new churches, of which the most prominent example is City Harvest Church, which use English and attract the young (W. Ma 2011:50–1). In this small but wealthy and globally connected nation, there is a strong emphasis on overseas mission.

Indonesia

The fourth most populous country in the world, spread across thousands of islands, and home to many different people groups, Indonesia includes former Hindu and Buddhist kingdoms but was incorporated into the Malay world from the tenth century. Indonesia was overwhelmingly Muslim but it nevertheless resisted Islamization when it gained independence from the Japanese in 1945 and while it fended off Dutch attempts to reclaim it. The constitution is based on five principles (Pancasila), which begin with belief in one God but guarantee equal rights. In the mid-1960s, the new government of President Suharto counteracted the threat of atheistic communism by requiring everyone to belong to one of five different religions – Islam, Protestantism, Catholicism, Hinduism or Buddhism. This decision resulted in rapid growth in the number of Christians, even among the previously resistant Javanese, who exhibit complex religious identities (Laksana 2014). Partly as a reaction against Islamization, tribal peoples, nominal Hindus and Muslims – among them communist sympathizers – and members of the economically powerful Chinese minority flocked to join the churches in some parts of the country. The generous European development aid that supported the work of the churches until at least the 1980s was also a factor in the growth of Christianity (Steenbrink 2010). As in many other countries in Asia, the number of Christians is a politically sensitive issue and figures quoted vary significantly. Today, according to census data, 23.5 million Indonesians are Christians, or slightly less than 10 per cent of the population. The Catholic Church may number seven million; the Communion of Churches in Indonesia, founded in 1950, has more than 60 member (Protestant) denominations. There are also many independent churches, often sparked by more recent evangelization initiatives by American, Australian and other Asian missionaries, and many indigenous churches, generally of a Pentecostal variety. The older denominations worry that the activities of some of these endanger the existing communal balance.

Christianity entered the Indonesian archipelago with Portuguese traders in the sixteenth century. Missionaries, including Francis Xavier, established Catholicism in Eastern Indonesia – in the Moluccas or Maluku Islands of Flores (now East Nusa Tenggara) and Dili or Timor. When the Dutch East India Company took over in 1695, it expelled the foreign Catholics and restricted missionary activities until after the Dutch government established Indonesia as a colony in 1800. Catholics were given freedom of worship but closely controlled, and Catholic missions were only allowed to return to the eastern part of the country after 1859. Catholic missions included, from 1913, the Society of the Divine Word (SVD), which pioneered methods of inculturation on Flores. Local people used this policy to retain traditional ancestor ceremonies and initiation rites. From the late nineteenth century until the Japanese occupation in 1942, a variety of Dutch, German, other European and American Protestant mission agencies worked in different parts of the islands. Few Indonesians were ordained until the twentieth century, and lay people were largely responsible for reaching others with the gospel (van den End 2001:377). During the Second World War, all foreign missionaries were expelled or interned, so the churches had to govern themselves anyway. However, after the end of the conflict, the Dutch tried to reassert their rule in Indonesia, and in the ensuing revolutionary war Christians were caught in a difficult position. Indonesian Dutch Reformed Christians took great risks to negotiate with the Dutch, while at the same time supporting the nationalist cause. A legacy of colonialism is that Protestant Christians still exert influence in the economy and the military.

As elsewhere in Southeast Asia, those who converted to Christianity were mainly from groups not incorporated into the major religious systems. In states of largely tribal population, there are large numbers of Christians. The state of Papua, which shares an island with Papua New Guinea, is more than 60 per cent Christian. Until 1975, the eastern half of the small island of Timor, which lies close to Australia, was a Portuguese colony. The indigenous people living there were 30 per cent Catholic. When it declared independence in 1975, Indonesia promptly annexed it and under the Indonesian system of compulsory religious affiliation, 90 per cent opted for Catholicism. Various agencies of the Catholic Church supported the East Timorese in their continuing resistance to Indonesia – first by humanitarian aid and eventually by advocacy of the people's rights. Since their economy was in the hands of Indonesians, the people were exceedingly poor, and they endured suffering and death at the hands of forces loyal to Indonesia. But due in part to the advocacy of Timorese bishop Carlos Filipe Ximenes Belo, who was jointly awarded the 1996 Nobel Peace Prize, East Timor was eventually recognized as an independent state in 2002 (Smythe 2004).

The largest Protestant community in Indonesia, with perhaps three million affiliates, is the Batak Christian Church in Northern Sumatra. In the late nineteenth century, German Lutheran Ingwer Nommensen befriended the progressive raja Pontas Lumban Tobing and they established a church with local leadership and indigenous form. Where once family ties overcame religious differences, today the paradoxical synchronic growth of both individualism and religious identities is putting a strain on Indonesia's plural society. There is pressure on Christians from Islamists, with some discrimination and, since the 1990s in some parts of the country, there have outbreaks of Muslim–Christian violence, in which Christians have also been perpetrators. These were most severe in Posso (Central Sulawesi) and Ambon (Maluku) around 1999, but there have been many other examples since (Schröter 2010) and the government has offered little redress to Christians. A group of women – Protestant, Catholic and Muslim – played a significant role in bringing about reconciliation in Ambon (Prior 2011:64). In such situations Christians naturally turn to foreign Christian support but this may exacerbate the problem (Titaley 2008).

Since all religious bodies are required to accept the Pancasila as the basis of national life, Indonesian theologians are challenged to theologize on the basis of it. Perhaps the greatest contribution of Christianity is 'a sense of human equity regardless of one's religious or racial background' (Titaley 2008:87). Catholic theologians particularly have sought to recognize and celebrate the diverse cultures of Indonesia in the church. In the churches of Sulawesi, women play a leading role. Marianne Katoppo (1979), a Catholic from the island, was one of the first to suggest that Asian feminist theology would not draw on the male-dominated major religions of Asia but on the folk spirituality of feminine power. In this immensely diverse nation, there is a range of Christianities by region as well as by denomination. SVD missionary John Prior suggests that, if they recognise this, Christians may be more open to collaborate with Islam, which is equally diverse (Prior 2011).

The Philippines

Moving even further east, the people of the Philippines, apart from some Muslim communities in Mindanao, followed local religions until the arrival of Christianity. Unlike the rest of East Asia, the first Catholic missionaries in this mass of islands were not Portuguese but Spanish priests who came across the Pacific Ocean from Latin America in the sixteenth century. They applied the same 'encomienda' methods as they had done in the Americas (see Chapter 5), although somewhat less oppressively. From the 1580s, Augustinian missionaries protected the natives from abuse. They used local languages with the result that a distinctive folk Catholicism emerged. The missionaries wrote down the languages for the first time, compiled dictionaries, translated literature and emphasized education. Saint Thomas University in Manila was established in 1611 and is the earliest extant in East Asia. The churches in the towns founded by the missions were in a baroque style but the creativity and techniques of local craftsmen make them unique. The institutional church was firmly in Spanish hands – and Protestantism was forbidden – until the revolution in 1896. The revolutionary movement was supported by local priests who were frustrated by colonial control of the Church as well (Francisco 2011). After the Spanish–American War the country became an American colony, although with continued resistance. Spanish bishops were replaced with American ones and Protestant missionaries flooded in. In 1902, nationalist fervour led to at least a quarter of all Catholics at the time forming the Iglesia Filipina Independiente (Philippine Independent Church) headed by a Filipino priest Gregario Aglipay, who had earlier been excommunicated for condemning foreign domination of the church. This large church is now in communion with the Philippine Episcopal Church. Nationalist feelings also led to the emergence of breakaway Protestant groups such as the Evangelical Methodist Church in 1909, and indigenous churches, including the controversial Iglesia ni Christo (Church of Christ), founded in 1914 by Felix Manalo.

The Philippines finally became independent in 1946, after occupation by the Japanese from 1942, but a close relationship with the United States was resumed. Many Filipinos were attracted to US-style Evangelicalism, which tends to see the inculturated Catholicism as compromised, and they formed the Philippine Council

Figure 2.5 Thousands of Filipino Catholics gather in Metro Manila, Philippines, for a parade honouring the famous statue of a black Christ. Image: iStock.

of Evangelical Churches as an alternative to the National Council of Churches of the Philippines (NCCP). Nevertheless, more than 80 per cent of the population remain Roman Catholic. Rather than the growth of independent Pentecostal churches, there is a strong charismatic movement that has cut across the Catholic and Protestant churches and blurred denominational boundaries. There continues to be foreign missionary activity in the Philippines; South Korean missions are particularly numerous, working with the poor and the more remote mountain tribes (J. C. Ma 2001). However, international links, knowledge of English and its status as 'the only Christian nation in Asia' has also made the Philippines a major missionary-sending country. Furthermore, millions of Filipinos who work abroad are active in spreading their faith (Tira and Wan 2014). Filipino women in domestic service may be inspired by the servant girl who directed her master Naaman the Syrian to seek healing from God's prophet in Israel (2 Kgs 5:1–8) to see themselves as missionaries.

The Roman Catholic Church, led by Cardinal Jaime Sin, the NCCP and many Evangelical Christians were involved in the 'people power' movement which in 1986 overthrew the military dictator Ferdinand Marcos and his wife Imelda (Linden 2012:167–74) and also in a second movement in 2001 that toppled President Joseph Estrada. Today the churches are working together through the Philippine Ecumenical Peace Platform to encourage greater democracy and to support the ongoing peace negotiations with the Moro-Islamic Liberation Front. Nevertheless, most of the nearly one hundred million population continue to live in poverty. Eleazar Fernandes has characterized Philippine theology not as a theology of liberation – for that is yet to be achieved – but as a 'theology of struggle'. The story of Jesus's pasyon (passion) is popularly retold in verse form not as passive endurance but ongoing resistance. Parallels are drawn between contemporary political figures and those who opposed Christ. The fact that Jesus's followers were poor and illiterate and yet changed the world is not lost on Filipinos (Fernandes 1994:103).

Summary

Asia is very diverse and the presence of churches is patchy. In general, the response to Christianity has been among populations following local religions and not the other world religions, which all originated in that continent. The major exception to this is South Korea where the political conditions have been exceptional. Many Chinese also, both within and outside China itself, have converted to Christianity. Within China, Christians in the registered churches are increasingly active in public life. In some regions unregistered congregations are increasingly visible but there remains an underground Catholic Church and Protestant churches that resist the authorities. Two concerns are characteristic of Asian Christianity: religions and poverty; and Christians are divided about whether Christian mission should address itself to the religious leaders (inculturation) or the needs of the masses (liberation). Asia is a highly religious continent, and Christians also are inclined to be religious but in a distinctive way. In the Confucian context of Northeast Asia, they have made great sacrifices for their faith and struggled for justice and human rights; at a popular level the churches help people deal with domestic problems through a life-affirming spirituality which relates to popular Buddhism, Taoism and Shamanism. In Southeast Asia, Christians are an overwhelming, but poor, majority in the Philippines, East Timor and parts of Indonesia. In Indochina they are a small minority (not so small in Vietnam) in predominantly Buddhist contexts. In Malaysia and Indonesia, Christian communities feel threatened by increasing Islamization. In South Asia, Christianity has a history stretching back to the first centuries, and a deep theological engagement has taken place with philosophical Hinduism. More recently the churches, the majority of whose members converted from low- or outcaste groups have been vocal in their opposition to caste and practical in their support for liberation movements. Hindu nationalism has caused Christians to reflect on their complicity with colonialism and also brought political restrictions on further conversions to Christianity. West Asia is the birthplace of Christianity and home to some of the most ancient churches which spread to India and China in the first millennium. For centuries Christian communities lived under the protective but marginalizing rule of Islam, for the most part in peace. However, the last two centuries have seen increasing discrimination against Christians along with a resurgence of militant Islam. In country after country, the numbers of Christians are decreasing, partly by emigration, and the future of Christian presence in the region is altogether uncertain.

Study questions and further readings

- Why has Christianity been attractive to Chinese in China and elsewhere in the past few decades?
- In what different ways have Indian Christians related to caste in India?
- Why is Christian conversion such a contentious issue in so many Asian contexts?
- How would you explain the variations in response to Christianity across Asia?
- What are the causes of the difficulties Christians face in West Asia?
- Discuss some of the indigenous forms of church in Asian contexts.
- What is the difference between inculturation and liberation theologies and why is there tension between them?

Armour, R. (2002), *Islam, Christianity, and the West*. Maryknoll, NY: Orbis.
Bays, D. H. (2012), *A New History of Christianity in China*. Chichester: Wiley-Blackwell.
Frykenberg, R. E. (2008), *Christianity in India*. Oxford: Oxford University.
Kim, S. C. H. and K. Kim (2015), *A History of Korean Christianity*. Cambridge: Cambridge University.
Moffett, S. H. (1998, 2005), *A History of Christianity in Asia*. Vols I and II. Maryknoll, NY: Orbis.
Phan, P. C. (ed.) (2011), *Christianities in Asia*. Chichester: Wiley-Blackwell.

3

African Christianities

Chapter Outline

In his foundational work on African religions and philosophy, John Mbiti (1969:229) commented that 'Christianity in Africa is so old that it can rightly be described as an indigenous, traditional, and African religion'. Furthermore, as Andrew Walls (2002a:90) insists, in view of the 'unbroken historical continuity of the churches of Egypt and Ethiopia of today and the ancient world', Christianity in Africa cannot be treated merely as a 'colonial leftover'. In the late nineteenth century 'Ethiopia' – a biblical word for Africa (Ps. 68:31) – became an inspiration for African nationalism and a justification for independent black African churches. 'Ethiopian', continues Walls (2002:91), 'stands for Africa indigenously Christian, Africa *primordially* Christian' so that 'African Christians today can assert their right to the *whole* history of Christianity in Africa, stretching back almost to the apostolic age'. The biblical world resonates with the people of Africa perhaps more than in any other continent, and inspires African Christian engagement with the age-old questions of spiritual power and the new questions of economic and political power raised by the encounter with the colonial and the globalized worlds.

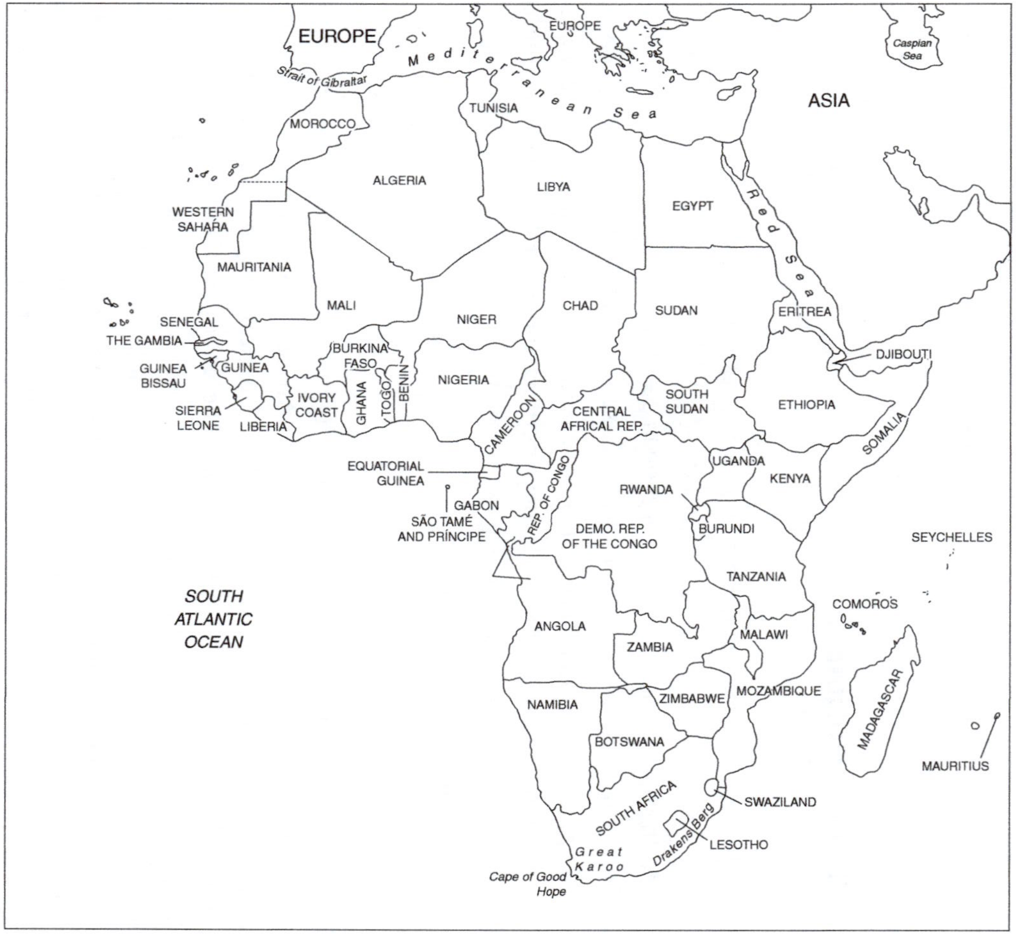
EUROPE
EUROPE
Mediterranean Sea
Strait of Gibraltar
Caspian Sea
ASIA
Red Sea
MOROCCO
TUNISIA
ALGERIA
LIBYA
EGYPT
WESTERN SAHARA
MAURITANIA
MALI
NIGER
CHAD
SUDAN
ERITREA
DJIBOUTI
SENEGAL
THE GAMBIA
GUINEA BISSAU
GUINEA
BURKINA FASO
SIERRA LEONE
LIBERIA
IVORY COAST
GHANA
TOGO
BENIN
NIGERIA
CAMEROON
CENTRAL AFRICAL REP.
SOUTH SUDAN
ETHIOPIA
SOMALIA
UGANDA
KENYA
EQUATORIAL GUINEA
GABON
SÃO TAMÉ AND PRÍNCIPE
REP. OF CONGO
RWANDA
BURUNDI
DEMO. REP. OF THE CONGO
TANZANIA
SEYCHELLES
COMOROS
SOUTH ATLANTIC OCEAN
ANGOLA
ZAMBIA
MALAWI
MOZAMBIQUE
MADAGASCAR
MAURITIUS
NAMIBIA
ZIMBABWE
BOTSWANA
SOUTH AFRICA
SWAZILAND
LESOTHO
Drakens Berg
Great Karoo
Cape of Good Hope

Ancient Christian communities in northern Africa

In the first seven centuries of Christianity, North and northeastern Africa were strongly Christian. Many of the key doctrines of Christianity were hammered out in the region in dialogue with Berber, Pharaonic and early Coptic and Nilotic cultures (Oden 2007). Tertullian, Origen, Cyprian, Athanasius, Didymus the Blind, Augustine of Hippo, Cyril of Alexandria – as well as some of their opponents – Sabellius and Arius – were North Africans and key doctrinal debates took place in Carthage, Alexandria, Hippo and Milevis that defined the methods of consensus that would be applied elsewhere.

Egypt

The Coptic Church in Egypt treasures the story of how the child Jesus was brought to their country when his family fled from the terror of King Herod (Matt. 2:16–18). In Alexandria the Christian community was certainly established early (Acts 2:10; 18:24). There was a sizeable Hellenized Jewish community in the first century and reputedly Jesus's disciple Mark was martyred there, although archaeological evidence exists only from the late second century. Alexandria was the source of several early theological developments. Christian Gnosticism, which regarded Jesus as a spiritual figure who only appeared to take on bodily form, had strong characteristics of the Egyptian mystery religions and Platonic dualism and was systematized by Basilides in Egypt. In keeping with these tendencies, Alexandrian theologians, who included Clement and Origen, developed an allegorical method of biblical interpretation. In the early fourth century Arius put forward his view that the *logos* or word, which became incarnate in Christ, was not eternal but the firstborn of creation. This was also opposed in Egypt by Bishop Alexander and condemned at the Council of Nicaea in 325. The next bishop Athanasius established the doctrine of *homoousios*: that Father, Son and Spirit shared the same substance. Rising nationalism in Egypt meant that apart from the 'Melkites', who favoured Constantinople, the Copts did not adopt the creed of Chalcedon, preferring to express their faith and national identity through the theology of Cyril of Alexandria that Jesus Christ had one incarnate nature. The ascetic community life practised by the anchorites, such as Anthony, in the deserts of Egypt attracted many others seeking a life of holiness through renunciation and fasting. So in the fourth century Pachomius drew up a rule for a desert community. It was modelled on an extended household with a father or mother, which was self-supporting and held all property in common. The communitarian (cenobitic) monasticism of the Egyptian desert was spread to Caesarea by Basil the Great, who integrated it into the life of the church and emphasized that monks and nuns should serve the poor and heal the sick. Athanasius popularized the movement during exile in Rome and Benedict of Nursia developed this African pattern of spiritual life in Western Europe (Lawrence 2001:1–38).

Christians were in a majority in Egypt until the ninth century, after which successive waves of Arab immigration, and persecution under the Mamluks in the thirteenth to sixteenth centuries, led to a greater decline in numbers, the clearing of large areas of their Christian populations and the demise of the Coptic language. Today Copts may number about 13 per cent of the population, although government figures are about half that. They make up the largest Christian population in the Middle East and underwent a renewal in the late twentieth century based in the monasteries and presided over by Pope Shenouda III of Alexandria. The Coptic Church, along with the smaller Greek Patriarchate of Alexandria, has been growing in sub-Saharan Africa because it is seen as authentically African. While priding themselves on their links back to the pharoahs, Copts also regard themselves as an integral part of Egypt, and they are known for their nationalism (O'Mahony 2010b). Nevertheless, they are discriminated against and churches have experienced violent attacks in recent years. As a result, Copts are disproportionately represented in the growing emigration of middle-class Egyptians in recent years. Nevertheless in the unstable situation since the Revolution in 2011, churches have been active and visible in serving society (Hulsman and Attallah 2015).

Nubia and Ethiopia

What are known today as Sudan – ancient Nubia – and Ethiopia were known to the Hebrews as Kush. This term was translated in the Septuagint as Ethiopia and used to mean the black race as a whole. The kingdoms of Nubia, which were beyond the borders of the Roman Empire, were evangelized by monks from the Egyptian desert and later by imperial missions sent from Constantinople in the sixth century. Eventually Nubia adopted non-Chalcedonian Christianity and was closely linked with the Coptic Church. After repelling Muslim invaders in 642, Nubia became a powerful Christian kingdom with a distinctive faith. King Kyriakos even invaded Egypt to rescue the patriarch from Muslim clutches. In the ninth century the Nubian king George I proceeded to Baghdad, fearlessly bearing the cross through Muslim lands, and in the tenth century George II consecrated the archbishop of Ethiopia (Anderson and Kalu 2007). But by the fourteenth century the country had succumbed to the Mamluks and soon afterwards Christianity appears to have disappeared. Today's Christians, mostly Roman Catholic, Anglican and Presbyterian, are the result of more recent missionary work among the black African tribespeople in the south of the country. Since independence from Britain in 1956, black Africans in the south, about half of whom are Christians, have resisted rule from the north and the country has been in a state of civil war. A ceasefire negotiated by the All Africa Council of Churches

Figure 3.1 Ethiopian Christian pilgrims carry a cross along the Via Dolorosa, commemorating the path Jesus took on the day of his crucifixion. Jerusalem, Israel, 13 April 2012. Image: iStock.

and the World Council of Churches (WCC) in 1972 held for ten years, but, since the discovery of oil in the Darfur region, violence has been intense. In an international attempt to end the violence, in 2011 a separate nation of South Sudan was created that is probably majority Christian but continues very unstable.

There may have been Christians even further south in the second century – the result of Philip's baptism of an Ethiopian courtier (Acts 8:26–40) or, according to tradition, a visit from the apostle Matthew. By the mid-fourth century Ezana, ruler of the kingdom of Axum, which was under Semitic rule, became (non-Chalcedonian) Christian through the mission of Frumentius, a Syrian, which was endorsed by Athanasius, bishop of Alexandria. He began translating the scriptures – including some books not recognized as canonical anywhere else – into the Ethiopian language of Ge'ez. The 'nine saints' – Syrian monks from the Egyptian desert – led the evangelization of the countryside, and the monastic tradition was a source of renewal in the fourteenth century (Persoon 2004). Although under pressure from the Mamluks, later Muslim armies and the Italians, Ethiopia (or Abyssinia) survived as an independent Christian kingdom. It had an 'umbilical' link with the wider Orthodox world through the appointment of its patriarchs by the pope in Alexandria until 1959 when it became autocephalous or self-governing (Walls 2002a:89). But in the communist revolution of 1974 the Emperor Haile Selassie was overthrown and the church was deprived of the wealth and lands it had held under the previous feudal structures.

Proudly independent since antiquity, the contemporary Ethiopian Church has a unique tradition which is closely connected with Judaism and pays special attention to the Old Testament, in which Ethiopia (Cush) is called to 'stretch out its hands to God' (Ps. 68:31). Why Ethiopian Christianity has such a Hebraic character has not been satisfactorily explained (Hastings 1994:11–17). The royal house claimed descent from Menelik, son of Solomon and the Queen of Sheba, who brought back the Ark of the Covenant from Jerusalem. The ark is said to be kept in Axum and a replica of it is necessary to consecrate each local church. When these replica arks are paraded at festivals, Ethiopian Christians dance to drumbeats as David danced before the Ark (2 Sam. 6:5, 12–16). Christians follow dietary and purity rules laid down in the Old Testament and they observe a Saturday as well as a Sunday Sabbath. The Ethiopian Church practices male circumcision as in the Bible and also female circumcision (or genital mutilation) according to African tradition. The church also reflects its African context in its attention to the spirit-world. Ethiopians give veneration not only to the Virgin and the saints but also to the angels, which have a special place in Ethiopian spirituality (Chaillot 2002:136–9).

In this populous country, since the nineteenth century, and especially since the 1980s, Protestant, Evangelical and Pentecostal churches have grown to reach nearly 20 per cent of the population. Founded in 1959, the Evangelical Church Mekane Yesu is the third largest Lutheran denomination worldwide – the result of an indigenous revival even under communism (Eshete 2009). Most of this growth seems to have come at the expense of the Orthodox Church and is due to a growing Pentecostal movement since the 1970s, which has permeated the other churches as well (Haustein 2011). Eritrea, which separated from Ethiopia in 1991, shares its long Christian history but there all religions suffer violations of their human rights (Mekonnen and Tronville 2015).

The Maghreb

The spread of Christianity westward across northern Africa first comes to historical attention through the records of martyrdom at the hands of the Romans from the late second century, such as that of the young mother Perpetua and her pregnant slave Felicitas in the arena in Carthage in 203 AD. It was in this context that the theologian Tertullian, who was from the same city, observed that 'the blood of the martyrs is the seed of the church'. He and his fellow North-African Augustine of Hippo wrote in Latin and defined the theology of the Roman Church. It was in this region that the Donatist schism occurred when purists, remembering the martyrs, refused to admit those who had collaborated with the Roman authorities even after Christianity had become an imperial religion. Arguing for unity, even if it meant using force, Augustine claimed that wheat and tares grow together and that, even though the priest is unworthy, grace is still imparted through the sacrament.

Despite the apparent strength of Christianity in the region, in less than a century from 639, Arab armies with their new faith of Islam had spread into Egypt and conquered the Maghreb, from present-day Libya to Morocco. They were helped by the facts that the non-Chalcedonian populations resented Byzantine rule and that the Donatists resented Rome. Muslim rulers at first used Christians to help them govern. However, gradually, in common with Muslim conquerors elsewhere, Christians were required to convert to Islam (and Muslims were forbidden to convert out of Islam) or to accept a lower status (as 'dhimmi'), pay land and poll taxes and face gradual exclusion from public office. Nevertheless, one of the challenges for historians of African Christianity is to explain how, in a matter of just five centuries, Christianity all but disappeared from the Maghreb. The usual explanation is that Christianity lacked indigenous roots, being largely confined to the towns. Other scholars point to factors such as the economic incentives to convert (Isichei 1995:44) and the opportunity to flee north to Spain and southern Italy. Perhaps Christianity's disappearance was rather because such world religions were understood to be bound up with different universal civilizations and so when the imperial power changed people replaced their religion as well (Ward 1999:193–4). Whatever the reason, over the centuries Islam has bonded with the local beliefs of the people and today these countries are almost entirely Muslim. Saint Francis of Assisi attempted unsuccessfully to preach in North Africa in the early thirteenth century. About 70 years later a lay member of the Franciscan order, Ramon Llull, made the first of several Franciscan missions to North Africa, hoping to reach Muslims by arguing the truth of the gospel. Otherwise little European missionary work was attempted until the nineteenth century. Apart from some Christian development work, today these countries generally resist or severely limit any form of Christian activity, and most Christians are expatriates. Many of those converted to Christianity more recently, such as Catholics in Algeria, have left, and there is a background of bitter memories of 'Christian' conquests by European powers.

Sub-Saharan African kingdoms and Portuguese colonies

It is not known how far ancient African Christianity penetrated south of the Sahara Desert before traders brought Islam in the eighth century. The local religions that existed in Sub-Saharan Africa before the coming of Islam and of Catholic Christianity in the fifteenth century should probably not be considered one 'African traditional religion', but there are some 'recurring, though not universal' patterns of belief and practice in Africa (Isichei 1995:96). These include some which differ significantly from the traditions of Western Christendom and the Enlightenment such as a cosmology that does not separate a heaven or a hell, belief in a cyclical rhythm of the environment rather than an end time, divination to heal and restore harmony when the rhythm is disrupted, and faith in the presence of ancestors and spirit possession necessitating exorcism (Mugambi 2002:56–73). In addition, questions of individual liberty, plural marriage, clan initiation, attitudes to land and property, and what constitutes appropriate religious behaviour are significantly different in most African societies than in the West. Nevertheless, traditional morality is strong and guarded by the elders of the society. However because it is 'by customs rather than by reason', the disruption of society and its traditions leaves individuals bereft of moral guidance (Moyo 2003:56).

The Africa encountered by the Portuguese in the fifteenth century, as they searched for new routes to the riches of the East that avoided Muslim empires, was very diverse. It was composed of thousands of different peoples, ranging from hunter–gatherer societies to structured clan groups, the Swahili city-states of the east coast and some larger inland kingdoms such as Kongo and Mali (Iliffe 2007:63–126). Although the Portuguese believed there was a Christian king (Prester John) in Africa, they did not encounter Ethiopia until the sixteenth century. Jesuits encouraged King Susenyos to convert to Rome in 1626 but retracted when the people rebelled against it. Portuguese activity in Africa in general was determined by 'the identification of national identity with Catholicism, and the hostility to Islam' (Isichei 1995:53). In search of gold, the Portuguese took their first colony on the North African coast in 1415 and established bases for their exploration of Africa on the west coast (modern Guinea Bissau) and also on the originally uninhabited Cape Verde islands, where mixed Portuguese–African communities grew up that provided many priests for missionary work. The alliances the Portuguese formed in order to set up trading settlements around the coast en route to Asia were confirmed by the baptism of the local ruler and insistence on adherence to Roman Catholic Christianity as a bulwark against Islam.

The small Christian communities established by the Portuguese were 'fragile, exotic plants, which did not always survive well in African soil' (Isichei 1995:52) and, with two significant exceptions, they appear to have left little trace. In 1482, the king of Kongo helped the Portuguese establish Angola. His son, baptized Afonso, established Christianity among the elite and also planned the evangelization of the whole country using mainly lay catechists. In the seventeenth century, Italian Capuchin friars serving under the Sacred Congregation for the Propagation of the Faith worked with them to expand Christian influence into the countryside, accommodating their message to local beliefs. Jesuits founded colleges in Angola and Kongo in the seventeenth century and produced a Kongolese catechism. The depth of Kongolese faith is shown by the fact that some who arrived as slaves in the Americas passed it on (Thornton 2002). Portuguese exploitation, especially through the slave trade, weakened the Kongo and in the late seventeenth century it was devastated by invasion. In this crisis several women prophets appeared, including Kimpa Vita (Beatrice), who claimed to be the medium of Anthony – the Portuguese patron saint. She taught that Jesus and the saint were black and called the people to restore the Kongo capital. Her growing power and unorthodox religion went too far for the Capuchins, and they persuaded a revival ruler to arrest her. She was burned as a heretic in 1706 (Hastings 1994:104–9). In the early sixteenth century the Portuguese took advantage of the relative weakness of the Mutapa state, which was down the Zambesi River from the impressive ruins of the kingdom of Great Zimbabwe that had been abandoned in the previous century, to establish Mozambique. They set up trading posts and large estates, which missionary priests – Jesuits and Dominicans – attempted to Christianize, although slavery was used to run them. For the next four centuries, the Portuguese, who exported slaves from their colonies, kept out missionaries of other nations, while their declining power meant they were unable to provide for the well-being of the church. Nevertheless, in the nineteenth century visitors reported that a syncretistic version of Christianity was still practiced in Kongo. The Portuguese government was forced to withdraw from both Angola and Mozambique in 1975, leaving chaos in its wake in both nations, an overwhelmingly Roman Catholic population in Angola and a much smaller Catholic minority in Mozambique. Today in both countries churches, along with other agencies, are heavily involved in humanitarian work.

Slavery, Islam and deliverance in West Africa

Much of the commercial interest in Africa centred on slaves. The Western slave trade saw between nine and fifteen million Africans exported to the Americas. Since for three and a half centuries the major contact between Europe and Africa was the slave trade, it is largely against this background that the spread of European Christianity there must be understood (Ward 1999:203). The debilitating effect of slave trading on African society, which slid into endemic war to keep up the supply of slaves, and the suffering caused to Africans, can hardly be exaggerated. However African societies survived it and new African kingdoms arose (Iliffe 2007:131–63). A long-term effect of the slave trade was the creation of the 'black Atlantic', a diaspora of people of African descent spread through the Americas and Europe, with a particular concentration in the Caribbean islands (Gilroy 1993), which plays an especially significant part in African Christian history.

The campaigns against European and Arab systems of slavery were intimately related to the Western missionary movement, both in Africa and at home. Catholic as well as Protestant missions struggled against slavery. For example, its eradication was one of the main aims of Charles Lavigerie, the first bishop of Algiers, who founded in 1868 the Missionaries of Africa, commonly known as the White Fathers.

Lavigerie hoped to link Algeria with the French colonies in Sudan and West Africa so the missionaries could work with the French government and its military to destroy the trans-Saharan slave trade (Shorter 2006:63–4). In Britain and the Caribbean abolitionist activities, led by Quakers and Evangelical Anglicans, included the establishment under the British Crown of Freetown in the former Portuguese colony of Sierra Leone in 1787 as a home for freed slaves, or Creoles. A group of former slaves founded the first Protestant church in Africa there in 1792 and helped to make Sierra Leone an exemplary black town (Walls 2002b). The Church Missionary Society (CMS) and the Wesleyan Missionary Society, with the support of local community leaders such as Samuel Lewis, were active in establishing a Christian society there after the pattern of Europe. Many freed slaves returned to Freetown for business or as missionaries with a desire to build up a colony as the Jewish Zionists were doing in Palestine. It became a centre for training Africans, who then spread the Christian message and Western education throughout West Africa. Like Sierra Leone, Liberia was also founded for ex-slaves, but by a US American abolitionist group in 1822, and it too became a centre of African American mission activity (Hanciles 2014). At least 115 black Americans are known to have served as missionaries – mostly of Western missions – in Africa in the last quarter of the nineteenth century. They were supported from the limited resources of churches of recently freed slaves. Jamaican Christians founded a mission to Calabar (Nigeria) in 1846 and West Indian missionaries worked on the Gold Coast (Ghana). Between 1880 and 1900, the African Methodist Episcopal Church had at least 60 missionaries in Africa (Hanciles 2014:43). Black churches also brought African students to study in the United States (Isichei 1995:166–7). Sierra Leonean missionaries were invited by rulers of Yoruba city states, who saw Christian connections as bringing trade and as a protection against rival groups and slave traders.

European missionaries suffered a high death toll due to their susceptibility to tropical diseases. Catholic presence along the west coast was continued through the black priests of the Cape Verdes. Conversely Europe proved inhospitable to Africans, as the (Anglican) Society for the Propagation of the Gospel discovered when they sent three Fante boys (from present-day Ghana) to study in England. The only survivor, Philip Quaque returned to Africa in 1765 as the first African Anglican priest. The (Protestant) Basel Mission began work on the Gold Coast in 1828 at the invitation of Africans and soon appointed local pastors. From 1819, the first female Catholic missionaries in West Africa, the Sisters of Saint Joseph of Cluny, arrived in Senegal from the revived French church. The growth of Catholicism in the region was helped by a movement of freed black slaves from Bahia in Brazil and Cuba to Lagos from the 1830s who built some of the earliest chapels in the region (Hanciles 2014:37). In all these cases, Europeans worked with Africans, many of whom they had freed from slavery, in a relatively collegial way, without the reservations about the suitability of Africans for mission and ministry they were later to display, and Africans reciprocated with great goodwill.

In the later nineteenth century, when advances in medicines and growing numbers of recruits led to greater European missionary presence, Europeans adopted a more superior attitude to Africans. This was encouraged by Darwinian theories of race, Enlightenment belief in the universality of European culture and the growing power of Western technology. In 1881, for example, a white Baptist missionary in Yorubaland could write back to his headquarters that no more black American missionaries were required (Isichei 1995:164). At the same time, European involvement in African affairs changed from trading to colonization. From about 1880, Britain, France, Germany, Belgium, Portugal, Italy and Spain engaged in a 'scramble' to take colonies in Africa, which they justified by the myth that it was 'the white man's burden' (Iliffe 2007:193–218). Some missionaries, such as Scots in Nyasaland and CMS missionaries in Uganda, encouraged this, believing that colonial rule would be best for the people (Ward 1999:216–17). By 1910 the entire continent, with the exceptions of Ethiopia and Liberia, was divided between Europeans.

One effect of these political changes was that white missionaries became increasingly involved in church and mission affairs on the ground. Whereas when their numbers were small, they were dependent on African hospitality, they now became part of a growing expatriate community and were often cut off from African society. The African leaders in Sierra Leone suffered acutely from this changed state of affairs, as they experienced increasingly little respect and autonomy. The most famous example is the treatment of Samuel Ajayi Crowther. He was a Yoruba who was captured and then rescued and released in Freetown. There he studied languages at the CMS college at Fourah Bay. He went on to publish a grammar book and Book of Common Prayer in Yoruba, and he began translating the Bible into that language. That work was finally completed in 1889 and laid the foundation of Yoruba literature and ethnic identity. In 1864, Crowther received an honorary doctorate from the University of Oxford in recognition of his language work, and he was also ordained as the first African bishop of the Anglican Church, with responsibility for the whole of 'West Africa beyond the Queen's Dominions'. However, his two decades of work there were clouded by accusations against his leadership by CMS missionaries which reinforced their theories that 'the African race' was not 'advanced' enough to hold high office. In 1890 Crowther was forced to resign and a European bishop was appointed as his successor. Europeans commentators agreed this was the best thing for the mission (e.g. Neill 1964:377–8), but African leaders were upset by Crowther's treatment and this encouraged independence movements in the church and wider society. Recent historians of African Christianity have shown how Crowther was extremely highly regarded by his contemporaries, but ill-supported and put in an impossible position by CMS. He was a victim of commercial interests and the racism of the period (Ajayi 1999). That missionaries are sometimes experienced as a hindrance rather than a help to the indigenous mission of local churches became apparent again in the late 1960s and early 1970s when All Africa Council of Churches meeting in Lusaka in

1974 called for a 'moratorium' on the sending of missionaries and money as 'the only potent means of becoming truly and authentically ourselves'. This suggestion was not seriously implemented across the churches, and in any case there were many indigenous churches without overseas support (Hastings 1976:22–4), but the long-term result of the moratorium call was greater reciprocity between (some) churches in the West and in Africa and the suggestion that Africans might also have a mandate for world evangelization.

The rivalry of Christianity and Islam has made the southern edge of the Sahara a flashpoint in Muslim–Christian relations. Countries on the west coast from Guinea northwards to Mauritania have mainly Muslims and very few Christian communities, and Mali and Niger have almost no Christians. However, Burkina Faso and Chad have substantial Christian minorities and the coastal countries from Sierra Leone to Benin are more Christian than Muslim statistically. Nigeria has roughly equal numbers of Muslims and Christians. Of the major tribal groups, the Hausa in the north are Muslim, the eastern Igbo are Christian and the Yoruba (in the west) are divided between the two faiths. This fact played a complex but significant role in the bloody Biafran war of 1967–70. The Igbo Christians tended to see themselves as declaring independence from a government which was pro-Islamic, whom they blamed for massacring tens of thousands in 1966 (Hastings 1979:197–200). Although the Nigerian state recovered from Biafra, matters deteriorated again in the 1990s when the predominantly Muslim states along the northern border implemented Shari'a law in the context of the growth of Evangelicalism. The city of Kano, a Muslim stronghold, and other northern cities have seen periodic rioting, with hundreds killed and thousands displaced. For the Islamist group Boko Haram the implementation of Shari'a was not rigorous enough; they kidnapped more than 200 schoolgirls in 2014 and allied themselves to Islamic State. The long-term result is the further diminishing of the Christian minority in the north.

The perception of West African history as a struggle between Christianity and Islam may reflect a Western missionary preoccupation (Sanneh 1983:210), but it is one that many African Christians also share. While many Christian leaders demonize Islam, the Programme for Christian–Muslim Relations in Africa (PROCMURA) has been aiming for faithful witness and constructive engagement since it was established through the agency of the International Missionary Council in 1959. Cyril Imo finds that, on the whole, the churches have responded politically to the imposition of Shari'a law in a constructive and ecumenical way to promote democracy. Furthermore, ordinary Christians have shown great restraint in the face of provocation and intimidation, adopting a theology of self-defence but not retaliation (Imo 2008). The growth of Christianity and Islam is mostly at the expense of African Traditional Religions, whose adherents are dwindling as they are the target of evangelism by both world religions. Sanneh has suggested that the latter may actually be the most enduring as they shape the two world faiths in African ways and may even offer hope for peace (Sanneh 1983:211), although it is doubtful that affirmation of African traditions will be acceptable to Arab Islam (Azumah 2001).

Apartheid, liberation and reconciliation in southern Africa

Whereas in West Africa Christianity was introduced by Africans or African Americans, in southern Africa in the same period the chief Christian presence was in the form of white settler populations. From 1652, the Dutch East India Company encouraged Dutch Reformed Protestants to settle there to grow crops and raise cattle to supply their ships on the way to Asia. The company also imported slaves from India and East Asia and struggling local Khoisan tribespeople were a source of labour. The British, who occupied the Cape from 1806, brought new settlers and encouraged 'Anglicization', although the presence of Scots among them later reinforced Dutch Calvinism with an evangelical fundamentalism which laid the foundations for the later system of apartheid (Saayman 1991:49). From about 1800, the Boers, who also included German settlers and Huguenots (French Calvinists) and were influenced by Pietism, began to identify themselves as 'Afrikaner'. Their experience of group preservation in the face of threats from both local tribes and colonial authorities led them to forge a strong identity as a 'white tribe', which was bound up with Calvinistic theology and inspired by the exodus of the people of Israel from Egypt into the Promised Land.

The Boers felt little sympathy for the Khoisan communities in the west and south, whom they deprived of their lands, but a Moravian mission was begun in 1737 and in 1792 established a community at Genadendal where the Khoisan were encouraged to settle and practise their crafts, free from the depredations of the colonists. Genadendal became a model for future mission stations in Africa. The Cape became the entry point for missionary work by other organizations across the whole of southern Africa. Criticism of Boer treatment of local people by missionaries of the London Missionary Society (LMS) resulted in some measures by the British government to give black and 'coloured' people access to the courts, but this did not change the underlying inequalities of the colonial system. Naturally this action soured the relationship between British and Afrikaners, and it was one of the factors that provoked the Boer 'Great Trek' of the 1830s to the 'Transvaal' to set up a new colony, displacing more black Africans.

As colonists spread eastwards they encountered the Nguni people, who were themselves in turmoil because of the expansion of one Nguni group, the Zulus. Among the first to respond to the missionaries' message were Mfengu refugees fleeing the fighting. The Xhosa also accepted Christianity on the advice of one of their number, Ntsikana, who claimed his conversion in 1815 was through a vision and on the basis of what he already knew about God before ever meeting a missionary. He preached and wrote hymns that expressed the continuity between African tradition and the God of the Bible. Ntsikana advised the king to make peace, rather than follow the warlike traditions of the ancestors, and Xhosa Christians joined the LMS mission church. However, they maintained their allegiance to 'the God of Ntsikana', and later leaders of the African National Congress hailed him as a forerunner of African nationalism. Other outstanding Christian Xhosa leaders include Tiyo Soga, who became the first black South African to be ordained as a minister. Because of his belief that God had given Africa to black people, he was later hailed as a pioneer of black consciousness (Saayman 1991:56–7, 62).

To the north, many Tswana became Christians following the reduction of their language to writing and the translation of the Bible by Robert Moffat, an LMS missionary. The neighbouring Ngwato and Sotho peoples also became largely Christian in the nineteenth century. Many Africans turned to Christianity at a time when their traditional way of life was almost destroyed by displacement and warfare, and the discovery of gold and diamonds in southern Africa in the late nineteenth century only exacerbated the pressures. Christian missions offered protection and a new, modern way of life which many accepted. However, even where they lived together, blacks and whites tended to be organized into separate congregations. In this way the foundations were laid for the separate black reservations or 'homelands', which became part of the later system of apartheid in South Africa (Hofmeyr and Pillay 1994:88). The 1910 constitution, agreed after the defeat of the Boers by the British in two wars (1880–81 and 1899–1902), set up a 'caste-like' society. The system of apartheid instituted by the National Party in 1948 built on this racial segregation and was accompanied by an ideology of separateness which amounted to a civil religion, for which the Afrikaner churches provided a theological basis. Furthermore, the Dutch Reformed missionary conference in 1950 advocated 'territorial apartheid' and prepared the ground for the notorious Group Areas Act and for policies of 'separate development' (de Gruchy 2004). However, leading English-speaking churches, Presbyterian, Congregational and Anglican which, while not free of discrimination, had mixed race congregations, opposed apartheid from the start on the basis that God had created all human beings in his image. Spurred on by the Sharpeville massacre of 1960, the WCC took up the issue through its controversial Programme to Combat Racism in 1970. In the aftermath of the Soweto uprising in 1976, the Reformed Church in the Netherlands broke with the Dutch Reformed Church of South Africa in 1978.

Influenced by James Cone and other black theologians in the United States and by African traditions, and encouraged by the Christian Institute of Beyers Naudé, a Dutch Reformed minister opposed to apartheid, Manas Buthelezi, Allan Boesak and others developed their own theologies of black consciousness and black power (Buthelezi 1976; Boesak 1977). In 1977, at the instigation of Buthelezi, a bishop, the Lutheran World Federation declared apartheid a heresy and the World Alliance of Reformed Churches followed suit. The appointment of a black Anglican bishop, Desmond Tutu, as its president reinvigorated the South African Council of Churches (SACC), which now became a focus of government attention. The Catholic Church had stood somewhat apart from the struggle against apartheid in South Africa. The Afrikaners were not Catholics and the ANC was dominated by Protestants, mainly Anglicans. Although the bishops' conference condemned racism in 1952, it took a gradual approach to integration and was slow to integrate the church hierarchy. It compromised with the philosophy of 'separate development', especially in its educational work, although Archbishop Denis Hurley repeatedly challenged government policies. However, in 1983 under the influence of liberation theology, shocked by events in Soweto and emboldened by the independence of the Portuguese colonies the same year, the bishops' conference opposed the new constitution. As militant action and government repression increased, Catholic, Baptist and Pentecostal churches that had tried to remain neutral began to collaborate with the SSAC (Linden 2012:174–98). Archbishop Hurley led a movement for contextual theology which brought together the Pentecostal leader Frank Chicane and Catholic theologian Albert Nolan who together drafted the landmark *Kairos Document* (1985). This was largely a black Christian response to the crisis. It called on all the churches to face the 'moment of truth' and reject apartheid and also any 'cheap reconciliation' as long as apartheid remained in place, urging direct Christian participation in the struggle. It was not long before the edifice of apartheid finally crumbled, and from 1990 the role of the churches changed from liberation to reconciliation and 'acting as a midwife' to the birth of democracy, in the words of the now Archbishop Tutu. The first act of church leaders toward reconciliation between black and white churches came at a meeting in Rustenburg in 1990, at which the Dutch Reformed Church confessed its complicity with apartheid. It is estimated that more than 90 per cent of South Africa's Christians and 70 per cent of its population were represented at that meeting (de Gruchy 2004:209).

Christians played key leadership roles in the peace-making initiatives and in the remarkable Truth and Reconciliation Commission (TRC) that followed the end of apartheid and was led by Archbishop Tutu. The churches were thoroughly involved and this gave access to grassroots networks and greater support for victims. What was initially a legal and political process became 'a morally and religiously sanctioned process of absolution' (van der Merwe 2003:274), a national 'baptism in tears' (Daye 2004:2). The international enthusiasm for the truth and reconciliation model was not entirely shared in South Africa. Some worried that this 'blurring of the line between politics and religion' may have been at the expense of legal justice, on the one hand, and of the churches' specific ministry, on the other (van der Merwe 2003:270). From a black South African point of view, theologian Tinyiko Sam Maluleke feared the work of the Commission was merely 'cosmetic'. The *Kairos Document* made the point that true reconciliation presupposes liberation yet Maluleke found that questions of justice, culpability and, most importantly, restitution were not sufficiently addressed. He feared that the South African commission, which was one of many worldwide since the 1970s, was part of the 'Euro-American human rights campaign' by which the Third World becomes the victim of the 'new world order' (Maluleke 1999). The TRC could only ever be part of the process of reconciliation and truth-telling; black theology, Maluleke suggested, will demand more: reconciliation to black cultures and worldview.

The seizure of the land of Africa by Europeans had a devastating effect on Africa, and land distribution is a burning issue in South Africa and other countries, as seen by seizure of land from white farmers in Zimbabwe that made Robert Mugabe so popular. All African religions have much to say about distribution and use of land, including Christianity, which includes the Hebrew traditions of the restoration of land to its original owners in the year of jubilee (Lev. 25). In a continent where the majority depends on the land for its sustenance and where land is associated with wealth, development cannot be reduced to economics while ignoring questions of justice and land ownership.

Domination, conversion and revival in East and Central Africa

It was from southern Africa that the famous explorer David Livingstone, initially an LMS missionary, pushed into the interior of Africa in the 1850s to stop the Arab slave trade in the east, which was now spreading further inland (Ward 1999:213). Livingstone succeeded in charting the river, but the Universities' Mission to Central Africa, which attempted to follow up his initiative, found the possibilities for commerce were overstated and soon withdrew to the coast. They later established missions in what are now southern Tanzania and Malawi. The coast being Muslim-dominated, missions there concentrated on freed African slaves. In western and southern Africa, revived Roman Catholic missionary activity arrived about a generation later than Protestants, but the east, being further from Europe until the opening of the Suez Canal in 1869, was reached later and Catholic missions had a greater presence there. The Holy Ghost Fathers established a settlement for slaves at Bagamoyo, now in Tanzania, in 1863, and in 1878 the Society of Missionaries in Africa, known as the 'White Fathers', was made responsible for the evangelization of the Great Lakes region (Shorter 2006). The large island of Madagascar, neglected except for a short-lived Jesuit mission in the seventeenth century, became an early focus of the attention of the LMS, which started work there in 1820. The education and Protestant work ethic they brought profoundly affected Malagasy society and set in train forces that led to years of persecution for the Christians (1835–61). However, in 1868 a Protestant queen, Ranavalona, was crowned, and mission work recommenced, with Catholic and other groups joining (Bechtloff 2002). Christians are now a large minority in Madagascar, where the traditional religion is also particularly strong.

In East Africa, faced with growing Muslim influence and threats from slave-traders from Egypt in the 1870s, Mutesa, king of Buganda (north of Lake Victoria in modern Uganda), asked for Christian missionaries – apparently more in the hope of getting arms and balancing Muslim with Christian advice than out of any willingness to become a Christian. CMS missionaries arrived in 1877, and were soon followed by White Fathers. The king found the Christian presence as threatening as the Muslim one and had the first Anglican bishop killed en route together with his entourage. In 1885–86 Mwanga, Muyesa's successor, blamed Christians for a series of misfortunes and martyred up to two hundred, including thirty-one men and boys – Catholic

Figure 3.2 Women chant in Christ Church in the centre of Stone Town, Zanzibar, Tanzania, 8 August 2014. This Anglican cathedral is built symbolically on the site of a former slave market. Image: iStock.

and Protestant – at Namugongo, which is now a shrine. After this Christians and Muslims united to overthrow king Mwanga but they could not agree on who should govern, the matter only being resolved – in favour of Protestant Christians – when the British intervened and took over the country. In a remarkably short time, having taken root among the African leaders like chief Stanislaus Mugwanya, Christianity became an integral part of Ugandan society and had 'a profound effect on the moral, intellectual and cultural life, both nationally and locally' (Ward 1999:215). Naturally this development did not satisfy Muslim leaders, and their resentment formed part of the background to the tyrannical rule of Idi Amin in the twentieth century, who created more Christian martyrs, including Anglican Archbishop Janani Luwum in 1977.

Although Western missionaries are prominent in the story of the growth of Christianity in East Africa especially, the day-to-day evangelization was largely the work of black catechists and evangelists, whose stories are only now being told, for example, in the online *Dictionary of African Christian Biography*. Louise Pirouet (1978) documented the stories of Ganda church workers, many of them employed by Western missions but hitherto given little recognition. Reverend Apolo Kivebulaya, for example, worked for CMS as an evangelist in western Uganda and then moved on to work with another people group in Congo. He was paid a tiny salary, most of which he gave away, and is remembered for his radiating happiness. Pirouet showed how many of these 'evangelists' were as much 'foreign missionaries' as any of their white counterparts because they worked far from home in different cultural and linguistic settings. From experience in Nigeria, Andrew Walls (1996:87) points out that 'the terminal connection through which the Christian faith passes into African society' is often not even an official church worker but lay Christians moving – individually or as a group – into into a new area and practising their faith, or a returning member of the village who has become a Christian elsewhere. Walls's research did not yield a single instance of a village congregation being founded by a missionary, white or black (similarly Hanciles 2008:218–20).

Many Africans embraced the Christianity brought by the nineteenth-century missions, but most were ignorant of it, indifferent to it, antagonized by its rejection of local customs or alienated because of Christian–Muslim tensions (Isichei 1995:155). Among sociological studies of why Africans converted, Robin Horton's (1971) thesis remains very influential. Horton argued that Christianity and Islam were equally 'catalysts' in the process of transition from the 'microcosmic' world view of village life to the 'macro-cosmic' view required by modernity. The specific content of the religions was largely irrelevant because converts were merely part of a process of change that was already under way. Horton's and most other studies from sociological and anthropological perspectives are unsatisfactory because they fail to take into account the religious factors involved. Even if Horton's thesis is accepted, the reasons that led Africans to convert arose out of their religious beliefs, especially their belief in the omnipresence of God and their association of religion with power. If they were convinced of the superior strength of the Christian God, they redirected their religion towards this higher divinity (Walls 1996:89). It may be argued that this response represents the teaching of traditional religion, not the teaching of Christianity in which 'power is made perfect in weakness' (2 Cor. 12:9). However, conversion is only an entry point to Christian faith; the influence of living in a Christian community and of religious education means that the reasons for retaining the new faith may be different from those for opting for it initially. African Christians are not simply practising their traditional religion under a new guise, although this is an accusation often made, especially against the African initiated churches by other Christians who fail to realize the Christian-ness of African Christianity (Jenkins 2002:161). Instead there are complex continuities and discontinuities in religious practice and world views when people convert to Christianity (Meyer 1999).

East Africa was the source of several significant movements within the mission churches that led to expressions of the faith that were more obviously African. The best known, the Balokole ('saved people') revival of the 1930s, was led by a partnership of CMS missionary Dr Joe Church and a respected African leader Simeoni Nsibambi, and inspired a radical egalitarianism (Ward and Wild-Wood 2012). The East African Revival began in Rwanda and Uganda but had a wide influence across East Africa and eventually worldwide from Brazil to the United States, Europe, India and Australia (Stanley 2013:79–85). As Ward (1999) points out, at one level it was a typical Evangelical revival movement, emphasizing repentance from sin and dependence on the blood of Jesus for salvation. But at another level it was 'profoundly African' because members saw themselves as a 'new clan', and expressed this, for example, by looking after widows and arranging marriages (224). However, the movement distanced itself from other African-led churches of the time by disallowing speaking in tongues, prophecy and healing ministries (Anderson 2001:144). In Kenya the 'brethren' (and sisters) became famous in missionary circles for their courage in refusing to take the oath of the Mau Mau rebels against the British in the 1950s, although the fact that, when forced by the British to choose, the majority of Kikuyu church people did the opposite raises questions about missionary perception of the issues (Casson 2000). The revival movement left behind a theologically conservative Church of Uganda, the second largest group after the Roman Catholic Church. However, unlike other mission churches in East Africa which generally follow the pattern of male leadership brought from Europe, across all the revival churches women's groups are particularly strong. Being relatively free from clerical control, they have provided church women with opportunities to express their faith in an African idiom (Isichei 1995:277). The church has been highly politically involved and tends to see itself as 'the conscience of the state' (Kasibante 1998:366).

New African religious orders in the Catholic Church include the Bannabikira (Daughters of the Virgin) and the Little Sisters of Saint Francis, both founded in Uganda. Women's organizations, wearing distinctive costumes, are a prominent feature in all the churches in Africa. In 2007, according to its website, a third of the 3.6 million members of the (Anglican) Mothers' Union were in Africa – about half of them in Tanzania.

African independent and African initiated churches

Throughout the colonial period, Europeans aimed to exercise a high level of control over church members' lives to 'civilize' them. There was a long period of preparation before baptism and most missions were slow to ordain African leaders. In denominations that did not make such a requirement in their homelands, this appeared as an implicit questioning of the genuineness of African faith. Until the colonial period, civilization generally consisted in creating Christian villages. Sometimes these involved the settlement of nomadic groups, sometimes freed slaves. Mostly they were places where converts could live together untainted by the world around them; in East Africa they became 'almost autonomous states' (Hinchliff 2002:485). Later, Christian education and boarding schools were seen as offering a similar opportunity to mould Africans after a European model. Missionaries in charge of these and other institutions were 'usually well-intentioned, sometimes harsh, even brutal, but always autocratic' (Isichei 1995:136).

During the nineteenth century, there was a 'withdrawal upwards' of missionaries into institutions and the creation of greater social distance between European clergy and 'natives' (Ward 1999:221). African peoples could even be described as 'child-races', although much missionary effort was put into proving that they could become equivalent to Europeans (Walls 1996:93). The gulf in world view between post-Enlightenment Europeans and most sub-Saharan Africans of the colonial period grew, especially with respect to causality. Missionaries were shocked by African witchcraft, invoking ancestors and belief in a spirit world, which evoked a pre-Christian 'dark' era in Europe and reminded them of practices condemned in the Old Testament. Many regarded traditional beliefs as a dangerous delusion; others gave credence to the beliefs but regarded them as devilish. Thus the traditional religion was either suppressed or demonized, or discounted as a religion by missionaries and by Africans themselves (Jenkins 2006:98–127). Few missionaries were able to engage traditional religion in a constructive way, and so they tended to take a tabula rasa approach. African Christians were expected to reject their previous way of life and to exist in a culture vacuum. Having abandoned their own ways of responding to problems, diseases, evil spirits and calamities, they discovered that often the mission churches could not provide alternative ways to deal with the problems. Furthermore, there were wide differences between the cultural customs of rural Africa and those of the largely urbanized missionaries, but most missionaries assumed that their customs were 'Christian'. Many missionaries were the products of movements in the West that emphasized 'holiness' in the sense of detachment from the world and moral purity, particularly sexual purity.

The social issue that arguably caused most misunderstanding was polygamy (or more accurately polygyny), which was widely practised in Africa but anathema to Europeans, and associated in their minds with Islam. Most missions had policies that male converts with more than one wife 'put the others away' before baptism; men found to be practising polygamy after baptism were excommunicated. Since these women had no protection outside marriage, this caused great suffering, and it often meant the most upstanding men of African society were denied baptism. John William Colenso, Anglican bishop of Natal in the mid-nineteenth century, was one of the first Europeans to oppose the social Darwinists and, influenced by the social Christianity of Frederick Maurice, argue for the respect of African – in this case Zulu – traditions and for African rights. Furthermore, the questions of his African students about the Pentateuch and the book of Joshua caused him to query their content and accuracy. Colenso's views on the Bible and on Africans dominated the first Lambeth Conference (of the worldwide Anglican Church) in 1867, but what Victorians found most shocking was his defence of polygamy. The 1888 Lambeth Conference ruled out polygamy in the church but, after a hundred years or so of discussion, at the conference of 1988 both Western and African bishops were sympathetic to the problem and agreed on a pastoral approach to be determined locally (Draper 2011).

Missionary paternalism and other 'failures of love' (David B. Barrett quoted in Walls 1996:112), coupled with increasing African knowledge of the Bible, led to dissatisfaction with missionary churches and their concepts of holiness. In the late nineteenth century, it became apparent that Europeans were less in control of the churches than sometimes appeared when Africans began to form churches independent of missionary control (Pirouet 1989:149). These are referred to as African Independent Churches or AICs – an acronym that is also construed as African Initiated Churches or African Indigenous Churches. The first stirrings took place in South Africa when, in 1872, 158 Sotho Christians left the Paris Evangelical Mission, only to return later (Isichei 1995:125). In 1884 in Transkei, Nehemiah Tile, a talented African leader who clashed with his Methodist superintendent, founded an ethnic Thembu church with their king as its head. This was intended as a political statement of 'the ultimate supremacy of the Coloured races throughout South Africa' (quoted in Saayman 1991:66).

The biblical references to Ethiopia were an inspiration to Africans and the name became a rallying cry for African independence. The West Indian Edward Blyden promoted 'Ethiopianism' in the African diaspora in the Americas and in West Africa as a form of pan-Africanism. 'Ethiopia' took on even greater connotations of African pride after the nation of Ethiopia defeated an Italy in 1896. In 1892 Mangena Mokone, a Wesleyan Methodist minister, and others founded the 'Ethiopian Church' in Johannesburg in protest at blacks and whites meeting separately at a Methodist conference. The 'Ethiopians' tried to join the US African Methodist Episcopal church, whose bishop, Henry McNeal Turner, promoted Ethiopianism as a form of black manifest destiny. They were unsuccessful but formed a rather ambiguous alliance with the (Anglican) Church of the Province of Southern Africa (Kalu 2006a). In West Africa there were calls for secession because of the ill-treatment of Samuel Crowther. His staunch defender, and protester at racial discrimination in Sierra Leonean Anglicanism, James Johnson, nevertheless resisted these, even when he was rudely dismissed as assistant bishop. Another six hundred formed the African Church Organisation in 1901 in protest and Lagos Baptists also separated in 1888. Similar new churches were founded in other West African countries and are sometimes distinguished from the Ethiopian churches in South Africa by the label 'African'. The new Ethiopian/African churches were (and are) more a statement of independent governance than an attempt to be churches in an African way; most retained the worship and theology of the mission churches (Ludwig 2002). Influenced by African Americans of the period, such as Booker T. Washington, they focused on education as a route to black emancipation. However, they were a statement that Christianity is African. Ethiopian churches were associated with the first rebellions against colonial rule, such as the one led by US-educated John Chilembwe in Nyasaland (contemporary Malawi) in 1915 (Kalu 2006b:200–3) and left a lasting legacy of dignity of being African and Christian.

A new wave of AICs arose in the period 1910–30 which may be termed 'prophet-healing' or 'spiritual' (Anderson 2001:16–18). They arose from a feeling that 'the Western God was spiritually inadequate and irrelevant to deal with the reality of many aspects of our lives', and a concern about 'how deep the Christian faith really is when so many of its affiliates still continue to visit the caretakers of the African traditional religions' (Organisation of African Instituted Churches (OAIC) quoted in Pobee and Ositelu 1998:68). African Christians turned to the Bible for their models because they 'did not want to imitate the practices of the mission Churches' (Ndung'u 2000:241) but demanded 'spiritual independence from the religious imperialism of Western extra-biblical ideas' (Mbiti 1986:29). What these churches have in common is that they represent a rediscovery of Christianity by Africans who, because of their African religious heritage, emphasize prophecy, healing and spiritual power. They are led by a charismatic figure – a prophet, who is known as a preacher and as a healer, combining African practices with Christian patterns of exorcism. The priestly role of Christian leaders is not stressed and the celebration of Holy Communion is not prominent in the AICs. Generally women are perceived to 'get more possessed', 'are prone to give more testimonies' and 'are more operative in initiating songs, dancing, jumping and clapping, than men' (Ayegboyin and Ishola 1997:30) but only a few movements have women founders. Most of the churches tolerate polygamy, and in their dress and activities they represent a turning away from modernity in favour of African culture. The new communities were formed by converts and often took on the features of a Christian tribe, resistant to or uncooperative with colonial institutions. However, it is difficult to generalize about what is a very diverse phenomenon, of which it is only possible to give a few of the most notable examples in each region.

West Africa: In this region the Harrist churches in Ivory Coast and Ghana take their name from William Wadé Harris, a Liberian Methodist lay preacher. He apparently received a call from the angel Gabriel, and later the gift of tongues, while in prison for political activities. After this, in 1913, he began an itinerant ministry. In many ways Harris is the classic example of the African prophet–leader. He walked barefoot from village to village with his companions. These included two women associates who led singing and dancing in traditional style. He wore a long white calico robe and white turban, carried a Bible, a rattle made from a gourd and a staff in the shape of a cross, which he used to perform miraculous acts of healing – although he destroyed it periodically so that people would not worship the staff itself. Harris's activities attracted a mass following – an estimated 120,000 baptisms in one year – among the people of Ivory Coast and Ghana. He tolerated polygamy but urged people to renounce traditional religious practices, burn fetishes and believe in the God of the Bible. Like John the Baptist (and unlike most missionaries), he immediately baptized those who responded, usually in a river, as is common across Africa. Harris did not intend to form a church but directed people to existing churches or, where there were no churches, to build prayer houses led by members of the village. Some joined the Catholic Church and others the Methodist Church, although groups later seceded from both. There are now several different Harrist churches, two of them founded by women. Western missionaries mostly failed to appreciate Harris's use of indigenous religiosity to spread the gospel. Seeing him as an independence leader, the French administration of Ivory Coast imprisoned Harris and deported him to Liberia in 1914. His followers were persecuted and many of their prayer houses destroyed (Sanneh 2008:193–211).

The 'Aladura' churches of Nigeria were the most prominent Christian expression in Nigeria by 1950 and very influential in society. They are so named because of their emphasis on prayer and fasting, especially as a means of healing without medication – traditional or Western. They grew out of prayer meetings in Yorubaland during the 1918 flu pandemic, led by Joseph Shadare and Sophia Odunlami, which were found unacceptable by Anglican church leaders. Some of these churches have since had contact with British and American Pentecostal groups, but only on their own terms. The movement is mostly urban and has several different branches. The Church of the Lord (Aladura) was founded by an Anglican schoolteacher Josiah Ositelu who had many visions, healed – sometimes by the use of 'holy names' and 'seals' – and exposed witchcraft by divine knowledge. His successor, Adeleke Adejobi, saw the church spread to Sierra Leone and

Ghana. He laid a theological foundation for the church and took it into the WCC in 1975. Of later foundation, the Celestial Church of Christ has distinctive taboos and its members go barefoot. Founded in the 1930s as the result of a revival led by the prophet Joseph Ayo Babalola, the church is now very involved in education and has good relations with government and the former mission churches (Adogame 1999).

Southern Africa: This region has more AICs than anywhere else – perhaps as many as six thousand denominations – and more than half the Christian population belongs to them. They are usually known as 'Zionist' or 'Apostolic' churches. They began in 1903 from a branch of a North American Pentecostal group, the Christian Catholic Apostolic Church in Zion, which claimed to liberate Africans and soon attracted several thousand Zulu followers. However the African church split off from the American movement because of racism. The South African government encouraged the growth of AICs as part of its policy of apartheid, and the Zion Christian Church, the largest in South Africa, was accused of supporting the regime, although there is evidence that its members did not (Anderson 2001:105–6). The church leaders are seen as 'Moses figures' who bring their people out of the slavery of sickness, oppression, poverty and evil spirits into the promised land. This new society is concretely expressed in the churches, which are called 'cities of Zion'. Like early Pentecostals, Zionists practise baptism by immersion, divine healing without medicine or doctors, encourage prophesying and speaking in tongues and do not take alcohol or smoke tobacco. Worship is the key marker of AIC identity and Zionist worship has certain traits that are widely shared. There is typically one worship service per week, either on Saturday or Sunday, that takes place outside under a large tree for shade and lasts from late morning until late afternoon. Leadership is generally male and begins with the bishop, under whom are prophets and healers, but weekly worship is a truly communal experience. It consists of singing and dancing accompanied by drums, rattles and trumpets; fervent prayer; frenzied exorcisms; Bible readings followed by lengthy, intense sermons by leading men; testimonies, which may be by women; prophetic words to particular members of the congregation based on a vision; and laying-on of hands for healing (Robert and Daneel 2007).

Central Africa: The most famous AIC in this region is the Kimbanguist Church founded by prophet Simon Kimbangu in the Belgian Congo in 1921. Kimbangu was denied the post of evangelist in the Baptist Missionary Society because he could not read well enough, but later in the village of Nkamba he reputedly performed miracles of healing and even raising from the dead. Soon crowds flocked to hear him, believing that a new African Pentecost had come, and other prophets began to appear. The colonial authorities declared a state of emergency, and Kimbangu was sentenced to death but eventually held until he died in prison thirty years later. The authorities, often with the help of European missions, persecuted his followers, and many were deported, although this only encouraged the spread of the movement. Led by Kimbangu's wife, Muile Marie, the church appealed to the United Nations for help, and was finally granted government recognition in 1959 (Martin 1976). It was accepted as a member of the WCC but the relationship has been tempestuous due to claims that Kimbangu is not only prophet but the black messiah who will restore the ancient Kongo empire. Today the Kimbanguist Church has perhaps seven million members – second only to the Catholic Church in Congo.

East Africa: In East Africa, Kenya is home to the largest secession from the Roman Catholic Church, Maria Legio (the Legion of Mary), which is spread throughout East Africa. It was founded in 1963 by a layman, Simeon Mtakatifu Ondeto, and a laywoman, Gaudensia Aoko, who denounced witchcraft and began mass baptisms. The church retains many aspects of Catholic liturgy in its worship and its leader is called 'pope', but it also shares many of the common features of African initiated churches. Within the Catholic Church, Emmanuel Milingo, Catholic archbishop of Lusaka from 1969 to 1983, practised a popular ministry of exorcism and healing, accepting the reality of the spirit world for the African (ter Haar 1992). He was investigated by the authorities and removed from his see, but while in Rome he caught the attention of the Catholic charismatic movement and was allowed to continue his ministry in Italy. In general, the Roman Catholic Church in Africa has avoided schisms but it has lost members to the new churches.

AICs are numerous in Kenya because of the 'Holy Spirit' movement, which began in a revival movement in the Anglican Church after the First World War and spread among the Luo and Luyia people. The Holy Ghost Church of East Africa (HGCEA) is one of the largest and most orthodox of its results. The church took root among poor people, originally peasants, who formed a 'church tribe' bound together by common worship and a shared millennialist and independence theology influenced by the Bible and African traditions. However they now take a longer-term view and they have seen some upward mobility. They have bought land cooperatively and built permanent houses and churches. These days their children go to school, and some to university, although they still resist medical intervention. Their high moral standards, simple lifestyle and hard work make them popular with employers. Nevertheless, the anti-colonial aspects of the movement are perceived to hinder the current Kenyan government agenda for development, which focuses on overcoming poverty, disease and ignorance. It is true that sometimes their enthusiasm for 'spiritual' matters and excessive fasting affects productivity and detracts from social responsibilities, but the real reason is their lack of cooperation with government and their countercultural lifestyle. The value they place on community and concern for the weakest over commercial gain are under pressure from the neocapitalist ethos of contemporary society (Mwaura 2003). Outside South Africa, AICs are declining. In their place have come the newer Pentecostal churches, which, with their emphasis on wealth, are more conducive to living in late or post-modernity.

From the start, African initiatives in Christianity were heavily criticized by missionaries and leaders of mission-founded churches that lost members, and they were sometimes suppressed by the authorities. There is always a concern whether, in dealing with the spirit-world, African churches are embracing African traditional beliefs or whether their intention is to confront the spirits with the power of the Holy Spirit. In the first Western study of the AICs, Bengt Sundkler damned them in the eyes of the West by describing them as 'the bridge over which Africans are brought back to heathenism', and calling them 'syncretistic' because they indiscriminately mixed Christian elements with those from African traditional religion. Others have viewed them as a 'witchcraft eradication movement', perceiving that they were preoccupied with overcoming the witchcraft which retains a powerful place in traditional African societies. Often AICs are labelled 'separatist' and seen as 'breaking away' from the churches founded by Western missions (Pobee and Ositelu 1998:29–30). In fact, groups such as the Aladura churches in West Africa were pushed out, and others were the result of movements founded as alternatives to the existing churches rather than splits from them. Some term the AICs 'nativistic', which usually means 'primitive and barbarous'. Others make fun of them for claiming to be African while imitating Western churches (2, 32, 53). But Sundkler later revised his opinion of AICs, and nowadays they are generally recognized by other Christians, although there are ongoing worries about their doctrines and practices, especially since few have developed tertiary-level theological training. There are many legitimate criticisms of these churches: for example, they suffer from cults of personality, frequent schism and poor administration. There is evidence that some leaders have alliances with witches and wizards and some abuse their positions to indulge in plural marriages and extramarital affairs (Ayegboyin and Ishola 1997:156–7). But as John Pobee, an Anglican theologian from Ghana, and the late Gabriel Ositelu, primate of the Church of the Lord (Aladura), insist, they also make important contributions. The OAIC themselves summarized these in 1996 as: awareness of the wholeness of creation and the power of sacred symbols; an appreciation for the generation and sharing of life; a sense of family and community; relatedness to our predecessors in the communion of saints; rediscovery of the church as a life-giving organ to society; renewal in the Holy Spirit leading to freedom from fear of other spirits; an emphasis on healing by the Spirit (Pobee and Ositelu 1998:70–1).

Churches engaging with health, development and politics

Decolonization came relatively late to most of Africa. Expectations were high, but there were the problems of drought, poor education and healthcare, rapid population growth and limited economic resources, and little preparation had been done to help Africans manage their own affairs (Meredith 2006). Furthermore, the nations of Africa were defined by territories drawn up by colonial map-makers with little regard for questions of ethnicity, language or African history. Nigeria, for example, 'had more linguistic, cultural, historical, and religious diversity than the whole of Europe put together' (Walls 2002a:105). Since independence, most African nations have followed a remarkably similar path: the independence leaders were authoritarian rulers, mostly at the head of one-party states; some survived there for several decades, others were overthrown earlier by military coup. Twenty countries have experienced or continue to experience civil war, but most nations have held together and several have instituted democratic reform in recent years (Iliffe 2007:267–72). Continued poverty, ongoing war, a refugee population comprising 40 per cent of the world's total, increasingly severe climates and the HIV epidemic are just some

Figure 3.3 Saturday morning church service at the United Church in the town of Chipembi, outside Lusaka, Zambia. The United Church was formed in 1965 by churches founded by four separate Protestant missions. Image: iStock.

of the problems facing African governments, and which concerned Christians try to address (e.g. Mugambi and Nasimiyu-Wasike 2003). Although recent reports are more optimistic about economic growth in sub-Saharan Africa, health and wealth remain a major concern for church leaders, but this is demonstrated in two different ways: the leaders of the former mission churches tend to work with governments on development programmes, whereas the leaders of more popular churches are inclined to help their congregations to better themselves by education, entrepreneurship and 'spiritual' means.

The emphasis on healing in AICs is an important distinguishing characteristic and a major reason for their spread (Walls 1996:97–100). Most of the prophets were regarded as healers, and many rejected medicine as a means of healing, thus heightening the power of God and the victory of Christ over the evil powers believed to be causing the sickness. Sickness is hardly less of an issue for Africans today than it was then. The scourge of AIDS, malaria, ebola and other pandemics is unabated, and disease due to lack of sanitation, unclean water and other preventable causes is rife. Although African governments now take the main responsibility, many churches in Africa continue to run hospitals, clinics and healthcare projects as they did in the colonial period, often supported by Christians in wealthier countries, including new missionary-sending countries like Brazil and South Korea. Because AICs tend to reject medicine and professional healers, Christians may need reassurance that 'it was God who gave doctors and scientists (including traditional medicine men) the skill and understanding of developing the many kinds of medicine that can cure sickness' (Kyomo 2003:150). For those millions of Christians who cannot afford access to healthcare, or whose health practitioners are unscrupulous, the belief that healing comes from God gives at least a ray of hope.

'[T]he African has a sense of the wholeness of life', declared Buthelezi (1997:85–6), in the sense that the living are in fellowship with the dead, the supernatural and natural interrelate, and the sacred and secular are not separated. Illness in African thought is disharmony in human and cosmic relations (Ela 1988:50–1). Since God is master of all the cosmic powers, for African writers healing disease is only a specific example of the wider life-giving work of the God (Kyomo 2003:148) and healing is holistic – restoring life (Stinton 2004:54–61). Healing in African traditional medicine and in the Bible is not a matter of treating the illness but of treating the person in their body and in all their relationships, including those with the 'natural world' (Walls 1996:98). So there is no discontinuity between healing and reconciliation, or between healing and creation (Kyomo 2003:149). African perceptions that illness is due to spiritual causes and that cure is wholeness offer challenges to Western theories and methods of health and healing that are reflected in international debate about church health services (Rookes and Rookes 2012). Furthermore, Buthelezi (1997:89) refused to separate health and wealth but went on to define 'poverty' as 'alienation from the wholeness of life' by being cut off from the life-sustaining gifts of God that we receive and share with others. The perception of African traditional religion that 'a people are only definable in terms of their total environment' is borne out in studies of different people groups in East Africa, for whom 'the integrity of this environment is defined in terms of "peace, harmony and prosperity" and depends on people's cooperation with one another. Therefore, when their environment is destroyed, people lose their identity, and even their name' (Kinoti 2003:10, 16).

Issues of land and the environment are nowhere more pressing than in sub-Saharan Africa, which has always been prone to drought and is likely to be hit most by climate change. Here the resources of African traditional approaches to land management, often mediated through the AICs, offer hope. For AICs it is natural to think of the Holy Spirit as the 'earthkeeping Spirit' who heals, protects and gives life, and therefore the AIC prophets condemn acts harmful to the environment as sin, and promote an understanding of baptism and the Eucharist as affirming the elements of creation. Partly as a result of the influence of its large African membership, the Anglican Consultative Council, which developed the 'five marks of mission' between 1984 and 1990, included as number five the aim 'to strive to safeguard the integrity of creation and sustain and renew the life of the earth' (Walls and Ross 2008). African theologians are prominent in theology of earth or creation care (Kaoma 2015; Conradie 2015) and African examples predominate in the encyclical of Pope Francis on the environment (*Laudato Si'* 2015).

Most leaders of independence movements and the first generation of government leaders were products of mission schools, who had learnt there how to 'play the foreigners at their own game' (Walls 2002a:106). In some cases, their plans for development could be ascribed in part to these influences, such as the 'African socialism' of Tanzania's Julius Nyerere (a Catholic; Parratt 1997:109) and the 'humanism' of Kenneth Kaunda of Zambia (a Presbyterian; Parratt 1995:143–8). On independence the mission churches became national institutions and 'seriously and self-consciously assumed for themselves a "nation-building role"' (Walls 2002a:106). However, after independence the roles became reversed. Governments stalled and weakened but the churches grew rapidly in numbers and strength. In the 1990s the structural adjustment programmes imposed on many African countries severely constrained the ability of governments to offer education, healthcare and other services and destabilized them (Iliffe 2007:288–99). In this context, churches and mission agencies took back many of the public roles which had been given into government hands at independence and assumed even greater socio-political importance. Examples where the churches have filled a vacuum until order was restored include: Uganda under Idi Amin, South Africa during apartheid and Kenya under one-party rule. There are many examples of brave and costly leadership by Christians. In the political turmoil of 1980s Kenya (Anglican) Archbishop David Gitari drew on the Hebrew prophets to denounce injustice from the pulpit and, at great personal cost, helped to change the course of political affairs (Gitari 1996). On the other hand, there have also been occasions when the churches have manifestly failed in their social responsibilities and have even been complicit in injustices. The most horrifying example was the Rwandan genocide of 1994 which took place in a country more than 90 per cent Christian. Though there were many cases of heroism by individuals, some Rwandan church leaders justified, orchestrated and took part in the killing, and betrayed their congregations, who were killed in their churches (McCullum 2004).

The transnational links of the churches were vital for sustaining development initiatives where local resources were so stretched (Gifford 1998:308–35). Since the Second Vatican Council and the end of colonialism, the Catholic Church and its related organizations have poured enormous investment into education, health, social projects in the continent. The situation of Protestant churches is changing. On the one hand, the 'mainline' Protestant churches whose links are with European churches have seen their funding dwindle. Many receive government funds, or funds raised from secular campaigns, that restrict their use to non-religious activities. On the other hand, some of the large independent Evangelical and Pentecostal churches are able to command greater resources, mainly from North America and East Asia, and mostly raised from the churches themselves. These newer agencies usually include evangelistic activities and also offer clergy training. As they receive much appreciated theological education, 'mainline' clergy also imbibe their ethos. Such is the attraction they exert that the other churches are drawn into their development initiatives, thus bridging the gap between the developmental and the spiritual approaches to health and wealth. However, the development programmes that overseas churches and other agencies fund in Africa sometimes detract from the work of the local churches themselves, and are often able to attract their most talented staff.

Because of the dominant twentieth-century theory that modernization inevitably led to secularization, governmental and non-governmental aid agencies have only recently become aware of the churches themselves as agencies for development and sought to engage them constructively (Rakodi 2015). In 2000 a conference on alleviating poverty in Africa was held in Nairobi between the World Bank and the Council of Anglican Provinces of Africa. In a joint statement, the World Bank and the churches 'recognized in mutual respect each other's role in addressing poverty issues' and both agreed that 'the spiritual dimension of life is an essential component of development'. Furthermore the World Bank recognized the church's 'ability to influence constructively, based on its numbers, its position as the moral conscience of nations, its closeness to the poor, and its own accountability to God' (Belshaw, Calderisi and Sugden 2001:8–9). The World Bank wields great power over African governments, but through the churches it stands to gain even greater power to effect its development aims in Africa. The needs of Africa are so basic that there is a large measure of commonality between the development aims of government and international bodies and the vision of the kingdom of God: education, health, good governance, economic growth, conflict prevention and post-conflict reconstruction were the main points the Anglicans and the World Bank agreed on. Only in the area of the use of condoms is there tension, especially between Catholic agencies and their secular counterparts. However, even there, African Catholic theologians such as Laurenti Magesa have been prepared to challenge the church's teaching and advocate the use of prophylactics to prevent the spread of HIV (Magesa 2003).

As we have seen, Christianity is a public religion in sub-Saharan Africa. For, example, as the Catholic churches in Africa acquired their own hierarchies, they became increasingly engaged in political life, as well as in dialogue and initiatives for justice and peace. Many of the new Pentecostal churches are also politically engaged and this can be seen as a continuation of the spiritual battles and power struggles in which they engage in worship services (Kalu 2008:167–246). A number of African political leaders have openly declared their faith, with varying effects. Frederick Chiluba, converted in prison and baptized in the Spirit at a Reinhard Bonnke 'crusade', not only saw himself as a Christian president of Zambia (1991–2002) but also introduced a new constitution that declared Zambia a 'Christian nation'. On the one hand, while the constitution also allowed personal religious freedom, in practice Chiluba suppressed the opposition (Mwamba 2000). Evangelicals and Pentecostals in Zambia became not merely politically engaged but dominant. On the other hand, Chiluba's declaration of a Christian nation established the democratic standards by which he was judged and by which he relinquished power peacefully after just two terms (Phiri 2008). Olusegun Obasanjo, who stepped down as president of Nigeria in 2007, was a Baptist who, despite – or perhaps because of – his openly religious language, commanded respect from the large Muslim community (Freston 2001:189). But a more recent Christian president Goodluck Jonathan was tainted with allegations of corruption and failure to deal with the aggression of Boko Haram. Since the 1990s good governance has been a crucial part of the development agenda for Africa. However, leadership in the churches may be as autocratic and self-seeking as in the wider society (Gifford 1998:343) and the continuance of widespread corruption in Nigeria, in particular, calls into question its 'Christian Revolution' (Burgess 2008:308–13). In this sense, the advent of democracies in many former dictatorships is seen as a challenge to greater openness in church affairs (Kahindi 2003; de Gruchy 1995).

African wealth, entrepreneurship and migration

Although expectations at independence were high, Africa economies faltered until in the 1980s tropical Africa's share of world trade was probably at its lowest for a thousand years (Iliffe 2007:261). As Africans got steadily poorer, the concern of popular Christianity shifted from health to wealth. Sub-Saharan Africa has seen a new wave of Christian-inspired movements, usually described as 'Pentecostal' or 'Pentecostal-charismatic', which are more concerned with social and economic success. Whereas the AICs were mostly countercultural, the new churches are public and often politically influential. Western Pentecostal churches have been in existence in Africa for nearly a century and some, such as the Assemblies of God, are large and widespread. Pentecostal missions began in South Africa as early as 1904, in Kenya in 1907 and in Sierra Leone in 1914. Missionaries were white or from the African diaspora in the Americas. In many cases they came as the result of invitations from African groups who had already experienced revival (Kalu 2008:41–64). Western revivalists also visited. The most prominent of these is the German evangelist Reinhard Bonnke, who has been leading large rallies or 'crusades' since 1967 that attract hundreds of thousands. The globalized communications systems that, from the 1980s, made the broadcasts of Western 'televangelists' available to African audiences were also significant. Not only did they

Figure 3.4 Worshippers gathered outside the Pentecostal International Worship Centre – Atomic, Accra, Ghana, after the morning service, 27 November 2011. The growing congregation belonging to the indigenous Church of Pentecost was meeting in the basement while the sanctuary was being completed.

spread Pentecostalism but the medium tended to encourage prosperity theology and personality cults (103–22).

In addition to classical Pentecostalism, there were local revivals in Evangelical churches from the 1960s that produced indigenous churches. In Nigeria, for example, a Pentecostal-charismatic movement arose among the Igbo in the context of their suffering and crisis of identity due to the Nigerian Civil War. Scripture Union groups in schools were the seed-bed in which educated Christians experienced revival and the energies released were spread nationwide during national reconstruction (Burgess 2008). The initiative is now with these newer churches, which differ from the older AICs in that they are largely an urban, middle-class phenomenon; they relate to modern Africa – a difference that is obvious in their dress and music styles; and they respond to the needs of a new post-colonial and post-modern generation. However, in their quest for spiritual power, they are like the earlier Ethiopian churches (Kalu 2008:32). Moreover, many of the AICs also have Pentecostal-charismatic characteristics, and indeed there is historical overlap between them in that many of the newer churches have AIC roots and share some practices (Anderson 2004:103–22). Furthermore, it could be argued historically that the AICs laid the foundation of charismatic ministries for the growth of Pentecostal Christianity (Asamoah-Gyadu 2005) and, theologically, that both movements show an indigenous 'pneumatic' response to the Christian gospel (Asamoah-Gyadu 2013). However, the older movements do not define themselves as Pentecostal so Ogbu Kalu urges a more differentiated view. In particular, he draws attention to the fact that Pentecostals have a more developed theology of discernment of spirits than do some AICs, which tend to retain more of African traditional religion (Kalu 2008:65–83). African Pentecostalism also shares the general characteristics of the worldwide movement. Pentecostals practise some of the church growth methods of Yoido Full Gospel Church in South Korea and use 'name and claim it' methods associated with some North American evangelists. But they have an African face, especially in their emphasis on deliverance from demonic forces associated with traditional religion. The most dramatic growth has been in West Africa, and some of the most prominent churches, which number their members in hundreds of thousands, are the Deeper Life Bible Church, the Redeemed Christian Church of God, Winner's Chapel and Living Faith World Outreach – all originating in Nigeria; Church of God International based in Benin; and Church of Pentecost in Ghana. These have spread in East Africa – especially Uganda, Central Africa – particularly Zambia, and to a lesser extent in South Africa. Moreover, Pentecostal churches are not just black but also white and Indian (Pillay 1994).

From the 1990s, Pentecostals 're-evangelized Africa' through internal mission that included not only church growth but also leadership training, the founding of Christian universities, evangelistic 'crusades' and social service missions to Muslims; and they transformed other churches (Kalu 2008:123–36). From a sociological point of view, the new churches have brought about a cultural shift: their emphasis on personal decision encourages individualism and the breakdown of the extended family. It reorders society for the benefit of youth and allows women leadership roles. Furthermore, the gospel of blessing legitimizes the accumulation of wealth, which might previously have been ascribed to witchcraft. The churches can also break down ethnic barriers, although equally they can demonize those outside. Paul Gifford (1998) describes Winner's Chapel in Accra, Ghana, where the most commonly used word is 'breakthrough'. One way to achieve 'breakthrough' is for each member of the congregation to wave a white handkerchief, called a 'mantle' (in reference to the prophet Elisha, 2 Kgs 2:9), which is given a 'double anointing' by the 'man of God' or 'prophet' leading the service. The congregation then waves their mantles over 'their instruments of destiny' – objects associated with their desired success (a pen for scholarship, for instance). 'Breakthrough', writes Gifford, refers to God's intervention to prosper his chosen followers. Biblical examples are given, such as Abraham, whose faith was (apparently) rewarded with wealth; Joseph, who went 'from prison to palace'; and David, who defeated Goliath. Winner's, which is part of a Nigerian multinational, and other large churches sponsor television and radio programmes and create videos, websites and mobile phone apps. They include many testimonies declaring what benefits people have received through their 'prophet', usually of a material kind, and sermons about achieving success.

Many commentators have drawn attention to the dangers of such expressions of faith. One is that in promoting 'big man' and 'big God', they lays itself open to corruption and public backlash (Kalu 2008:136–46). Gifford is similarly critical of these new 'prophets' whose gospel is open to abuse and which does not, in his view, address the underlying problems of Ghanaian society. However, he recognizes that one of the most successful prophets, Mensa Otabil, preaches about success brought about by hard work, assuming responsibility and obtaining education. Otabil does not dismiss witches and spirits but rises above people's personal fears to address social ills and make calls for political reform. While others have been exposed as corrupt, Otabil's personal integrity and careful negotiation of politics has been, in Gifford's (2005) view, a widespread influence for good. Furthermore, Otabil and others inspire self-help and hope of success. Whereas, for several decades sub-Saharan Africa has been the focus of attention for international aid and a symbol of hopelessness, these newer churches demonstrate the vibrancy of the region and its potential for self-development, of which there is a growing global awareness, especially under the influence of the Obama administration in the United States. In short, the prosperity gospel in Africa leads people to succeed in the capitalist economy, which is what is currently meant by 'development' (Freeman 2015). Although Western commentators may worry about the pursuit of wealth in Africa today in the context of late capitalism and compare it to Christian traditions of renunciation, African theologians are less worried about materialism – the material has not been separated from the spiritual in African faith – but they are concerned that the ideal of what constitutes wealth is far from the holistic vision of the ancestors (African and Christian) and that the Christian and African demand to share wealth is undermined (Getui 2003; Moyo 2003).

Churches of this new generation are more likely to call themselves 'global' or 'international' than 'African'. They express the aspirations of an entrepreneurial generation and also have branches in Europe, North America and in other continents, facilitated by the African diaspora. Forced migration for slavery by European powers from the fifteenth to the nineteenth centuries created the 'black Atlantic'. Largely undocumented has been the considerable migration within Africa, such as that brought about by the ongoing war in the Democratic Republic of Congo. Migration reshapes community identities, including religious identities (Wild-Wood 2008). Today, Africa has the highest population growth of any region and is ranked lowest in the Human Development Index. In the era of globalization, it was therefore bound to expand into other continents (Hanciles 2008:207–28). African migration is due to the search for resources, education and a better life; but also the disruption caused by famine and conflict; the need for work; neocolonial land-grabs; segregation; urbanization; environmental degradation; forced labour and trafficking. The level of desperation shown by recent refugees from Africa attempting to cross the Mediterranean Sea, often with the 'aid' of traffickers, gives the lie to the distinction between forced and voluntary migration and reveals the extent of the fears and the repressed hopes of young, mostly educated and skilled, Africans.

Among African migrants and refugees to the West are many Christians. Africans from older denominations may join existing churches in a new country. This is particularly so in the case of Catholics, and if the numbers justify it, the Church may provide opportunities for congregations and services based on language and ethnicity. But AIC and Pentecostal African migrants in Europe tend to form new congregations. Studies of these draw attention to the strength of their religious identity and the missionary motives of lay Africans as well as clergy (e.g. ter Haar 1998; Währisch-Oblau 2012). Nearly half of African migrants are female and their powerful networks are also extended transnationally (Adogame 2013:138–44). In the case of the United States, Jehu Hanciles shows that those who make it are mostly Christian, or become so after arriving. Independent African churches in the United States tend to be led by dynamic, well-educated Anglophone West Africans with backgrounds in business who came to the United States for other reasons but experience a call to mission as a result of observing that their adopted home is a mission field. They complain that US Americans exhibit complacency, 'materialism', a lack of 'fire' and a falling away. Given that they feel they are treated as inferior by the white majority, their African identity is part of their motivation to successful ministry. Thanks to mobile phones and the internet, they can maintain constant touch with the churches back home. The migrant churches mirror these and, like them, have a strong missionary orientation (Hanciles 2008). Afe Adogame (2013) finds that Africans are not only in 'reverse mission' to the West in the sense of seeking to convert people of European descent to African Christianity but also that African Christianities have considerable social, cultural and spiritual capital which they contribute in diaspora. So in the West they challenge the colonizing antecedents that led to John Gatu's call for a moratorium on missions to Africa. Furthermore, this capital is available to their churches at home as a 'spiritual remittance' to their home continent (101–22, 169–89). Of course African migration and intercontinental mission is not only to the West. The impact of African Christians on other continents is still largely an untold story.

Reading the Bible in Africa

Before European missionaries arrived, West African cultures were linguistically rich, politically intricate, artistically vibrant and musically distinctive. Many, like the Yoruba, had a substantial collection of oral literature but they did not have a system of writing, and it was this aspect of European culture that most impressed Africans. Those who became Christians also became literate, and school teachers were synonymous with evangelists. The freed slaves who settled in Sierra Leone were so convinced of the importance of education that by the mid-nineteenth century they had a higher rate of literacy than most Western countries and many were better educated than the Europeans among them (Walls 1996:102–4). The most lasting legacies of the missionary period in West Africa were the schools and colleges founded, the spread of literacy and the reduction of African languages to writing. This both facilitated African access to modernity and also contributed to the formation of national and ethnic identities. The long-term result of this was both national independence and also indigenous churches.

Not only did Africans emphasize the importance of reading, but they also laid claim to the Bible in particular, which they recognized as an African book, and which provided 'indispensable guidance at a crucial period at which they would otherwise have been inarticulate' (Mbiti 1986:29). It is noticeable in the descriptions above that the AICs have connected particularly with sections of the Old Testament – often with parts which make least sense in the cultures of the West, such as the genealogies of Genesis and the food and purity laws of Leviticus. Reading the Hebrew scriptures, Africans discovered that polygamy was practised by the patriarchs; that the people of Israel approached God through their ancestors (Mafico 2000:488); that they danced and used a variety of percussion and musical instruments in their worship; and that dreams, visions, prophetic messages and miraculous signs are means by which God communicates with his people. But the most interesting aspect of African reading of the Bible is the intense identification with its characters and events. This is especially so since many stories mention the people and places of Africa, which gives

African Christians a sense of participation in biblical history (Holter 2000:579). As the Ethiopians believed themselves to be the heirs of Judah, so the Akurinu Churches of Kenya understand that Mount Sinai, on which the law was given, is Mount Kenya (Ndung'u 2000:241). African Christians seem to feel part of the biblical world and in continuity with its people; the two worlds 'interpenetrate' (Mbiti 1986:228). The wisdom of the figures of the Bible has joined the wisdom of the ancestors (Jenkins 2006:35). For AICs, the Bible 'functions primarily as a repository of narratives' that illustrate God's intervention on behalf of his followers (Gifford 2003:86). This intervention is particularly needed because of the sense of living in a world of spiritual powers, in both the African and the biblical worlds (Parratt 1995:59). A bound copy of the Bible was itself a symbol of power over evil when brandished by William Harris and other prophet leaders. The text may function as an incantation, as, for example, in the Church of the Lord (Aladura), in which certain of the Psalms are believed to be effective for specific purposes. For example, the imprecatory Psalms (particularly Ps. 55) are considered to protect from evil ones. Other Psalms are regarded as therapeutic (e.g. Pss. 6, 20 and 40) and are used in conjunction with traditional methods of healing. Some Psalms (such as Pss. 4; 119:9–16) are identified as efficacious for success in the passing of exams, getting jobs and so on. Careful instructions are given as to how these should be used in a ritual setting to attain the desired results (Adamo 2000). AICs 'sought to establish a Christianity of the Bible as we saw it, without Western additions and in harmony with our own cultural heritage . . . to make the Christian faith come alive to our own thought and culture' (OAIC quoted in Pobee and Ositelu 1996:68).

Since most of the members of African churches prioritize oral rather than a literate understanding of the Bible, it is 'meaningless to discuss the interpretation of the text by itself'. Instead African hermeneutics is the 'enlarging' of the meaning of the text being interpreted based on the belief that 'God is speaking' directly through the Bible and that the Bible relates to daily experience (Anderson 2000:133–4). This approach is often referred to as 'fundamentalist' and is related to the attitudes of the more conservative of colonial missionaries (e.g. Parratt 1995:62). However, there are many other factors in African cultures that may have a bearing on attitudes to sacred texts, such as African oral traditions and Muslim use of the Qur'an. The controversies which produced Christian fundamentalism in the West have not taken place in Africa. As Philip Jenkins (2006) stresses, Africans are not being 'ultraconservative' in their reading of scripture because, on the whole, they are not taking a political or social stance against 'liberalism'. They may in fact be restoring (legitimate) traditions of interpretation long lost in Europe (17). Biblical interpretation and the methods of biblical interpretation serve the ends of the politically powerful – as the furious reaction to Colenso revealed. Yet equally they may be powerfully appropriated by those at the margins – as in the case of independence leaders and South Africans under apartheid, who 'read the Bible back' to their oppressors (Sugirtharajah 2001). Africans give the Bible authority because they choose to do so. They are not untouched by the Enlightenment – only resistant to its shortcomings (Bulangalire 2006).

Anglicanism is stronger in Africa than in any other continent, and African reading of the Bible, particularly on issues of sexuality, is currently at the centre of the controversy that is dividing the Anglican Communion. Whereas in the nineteenth century, Europeans slated the African custom of polygamy, in the twentieth century many African church leaders were shocked by Western Christian willingness to tolerate homosexuality. At the Lambeth Conference of 1998, at which African bishops were in a majority, a motion was passed overwhelmingly that homosexuality was 'incompatible with Scripture'. The strongest defender of that statement was Archbishop Peter Akinola of Nigeria. Akinola's pronouncements were very strongly worded, and after the Episcopal Church in the United States (ECUSA) consecrated a practising homosexual, Gene Robinson, as bishop, he declared the Church of Nigeria to be in a state of 'impaired communion' with it. The incident also led to the formation of the breakaway Anglican Church in North America. The issue raises important questions about the nature of Christian communion and Christian attitudes to homosexuality, but here we will highlight the clash between what appears to be the dominant African approach to biblical interpretation and the Western one – at least in the Anglican Communion.

The *Africa Bible Commentary* (Adeyemo 2006), authored by Evangelical African scholars, states that '[t]he Bible clearly defines homosexuality as a sin' (Turaki 2006:1355). To appreciate the predominant African position, it is important to realize that homosexuality is against the law in most African states and that the responsibility to marry and have children is a very strong expectation, supported by traditional African and biblical world views (Gen. 1:28; 9:7). It is also the case that there are passages in the New Testament, especially Romans 1:24–7, which are most straightforwardly understood as condemnations of homosexual practice and orientation. For people who see themselves as inhabiting the world of the Bible, the message seems plain. Furthermore, ECUSA's actions seemed to be disrespectful both of the clear message of Scripture and also of African views (Kaye 2008:175–95). It is true that Akinola and others disregard scientific and cultural considerations, not to mention the experience of homosexual people – including many African Christians (T. Brown 2006). But if there is to be reconciliation on the issue, one of the conditions must be that other Christians make a case on the basis of what is written in the Bible. Taking the Bible as a whole, without disregarding the difficult passages as liberal theologians tend to do, Kenyan Anglican theologian Esther Mombo nevertheless shows that it is unreasonable to draw the conclusion that God condemns homosexual practice and homosexually oriented people (Mombo 2006).

Robinson was not invited to Lambeth Conference of 2008 but even so more than two hundred bishops opposed to accommodating homosexuality declined to attend. Instead Akinola and six other primates held the Global Anglican Future Conference

(GAFCON) in Jerusalem one month before it. There they created a Fellowship of Confessing Anglicans (FCA). FCA is not only an African initiative but an alliance of moral conservatives from across the Communion, including particularly North America and Australia. Within Africa, many churches and Christian organizations are addressing the related issues of African constructions of masculinity and the spread of HIV, and their relation to sexuality and male power. These include, for example, Pentecostal pastors who, taking an increasingly public role, advocate a 'born-again masculinity' that inculcates a sense of responsibility (van Klinken and Chitando 2015).

African Christian theology is usually described as having two strands: 'African theology', related to traditional African culture; and 'black theology', developed at first in South Africa, with respect to political concerns and relating to the black liberation theologies of North America. In both cases, the approach to theology has paid close attention to the Bible. African theology as an engagement with traditional culture and religion arose in the independence period. In the face of criticism that this was a distraction from dealing with pressing social and political issues, Ghanaian theologian Kwame Bediako (1997:427–8) argued that African culture, more than any other, had been so vilified by missionaries and colonialists that it was necessary first to recover it and affirm that it could be considered a *praeparatio evangelica* – an entry point for the Christian gospel. Missionaries such as Placide Tempels, Geoffrey Parrinder and John V. Taylor produced the first studies of African religion and culture. The first modern generation of educated African Christians from the mission churches began their theology by considering its relationship to the Western Christianity they had received (Parratt 1995; 1997). To cite a few examples: Harry Sawyerr, a Protestant from Sierra Leone, was concerned that theology should function to give expression to the Christian gospel using, as far as possible, the religious ideals and rituals of African thought. Charles Nyamiti, a Catholic from Tanzania, with a similar intent, applied African thought, to the doctrine of God, where he saw that African concepts of the motherhood of God could complement Western emphasis on Fatherhood, and to Christology in a typology of 'Christ our Ancestor'. Noting the relevance of the Old Testament in Africa, Kwesi Dickson, a Methodist from Ghana, showed how African traditions, such as the understanding that death 'binds up relationships in society', reinforce the Hebrew background to Christian concepts such as the atonement. John Mbiti's (1969) thorough study of African religions and philosophy, and his concern that Western theology was 'impotent' in dealing with the African spiritual powers (1976), informed his conclusions that African eschatology was past- rather than future-oriented (1971). Theologians differed in the degree of continuity they saw between African culture and the Christian gospel. Opinions ranged from the Nigerian Methodist Bolaji Idowu at one end of the spectrum, who described African traditional religion as 'monotheistic' and used this to inspire pan-African cooperation, to Zairean Catholic Vincent Mulago, who saw African culture as merely an 'embellishment' to the Christian tradition (Parratt 1995:30), and Zairean Evangelical Byang Kato at the other end, who rejected African traditional religion altogether.

Because the focus was on the validity of African traditional religion as a vehicle for theology, the early studies tended to highlight pan-African concerns and not the distinctive aspects of the Christian message. Much of the initial discussion was on the nature of God, but once African theologians moved beyond missionary criticism and began to do theology on their own terms, African visions of Christ began to emerge. These were not so much concerned with biblical Christological titles, such as Messiah or Son of Man, but more related to 'the deeds of Jesus in relation to the individual believer' (Parratt 1995:78–81). A large part of African theology has to do with relationships and this is reflected in the some of the most common names for Christ: Ancestor, Elder Brother and Intercessor or Mediator. Another prevalent image is of Christ as healer (Healey and Sybertz 1996:82–87; Stinton 2004:54–61). Although African Christian theology is criticized as an 'elite academic theology' out of touch with grassroots Christianity (e.g. Gifford 1998:333), Diane Stinton's (2004:80–103) work has shown that Christ as healer, or life-giver, is also a common view of ordinary church members. This is supported by the fact noted earlier that healing is also the chief concern of the AICs. In describing Jesus as healer, the African Christians Stinton interviewed understood Jesus as one who recreates wholeness in all aspects of life and is supreme over every form of evil operating in the universe as saviour, liberator and redeemer (71–5).

In the second generation of African theology, women theologians came to the fore, especially through the 'Circle of Concerned African Women Theologians', which was inaugurated in 1989 by Ghanaian Methodist Mercy Amba Oduyoye (2008). African feminist theology is 'concerned with women's role in the wholeness of a single humanity rather than in feminism as a revolutionary countermovement' (Parratt 1995:51). Oduyoye (1986:44) declared that 'the cry for salvation/liberation in Africa is primarily a cry for health and wholeness' and this is necessary because of the brokenness of life. Musimbi Kanyoro (2001:112) observed that, though the male theologians who started African Christian theology regarded African culture as lost and in need of recovery, from the point of view of African women the culture continues, only with certain extra Western elements added on. The reflections of the Circle on a wide range of topics demonstrate the truth of this in the way that they combine African women's wisdom with biblical texts and current issues in new and imaginative ways. In one publication Musa Dube (2001a) tells the story of post-independence Africa in parallel with that of the bleeding woman who touched Jesus's robe for healing, and then she applies a method she likens to traditional divining to the book of Ruth to see the consequences for international relations (Dube 2001b).

The bewildering growth of African initiated and Pentecostal churches has left the historic churches with a challenge. In this context, the 'up-dating' of the Second Vatican

Council was embraced by the Church in Africa that aimed to become 'self-governing, self-ministering and self-supporting'. Several bishops' conferences in Africa took the image of the church as the people of God seriously. Pastoral life was organized around Small Christian Communities (SCC) and the Bible became the basis of instruction (Baawobr 2015). Recently two synods (1994 and 2009) and subsequent papal apostolic exhortations – *Ecclesia in Africa* (John Paul II, 1995) and *Africae Munus* (Benedict XVI, 2011) – have been devoted to the continent. They revealed some tensions between African leaders and the interests of the Roman curia and the magisterium, but they also reflected African themes. *Ecclesia in Africa* developed the image of the church as the 'family of God', which 'emphasizes care for others, solidarity, warmth in human relationships, acceptance, dialogue and trust . . . avoiding all ethnocentrism and excessive particularism' (para. 63) and *Africae Munus* recognized 'the African vision of life' in service of reconciliation, justice and peace. As Agbonkhianmeghe Orobator (2011:2) points out, the synods were not only directed at African problems but also defined Africa's part in the global mission of the Church.

It is important to bear in mind that most African Christians continue to belong to traditional denominations – Roman Catholic, Anglican, Methodist and so on – or have dual identities (Ward 1999:234), so there is considerable overlap between the AICs, Pentecostal and mission churches. The latter are far from being dead and formal, and are also shaped by their African context. As shown graphically in the documentary *African Christianity Rising* (Ault 2013), almost all the churches now incorporate Pentecostal-charismatic style worship, including deliverance ministry. Although initially resisted by the 'mainline' churches, this was a necessary concession to popular demand, and Charismatic Christians are increasingly found in their leadership (Omenyo 2003:19). Charismatic movements cut across the churches and express the concerns for both health and wealth (Magesa 2003:27). As this suggests, Africans do not divest themselves of their world view even when they enter the mission churches. A study of belief in witchcraft illustrated this when it was found that African Lutherans held a traditional world view and understood Christian teaching within that, rather than within the context of Western Christian anthropology and the tradition of original sin. Even within this church, which maintains relationships with churches from many different parts of the world, Christianity 'is already a uniquely African form' (Vanden Berg 2005:49).

Summary

Since the time of the ancient Ethiopians, whose descendants still practise an ancient Hebraic form of Christianity today, Africans have claimed Christianity as African and understood it as the answer to the questions they were asking, questions about spiritual power, deliverance, liberation and life. Since the Bible was reintroduced to Africa, sub-Saharan Africans have recognized themselves and their societies particularly in the narratives, genealogies and wisdom of the Hebrew Bible and found in Jesus Christ one who revealed the God they already knew, became part of that history as an ancestor and at the same time confronted its demons. Christianity has grown less in areas already reached by Islam, some of which are flashpoints of religio-ethnic tensions. In the countries of North Africa, which were Christian in the first seven centuries, there is little Christian witness except for the Coptic community in Egypt and the Ethiopian churches. African encounters with Christianity in European forms were seldom affirming to African identity; on the contrary, they were often experiences of aggression and domination. Nevertheless, a majority of black Africans appropriated what was useful in the message translated into their context, celebrated the freedom it brought and some made it into a tool of liberation from oppressors and of social transformation. Most did this within the colonial churches, which Africans now lead, but others exercised a prophetic ministry from outside in African initiated churches. In South Africa different kinds of churches (though not all of them) worked together to overthrow the system of apartheid and led in the process of truth and reconciliation. Although traditional African spirituality was mostly condemned by the mission churches, aspects of it were used in the new churches and have found their way into the older ones, giving African Christianity a unique aspect, particularly in terms of music, bodily participation in worship and expectation of God's involvement in the whole of life. Sometimes described as 'Pentecostalism', in most cases this is a development independent of Western Pentecostal denominations. Particularly as developed in West Africa, these new churches are growing worldwide. The legacy of the slave trade and colonial exploitation, an unequal global economic system, disease and climate change pose social problems, within which overseas missions and local churches are working to bring relief and improvement. In the context of corrupt leadership within the churches and in government, some African Christians have taken risks to speak out for justice and others have sought to exercise political power in the name of Christ. In the context of late capitalism there has been a shift in the concern of popular Christianity from health to wealth. On the one hand, many African church leaders and theologians struggle to balance this preoccupation with emphasis on education and ethical behaviour. On the other hand, many Pentecostal churches are upwardly mobile and empowering members to thrive in globalized society. With confidence in their faith, African Christians increasingly question the descendants of those who brought the gospel in the colonial period, rethinking the gospel for themselves and raising difficult questions about biblical interpretation, sexuality and reparation for past injustice. Created through slavery, modern migration and mission initiatives, an African Christian diaspora is re-shaping Christianity around the globe.

Study questions and further readings

- In what way does Christianity in Africa answer the questions Africans are asking?
- What is distinctive about the ways African Christians have interpreted and applied the Bible?
- Assess how Christianity has hindered or helped sub-Saharan African socio-political life.
- How significant is the rise of African Initiated Churches for Christianity in Africa?
- Discuss ways in which African Christians have responded to ethnic conflicts, political injustice or economic problems.
- What are key motifs and themes of African worship and theologies – and why?
- In what ways has African migration impacted Christianity globally? (See also Chapter 6.)

Adogame, A. (2013), *The African Diaspora*. London: Bloomsbury.

Asamoah-Gyadu, J. K. (2013), *Contemporary Pentecostal Christianity*. Oxford: Regnum.

Isichei, E. (1995), *A History of Christianity in Africa*. Grand Rapids, MI: Eerdmans.

Kalu, O. U. (2007), *African Christianity*, Trenton, NJ: African World.

Stinton, D. (2004), *Jesus of Africa*. Maryknoll, NY: Orbis.

4

European Christianities

Chapter Outline

The Christians of what is today Europe fall under the ancient patriarchates of Rome and Constantinople, which, although they both ratified the early councils, from Jerusalem to Chalcedon, gradually separated from each other due to cultural, political and economic factors into the Catholic and Orthodox churches. The first Protestant churches were born later from Catholicism. The heartlands of these three different ecclesial cultures roughly correspond to Southern, Eastern and Northern Europe. Christian experience in Europe is distinct from that in most other parts of the world in one obvious way: it was in Europe that (some) churches shared political power in what was known as Christendom. The precedent for an interdependent relationship between church and state was set in Rome 300 years after the birth of Christianity and carried over into the Byzantine and Holy Roman Empires in Europe but such an arrangement is not necessarily integral to Christianity. Questions of church and state still loom large for European churches, especially as those relations have been challenged by another powerful movement which has its origins in Europe: modernity. Each of the three forms of Christianity has encountered modernity in a different way and, brought together in a new united Europe since 1990, they each find themselves in a new and unfamiliar situation.

1. LIECHTENSTEIN
2. MONTENEGRO
3. KOSOVO
4. REPUBLIC OF MACEDONIA
NORTH AMERICA
ICELAND
Norwegian Sea
NORWAY
SWEDEN
FINLAND
Barents Sea
RUSSIAN FEDERATION
L. Vanern
ESTONIA
LATVIA
LITHUANIA
RUS. FED.
Baltic Sea
DENMARK
North Sea
UNITED KINGDOM
IRELAND
NORTH ATALANTIC OCEAN
NETHERLANDS
BELGIUM
LUXEMBOURG
GERMANY
POLAND
BELARUS
UKRAINE
MOLDOVA
CZECH REPUBLIC
SLOVAKIA
AUSTRIA
HUNGARY
ROMANIA
FRANCE
SWITZERLAND
SLOVENIA
CROATIA
BOS-HERZ.
SERBIA
BULGARIA
SAN MARINO
MONACO
ITALY
ALBANIA
GREECE
VATICAN CITY
PORTUGAL
ANDORRA
SPAIN
MALTA
CYPRUS
Black Sea
Caspian Sea
ASIA
AFRICA
Mediterranean Sea

Eastern Orthodox Christianity: Trinity and unity

Byzantium

The Eastern Orthodox Church, which began from the Greek-speaking church, sees itself in continuity with the New Testament. The missionary work of the apostle Paul to the Greeks straddled what we now see as a continental divide. But when Paul responded to the call of the Macedonians (Acts 16), there is no mention in the text that he was crossing from Asia into Europe. The Greek Church stretched across the Roman Empire, used the empire's common language and saw itself as universal. In 324 AD the first Christian emperor, Constantine, established his capital Constantinople in the Greek-speaking heart of the Roman Empire. The city became known as Byzantium and now Istanbul, and it is still the seat of the Ecumenical Patriarch. The patriarch presided over the seven ecumenical councils, all of which were held in the same region, the first and the last being at Nicaea in 325 and in 787. The Orthodox regard these councils, which systematized Christian thought in the language and culture of the Hellenistic world, as complete and, along with the Bible and the writings of the Fathers, as foundational to their tradition (McGuckin 2008). The councils defined key Christian doctrines: the Trinity and the divine–human nature of Christ. The last council stressed the unity of spiritual and material, soul and body, heaven and earth, which was grounded in the incarnation, through its affirmation of the veneration of icons. The church in Rome, which used Latin, the language of the elite, ratified all seven councils but the churches of Asia and Africa beyond the empire did not accept the Council of Chalcedon (451) or any subsequent ones.

As the Roman Empire disintegrated in the West in the late fifth century, the Eastern or Byzantine Empire flourished and also encompassed the patriarchates of Alexandria, Antioch and Jerusalem. When the latter came under Muslim rule from the seventh century, the patriarchate of Constantinople was without rival in the Byzantine church, although its territory was much reduced and Constantinople or Byzantium was itself under threat from Muslim armies. In the Middle Ages the splendour of Byzantium was legendary. Church and state were said to work together in 'symphony', like soul and body, and the whole was understood to be 'heaven on earth' (Ware 1993). The monasteries of Byzantium, particularly on Mount Athos in modern Greece, were renewed from the tenth century by Hesychasm, or a spiritual practice of stillness.

The status of the Patriarch of Rome as first among equals had been established by the fifth century. Gradually, due to the domination of Islam in the Eastern

Mediterranean and the rise of Southern and Western Europe as the Holy Roman Empire, the Roman Church became the more powerful and the pope began to claim an absolute primacy. In 1054 a papal delegation to Constantinople excommunicated the ecumenical patriarch for not submitting to the jurisdiction of the bishop of Rome. The action was reciprocated and increasingly the Orthodox saw the Western Church as heretical. They had three main complaints: elevating the pope, unilaterally adding the clause 'and the Son' (filioque) to the Nicene Creed, and using unleavened bread in the Eucharist (McGuckin 2008:21). When, threatened by Turkish forces in the late eleventh century, the Byzantines requested help from the pope, the leaders of the crusading army took the opportunity to impose Latin rites on the Eastern churches and even appointed Latin bishops over the existing Orthodox ones. There were skirmishes between Christians, and in 1204 a largely French army sacked and burned Constantinople itself, appointed a pro-Latin patriarch and stripped it of its wealth. The Western forces held Constantinople for fifty-seven years. The antics of the Catholic Europeans undermined rather than strengthened Constantinople, which was eventually taken by the Ottoman Turks in 1453 and renamed 'Istanbul'.

During several centuries within the Ottoman empire, Christians were a dhimmi, or a 'protected' religious minority, but they faced taxes, restrictions and sometimes the forced marriage of their women to Muslim men (Irvin and Sunquist 2012:127–30). Since Muslim rulers did not distinguish religion and politics, the Orthodox Church became a civil as well as religious institution, a situation that persisted in Turkey until 1923 and in Cyprus until 1977. In this way Greek identity was preserved, but at the expense of the church being bound up with Greek nationalism (Ware 1993:89). The other patriarchates within the Ottoman Empire resented the fact that the Turks gave Constantinople jurisdiction over them as well. So, at the end of the nineteenth century, as the Ottoman empire gradually broke up, nationalist Greeks, Bulgarians, Serbs (with Russian support) and Romanians demanded autocephalic (self-governing) status. The Greeks were first to attain it in 1850. The attempt to bring the remaining Greeks of the Ottoman Empire within the Greek state led to the massacre of thousands by Turks in Smyrna in 1922. This was followed by population exchanges between Greece and Turkey. A Greek community was allowed to remain in Istanbul with the ecumenical patriarch, although it has almost disappeared today. After the First World War, the collapse of the Russian and German empires led to new Orthodox churches coming into being made up of believers in Poland, Finland, Lithuania, Latvia and Estonia, some linked to Constantinople and others to Moscow. The Orthodox world became largely a collection of national churches, which left the Ecumenical Patriarch in Constantinople with limited jurisdiction, and the Turkish authorities now question the patriarchate's status and presence.

The Russian Church

The loss of imperial lands east of Asia Minor to Muslim armies by 634 meant that the Orthodox faith could no longer spread eastwards. However, the Slavs and the Bulgars, who from the sixth century had moved into territory north of Constantinople, adopted Christianity in the ninth century. This was facilitated by the mission of Constantine-Cyril and Methodius from Constantinople. In accordance with Greek practices, the missionaries translated Christian literature into the local languages – devising the Cyrillic script in order to do so. However, their efforts were opposed by Frankish (German) missionaries, who regarded Latin (or conceivably Greek and Hebrew) as the only proper language for the liturgy. In 867 the Franks were overruled by the Roman pontiff, but they prevailed eventually, and by the end of the ninth century the Moravian church was increasingly Latinized. A Slavonic church gradually came into existence in the lands of the Rus people, who lived north of the Black Sea. The Kievian Rus were impressed with the wealth of Constantinople and raided it several times before coming to see the value of its religion. Prince Vladimir, whose mother Olga had become a Christian (Helena), investigated other religions before taking baptism in 988. Vladimir appreciated the unifying potential of Christianity

Figure 4.1 Infant baptism service in a Russian Orthodox Church, Nizhny Novgorod, Russia, 22 April 2007. The priest is anointing the baby, who is held by its godmother. Image: iStock.

and built a strong Russian national identity on the basis of Orthodox Christianity. He Christianized social structures, gave alms and exercised mercy, and encouraged the migration of monastic communities into the country.

While the other Orthodox communities were under the Ottoman Empire, a Russian empire, centred on Moscow, emerged from the Mongol rule that had been imposed since 1240. Under the Mongols the church had held the Russian people together, particularly through the monasteries, which practised a revived Hesychasm and were closely integrated into community life. It was monks, such as Saint Stephen of Perm, and monastic communities who pioneered the expansion of Russian settlement north of Moscow. Since the Russian Orthodox Church regarded Rome as heretical, and Constantinople as infidel for capitulating to the Turks, it began to see itself and the nation as the sole remaining protector of Orthodoxy, and Moscow as 'the Third Rome'. The church and monasteries gained a great deal of territory, despite the protests of the 'non-possessors', and church and state became closely integrated, especially under Ivan IV, the Terrible, in the sixteenth century. In 1666, the 'Old Believers' separated from the church as a protest against the reforms introduced by Patriarch Nikon.

For several centuries the Russian Church was largely cut off from other Christians but from the late seventeenth century several Western European influences came in: first, Peter the Great's reforms of the church incorporated some Westernization of its political structures: the church was subordinated to the state, the patriarch was deposed, and there was a church council effectively ruled by the emperor's representative. Second, Enlightenment learning attracted the intelligentsia of the Orthodox churches, and the seminaries borrowed Western models and taught Latin, scholastic thought and rationalism. However, the rise of romanticism convinced many intellectuals to return to the roots of their own tradition and sparked a Hesychast revival in nineteenth-century Russia based at the monastery at Optino (Hackel 2002:551–3). The power of this mystical and eremitic spirituality based on the repetition of the 'Jesus prayer' – 'Lord Jesus Christ, son of God, have mercy on me, a sinner' – soon spread throughout the Orthodox world through the monasteries. Third, when Tsar Peter expanded Russian territory over vast tracts of Central Asia and Siberia as far east as the Pacific Ocean and Alaska, he followed a Western model in using missions to convert conquered people. Under Catherine the Great in the late eighteenth century, the Russian empire also expanded westward. It incorporated parts of the then greatly enlarged Poland, bringing in Orthodox Ukrainians and Byelorussians, whose churches were incorporated into the Russian Orthodox Church. In the mid-nineteenth century, missionaries evangelized Muslim tribes in the Volga and Ural regions. Moreover, following Western patterns of evangelism beyond national territory (and in accordance with national interests), by 1899 missions had been established in Persia, China, Japan and Korea. There was also continuing work in Alaska – by now US territory. Inside Russia, the church began a Bible Society in 1814 and established various charitable organizations. In 1870, the Russian Missionary Society was established, and it supervised much of the work until its closure in the aftermath of the 1917 Bolshevik Revolution (Stamoolis 2001).

Despite Peter the Great's attempts at Westernization, in the nineteenth century the Russian Orthodox Church, burdened by state bureaucracy and suffering from corruption, tended to maintain tradition without relating it to modernity. Orthodoxy was treated as a marker of national identity and a hereditary characteristic, and apostasy from the Russian Orthodox Church was a punishable offence (Knox and Mitrofanova 2014:40). But as the twentieth century dawned, there was widespread anti-clericalism in Russia, fuelled by the Westernized and Marxist-influenced intelligentsia. In response in 1905 Tsar Nicholas II gave a measure of religious freedom and elements within the church pressed for reform. In 1917 the Russian Church put in place the vision of sobornost: a conciliar administration of patriarch, bishops, clergy and laity. However, the Bolshevik Revolution later that year meant that most of these plans were never implemented. Instead Orthodox theologians – such as Serge Bulgakov, Nicholas Berdiaev and Vladimir Lossky – joined other émigrés in Paris where they brought Orthodoxy into dialogue with Western theology (Noble et al. 2015) and influenced particularly Catholic ressourcement theologians, who were revisiting biblical and patristic sources (Dupuis 1999).

Orthodoxy under communism

The leadership of the Union of Soviet Socialist Republics (USSR) espoused militant atheism and persecuted the church to an unprecedented extent. It regarded the church as its most dangerous threat and attacked it physically by persecution, mentally by the re-education of the masses and politically by subverting its leadership (Lupunin 2010:19). By the beginning of the Second World War there was not a single monastery or convent left in Russia. Barely a hundred places of worship were open in the whole country and hundreds of thousands of Christians had been liquidated (Hackel 2002:552, 558). The church was forced into silence in public; its life was limited to cultic activities at the most; its icons were burned. Nevertheless, at the height of Stalin's purges in 1937, millions in the Soviet Union risked their livelihoods and lives to answer 'yes' to a census question asking whether they believed in God. Only with Soviet entry into the Second World War did the government recognize the patriotic value of the church, which came out in support of the state and thereby bought itself some reprieve. Orthodox churches also suffered under fascism in Europe. During the Second World War, Orthodox Serbs in Croatia were forcibly converted to Catholicism as part of a policy of genocide, and the 350,000 who resisted were slaughtered.

In the aftermath of the war, many more European Christians found themselves under communist regimes. Communist leaders in Russia changed their attitude to the Church and began to regard it as a vehicle for the expansion of communism in the Eastern bloc. Smaller Orthodox churches in the Soviet Bloc – Polish, Latvian and Estonian – were subsumed under the Russian Church. The Eastern Rite Catholic Churches (Uniate) in Ukraine, Poland, Czechoslovakia and Romania were abolished. Working with government, the Russian Patriarchate celebrated the five-hundred-year anniversary of its autocephalous status in 1948. It challenged the authority of Rome and Constantinople and pressured other Orthodox churches to follow suit. In fact, the relationship of churches and governments in Eastern and Central Europe varied: at one extreme the church in Albania, whose leaders had opposed communism during the Italian–German occupation in the Second World War, was persecuted and disbanded (Pano 2014); at the other, the Romanian Church benefited from collaboration (Leustean 2010b). From the communist point of view, the church was useful to control the masses, give the impression internationally of religious freedom and monitor the Orthodox diaspora (Leustean 2010a:6–7) Orthodox churches outside the Communist Bloc held varied attitudes toward it: Alexandria and Antioch supported it but the Church of Greece was opposed, and the Orthodox diaspora in the West worked for the overthrow of communism.

Particularly during Nikita Khrushchev's rule, repression was renewed in the USSR and also in the Eastern bloc, especially in Bulgaria and Romania. In this period of enforced interiority, as the churches were 'aligned . . . with Isaiah's Man of Sorrows as never before', worship gained 'exceptional dignity and power' (Hackel 2002:559, 562). However, with few if any young people being brought up in the church and trained for ministry, the damage inflicted on the ancient religion was not to be easily undone. Christian delegations from communist countries were sometimes permitted to attend conferences, but not to reveal the situation of the churches there (Walters 1999:316). The Christian attitude to the regime varied. Most of the Orthodox Church leaders of Eastern Europe drew on the tradition of a 'symphony' of Orthodoxy, autocracy and nationhood. They sought to maintain the traditions of the 'true' faith (Orthodoxy), regarding the state as temporary but nevertheless put in place by God (Leustean 2010a:1). In international forums they condemned the actions of the West and they promoted their alternative Christian Peace Conference. However, there was also underground resistance by monasteries, charismatic monks and nuns and religious intellectuals, for example, in Serbia where there had been a strong inter-war peasant movement Bogomoljci (Buchenau 2010:67–71). Christians in the West sought to help. In the Protestant case, the Keston Institute in Oxford founded by Anglican priest Michael Bordeaux monitored the abuse of human rights on the other side of the Iron Curtain and the Dutchman 'Brother Andrew' (Anne van der Bijl) smuggled Bibles to underground Evangelical churches. Following the Helsinki Peace Accords in 1975, dissidents and diaspora Orthodox increasingly raised the issue of human rights. Communism was unable to eradicate the churches for several reasons: because of the large size of the communities; because the churches effectively campaigned for religious freedom; and also because the regimes saw the church as useful during the Cold War (Leustean 2010a:6–7). In fact by continuing to provide an ethical alternative to communism, by existing as the only public institutions (and buildings) not controlled by the party and by helping to preserve national identities in many cases, the churches contributed to the end of communism (Walters 2006:352–3).

Roman Catholic Christianity: Christ and church

Roman Christianity

The apostle Paul claimed to have preached the gospel from Jerusalem as far west as Illyricum and had plans to go on to Spain – the end of the known world at that time (Rom. 15:19, 28). There was already a church in Rome before the Apostle Paul wrote to it or was taken there in chains (Acts 27–28). The extent of Christian presence in Rome – at the heart of the empire – became clear in 64 AD when the emperor Nero executed hundreds in the Colosseum. According to tradition, not only Paul but also Peter was martyred in Rome. So the patriarch of Rome could claim to be the successor of Saint Peter, the rock on whom Jesus said he would build his church and to whom he gave the keys of the kingdom of God (Matt. 16:18). After the destruction of the temple in Jerusalem in 70 AD, it became the pre-eminent Christian centre, despite the shift of Christian imperial power to Constantinople.

The city of Rome, like any imperial capital, was a microcosm of the empire and within it were migrant churches from across the whole world. They each had their own customs and ways of practising their faith, for example, different dates of Easter, which meant that, while some were fasting, others were feasting. This state of affairs was problematic for Christian fellowship and threatening to Christian legitimacy. The lack of unity, the need to defend Christianity against persecution and also the desire to influence Roman society for the better, encouraged the diverse churches in the city to come together and appoint a single bishop, Victor – a North African – in 189 AD. He insisted on unifying the church calendar – even at the expense of excommunicating many from Asia Minor who wished to maintain their own tradition – and laid the Latin foundations of the Church of Rome. The church in Rome was increasingly Gentile in composition and Jews and Christians distanced themselves from one another. Although the split was gradual over several centuries, already in the mid-second century Justin Martyr declared in Rome that the two religions were separate and that Christians were the sole inheritors of the promises to Israel. In the same period, Marcion (originally from Asia Minor) gathered support in Rome for his view that Christians should reject the Hebrew scriptures and a number of the teachings of the apostles because of their Jewish origins. He drew up the first list of a canon of Christian scriptures. However, his views were rejected as part of the finalization of the canon, which also seems to have begun in Rome. In the early third century, Hippolytus laid down what he believed was the apostolic church structure of deacons, presbyters and bishops which was adopted by the Roman church.

After the Christian faith was established as an official religion of imperial Rome, following the conversion of Emperor Constantine, people flocked to the churches for baptism and church leaders became increasingly taken up with teaching and pastoral care of the local people. The basis of the theology of the Western church was developed by Augustine of Hippo at the turn of the fifth century. He was trained in Roman law and largely separately from the deliberations of the Greeks. His theology differed from that of the East most significantly in his theology of the Trinity. Where the Eastern Fathers discussed the complementary roles of all three divine Persons, in his dispute with Arians, Augustine insisted on the unified action of the Godhead. Acutely aware of his own sinfulness and in dispute with Pelagius, Augustine stressed the necessity of grace for salvation – or justification, which he connected particularly with sacrifice of Christ. And in dealing with the Donatists of North Africa, he defended the Roman church as made holy by the blood of Christ and taught that it was the only source of salvation. In contrast to the Orthodox, Augustine separated the earthly city from the city of God and allowed for a world outside the church, which needed to be converted. Where the Orthodox tended to totalitarianism, Catholicism tended (contrary to its name) to exclusivism.

Evangelization of Europe

From Rome the Christian faith could rapidly be disseminated further west and south through the excellent communications network of which it was the centre. By 180 there were churches as far apart as Lyons (modern France) and Carthage (North Africa). Christianity also spread to Britain under Roman occupation. After the establishment of Christianity as a legitimate religion, the church cooperated with the state to evangelize the Barbarian tribes who were causing trouble along the empire's borders and so turn its enemies into Christian brothers. The migrants and invaders who settled within the empire – Germanic tribes and the Visigoths in Italy – were persuaded to adopt Catholic Christianity. The evangelization of Northern Europe was mainly by missions from Rome, although there were exceptions to this pattern. The most notable was the mission of Patrick who followed a Celtic rather than Roman pattern of belief and worship which he had learnt in Gaul and evangelized Ireland in the fifth century without imperial backing. The peoples to be evangelized included the Franks, a Germanic group along the Rhine who later spread into Gaul (which became France) and to Spain, whose king Clovis was baptized a Catholic around

500 AD. Their conversion began the long alliance between the ruler of the Franks and the Roman pontiff that reached its height under the Emperor Charlemagne. It unified Europe, preserved the Roman language especially through Jerome's translation of the Bible into Latin (the Vulgate) and came to be called 'the Holy Roman Empire'. However, missionary activity was now backed by force. For example, under Charlemagne, the Franks forced the Saxons of what is now northern Germany to be baptized on pain of death.

The Angles, Saxons and other groups who had migrated into Britain from the North German plains were the object of a mission sent from Rome by Pope Gregory the Great in 596 and led by Augustine of Canterbury. However, another mission to Britain had been initiated from Ireland by Columba, who established a base on the island of Iona off the Scottish coast and from there came into northern England. When the two missions from north and south encountered each other, it was found unthinkable that British Christianity should follow more than one set of practices. At the Synod of Whitby (663–64), under Abbess Hilda, it was decided that Britain would come under the authority of Rome. After this, England became a base for wider missionary activity by missionary monks in the seventh and eighth centuries: Wilfrid led the evangelization of the Saxons in England, Willibrord was sent to the Frisians

Figure 4.2 Procession at the installation of Dominik Jaroslav Duka OP as the thirty-sixth archbishop of Prague, St. Vitus Cathedral, 10 April 2010.

and Boniface was the Apostle of Germany. In the tenth century, the Saxons expanded their power and Christian faith northwards into Denmark, south to Italy and east into Poland. The Vikings, who had been raiding Christian settlements around the North and Irish Seas, gradually adopted the faith and spread it back to Scandinavia in the ninth and tenth centuries. In the year 1000, after long deliberations by the elders of the community and shamanistic-style divinization, the people of Iceland opted to become Christians. The Finns and other peoples of the Baltic were the last to become Christians (under Swedish rule) but by about 1400 virtually all the people of Europe professed Christianity (Irvin and Sunquist 2001).

As with subsequent missions to tribal people in many different parts of the world, signs and wonders were effective in proving the superiority of the Christian faith in encounter with their traditional gods. This is an approach that seems to be advocated in the closing words of Mark's gospel, which records signs which 'will accompany those who believe', including exorcism, new tongues, freedom from harm and healing (Mark 16:15–18), and recalls the challenge of Elijah to the prophets of Baal (1 Kgs 18:20–40). Boniface is popularly remembered for having demonstrated the power of the Christian God over the old ones by chopping down the sacred oak of Thor, God of thunder, and using the wood to make a church. If so, this was not an impetuous act but carefully thought out after much reflection on cultural issues and how to argue with polytheists (Mayr-Harting 2002).

The Christianization of the European people was carried out mainly through the monasteries, for which in the West the norm was the Rule of Saint Benedict of poverty, chastity and obedience. The monasteries were centres of education and learning; they introduced new technological developments, especially in agriculture; they provided healthcare, gave alms and other help to the poor and offered hospitality to pilgrims and other travellers. Generally the life of the monks was an example to the local population and the monasteries were, at their best, the centres of a rural mission movement, which followed a centripetal model of witness that drew people into the Christian community (Bosch 2011:235–41; Bevans and Schroeder 2004:119–29). The monasteries attracted support in the form of endowments from the wealthy in the hope of accruing vicarious merit according to the medieval penitential system, for spiritual protection and for other reasons including their colonizing role (Lawrence 2001:66–73). The great abbey of Cluny in France extended its power to include the shrine of Santiago de Compostella in northwestern Spain and controlled the pilgrimage routes there. At the same time – the tenth century – Pope Gregory VII instituted moral and structural reforms. The church came out from under the protection of local lords in many parts of Europe and became a pan-(Western) European body. It assumed temporal as well as spiritual powers, and the hierarchy took the initiative in Christianizing Europe, changing the laws, institutions and customs to conform more closely to the law of Christ as they understood it. Through the Peace of God (Pax Dei) movement, which began in southern France in the tenth century, the church counteracted the violence of feudalism by offering protection to non-combatants and restricting violence. The church also accommodated itself to feudal society by controlling and providing for the – now settled – people of Europe through a system of parishes, which clothed Europe in what a French monk described as 'a white mantle of churches' (MacCulloch 2009:365). People were baptized into the church in childhood and households contributed a tithe (tenth) of their income. In return, the church pronounced forgiveness, interceded with God for the people and in the name of God legitimized rulers, governments and systems of justice. In addition to their religious duties, priests took on clerical roles, such as recording marriages and deaths. Within the boundaries of this 'notionally unbroken Christian territory' of 'Christendom', alternative forms of public worship were not permitted and idolatry, blasphemy and heresy were not tolerated (Walls 2002a:198).

By the twelfth century, the great monasteries of the earlier period were not adaptable to the needs of the growing towns and they seemed far from the simplicity of the monastic ideal. In this situation there emerged orders of friars, notably the Franciscans and Dominicans, who followed a mendicant model of ministry (cf. Luke 10:7) and went out (centrifugally) from their respective religious communities to preach and meet the needs of people. They followed the instructions of Jesus when he sent out the disciples to carry no purse but to receive their living from those to whom they ministered (Mark 6:7–13, and parallels) (Bevans and Schroeder 2004:141–60).

The Gothic splendour of medieval church buildings in Western Europe showed both the glory of God and the power of the church. Although the church actively tried in this period to separate ecclesiastical and secular, in some respects it behaved like an imperial government. The papal bull *Unam Sanctam* of Pope Boniface VIII in 1302 asserted that there was only one, holy, Catholic and apostolic church, outside which there was no salvation. Christ appointed one head of that church, Saint Peter, and the pope is his successor, to whom all human beings must be subject if they wish to obtain salvation. Furthermore, the church had not only spiritual but also temporal power, just as Peter also held the sword (Matt. 26:52) (Irvin and Sunquist 2001:480). With its increasing power, the church came to see itself as 'mother' to the faithful, particularly in its teaching role (Ward and Evans 1999:110) and 'king' in its 'fullness of power' (Morris 2002:217). It assumed an increasingly hierarchical structure, a militaristic posture and a juridical theology.

Catholicism and Islam

The self-assertion of the church was a proclamation of a new society in Europe in which the old pagan past was rejected and the kingdom of God and millennial light was instituted on earth (Hastings 1999b:335). But this stance was not only so that the people of Europe and other church leaders knew where they stood, it was also due to an external enemy. Although different Muslim empires were involved, Islam as a whole was perceived to be the enemy. It had conquered many Christian lands, including near ones such as Spain, Portugal and Southern Italy. It threatened Constantinople, which fell in 1453, and even Vienna, until turned back in 1683. It was the spread of Islamic rule that turned Europe into 'Christianity's main base' for the next thousand years (Davies 1996:257). And it was while fighting together in the Crusades, away from their own communities, that Europeans began to express a common identity as 'Westerners', 'Christians' or members of 'Christendom'.

At first, Europeans viewed Islam as a new heresy that needed correction by the church for its denial of the crucifixion and Christian beliefs such as the Trinity, and its rejection of the authority of the church. But Islam defined itself over against Christianity (and Judaism) as the pure faith of Abraham and God's last testament with humanity. So gradually Christians came to regard Islam as lying outside the Christian tradition altogether. By the logic of Christendom therefore, Muslims had no place in Christian territory. Rulers anxious to channel the energies of the warrior class encouraged Christians to participate in driving Muslim rulers out of what had once been Christian lands, beginning with the Iberian Peninsula and Sicily. Christian rulers fought these campaigns in the name of Christ and received the church's blessing. However, when in 1095 Pope Urban II called for a military campaign under the sign of the cross (Crusade) to recover the Holy Land because 'God wills it', this marked an unprecedented step. For the first time war was made part of the task of the church – and Augustine's distinction between the church and the kingdom of God was lost (Burrows 1996:123). Material gain was a major incentive for many crusading knights, but the series of crusades over two centuries were supported by the populations of Europe for religious reasons: as a form of pilgrimage (Johns 2002:177) and as 'the ultimate form of penance' (Irvin and Sunquist 2001:396). The church very soon lost control of crusaders' activities and all manner of atrocities were committed against Muslims and Jews, and even Orthodox Christians, in the name of Christianity. This episode continues to bring disgrace to the name of Christ and the symbol of the cross. The ongoing political fallout in a globalized world is often not appreciated by Christian missionaries, who identify their organizations or activities as a 'crusade', although several international organizations have taken steps to change this designation in recent years.

The Crusaders had not intended to convert Muslims, and indeed hardly any such attempt seems to have been made until the thirteenth century when Francis of Assisi, who was known for his holy life, extended his preaching to include Muslims (Armour 2002: 61–79, 87). Since there was little response but more Christian martyrdoms, in the fifteenth century the Franciscan John of Segovia suggested a shift in Christian–Muslim relations from the goal of conversion to encouraging dialogue about matters of mutual concern and an emphasis on the common ground shared by the two faiths. Ironically, it was during the Crusades that Arab learning, building on the ancient civilizations of the Mediterranean and West Asia, was filtering into the universities established (on an Arab model) in Spain. The great Scholastic theologian Thomas Aquinas drew on Arabic translations of Aristotle and Arabic scholarship itself. Aquinas's distinction between natural law, deduced from empirical evidence, and God's law, made known by revelation, allowed him to benefit from Islamic learning while also arguing against Islam itself, and so laid foundations for secular scientific enquiry.

The final crusade ended in 1291, and there was no significant European influence in the Holy Land again until the twentieth century, although Eastern Christians continued to live there. However, not only had Islam been decisive for European identity (Davies 1996:258), it had also shaped the medieval church and aspects of Catholic theology. The crusading mentality continued in Western Christendom in three ways. First, European Christians re-conquered the lands they regarded as originally Christian (reconquista). The last Muslim kingdom in Iberia fell in 1492; the Moors were pursued into North Africa and the Jews were expelled. Second, crusades turned inward against Jews and heretics within Europe and against new groups deemed heretical, such as the Waldensians in Italy and the Cathars in southeastern France. In the fifteenth century, the pope was supported in these measures by the rulers of the re-Christianized and rising European powers Spain and Portugal. The Inquisition was set up by Queen Isabella of Spain initially to root out Jews, but this was soon extended to exposing all heresy. When biblical justification of force was called for, it was found in Luke 14:23, where the disciples are to go to the poor from 'the highways and byways' and 'compel them to come in'. At the turn of the twelfth century, Dominic Guzmán tried an alternative way to counteract heresy by a combination of word and deed: preaching and demonstrating a pure Christian life. The Dominicans, or Order of Preachers, developed a theology that stressed the connection between reason and faith, and therefore promoted scholarship, but they also became heavily involved with the Inquisition. Third, the crusading mentality was harnessed to spread Christianity, especially to the territories which emerging European nations were gaining in Africa and the Americas after discovering alternative ways of reaching Asia. The fact that 1492 was also the year that Christopher Columbus set sail across the Atlantic looking for a westerly route to Asia underlines the way in which the Portuguese acquisition of colonies in Africa and the Spanish conquest of the Americas were, in the minds of the conquistadors, a continuation of the reconquista of Europe.

Evangelization of Latin America

In the next few centuries, the growth of Europe as a world power and of Christianity across the world went largely hand in hand. The aggressive seizure of the lands of

Latin America cannot be blamed on Spain and Portugal alone. It was part of a greater European enterprise through which the mercantile economy developed into the global capitalism of today. It was also the product of the older feudal system in which the earthly lords and the Lord God were believed to be working together for the furtherance of the honour of both (Dussel 1990:32–6). During the overthrow of the Moorish kingdoms in Spain and Portugal and in the Americas, the conquistadors were rewarded by being granted (by the crown) the conquered land and the labour of those living in it, 'in trust' – encomienda. Encomienda also became the basis of the system of 'patronage' set up in the sixteenth century to stop the squabbling of Spain and Portugal over territory. In the bull *Inter Caetera* (1493) Pope Alexander VI drew a line on the world map from the North to the South Pole, declaring that colonies to the east of it, including Brazil and Africa, were under the jurisdiction of Portugal and those to the west belonged to Spain. The respective monarchs were charged with baptizing and Christianizing the people, for which they called in the mobile mendicant priests (who came with their corresponding women's orders).

There was no shortage of recruits, as sixteenth-century Spain saw a renewal of spirituality which produced famous mystics including John of the Cross, Teresa of Avila and Ignatius Loyola (founder of the Jesuits). At Spain's new universities, the Scholastics defended the conquest by appeal to Aristotle and natural law, to which the church and theology were subordinated (Richard 1990). They argued that the indigenous people were 'slaves by nature', and so they justified armed conquest and subjugation. This view was translated by missionaries into the tabula rasa or 'clean slate' approach. This eradicated the expression of traditional customs and beliefs in order to inculcate what they believed was the Christian way of life. However, many missionary friars and some bishops tried hard to protect the people from the predations of the colonists and traders, and protested the treatment of the indigenous people (Salinas 1990). The most outstanding example was the Dominican Bartholomé de las Casas. At the University of Salamanca, Francisco de Vitoria provided academic grounding for Las Casas's work, both by producing an evaluation of Indian culture and by disputing that the conquest constituted a 'just war'. Vitoria's work laid the groundwork for the later development of European concepts of human rights (Gutiérrez 1990). When the drastic decline in the Indian population led to a shortage of labour, there was no comparable debate in Europe about whether Africans could be enslaved. Already the myth that Africans were the descendants of Ham, who was apparently cursed by his father Noah to be the 'lowest of slaves' (Gen. 9:18–29; 10:6), allowed for a theological justification to be made for the practice, and led to the development of the anthropology of the 'negro' as suitable for slavery because he was savage and barbarous (Hurbon 1990:91, 96).

By the sixteenth century, new powers were emerging in Europe north of the Alps, in Holland, France, Britain and the princedoms of Germany. The papacy was weak, increasingly Italian and unable to correct obvious abuses of religion, and yet the church demanded allegiance and commanded wealth that was the envy of secular rulers and accrued by exploitation of the peasants. The church could not relate to the aspirations of the people of Northern Europe, who were experiencing the beginnings of the capitalist economy, increasingly well informed by printed material, and craving for social justice and self-determination. Peasant uprisings, new religious movements and outspoken criticism of the church signalled the rise of Protestantism. In response to the crisis of the Reformation, the 'counter-' or 'Catholic' Reformation expressed at the Council of Trent (1545–63) refuted Protestant doctrine. Although it recognized the biblical testimony as to the priority of grace and the response of faith for justification, it stressed the ongoing dimension of justification and the importance of the tradition of the church for salvation. With regard to the church's inner life, new disciplines were imposed and abuses stopped, but with regard to the outside, the council signalled a restoration, which affirmed the unique sacramental role of the Catholic Church and the authority of its hierarchy (Küng 1995:483, 493). Furthermore, this restoration was implemented politically and militarily where possible, with disastrous results for the peace of Europe.

Evangelization of Asia

In this time of Catholic renewal, several new religious communities were founded, including the Jesuits. Ignatius conceived the Society of Jesus as a mobile and flexible body to be 'sent' – the Jesuits were the first to use the term 'mission' in this sense – by the pope (not a local ruler) wherever in the world they were needed. He emphasized centralized authority, obedience and training through the 'spiritual exercises' and education. The Jesuits engaged with contemporary philosophy in Europe, became spiritual advisors to powerful leaders and founded schools with a reputation for excellence. A major theatre of Jesuit activity was Asia, where conditions were very different from those in the Americas. European conquest of the great empires of Moghul India or China was not (at this time) considered, much less attempted, therefore '[i]t was necessary to accommodate the Christendom idea to political and military reality' (Walls 2002a:199). Through Alessandro Valignano in the sixteenth century, the 'the gentle way', which required missionaries to explain the Christian gospel in a way appropriate to the cultural context, became Jesuit policy in Asia. Under Valignano's influence, in 1622, the church set up the new Sacred Congregation for the Propagation of the Faith (SCPF) to prevent mission activity being perceived as an arm of foreign power by training local clergy. Reflecting the rising power of France, the SCPF established the Paris Society for Foreign Missions (Société des Missions étrangères de Paris) in 1658–63. This was the first of a new style of Catholic mission organization. Instead of being a religious institute made up of people who have consecrated themselves to community life by vows of poverty, chastity and obedience, it comprised secular priests and lay persons who shared a common purpose of foreign mission (today described as a 'society of apostolic life').

Following SPCF policy, Matteo Ricci identified with the Confucian scholars, or literati, in China. However Ricci's decision to use a Chinese word for God and assertion that the Confucian practice of ancestor veneration was a social rather than a religious act (and therefore compatible with Christian faith) were criticized in the seventeenth century, particularly by Dominican missionaries entering China, who saw this as a compromise with pagan religions. Chinese Christians were also divided on the matter. When these concerns were taken back to Europe they erupted into what became known as the 'Rites Controversy', which pitted the Portuguese Jesuits against French Jansenists, who were much more negative toward human nature and culture. Pope Clement XI's decision in 1715 against the rites contributed eventually to papal suppression of the whole Jesuit order for forty years from 1773 (Moffett 2005:105–42; Bays 2012:28–32).

The Rites Controversy shows that in addition to the paradigm of 'missionary war' followed by the church both within and outside Europe (Bosch 2011:241–2), there was another paradigm of 'radical inculturation' (Burrows 1996) at work, which followed the Apostle Paul's advice to be 'all things to all people' (1 Cor. 9:22). This broke away from the Rome-centred, or Eurocentric, mindset and, anticipating the 'culture principle' of later cultural anthropology, approached other societies and new movements 'from within' (Bevans and Schroeder 2004:203). Of course, this approach depended on the separation Jesuits perceived between what was 'cultural' and 'religious'; there was no accommodation in the latter sphere. However, one of the chief objections of the Dominicans and Franciscans was that the Jesuits chose not to disclose aspects of revelation, such as the crucifixion, which they knew Confucians would find unacceptable. Although the church hierarchy rejected inculturation, it continued to be widely practised by Catholic missionaries in the mission field until eventually it resurfaced in the twentieth century. Following the development of the culture concept in Europe and in the context of persecution in China, the objection to the Chinese Rites was revoked in 1935. In the wake of Second Vatican Council (1962–65), it was decided to translate the words of the mass, still said almost everywhere in Latin, into vernacular languages. Pope Paul VI insisted on a 'synthesis' between faith and culture (Shorter 1999:57, 55) and the term 'inculturation' was endorsed by John Paul II in 1990 (*Redemptoris Missio*), who described it as an act of incarnation. Although, there are continuing tensions within the church about the extent of inculturation and about whether faith or culture should be the starting point for the process, Pope Francis – a Jesuit – has recently emphasized its importance (*Evangelii Gaudium*).

Protestant Christianity: Bible and society

The Reformation

In the face of the intransigent and corrupt Catholic Church of the early sixteenth century, the people of Northern Europe inculturated the gospel for themselves in a new theology and a new form of church known as Protestantism. Through the Reformation, many of the new churches became closely linked to the different linguistic, ethnic and national identities of Northern Europe. The Reformation had many aspects – political, social and economic – as well as the religious. As their name implies, the Protestant churches were originally a protest movement, which aimed to reform the Roman Catholic Church. The Protestant paradigm, as articulated by the Augustinian monk Martin Luther in Germany beginning in 1517, did not depart from the juridical approach of Augustinian and Scholastic theology, or from the Catholic doctrines of the Trinity and Christology. It offered a new understanding of how believers are reconciled with God which emphasized sola gratia: God's grace or initiative in revelation toward humankind as the only ground for knowing God; sola fide: faith, rather than religious ritual, as the way to approach God; and sola scriptura: the Bible rather than the magisterium or teaching office of the Catholic Church as the authority for teaching and formulating doctrine. Luther clarified therefore that it is not the role of the church to grant salvation, but primarily to give instruction as to how salvation may be received and lived out.

Luther's Reformation was a national event that unified the German people through his translation of the Bible, and it developed as a communal event in the 'Peasants' War of 1525 (Blicke 2007). Subsequently, to varying extents Protestants reduced the sacramental role of the church and priesthood, laying emphasis on the clergy's role in preaching the Word of God. Although Protestants formed new churches, they continued to believe – like Catholics – that the doctrine they held was absolutely true and universally applicable (Bosch 2011:245). For leading Reformers it was not the Bible itself but its interpretation by church leaders educated and ordained in their Reformation tradition that was binding on the faithful, but other more radical movements gave greater freedom to the Holy Spirit and to individual interpretation. In the case of the Anabaptists the biblical text itself assumed greater importance (McLaughlin 2007).

The theology of Martin Luther is the basis for the Lutheran churches of Germany and Scandinavia. Another German, Huldrych Zwingli, founded the Swiss Reformed Churches. The French reformer John Calvin became the leading theologian of the Reformed churches, who aimed to 'educate' the world to 'hear'

God's Word, in a 'personal, dynamic and life-changing' way (Greengrass 2007:113). The Scottish Reformer John Knox was an associate of Calvin and the Church of Scotland adopted Knox's interpretation of Reformed polity – Presbyterianism, which stressed lay leadership by presbyters who were 'elders'. The theologians of Anglicanism (or Episcopalianism in North America), such as Thomas Cranmer, followed Luther more closely. But the English Reformation had more of the nature of a political compromise. Anglicanism was defined in the Elizabethan settlement of 1559 which (re-)established the Church of England and it developed through the Enlightenment as a reasonable and broad religion with a social mission (Spencer 2010). The Lutheran and Anglican churches have retained (or can choose to retain) more of the sacramental cult of Catholic worship, such as a strong emphasis on the Eucharist, a priestly role for their 'ministers' and an ornate sanctuary. Generally speaking, the Reformed churches represent a more thoroughgoing reformation of worship than the Lutheran and Anglican churches. The Reformers stripped the churches of many of the things they regard as non-essential in order to focus on the Word. Buildings are relatively (and sometimes very) plain in style; there is less emphasis on the celebration of the sacraments and more on preaching. There were also more radical Reformation groups such as the Anabaptists (whose main representatives today are Mennonites). Subsequent protest movements in Europe and North America led to the formation of the Society of Friends (Quakers), and also Methodist churches, Baptists and many other denominations. These accommodated to aspects of modernity, particularly emphasizing education and intellectual assent to faith.

National Christianities

When the reforms suggested proved unacceptable to the Catholic Church, the Reformers became hostages as European monarchs and local rulers assumed responsibility for reforming the church, and at the same time submitted it to their jurisdiction. Since leadership of the Protestant churches was bound up with the interests of local powers, and neither Catholics nor Reformers nor princes could conceive that there could be more than one true church or one true doctrine within a defined territory, Catholic rulers persecuted Protestants and vice versa. Europe entered a period of wars that devastated life and property across the western part of the continent from Britain to Poland and Germany to Italy for more than a century. Since each ruler took a particular religious view, these were later dubbed 'Wars of Religion'. Eventually a workable solution was found in the Peace of Westphalia in 1648, which reconfirmed the principle of the Peace of Augsburg (1555) that each region should follow the religion of its ruler but added to Catholicism and Lutheranism the option of Calvinism as well. Scandinavia was recognized as Lutheran, Poland, France, Austria and lands to the south as Catholic, parts of the

Netherlands and Switzerland as Reformed, and residents of the German-speaking kingdoms as either Lutheran, Reformed or Catholic. On the same pattern, Britain, England and Wales were recognized as Anglican, Scotland as Presbyterian. As this suggests, these 'established' churches maintained a close relationship between church and state. In most cases, the state collected church taxes, paid clergy and controlled appointments.

Despite the close church–state relationship, the Peace of Westphalia was the first 'breach' of the principle of Christendom because, as nation-states grew, Christianity became increasingly nationalized (Walls 2002a:211). The only self-consciously transnational churches were the Roman Catholic Church and the Anabaptists who, as their name implies, did not accept the validity of the baptism of the Roman Catholic or any other church, and insisted that believers be 'baptized again'. They were seen by governments as a particular threat because they wandered, in family and community groups, across Europe, preaching the gospel in the belief that 'the earth is the Lord's, and all that is in it' (Ps. 24:1). This attitude also infuriated the leaders of the established churches, who regarded the Anabaptists as encroaching on their territories (Walls 2002a:37).

As well as breaching the territorial unity of Christendom, the Peace of Westphalia also signalled an important stage in the secularization of Europe. International relations were no longer conducted on the basis of religion; the state was the dominant actor (Thomas 2005:33). Furthermore, there was an understanding that the established churches would support their state and curb any religious enthusiasm that might disturb the peace of Europe. Dissenters, radicals and independents who set up their own churches and interpreted the Bible in their own way, were dealt with ruthlessly as enemies of the state, and those who did not conform to the established religion were now denied opportunities for government service. The search for freedom to practise the religion of their choice was the reason many groups migrated to North America in the seventeenth and eighteenth centuries.

The effect of the Reformation on Europe was to establish separate national churches which defined themselves (or redefined themselves in the case of Catholicism) against one another, rather than in terms of the world in which they were set (Bosch 2011:253–4). The antagonized differences between Catholics and Protestants were exacerbated by the politicization of religion, and any possibility of an early reconciliation was prevented by the structure of the nation-states. The Protestant churches understood themselves as maintaining and correcting the faith of the nation in which they were established. Although John Calvin attempted to wield juridical as well as religious power in Geneva, most Protestant churches renounced violence and state control as a means of Christianization and relied instead on the proclaimed Word of God to effect the change they expected to see in individuals and the transformation of society.

Renewal movements: Pietism and Evangelicalism

From the turn of the eighteenth century a series of movements of religious renewal among Protestants led to new initiatives not always under the direct authority of the national churches. Because these deepened the faith of those involved, the revivals brought them together but separated them in this respect from others who had not experienced renewal. So these movements for 'real' Christianity challenged the assumption that everyone within Christendom was Christian. Furthermore, they encouraged transnational – and therefore trans-church – activities and even churches (Walls 2002a:211–14). Some of these were directed locally and others globally, but the same individuals tended to be involved. The first type of renewal movement was Pietism in the seventeenth century, a movement which 'combined the joy of a personal experience of salvation with an eagerness to proclaim the gospel of redemption to all' (Bosch 2011:257). Beginning from the work of Philipp Jakob Spener within the Lutheran church of Germany, it spread across Northern Europe, and also overseas, beginning with India in 1706. Pietism marked the emergence in Protestantism of Christian organizations. At first these were within the churches but separate from their hierarchies and with alternative sources of funding. They took the form of voluntary societies, which became the Protestant, activist equivalent of the Catholic religious communities, which could address the shortcomings of the churches and overcome their limitations. Voluntary societies are integral to Protestant missionary method – both as part of and parallel to denominational structures – to the present day (Walls 1996:241–54). The catalyst for this development was the need of the church overseas, and the first examples were the societies set up in 1699 and in 1701 by Thomas Bray, an Anglican clergyman. The first was for the 'propagation of Christian knowledge' (SPCK). The second was for the 'propagation of the gospel in foreign parts' (SPG; O'Connor 2000). That is, among the inhabitants of the colonies – Europeans, natives and slaves – the link between religion and territory being maintained (Bosch 2011:249–50). Bray's missionaries were ordained clergy, always men, but – unlike Catholic priests – often married with families.

The second type of renewal movement, known as Evangelicalism, was influenced by Pietism but became a transatlantic, mainly Anglophone, phenomenon. The 'Evangelical Revival' in Britain (1735–45) was led by John Wesley, a Church of England priest, and another priest George Whitefield, who carried it to the United States, where it issued in the 'Great Awakening'. Wesley's Anglo-Catholic faith had led him to seek spiritual perfection by self-denial, and so he had dedicated himself to serve with SPG in the American colony of Georgia. Crossing the Atlantic on the boat home after only three years, feeling he had failed, Wesley was impressed by the spiritual vitality of a group of Moravian missionaries. The Moravians were a community whose origins lay in the ministry of the early Czech Reformer Jan Hus and who were also influenced by the Pietism of their patron Nikolaus von Zinzendorf. They exhibited a Pentecostal-type spirituality – the result of an intense and radical revival at their community of Herrnhut in 1727. This inspired them to share their faith globally in a self-sacrificial way (Podmore 1998). A decade later Moravian missions had begun in the West Indies, Greenland (a Danish territory), Georgia (North America), Lapland, Suriname (Dutch Guiana), South Africa and Gold Coast (modern Ghana). The Moravians supported themselves and worked among the poor and marginalized (Gallagher 2008). Through the Moravians, Wesley experienced for himself a more 'affective' or emotional expression of faith. Returning to ministry in Britain, Wesley's passion became to revive the Church of England, which he saw was failing to reach and care for the urban poor. His watchword, 'the world is my parish', referred primarily to his challenge to the territorial jurisdictions of the established church, but it also signalled a willingness to 'go into all the world', which Evangelicals later put into practice, and a catholic (or inclusive) spirituality (Rack 2002:189). The direct effect of Wesley's work was Methodism, which separated from the Church of England in the American colonies and then also in Britain. Named because of the methodical prayer and Bible study in small groups that the Methodists organized, Methodism became a separate Protestant 'denomination'. Evangelicals in general, in awareness of personal sinfulness, practised a strict moral code and, grateful for the grace of God shown in Jesus Christ, they sought to share the good news by preaching, teaching and taking practical steps to improve society. Pietism and Evangelicalism 'conditioned the earnestness of what in England was called the Victorian ethos' (O. Chadwick 2002:351) and the voluntary societies they established were quintessentially modern in their structures and their pragmatic outlook. But unlike the other forms of Protestantism, Methodism was not the established church of any nation-state. Freed from Anglicanism, it tapped into the anti-establishmentism of the era and became an 'empire of the spirit' (Hempton 2005:203–4).

Modern Europe: Cross and flag

Modernity is a complex phenomenon, the result of social, scientific and industrial revolutions led by Northern European peoples, mainly French, British and German, but resourced by lands far from Europe. Although developments in Europe profoundly influenced other parts of the world, Europe also absorbed ideas from elsewhere (Ramachandra 2006:219–22) and was changed by them (Frykenberg 2008:142–68). Medieval church scholarship and the encouragement to literacy and intellectual freedom of the Protestant Reformation may both be regarded as contributing to the emergence of modernity but, although the established churches continued to be powerful institutions for most of this period, they were now subject to secular rulers. Moreover, in the development of science and philosophy on a secular basis, the initiative moved away from Christians, who were increasingly put on the defensive. Modernity brought new challenges for the (now several) churches of Europe, particularly in terms of their task, thought and morality.

The form of European faith that thrived most in early modernity was Evangelicalism. Further transatlantic Evangelical revivals or awakenings continued into the mid-nineteenth century and resulted in a loose grouping of denominations or groups within denominations who shared four common characteristics: conversionism – the need for individual change of life – being 'born again' – because of sin; activism – through evangelistic and missionary efforts; biblicism – attaching a special importance to the Bible as authority for belief and conduct; and crucicentrism – belief in Christ's death on the cross as of central significance for human salvation (Bebbington 1989:2–17). Each revival produced a new wave of voluntary societies for work at home and overseas. The most prominent social result of the first revival was the abolitionist movement. British Quakers, a breakaway group from the English Puritans, in the late eighteenth century formed a loose coalition with the Clapham Sect, a group of Anglican Evangelical activists. It included freed slaves such as Olaudah Equiano. After William Wilberforce steered through parliament a bill for the abolition of slaveholding in 1807, the campaign was revived in order to eradicate slave-trading. This became a major motive for nineteenth-century missionary activity, particularly in Africa. Abolitionists from Britain and the United States established the two West African colonies of Sierra Leone (1787) and Liberia (1822) (respectively) as homelands for freed slaves. They then tried to penetrate the interior to improve conditions for Africans so that there would no longer be any economic incentive for slave-trading, and also to reach with Christianity populations who might otherwise become Muslims (Robinson 2004:71). The campaigns against slavery were closely linked with movements to bring the slaveholders and other colonists to the Evangelical faith (because they would then give up slavery) and to bring the gospel of liberation to the enslaved and others in the colonies. A second Evangelical revival at the end of the eighteenth century led to a mushrooming of voluntary societies for overseas mission. Among the European societies were the London Missionary Society (LMS; 1795), the (Anglican) Church Missionary Society (CMS; 1799), the British and Foreign Bible Society (1804), the Netherlands Missionary Society (1797), the Basel Mission (1816), the Danish Missionary Society (1821), the Berlin Missionary Society (1824), the Swedish Missionary Society (1835) and the North German Missionary Society (1836).

The archetypal 'modern mission' is the Baptist Missionary Society (Stanley 1992), founded in 1792 by a group including William Carey, who then went to India as its first missionary. Carey argued, first, that it must be practically possible to go overseas because explorers, traders and Moravians and others were doing so already and because of the advances in knowledge and technology of the Enlightenment. Second, he insisted that not only the first apostles but also modern Christians were mandated by Jesus's Commission to take the gospel to 'all nations' (Matt. 28:18–20). Being a Baptist who rejected the established church, which had tolerated Baptists only since 1689, Carey's aim was not to revive the faith of the colonists but to reach the local people. He founded new local churches that were only loosely linked together and were more dependent on the mission than the parent denomination. Carey's ministry was ambitious and typical of the era. In the Danish colony of Serampore, Carey set up a mission compound with missionary homes, a church, school and hospital, such as were soon multiplied across the world. Carey's compound exemplified 'Christian' or European living, provided a safe haven for converts and accommodated mission work. The latter comprised codifying Indian languages, Bible translation, printing and initiatives in education, healthcare and agriculture. Such voluntary societies, in which the Bible did not always go with the flag (Stanley 1990), were much less easily contained by the Protestant churches than the missionary communities or apostolic societies were by the Catholic Church. The autonomy of the voluntary societies, combined with the nation-bound nature of most Protestant churches, led to a greater separation between church and overseas missions than was possible in the Catholic Church, in which the church beyond Europe was an extension of the one church.

Under the influence of the Holiness revival movement of the mid-nineteenth century, in 1865 James Hudson Taylor, a member of the independent Brethren, founded the China Inland Mission (CIM; now OMF International). It was the first of a new generation of missions: 'Faith Missions' (Fiedler 1994). Taylor introduced a number of innovations. The society was non-denominational but required missionaries to sign a statement of faith (doctrine). The aim of the mission was not to plant churches but only to convert individuals and then leave it to them to organize churches. The society would not clash with established missions by soliciting funds but would be supplied 'by faith alone' – in other words by donations from individuals convicted by prayer. Calling rather than qualifications constituted the missionary. Rather than general mission activity, CIM undertook a specialist task where there was not already a church – in this case, mission to inland China. Unlike the missionaries to China whom Taylor observed congregating in the treaty ports among other ex-patriates, CIM missionaries were expected to identify with the people, so as not to put any unnecessary barriers in the way of the gospel. Whereas in most societies they were invisible, in CIM single women and wives were treated as co-workers. And Taylor insisted that the work in China should be directed not from London but on the ground in China. Soon other independent societies were begun to do specialized mission work in particular regions, such as the North Africa Mission (1881) and the Sudan Interior Mission (1900), which borrowed from Taylor's methods. The Faith Missions were particularly influenced by premillennialist theology that the world would soon be destroyed and only believers would be saved – hence Taylor was not greatly concerned about long-term civilization. The different structures of the Faith Missions reflected a divide among Protestant missionaries that opened up at the end of the nineteenth century between the priorities of 'evangelism' and 'social action'. The missions grew particularly in the United States among the independent churches there.

Carey epitomized the modern Protestant mission paradigm (Bosch 2011:286–7), which began with awareness of the need of the 'heathen', who were regarded as calling out for Europeans to 'come over and help us' (Acts 16:9), and the motive of obedience to 'the Great Commission'. Although missionaries were the first cultural anthropologists, and were instrumental in preserving cultures and languages threatened by globalizing forces, they generally intended to use that knowledge to persuade people to convert. With notable exceptions, the two activities of converting and civilizing were largely synonymous because Pietistic Christian faith had strong implications for moral behaviour and way of living. Missionaries were increasingly co-opted by colonial governments as a cheap way of 'civilizing' their populations by providing education and healthcare, and introducing Western standards of hygiene, agricultural methods and other technologies. Whereas some missionaries challenged colonial policy, most, as people of their time, did not question colonialism itself.

Earlier Catholic and Protestant missions were more willing to ordain local people as clergy. In the first half of the nineteenth century, Henry Venn of the CMS (Ward and Stanley 2000) developed the 'three-self' missionary strategy. Under this plan, local churches established by missions were encouraged to be self-governing, self-supporting and self-propagating. Venn believed this would eventually obviate the need for missionaries and lead to the 'euthanasia of the mission'. However, due to the influence of social Darwinism, and as even China, which had been regarded as 'civilized', began to crumble before the onslaught of modernity, later missionaries increasingly doubted the character and ability of 'the natives'. Furthermore, having better resources, more personnel and the long view of the imperialist, they did not regard indigenization as a priority. Missionaries, who were portrayed as heroes at home, also neglected to give credit to the role of local evangelists in the growth of churches overseas. A rare protest against colonialism in the church came from Roland Allen, an SPG missionary in China in the early twentieth century, who unfavourably compared contemporary mission methods to the pattern established by the apostle Paul. He found that Paul's confidence in the power of the Holy Spirit to guide new believers and willingness to let them discover their new faith for themselves contrasted strongly with the paternalism of the missions (Allen 1956[1912]).

Protestant societies first emerged at a time when Catholic missionary activity was diminished because of the weakening of Spain and Portugal, the suppression of the Jesuits and other factors. However, at the beginning of the nineteenth century a renewal of Catholic mission was stimulated particularly by the revival of French political power in the Napoleonic era and also French spirituality. The latter took the form of devotions to the Virgin Mary, to the Sacred Heart of Jesus and to the Blessed Sacrament, by lay people and especially women (Heimann 2006). New French missionary orders were founded for men and for women, such as the Society of the Sacred Heart (1800), the Sisters of Saint Joseph of Cluny (1807) and the Oblates of Mary Immaculate (1816–26). Other developments were the restoration of the Jesuit order in 1814, the reconstitution of the Sacred Congregation for the Propagation of the Faith in 1817, whose main arm had become the Paris Society for Foreign Missions, and the renewal of older congregations such as the Franciscans and Dominicans. From 1831 until the turn of the century, a series of popes supported modern mission work. It was no longer limited to Catholic-ruled places but planted churches as well as evangelized society. The middle of the nineteenth century saw the founding of another raft of new Catholic organizations, including the Spiritans (1848), Comboni Missionaries (1864) and the White Fathers (1868).

With so many different groups in the 'mission fields', there was inevitably competition between them in some regions. These problems tended to be worked out locally by systems of 'comity', or agreement between the main groups to divide up territory and work in different areas. The interdenominational Protestant (and Anglican) missionary conference at Edinburgh in 1910 to discuss cooperation on the 'mission field' (i.e. outside Christendom) led eventually to closer working relationships between the Protestant churches in Europe. Almost all the organizations mentioned in this section still exist today, some in a modified form, and the paradigms they grew out of still manifest themselves.

Modern Europe: Faith and reason

The experience of the churches in Europe in the nineteenth and twentieth centuries was one of 'attack' and 'persecution', which undermined their confidence as bearers of Christianity to other parts of the world (Chadwick 2002:349). Those which had authority and privileges saw them stripped away in the interests of progress and commerce. In some cases misrepresentation, suppression and outright persecution were used against Christians to advance vested interests. The churches deserved much of the criticism directed against them for their collusion with unjust government, self-interested attempts to preserve their privileges, abuse of the trust placed in them, intransigence, lack of respect for popular opinion and attempts to gain popularity at the expense of truth. However, they were also the victims of ideological and commercial agendas. Whatever the rights and wrongs of the matter, in many respects the churches felt themselves to be under attack; they found themselves marginalized in public life, and on the defensive. The 'attack' was first on the church's doctrines and then on its morals. Both were challenged by the rise of modernity: doctrine by the new intellectual approaches of modern science and morality by the new social context of democracy and capitalism.

The effect of the Enlightenment, or Age of Reason, on the European elites was profound – although the thinking of the peasants was probably little affected. In Western Europe, the self-proclaimed 'enlightened ones' of the seventeenth century blamed the turmoil of wars since the Reformation on something called 'religion', which was increasingly separated from public life and was defined by the Peace of Westphalia as a body of beliefs rather than as a human community (Thomas 2005:25). The solution to European problems and the means to achieve 'tolerance' was therefore deemed to lie in playing down the differences in doctrines of Catholicism and Protestantism and emphasizing the developments in empirical science that seemed to offer 'universal truths' that all 'rational men' would be bound to agree upon. However, since scientific method could not prove any of the basic Christian creedal statements of the incarnation and exaltation of Jesus Christ, the lowest common denominator of Deism was all that was left for Enlightenment thinkers. Christian doctrines became matters of conjecture or opinion and could not be classed among the 'facts' on which all must agree (Newbigin 1986). Furthermore, the Enlightenment subtly altered the basis of Western thought, putting it out of step with almost every other society in the world. No longer was religion assumed true unless proved otherwise; by the nineteenth century the burden of proof had shifted from the doubter to the believer (Heimann 1999).

Further intellectual challenges for Christians arose in the nineteenth century. The opening of the universe to scientific investigation and its explanation in terms of laws which did not need recourse to God removed the category of the 'sacred' from philosophical thought. The Bible and the church were demystified and laid open to study not only by the methods developed within Christian tradition but by secular methods of historical science. When the Bible was read, along with other ancient texts, by F. C. Bauer and others of the Tübingen school, what struck the scientific eye tended to be internal contradictions, uneven style and unprovable claims rather than God-given truth and guidance. Charles Darwin's *The Origin of Species* removed the need for belief in God one stage further by filling in many of the 'gaps' for which God had been invoked and providing scientific explanation for the 'wonders of creation'. His *The Descent of Man* reduced human beings to the purely material and questioned the existence of what Christians called 'the soul'. 'Natural theology' was now replaced by 'natural science' or just 'Science' (with a capital 'S'), and Science seemed to be in opposition to something called 'religion', which was as obscure and subjective as Science was clear and objective (Heimann 1999:497).

In the face of aggressive scientism, which declared Christianity to be 'untrue', or at best superseded, European Christians took one of four positions: traditionalism or modernism, evangelicalism or liberalism. The first two were associated with Catholicism and the second pair with Protestantism. In the eighteenth century there was a strong climate of anti-clericalism in France, which culminated in the French Revolution (1789–99). It attempted the complete overthrow of traditional society, de-Christianization and the construction of a new society based on pure reason. Hundreds of priests and lay Christians were killed in the attempt (Tackett 2006). In this context, French Roman Catholic theologians were the first to question the motives of 'the Lights' (Les Lumières), the French Enlightenment philosophers. Discussion between them centred on whether or not miracles occurred. The Archbishop of Lyons, Antoine de Montazet, argued that scientists who dismissed miracles on the grounds that the laws of nature could not be broken were not being objective and examining the historical evidence, and he further refined the methods for verifying reported miracles.

Despite the opposition of the Jansenists, who taught that the philosophies of the Enlightenment were 'pagan' and anti-Christian, the challenges of biblical criticism and the theory of evolution were not as threatening to Catholic theology as to Protestant faith. Catholicism was based first and foremost on the traditions of the church which acknowledged an ongoing revelation. Nevertheless Catholics were bound to defend the church and its historic teaching from what was also an attack on its political power. The church asserted its doctrinal authority and further centralized power in the Vatican. In the 1864 *Syllabus of Errors* the church declared itself against most aspects of the modern world, and at the first Vatican Council in 1869–70 Ultramontanists, who supported greater papal authority, triumphed when the pope was declared 'infallible'. This declaration was in defiance of the fact that, as part of the unification of Italy, the extensive papal lands were seized and the council had to end abruptly. For the next few decades Catholic theologians who wished to engage in dialogue with the modern world were regarded with the suspicion that they were falling into agnosticism, and in 1907 Pius X labelled them 'modernists'. The future John XXIII, later to open the church to modernity through the Second Vatican Council, was cast under a cloud in this period.

While many Catholics retreated into church tradition and looked to the authority of the pope to support them, Protestants read their Bibles and rediscovered aspects of the experience of the early church in the movements known as Pietism, Methodism and Evangelicalism. These movements, like romanticism, represented a rejection of dependence on reason as the only arbiter of truth. Rather than law or logic, they stressed the unpredictable and the amazing work of God. However, they did not reject reason altogether, but to the sources for theology recognized by Enlightenment thinkers – scripture, tradition and reason – they added the category of experience (the 'Wesleyan quadrilateral'). Methodism particularly gave rise to all sorts of 'enthusiastic' behaviour, often among the new industrial working class. Its apparent irrationality called forth scorn from the 'enlightened' establishment. There were similarities between the behaviour of the Protestant Evangelicals and the Jansenists in the Roman Catholic Church. The latter's uncontrolled behaviour and their unreasonable assertions of untested miraculous occurrences contributed to their suppression by the church authorities in the 1730s.

The strength of the initial reaction of Western church leaders against the new movements showed the extent to which they were under pressure in eighteenth-century society to conform to Enlightenment reason. However, the shock of the horrors of the French Revolution drove those European elites who remained in power back into the arms of religion. For leaders of Protestant nations – both Christian and Deist – the faith, and especially the morality, of the Spiritual and Evangelical movements offered an attractive alternative to the chaos of revolution. Furthermore, the Evangelicals were also an essential force in the growth of the capitalist economy, as Max Weber (1930[1905]) was later to argue. For the leaders of Catholic nations, traditionalism prevailed. Therefore, during the nineteenth century most European states took steps to protect their churches as a bulwark against revolution. In France the restored empire made peace with the Roman Catholic Church, and a revival of popular spirituality followed. In Prussia in 1817, the Reformed and Lutheran churches were brought together to form a single Evangelical Church supported by the state. As well as the Evangelical movements, in England and Germany there were reactions against them, which aimed to restore a pristine version of the faith through Anglo-Catholicism (the Tractarian or Oxford movement) and neo-Lutheranism.

However, the leading Protestant theologians of Germany and Britain, who were schooled in their best universities, generally supported what was seen as 'progress'. They tried to work out a compromise that took into account the latest intellectual developments while preserving as much of traditional doctrine as possible. Nineteenth-century liberals encouraged open debate and the use of critical methods to read the Bible and examine Christian doctrines. Their faith was not undermined since, following the lead of the German thinker Friedrich Schleiermacher, they tended to play down Christian doctrine and give greater importance to the experience of faith. However, the results of their enquiry profoundly disturbed the faith of educated Christians. The views arrived at about the dates of biblical writings, the authenticity of documents and what could be known about the historical Jesus were much more sceptical than the consensus today, but, more than that, the liberal assertion that human knowledge could take precedence over biblical revelation was deeply troubling, especially to Protestants (Heimann 1999:490). This intellectualization and rationalization of faith led to a separation between theologians and Christians in churches; causing the latter to look to other sources to sustain their daily Christian practice. Now that science began to take precedence over religion, liberal theology became captive to developments in the former. Furthermore, some of the fervour once reserved for religion became transferred to science, which came to resemble a new religion and embody hopes for the future. The assertion of the pre-eminence of science over religion had a profound effect on European relationships with the rest of the world in the later nineteenth century. It formed part of the positivist philosophy that all knowledge passed through different stages of evolution before arriving at scientific knowledge. This supported the supposed superiority of European (or rational Christian) civilization and its colonization of other parts of the world that were perceived to be benighted by dark forces of irrational religion as Europe had once been.

Modern Europe: Righteousness and justice

In the nineteenth century in Protestant countries, what is known in Britain as the Victorian era was one in which religion was the mark of respectability. Although the intellectual problems remained, religion was valued again as making an important moral contribution in maintaining civilized society. So it not surprising that it was chiefly the morality of Christianity that came under attack in the nineteenth and twentieth centuries. Karl Marx criticized religion for drugging people into quiescence and acceptance of the will of the powerful. The atheism of Bolshevism, which triumphed in Russia after the overthrow of the monarchy in 1917, and the spreading of Stalinism across Eastern Europe after 1939, which caused so much suffering to Orthodox and other Christians there, tended to be used in Western Europe by right-leaning governments to gain Christian support. However, many church people, remembering the communal sharing of the early church and the concern of Jesus for the dispossessed, were challenged by the communist call for justice, and recognized its criticism of church complicity with oppression. Leaders of the established churches were also aware that the churches were barely present among the urban poor, especially in the newly industrialized cities of Europe. Evangelical missions and Catholic religious orders responded most quickly on the ground to the call for a 'home mission' to Europe, or into the heart of what William Booth, founder of the Salvation Army, called 'darkest England'. Churches in different parts of Western Europe were able to bring a sense of identity and moral support not only through their religious activities but also through initiatives such as workers' cooperatives. Religious revivals helped to establish a moral order in the new working-class communities through the temperance movement, friendly societies and a rejection of violence, gambling, and other forms of antisocial behaviour. Churches encouraged education and facilitated it through Sunday school movements, libraries and public institutes. People turned to the churches in times of crisis, such as epidemics and war, and they were able to build solidarity in the face of adversity (McLeod 1997:76–83).

This practical work, both at home and overseas, was justified among Protestants in the nineteenth and early twentieth centuries by two theologies: Evangelicalism in the first part of the nineteenth century and the 'social gospel' of liberal theologians in the late nineteenth and early twentieth centuries. What was known as 'Christian

Figure 4.3 'Campaigners for 'Make Poverty History', Edinburgh, while G8 leaders were meeting in Scotland, 3 July 2005. The campaign was initiated by Christian churches and organizations in partnership with others and attended by some 225,000 people from all over Britain.

socialism' in Britain, 'religious socialism' in continental Europe and the 'social gospel' in North America was developed under the influence of Hegelian idealism, Darwinian theories of evolutionary progress and studies of comparative religion. It grew further in reaction to the rise of individualism in religion and society. The Anglican theologian Frederick Maurice and those who followed him were more concerned with the historical Jesus than the doctrines about him, and saw the role of the church as ushering in, or even building, the Kingdom of God or the New Jerusalem on earth (Phillips 1996:1–8). This resulted in movements of social compassion, because Jesus Christ came to give life in all its abundance (John 10:10), and efforts toward social and church unity, because Christ prayed 'that they might be one' (John 17:21). Christian socialists saw a unity between sacred and secular, God and humanity, and church and state through their theology of the incarnation, and so they overrode any Christian misgivings about working with government at home or the colonial authorities abroad. Between 1880 and 1940 the movement developed from almsgiving and philanthropy to organizing trades unions and social democratic political parties, and advocating state intervention abroad to protect populations. It also led to movements of pacifism and reconciliation in the aftermath of the world wars. Their altruism and ethos of service led social Christians willingly to transfer their projects to secular authorities and to work with groups which did not share their Christian belief. In this respect, they tended to secularize Christianity, but nevertheless this was a religious movement, which understood Christian faith as service in the fulfilment of human aspirations, and fused civilization with the purposes of God in Christ.

Friedrich Nietzsche made the opposite criticism to that of Marx: that Christianity protected the weak. Under the influence of Darwinian 'survival of the fittest', Christianity was described as a 'crutch' for those unable to walk, and therefore dispensable by a mature humanity. The Roman Catholic Church particularly became a scapegoat for those pushing forward liberal democracy. In Catholic Europe, the conservative reaction to the French Revolution was so strong that further revolutions occurred in France, Sicily, Poland and the Hapsburg Empire. Across Europe the Catholic Church was feared as reactionary, dogmatic and centrally controlled, and it began to be persecuted as the enemy of the nation-state and democracy. Anti-clericalism persisted in France, Spain, Portugal and Italy, and these states insisted on wresting control of education and youth movements out of the church's hands. In the newly united Germany, the chancellor Otto von Bismarck's Kulturkampf was intended to keep Catholics out of public life, and in early-twentieth-century France Catholic schools were secularized, monks and nuns expelled, the church disestablished and its property nationalized (O. Chadwick 2002:370). This extreme situation did not last and during the twentieth century the situation of the Catholic Church improved, especially after the Italian fascist dictator Benito Mussolini signed the Lateran Accords (1929), which recognized the sovereign rights of the church within the Vatican City. Now the pope was no longer imprisoned in the Vatican without recognized international status, the Holy See began to build diplomatic relations around the world and until today the Vatican state has links to most other states and even permanent member status at the United Nations.

The German dictator Adolf Hitler despised both Catholic priests and Protestant pastors because he believed they had Judaized the message of (an Aryan) Jesus and were therefore the enemies of nationalism. The Nazi party at first tried to co-opt the German churches; some Protestants – the German Christians – seriously tried to reconcile Christianity and National Socialism. They denounced opponents as un-German, sang hymns to Hitler, purged liturgy of references to Israel and supported Nazi racial policy (Berger 1996). However, in 1934 Protestant leaders of 'the Confessing Church' opposed them with the 'Barmen Declaration'. This was inspired by the neo-orthodox theology of Swiss Reformed theologian Karl Barth. Re-reading the letter to the Romans, Barth denied that human beings could reach God by means of religion or human progress and asserted that knowledge of God was only possible through God's revelation in Jesus Christ. His work is still widely used by Evangelicals and others (including Catholics) who wish to construct theology on the basis of

Christian sources rather than 'the world', and often criticized by those who, often following his fellow countryman Paul Tillich, seek to engage cultures and religions more constructively. One of the Protestants who suffered martyrdom for opposing Hitler, Dietrich Bonhoeffer, greatly encouraged fellow Europeans struggling to profess Christian faith in modern secular society in the post-war years, through his emphasis that the grace exhibited on the cross is never 'cheap' and by his honest wrestling with faith in a world in which God is not a given (Reimer 1999).

For West European Protestants in the first half of the twentieth century, the main struggle was against fascism; for Orthodox Christians in Eastern Europe, it was against communism; and the Roman Catholic Church struggled on both fronts. In 1933 Pope Pius XI made a concordat with Hitler which he hoped would allow the church to continue its activities and save Catholic communities from persecution in return for the church's withdrawal from the political field. However in his 1937 encyclical, *Mit brennender Sorge* (With Burning Anxiety), he condemned breaches of the agreement, criticized Nazi mythology and ideology, defended the Jewish heritage of the Christian faith and upheld the dignity of the human person. In the same year, the pope also condemned communism. After the Second World War, the Catholic Church campaigned fiercely for containment of communism and in 1949 Pope Pius declared that Catholics joining the Communist Party would face excommunication.

The Catholic struggle against communism on the one hand and fascism on the other is further demonstrated in the development of Catholic social teaching (CST) over the past century (Curran 2002; Deberri and Hug 2003). It began from concern for the urban poor and conditions of labour, as expressed by Leo XIII (*Rerum Novarum*, 1891), and grew as a result of the involvement of Catholic priests and laity in social work through Catholic Action and more recently in international development through organizations connected with Caritas. CST begins with economics and a concern for the poor, and proceeds on the basis that 'the goods of this world', given by God, 'are originally meant for all'. It does not oppose the present capitalist system as a whole, and indeed it encourages private property but only as a way of safeguarding the earth's resources for all, and the individual accumulation of wealth only as part of human development. CST opposes both economic collectivism and individualism, criticizing socialism and Marxism for failing to recognize the sacredness of the human person, and liberalistic capitalism for neglecting the social aspects of the human person. The political implications of this approach are: to affirm the state which exists to bring about public well-being and private prosperity; to respect different levels of society – from the family to the state – in the principles of 'subsidiarity' and 'mediation' (as a bulwark against totalitarianism); and to uphold human rights (economic and social as well as political and civil) in so far as they uphold human dignity, are related to duties and are considered along with other values such as truth, justice and charity.

CST is addressed to 'all people of good will' on the basis (established by Aquinas) that there is a 'natural law', drawn from human reason and a 'common good' for all human beings. CST sets forth what the church believes to be a universal framework for human societal behaviour and relations, beginning from the understanding that all human beings have a fundamental and equal dignity because they are made in the image of God. Furthermore, they are social beings, who live in community with others as children of the same heavenly Father, and in relationship with the whole creation. During the Cold War, successive popes had found that communism could not be intimidated, mitigated or appeased but the Polish pope John Paul II understood that it could be subverted by making its positive ideals Christian ones and incorporating the 'option for the poor' of the liberation theologians part of Church teaching (Walters 2006:354). The latest development in Catholic social teaching is the encyclical of Pope Francis, *Laudato Si'* (2015), which adds care for creation to the range of its concerns.

The new Europe: Ecumenism and diversity

The confidence of Europe, built up from the Middle Ages, was shattered by the experience of by the two major wars of the first half of the twentieth century. For Christians of Central and Eastern Europe, further hardship was in store, but Western Europeans, who had more opportunity to reflect on the war itself, were stunned, with others, at the revelations of the Holocaust. Although some Christians had actively helped Jews to hide or escape – often at great risk to themselves – the German churches had made no public protest at their treatment. Furthermore, the realization that anti-Semitism might lie at the heart of Christianity caused a great deal of soul-searching. It prompted a rediscovery of the Jewishness of Christian faith, the recognition of a Judaeo-Christian tradition and attention to the theme of Jew–Gentile reconciliation in the letters of Saint Paul (Ochs 1997). At the Second Vatican Council, the declaration on the relationship of the church to non-Christian religions (*Nostra Aetate*, 1965) began by expressing the church's ongoing relationship to the Jewish people. It also laid the foundation for dialogue as the chief way of relating to other faiths that was formalized during the pontificate of Pope John Paul II.

Church unity and world peace

Christian churches committed themselves to the reconstruction and reconciliation of Europe. As well as the many aid and development activities of Christian organizations and the rebuilding of churches, religious initiatives aimed to bring people together. Examples include the International Centre for Reconciliation at Coventry in England and the lay religious community at Taizé in France which bridged the Catholic–Protestant divide through its worship life. Quakers, founded the first modern peace society in 1816 and in the first half of the twentieth century there was a close relationship between the social gospel and the peace movements (Cortright 2008). 'The Troubles' in Northern Ireland were construed by the media as a late-twentieth-century vestige of the Wars of Religion and Christian efforts toward resolving them involved the four mainstream churches – Methodist, Presbyterian, Catholic and Anglican. They worked together to stay the hand of the paramilitaries, comfort the victims, campaign for justice and create safe places for dialogue (like the Corrymeela Community). The political solution based on the 1998 'Good Friday Agreement' recognized in its name the religious resources for a solution to the conflict, but it is not in itself a reconciliation. That requires a painstaking process of truth-telling, healing and positive engagement of the communities which is not yet over (Liechty and Clegg 2001).

Since the division of Europe into nation-states was closely related to the divisions between the churches, reconciliation between the churches presented itself

Figure 4.4 'Reconciliation' sculpture by Josefina de Vasconcellos in Coventry Cathedral, UK. Photograph by Jonathan Kim.

as the way to achieve peace in Europe. Moreover, given that the two world wars resulted from European disputes, the unity of Europe was seen as a route to world peace. Stimulated by the missionary conference of Protestants in 1910 and its ongoing International Missionary Council, after the First World War two commissions were founded: a commission for Life and Work to look at ways the churches could work together in public life and another for Faith and Order to discuss matters of doctrine and liturgy that divided the churches. The latter two bodies, which included European-initiated churches across the world, agreed in 1937 to form a World Council of Churches (WCC) but war intervened. Nevertheless, the WCC 'in process of formation' was active in post-war reconstruction in Europe (Visser 't Hooft 1993) and also in the formation of the United Nations (Nolde 1993). The organization was finally constituted in 1948, with its headquarters in Geneva. The Catholic Church invited Orthodox and Protestant observers from other churches to the Second Vatican Council and in 1965 Pope Paul VI and the Ecumenical Patriarch Athenagoras lifted the mutual anathemas of 1054. There were high expectations that historic divisions could be overcome and that visible unity could be achieved between Catholic and Protestant churches. Although, the Roman Catholic Church did not join the WCC, provision was made for Catholic involvement in almost all its activities. Some unions of Protestant churches have subsequently taken place, and Anglicans and Lutherans in the Nordic and Baltic region are now in communion with one another (the Porvoo agreement), but organic union is not expected. However, there is a commitment to continuing dialogue (May 2004) and increasing desire to collaborate in mission (Gibaut and Jørgensen 2014).

Although the magisterium (teaching office) of the Catholic Church had resisted the modern world for several centuries, movements of renewal were taking place in Catholic theology in the twentieth century. French Dominicans and Jesuits, including Yves Congar and Henri de Lubac, inspired by returning to the biblical and patristic sources of Christian faith (ressourcement) suggested liturgical and theological reforms which moved away from the scholastic models that had dominated the church since the middle ages and enabled dialogue with Protestant and Orthodox theologians (Flynn and Murray 2012). At the same time as the ressourcement scholars looked back, some such as Jacques Maritain and Marie-Dominique Chenu were looking forward, wishing to update the church through an open-minded engagement with the modern world (aggiornamento) (Komonchak 1999). When John XXIII opened the Second Vatican Council (1962–65), he encouraged both approaches (O'Malley 2010). A third influential European theologian at the Council was the German Jesuit Karl Rahner, whose transcendental approach to theology brought together the theology and spirituality of the church and also facilitated an inclusive approach to other Christians and to people of other faiths. This opened the church to the ecumenical movement, including collaboration with the WCC. For a time there seemed to be a real possibility that reunion of at least some Protestant churches with Rome might take place. The Anglican Church, which uniquely had broken with Rome but not with the Catholic faith, engaged in dialogue from 1970 (Küng 1995:589–97). However, although the unity of the churches remains a specific objective of the Catholic Church, it envisages this as the integration of all churches into the one Catholic Church, and the papacy was not a subject for discussion in ecumenical dialogue. The publication in 2000 of the letter (*Dominus Iesus*) from Cardinal Joseph Ratzinger – later Pope Benedict XVI – underlined 'the limits to ecumenism' and was a further retreat from the rapprochement of the Second Vatican Council (Vischer 2004:29–30). However, Pope Francis has shown a more open posture and even reached out to Pentecostals in his own Argentina.

Christian solidarity across political borders meant that churches were one of the main means by which, during the Cold War, people of East and West could have contact with one another. In 1961, the Russian, Romanian, Bulgarian and Polish Orthodox churches joined the WCC. Orthodox churches have long experience of attempts by other religions and churches to convert their adherents. For political as well as theological reasons, Orthodox churches made a condemnation of such 'proselytism' by the WCC a condition of their joining it. Today Orthodox theologians promote an understanding of mission as witness and service that works with the Holy Spirit to promote the kingdom of God and build unity (Vassiliadis 2013). Under the policies of glasnost and perestroika, the Russian Church celebrated its millennium in 1988 and reached out to the Ecumenical Patriarch (Leustean 2010a:6). The churches of the two Germanys were able to maintain the closest contact and they jointly campaigned and prepared for reunification through democratic socialism, the movement for civil rights and social service. These activities were significant in bringing about the fall of the Berlin Wall in 1989, which precipitated the end of the Cold War (Sauer 2008).

Rethinking Christian mission

The aftermath of the Second World War saw a withdrawal from empire by West European countries that necessitated the rethinking by European churches of relations with the churches founded by their missions. At the same time, their mission work was being criticized by secularists and the formerly colonized. Moreover much of their work was being replaced by the secular enterprise of international development. Through a series of conferences from the late 1940s until the 1950s, churches and mission agencies connected with the WCC achieved considerable consensus about theology of mission and articulated what amounted to a new ecumenical paradigm that was profoundly affected by the Trinitarian theology encouraged by the Orthodox churches (Bosch 2011; Newbigin 1995a). The new understanding of mission drew on John's gospel rather than Matthew's. Instead of starting from the commissioning of the disciples, it begins with the sending by the Father of the Son

(John 3:16) and by both of the Spirit (John 20:22), and so it is referred to as missio Dei (God's mission). In this view mission is 'participation in Christ' and 'joining in with the Spirit'; in other words it is central to Christian life, and part of Christian spirituality, to witness to the world. The new paradigm promotes a more humble view of the church not as an authoritative institution representing God's will on earth but as a 'sign, sacrament and instrument' of God's will and in the service of others (Bosch 2011:383–5).

Although there are differences in the way it is interpreted, depending on the scope allowed for the Spirit's work, missio Dei has had important ramifications in the theological and practical life of the mainstream churches. For example, Europe was now understood to be as much a mission field as any other continent. If not persuaded by theological argument, then Europeans recognized this when they were increasingly on the receiving end of missions from Billy Graham and other US evangelists. So mission could no longer be thought of as 'from the West to the rest' but must be 'from everywhere to everywhere'. Furthermore, since mission was no longer one-way, the relationship between the 'older churches' of Christendom and the 'younger churches' should now become one of equality, reciprocity and 'partnership in mission' (Nazir-Ali 1991). Although missionary paternalism has proved very difficult to overcome and continuing economic inequalities have made the implementation of partnership challenging, European churches all now enjoy some sort of a conciliar relationship with their former mission churches in other parts of the world through 'families' of Protestant Christians, such as the Anglican Communion, the Lutheran World Federation, the World Methodist Council, the World Communion of Reformed Churches and the Baptist World Alliance, which have programmes of exchange and mutual sending between national churches and joint programmes of mission activity. At its most radical, partnership is expressed in the reconstitution of mission bodies as councils of churches with shared financial resources (as in the case of the LMS which is now the Council for World Mission). While the older European missions have been forced by their partners to confront their colonial past, the same may not be said of wider European society. Europeans tend to interpret the twentieth century as a struggle against fascism and communism in the name of progress whereas the fact that these extremes arose in Europe could be seen conversely as a failure of the Enlightenment project. Furthermore, the colonial enterprise was so integral to the Enlightenment view of the world that European relations with the rest of the world continue to be strained and the myth of the superiority of European thought and culture remains (cf. Ingleby 2010).

The Roman Catholic Church has been through a parallel process of rethinking mission (Bevans 2013). Prior to the Second Vatican Council, 'mission' referred to the mission ad gentes, that is, to the parts of the world designated mission fields. The Council's decree on the church's missionary activity (*Ad Gentes*) opened by declaring the missionary nature of the church and setting the missions within the sending of the Triune God as the WCC had done. This allowed for the whole world to be considered a mission field. In the decree, a major aim of mission is the establishment of Christian communities by both preaching the gospel and planting churches. However, it is recognized that this activity does not take place in a vacuum but in the context of the work of the Spirit who has already planted 'seeds of the Word' in the cultures and values of all peoples. Proselytism is condemned and the tone is of respect for others (Oborji 2006). The decree laid the ground for the development of inculturation and dialogue and the concept of evangelization, articulated by Paul VI (*Evangelii Nuntiandi* 1975) and recently developed by Pope Francis (*Evangelii Gaudium*, 2013), by which not only individuals but societies and cultures are transformed by the good news.

In the postcolonial period, missionary experience from overseas is being put to use in Europe. For example, theologies of religion and patterns of dialogue established on the 'mission field' have provided a resource for European Christians seeking to relate to their growing number of neighbours of other faiths. A theology of mission as Christian presence was developed by Anglican missionaries in Islamic contexts in which there was little hope of conversions (Yates 1994:141–2). They realized they needed to become learners of Islam before (if at all) they could expect a hearing (Cragg 2000) and so they encouraged the foundation of Christian schools of Islamic studies, often now incorporated into universities (Siddiqui 1997:194–200). As shown by the controversy over the Danish newspaper cartoons (2006) and Charlie Hebdo incident (2015), Westerners tend to emphasize freedom of expression over Muslim insistence on the proper respect for faith. Christians who have made the effort to live alongside Muslims and respect their faith, like the British Anglican Kenneth Cragg and the Dutch academic Antonie Wessels, interpret Islam sympathetically to Europeans and suggest how Muslims and Christians can find ways to live together (Wessels 2006). They also suggest that the example of the Arab Christians has a great deal to teach European ones about bearing witness to Christ in a hostile environment (Cragg 1992; Wessels 1995). As well as prompting European Christians to rethink their methods of evangelism, if not voluntarily then under pressure from governments anxious to preserve religious harmony, the increasing Muslim presence in Europe is already having other effects on Western European Christianity. For example, Christians increasingly see themselves together with people of other faith; not only as Judaeo-Christian but with Muslims as 'people of the book' or 'children of Abraham'. On the other hand, accommodation by the authorities to Muslim sensitivities has led to greater assertiveness by Christians of their right to profess faith publicly and of the contribution of Christianity to European heritage (Jenkins 2007:260–5). Either way, once again, awareness of Islam is increasing Christians' sense of identity and prompting a new discovery of the character of Christian faith.

The new Europe: Christian decline and growth

The most fundamental development of the Second Vatican Council was the redefinition of the church as 'the people of God' – the hierarchy, the religious and the laity. This apparently abrupt departure from clerical dominance had profound effects throughout the Catholic world and empowered lay people, as seen in the subsequent movements of liberation theology, charismatic renewal and popular religiosity. However, although the whole church was energized by it, after the council attendance and vocations in Western Europe declined rapidly. Since a similar pattern has been seen in other churches in Western Europe, the reforms of the council may not have been the main cause of the drop.

The 'crisis' in the church

Much has been made of the crisis of faith in Western Europe although, according to McLeod (1997:83), it has been talked about since the 1790s. The perception that churches are emptying may be ignoring the fact that most of the church buildings, built at times of revival and optimism, had never been full in any case (Gill 2003). Furthermore, there had been a gradual decline in church attendance over decades and this correlates with the changing demography of Christianity in Europe both in age and inherited religious tradition. British census figures, which show a drop between 2001 and 2011 in those declaring themselves Christian from 72 per cent to 60 per cent, confirm that decline is continuing, although church attendance figures seem to be bottoming out. Callum Brown (2001:1) anticipates 'the death of Christian Britain', which 'took several centuries to convert' and 'less than forty years' to forsake Christianity. He is far from the only one prophesying the doom of the traditional churches.

There was a real and precipitous decline in attendance at all the mainline churches from the 'cultural revolution' of the 1960s. This is partly attributed to the search for greater individual freedom, which led to rejection of moral and doctrinal codes and authority, but it was aggravated by social changes such as rapid decline in rural cultures, changes in work and leisure patterns and loss of association of social identity with the church (McLeod 1997:141–3). In the British case, another factor was that women, who are the majority and the most consistent of church members, stopped attending church and, moreover, sending their children to Sunday school (Brown 2001). The loss of women from the church has been blamed on the opposition of the Catholic Church to abortion and almost all methods of birth control, which, expressed bluntly by Paul VI in the encyclical *Humanae Vitae* in 1968, seemed to run counter to that decade of growing freedom for women (191), together with the slowness of the established churches to respond to growing demands for women's ordination. The conservative stance of most churches on divorce and sexuality was another contributing factor, although in Britain Anglican clergy led the struggle which brought about the decriminalization of homosexuality in 1967 (MacCulloch 2009: 987–8). The more recent revelations about abuse of those in church institutions and sexual abuse by priests have further undermined the credibility of the church.

Deeply ingrained in Western Europe since the 'Wars of Religion' is the perception that the churches are authoritarian, reactionary and anti-progress. The ubiquitous physical presence of stone-built churches evokes the kind of rigid authority, conservatism and immutability that the youth of the 1960s rebelled against. The sociological manifestation of this perception is the theory that modernization and secularization go together, which originated with the Enlightenment despisers of religion. This theory appears to have been vindicated in Western Europe. However, in a worldwide perspective, the relationship between modernity and the decline of religion is much less obvious. It even appears that Western Europe is the 'exceptional case' since Christianity accompanies modernization in other contexts – even the United States (Davie 2002). The situation becomes even more complicated when we look further than church attendance and religious allegiance and attempt to assess religiosity. Decline in attendance does not necessarily indicate decline in belief. Grace Davie (1994) showed in the case of Britain that there is a tendency to 'believing without belonging' and that even in Protestant Europe there is a vicarious sense of religion – associated with older patterns of priesthood – by which 'a relatively small number of people . . . "look after" the [Christian] memory on behalf of others' (2000:177). The growth of New Age religion, the revival of Paganism, interest in supposedly 'non-theistic' religion like Buddhism and the continued popularity of belief in the paranormal and horoscopes show that people are much more religious than might be expected three centuries after the Enlightenment (cf. Bruce 1995:54–5).

Then the real question in Europe is why, when people want to believe, they do not choose traditional Christianity. It may be that this has less to do with intellect and more to do with a search for a different kind of religious experience. An extensive French study found many who turn away from traditional Christianity to find meaning in Eastern religions have 'an axe to grind . . . with the institutional church', which they see as 'dogmatic', 'moralistic', 'having disdain for both physical and emotional life', 'too prescriptive' and hypocritical. In part, this is a rejection of the Enlightenment heritage in favour of Paganism and Gnosticism, but it is also influenced by a humanist anthropology (Ugeux 2006:325). Vandana (1991:99–105), one of the leaders of the Catholic ashram movement in India, observed that European young people looking for religious experience tended not to expect to find it in their home churches but in what is exotic to them: the Eastern religions of Hinduism and Buddhism. From their study of this phenomenon in the English town of Kendal, Paul Heelas and Linda Woodhead (2004:1) suggested that the growth of holistic, therapeutic religious experience and other alternative forms of religion represents a shift from 'religion' to 'spirituality'. They see this as part of the wider 'turn' of modern culture from 'life lived in terms of external or "objective" roles, duties and obligations . . . towards life lived by reference to one's own subjective experiences' (2).

Even if Heelas and Woodhead's prediction of a 'spiritual revolution' spelling the end for 'religion' comes true, it does not imply the end of Christianity in Western Europe, because many of the examples of the new spirituality which they include are Christian churches or groups which have adapted to the needs of the new generation by offering alternative forms of worship. These are charismatic forms of older churches or new Christian groups such as 'house-churches'. The latter are Pentecostal–charismatic groups which do not have a building, denominational affiliation or institutional presence but offer 'fellowship', alternative forms of worship and a post-modern Christian identity (Kotila 2006). Migration of people into Europe means that 'religion' no longer refers to Christianity and that all forms of religion are diversifying and becoming more transnational. Woodhead's work further suggests that religion in post-war Britain has moved out of the sphere of the church and the state and into the marketplace and the media (Woodhead and Catto 2012). This is a realm in which Christianity has a high profile among religions – although most often in its North American form.

Christian renewal and public engagement

Another difficulty for secularization theory is that the decline of Christianity is not experienced by all Europeans. The attention given to church attendance and membership of many of the older churches in Western Europe masks a much larger reality of European Christianity in the twenty-first century. After the fall of communism, the countries of the former Communist Bloc found themselves coping not with decline but with rapid growth. Although growth rates have slowed in this century, in every country of the former Soviet Bloc, Christianity underwent a significant revival. Even in Albania, where there were no longer any living priests, the church was revived, especially through the ministry of Archbishop Janullatos (Yannoulatos), a Greek, appointed by the Ecumenical Patriarch (Pano 2014). Today, everywhere except the Czech Republic, more than 70 per cent are Christians. Figures given for Moldova, Poland and Romania show nearly 100 per cent; however this reflects cultural identity and not necessarily Christian practice. Today the populations of Russia, Ukraine, Belarus, Romania, Serbia, Macedonia and Montenegro are mainly Orthodox. Poland, Croatia and Slovenia are largely Roman Catholic. The Baltic States, Hungary and Slovakia have large Catholic and Protestant populations.

In former communist countries, the churches have been actively engaging with public life. Religious freedom was one of the main factors delineating the communist

Figure 4.5 Bulgarian Orthodox servers hold an icon of Saint Sophia the Martyr during the celebrations of the saint's day. Sofia, Bulgaria, 17 September 2013. Image: iStock.

and post-communist eras (Leustean 2014:2). In the new Europe relationships with the state and roles in the public sphere have to be negotiated anew. Instead of resisting modernity in the shape of communism, the churches are invited to engage with it in the form of democracy and capitalism. Moreover, the ancient churches have new competitors and all must adjust to a situation of religious pluralism.

The reinstatement of religion was nowhere more obvious than in Moscow where in 1997 the Cathedral of Christ the Saviour, which had been razed to the ground in 1931 as part of Stalin's assault on religion, was rebuilt and consecrated. Its size and prominence shows the special status of Orthodoxy in today's Russia (Knox and Mitrofanova 2014:38–9). Orthodoxy has become a popular movement with millennialist characteristics. Since there is a lack of trained clergy, it has charismatic leadership and beliefs are mixed with pre-Christian ones (53–7). After the fall of communism, the church was ill-equipped to reclaim its position at the centre of Russian culture and it was facing vigorous competition from Catholic, Evangelical and Pentecostal missions. But it was helped in 1997 by the passage of a law which recognized the special position of Orthodoxy and curbed the activities of other groups. Anxious not to repeat the mistakes of the past, under Patriarch Aleksii II the church sought and gained greater independence from the state and kept its distance from nationalism. Instead in 2000 it proclaimed itself higher than the state and it also gained access to education and the military. President Vladimir Putin sees the church as the guarantor of Russia's spiritual (or ideological) independence – a view dramatically opposed by the Pussy Riot punk group in the cathedral in 2012. He has used the strength of Russian Orthodoxy to assert Russian authority over other Orthodox countries (43–9). In 1995, the church restored its missionary department. But it is engaging in a mission aimed at conversion, catechization and Eucharistic participation while it actively prevents other churches from proselytizing in its 'territory' (Kozhuharov 2015). The Russian Church is also deeply involved in activities in Africa, Asia, Latin America and the West. This worries some other Orthodox, who fear the perennial link between ethnicity, nationalism and religion (Clapsis 2004). Moreover, the church has yet to find a constructive way of engaging with Islam – so long resisted – or Buddhism, which are dominant in parts of the Russian Federation (Cousins 2004).

Most of the Orthodox peoples of Central and Eastern Europe, whether in Russia or in the Ottoman Empire, did not experience the effects of the Enlightenment or the industrial revolution to the extent that Western Europeans did until the twentieth century when they were mediated to them through atheistic communism. This negative experience of modernity, together with the strength of the Orthodox tradition, maintained through centuries of minority status under Muslim rule or atheistic regimes, means that Orthodox Christians are only now, in the context of European unity, coming to terms theologically with the post-Enlightenment intellectual climate. Greece, which remained free of communist control, has a significant role in bridging East and West but even so it has many hardline Christians who refuse any compromise with modernity or relations with other churches. Furthermore, there is a great deal of tension between the Russian and Greek Orthodox churches. This is due to long-standing historic differences between Greeks and Slavs and also to Greek resistance to communism and support of the West in the Cold War (Makrides 2010). Orthodoxy is a strong marker of Greek identity vis-à-vis both Turkey and the Slavs and the Orthodox Church is strongly supported by the state. In Greece, as in Russia, minority Christian groups, let alone Muslims, find it difficult to establish a presence or find a voice.

Twenty-five years after the end of communism, the role of Christianity in Central and Eastern Europe is far from clear but, as in other areas of life, Christian practice too has started to equalize across the continent. For example, on the one hand, the migration of Central and Eastern European Christians is swelling the numbers of Catholic churches and establishing new Orthodox and other churches in the west. On the other hand, interaction especially among the young through social media spreads the same kind of suspicion of religion that has been growing in Western Europe.

The minority status of the West European churches and the new possibilities opened up in the East since 1989 have resulted in a renewed mission activity in Europe. Western European Christianity is being buoyed up by migrants from other continents who are giving the church in Europe a more diverse and more Pentecostal complexion, and perhaps hold the possibility of reviving it (Jenkins 2007:96–9). In particular, there is a trend toward 'mission in reverse' from countries that were evangelized by Europe in the past few centuries, but who are now shocked and dismayed by what they see as the decline of Christianity on the continent and come with missional intent. A few of these arrive through exchange programmes such as organized by the Church of Norway, some through the Catholic Church as priests to supply vacant European parishes, some through mission agencies such as CMS (Catto 2013) and missionary congregations but many find their own way. Examples could be given from the Netherlands (Paas 2015), Germany (Währisch-Oblau 2012) and other places in Western Europe but the most extraordinary case is that of the Embassy of the Kingdom of God Church for All Nations in Kiev which was founded in 1993 by a Nigerian, Sunday Odulaja, but has a majority Ukrainian membership. Odulaja studied in Belarus and started a Bible study group after the fall of communism with seven members which, despite the opposition of the authorities, has grown to twenty thousand in Kiev today with daughter churches across Russia and Eastern Europe and worldwide (Adogame 2013:163–6, 184–9). Another growing Christian movement today is Pentecostalism among the Roma (or 'Gypsy') people who have long been marginalized from European society.

Local European churches also increasingly regard Europe as a mission field. Of the local initiatives, some are primarily directed at addressing declining numbers; they seek to inspire Christians with confidence to proclaim their faith and bring others into the churches. In the Catholic Church the 'new evangelization' was set out by John Paul II and promoted by Pope Benedict with a view to re-evangelizing Europe. It encourages a personal encounter with Christ, public demonstrations of faith and popular religion such as pilgrimages (Grogan and Kim 2015). A famous example among Protestant churches is the Alpha courses originating at Holy Trinity Brompton in London and now a global phenomenon, designed to draw individuals into Christian faith in a low-key way (Brookes 2007). Traditional churches have been looking at ways to make themselves 'mission-shaped' (Cray 2004) by processes of restructuring and reorienting church life to those outside rather than internal church concerns. In the case of the Church of England, this has resulted in 'Fresh Expressions' of the church to suit contemporary lifestyles and spirituality. Alongside such initiatives in church growth, there are equally desires to change lives by practical service and to address issues in the public sphere. Liberation Theology, developed in Latin America and mediated through the Catholic Church, resonates with social Christianity. As a result, Christian churches may be associated with left-wing politics and are not so easily accused of political conservatism. Since the economic crisis of 2008, the churches of Europe have been heavily engaged in social service – often making up shortfalls in government provision – and in challenging austerity policies. Beyond the debate about numbers, Christianity in

Europe plays significant roles in identity formation, cultural transformation and the promotion of virtue (Garnett et al. 2006).

The end of Christendom

The different aspects of modernity challenged the churches of Europe profoundly and at many levels, although at a rate and in a way which varied considerably across Europe. In the post-war period Christians in Western and Southern Europe find themselves in a new position. First, although Europe is united to an extent it has never been before, it is no longer Christendom, and at the end of the twentieth century doubts would be raised as to whether European society was, or had ever been, a 'Christian continent' (Wessels 1994). A raft of social changes, including breakdown of community, the loss of a common world view, the rise of rationality and secularism and the predictability of modern urban life compared with pre-industrial rural society, have made traditional Christianity an option, not a necessity, and often an irrelevance for most Europeans. In several countries in Europe – Norway, Denmark and Greece are major examples – it is still the case that nation and membership of the national church are closely identified legally. In Southern and Eastern Europe, religion is closely identified with identity – Catholic or Orthodox. But with the exceptions earlier, European governments no longer assume their citizens are Christians by birth. In place of parish records, civil registers of births, marriages and deaths are kept and faith is a matter of personal choice. The disestablishment of churches from the late eighteenth century onwards signalled, in most countries, the end of the privileged relationship one particular Christian church had held with government in each territory. Although the former state churches usually remain the largest, most governments now recognize the legitimacy of many other churches and religions and adopt policies of religious toleration. Established Protestant churches remain in England and Scandinavian countries, except Sweden where the link with the state was ended in 2000. In Germany, Denmark, Sweden, Finland, Iceland, Italy and a few other countries, religious bodies receive contributions through the tax system, but in most citizens can opt out. Otherwise church taxes were either abolished or are paid to the government. Education, health and other services once delivered by churches are largely in government hands, although some Protestant countries like Britain have strong networks of faith schools. Increasingly churches are treated like other non-governmental bodies: as charities or social service organizations. The plurality of religions available and the possibility of making a choice, or not doing so, mean there are now 'societies of Christians' rather than 'Christian societies' (Bruce 1995:2).

A second change is that, with the notable exceptions of Russia and Greece, the place of Christianity is shifting from the public to the private sphere of life. Governments no longer necessarily seek the church's blessing or advice, public ceremonies no longer always use Christian or even religious language, and religious broadcasting is limited. One aspect of this is that the presence of Christian theology in the academies is questioned, even though the most ancient and prestigious were founded for training clergy. Mathematics has replaced theology as 'queen of the sciences'. Other foundational assumptions in a Christian world view such as the creation of the world by a loving God and God's exercise of judgement over the world are no longer a basis for philosophical or legal thought. Departments of theology, where they have survived, have mostly diversified into departments of religion, using historical, sociological or philosophical tools. Theology as the study of the self-understanding of the Christian religion and its development may not be regarded as a proper activity for a university.

As Europe draws closer together, and modernity gives way to what is sometimes called 'post-modernity', the churches in East and West find themselves in a changing intellectual climate, and one which is in some ways less hostile to faith. While it is difficult to stake a truth claim in an age of suspicion of 'meta-narratives' (Kirk and Vanhoozer 1999), it is also more difficult to establish ground on which to deny Christian experience. The Christian story may play alongside many others, but it can be told much more straightforwardly than in the recent past and Christian worship can be made attractive in the marketplace of religious experience. The danger for Christianity is that, in an increasingly fragmented society, it will be tolerated but not engaged by those outside its network. The churches have no option of 'missionary war' or an authority that is not earned. As they seek to be 'all things to all men' and inculturate the gospel in Europe, they may have 'proper confidence' that the Christian gospel is a plausible view of history which challenges modern thinking (Newbigin 1995b), but they must learn to use persuasion rather than fear and they have to live the gospel they proclaim. The renewal of Christian witness in Europe is being further enriched by interaction with Christians from other continents as part of global church and mission networks (Engelsviken, Lundeby and Solheim 2011; Währisch-Oblau and Mwombeki 2010). It is part of a de-centring of Europe and its integration into world Christianity.

Summary

Christianity in Europe has had a rather different history from elsewhere because, following the pattern of the Roman Empire, it was favoured by rulers and governments and grew alongside the ruling powers. The Roman Catholic Church and the Orthodox Church developed systematic theologies in European contexts. With the encouragement of monarchs and rulers, the peoples of Europe were evangelized through the work of apostles or missionaries: monastics, friars, priests, preachers and revivalists. The Protestant churches arising after the Reformation became, after the wars of religion, linked with particular ethnic groups and nation-states. There were occasions when the churches were deprived of temporal power under the Moors, the Mongols, the French Revolution. And there were some Christian communities who dissented from the established confession. But generally speaking it was only in the twentieth century that churches of Europe as a whole underwent what has been the experience of most Christians down the centuries: a climate indifferent or hostile to Christian faith and marginalization from political power.

When the nations of Europe gained global ascendancy, in their position of shared power, its churches carried the gospel to other parts of the world using several different models: 'missionary war', 'radical inculturation', colonial 'civilizing' and church planting, the 'social gospel' and 'proclamation'. This resulted in the extension of European churches to most other parts of the globe, largely without regard to the ancient churches already present in Asia and Africa or other pre-existing traditions and beliefs. However, modernity, in the form of secular science and secularist or atheistic philosophies, challenged European Christian confidence and resulted in changed circumstances: privatized religion in the West and suppression under atheistic communism in the East. In the post-war, postcolonial period, the churches in Western Europe are still coming to terms with their decreasing numbers in many countries and newfound power in others. They are experiencing a new relationship with churches in other parts of the world and a resurgence of other religions. Movements toward church unity and the rise of the Ecumenical movement were a major Christian response to Europe's fractured political experience and contributed to the unification of Europe. Since 1989, in Central and Eastern Europe, the churches no longer face persecution and are popular, but face new challenges in democratic and capitalist societies. Christians long separated from one another are brought together in the new Europe, along with an increasing variety of Christians from other parts of the globe, and are challenged to live out their faith in a secularized and pluralist society.

Study questions and further readings

- In what ways does Europe today reflect the long influence of the Roman Catholic Church and/or the Orthodox Church?
- Discuss the impact of the Reformation on socio-political life in Europe.
- How close was the relationship between colonialism and the missionary endeavour of European churches in Africa, Asia and Latin America?
- How has the involvement of the church in public life in Eastern Europe changed since the onset of modernity, and what have been the implications of this for Christian witness?

- What are the European factors which encouraged the Ecumenical movement in the twentieth century and to what extent did it succeed?
- Discuss the implications for the European churches of the expansion of the European Union and increasing migration.

Bosch, D. J. (2011[1991]), *Transforming Mission*, second edition. Maryknoll, NY: Orbis.
Davie, G. (2000), *Religion in Modern Europe*. Oxford: Oxford University.
Irvin, D. T. and S. W. Sunquist (2012), *History of the World Christian Movement*. Vol II. Maryknoll, NY: Orbis.
MacCulloch, D. (2009), *A History of Christianity*. London: Allen Lane.
McGuckin, J. A. (2008), *The Orthodox Church*. Oxford: Blackwell.
Ward, K. (2006), *A History of Global Anglicanism*. Cambridge: Cambridge University.

5

Latin American and Caribbean Christianities

Chapter Outline

We have chosen to define America from Mexico southwards by its 'Latin-ness' because many of its common features in the present day are traceable to its colonization by the rulers of Spain and Portugal. The label 'Latin' also expresses a contrast with North America, which has been shaped more by the cultures of the Reformation and the Enlightenment. However, the colonial title 'Latin' disguises many other influences, such as the cultures of the indigenous peoples and of the millions imported from Africa as slaves, as well as of later migrations of people from Northern as well as Southern Europe. Global processes in religion as well as economics, politics and technology also shape contemporary 'Latin' America and have resulted in new religious movements. Nevertheless, we will take Latin-ness as an important key to understanding this part of the world, because it also refers to the dominant form of Christianity, which has been a stabilizing and integrating force. Not only do 80 per cent of its population belong to the Catholic Church, but all areas of Latin American life are 'infused with Catholic-Christian beliefs' (Wiarda 2001:9, 351).

UNITED STATES
MEXICO
THE BAHAMAS
NORTH ATLANTIC OCEAN
CUBA
DOMINICAN REPUBLIC
JAMAICA
HAITI
PUERTO RICO (US)
BELIZE
ANTIGUA & BARBUDA
GUATEMALA
HONDURAS
DOMINICA
ST. LUCIA
NICARAGUA
BARBADOS
EL SALVADOR
COSTA RICA
VENEZUELA
GUYANA
SURINAME
PANAMA
NORTH PACIFIC OCEAN
COLOMBIA
FRENCH GUIANA (FR)
ECUADOR
PERU
BRAZIL
BOLIVIA
PARAGUAY
SOUTH PACIFIC OCEAN
CHILE
ARGENTINA
URUGUAY
SOUTH ATLANTIC OCEAN
Cape Horn

Latin-ness also extends to the Spanish-speaking part of the Caribbean, including Cuba, the Dominican Republic and Puerto Rico. However, that region contains in addition three other language areas due to other European colonization. The islands of Guadeloupe, Haiti and Martinique are Francophone. There are several Dutch-speaking islands, including Aruba, Bonaire, Sint Maarten and Curaçao (and also Guyana on the South American mainland). The Anglophone Caribbean, the former West Indies, which is the most extensive, comprises the remainder. This meeting point of cultures has resulted in many expressions of hybridity and interculturality. For example, the creolization of European languages and the creation of further distinct languages and dialects which mix words from different European tongues. The common denominator of Caribbean reality is of 'peoples and spaces' created by slavery, colonization and forced migrations (Williams 1994:62–5). This feature it shares with the rest of Latin America and so we include it in this chapter.

The Christianization of the Americas

The first inhabitants of the Americas probably arrived there across a land bridge from northeast Asia perhaps as much as forty thousand years ago and spread southwards down the Pacific coast, becoming cut off from Asia as sea levels rose. Except perhaps for a few Viking explorers around 1000 AD, it seems unlikely that the peoples of the Americas had had contact with Christians before the end of the fifteenth century when Europeans arrived. Whereas in North America it is estimated there were only about 3 million Native Americans loosely organized into tribal groups, in Latin America there were several large-scale societies and probably ten times as many people (Wiarda 2001:104). The Mexica or Aztec civilization in what is today Mexico was a loose association of city-states, some of them among the largest in the world at the time, paying tribute to the ruler in the capital city of Tenochtitlan, where the present-day Mexico City lies. Their lingua franca, Nahuatl, is still spoken by some 1.5 million people. The even larger empire of the Incas to the south had its capital at modern Cusco in Peru, and included large parts of modern Ecuador, Bolivia, northern Argentina and Chile, and Colombia as well. Its official language, Quechua, continues to be spoken by about 10 million people in South America. Both civilizations were highly structured and organized, but outside them were large numbers of independent or semi-independent groups. The new arrivals were Spanish noblemen excited by their recent reclamation of their own country from the Muslim Moors and confident that God was granting them new lands for the exaltation both of the Christian faith and the glory of Spain. In their eyes, the destiny of the nation and the destiny of the church were united: Spain was a temporal messiah, and the purpose of the Spanish crown was 'essentially missionary' (Dussel 1981:38–9). The arrival of Europeans took the indigenous people by surprise and they were ill-prepared to resist.

The Taíno people, who found Christopher Columbus on Guanahani (in the modern Bahamas) in 1492 and helped him and his men when he first made landfall, were spread across the Caribbean islands and northern South America. Columbus was motivated to preach the Christian gospel with a sense of urgency because he understood his mission to contribute to the eventual conquest of Jerusalem and the end of the world (Chidester 2000:383–5). A papal bull (*Inter caetera*) the following year made clear the obligation on Spain to bring these and other peoples of the newly discovered lands to Christian faith. Bishoprics were established from 1511. Although the Portuguese were eventually given jurisdiction over what is now Brazil, they were occupied in Asia and did not develop their transatlantic lands at first. Spanish conquistadors were able to seize lands in the Caribbean, Mexico, Central and South America rapidly because the centralized empires collapsed, but groups of Native Americans outside the empires held out for longer, and isolated groups remained in the rainforests of the Amazon even into the twenty-first century. The conquistadors brought to the conquest of the Americas the 'energy, crusading spirit, militarism, missionary fervor, and social and political institutions that had carried [them] to victory' in Iberia (Wiarda 2001:77). Their social vision was essentially feudal but also militarized, as a result of the period of 'reconquista' or reconquest of Christendom from Muslims, and centralized as a consequence of the policies of the unification of the many Iberian kingdoms into two (98). The conquest was justified by scholastic philosophy but, under the system of papal patronage, its execution was in the hands of the monarchs of Spain and Portugal.

In feudal society the acquisition of land carried with it the labour of its inhabitants and so, on each encomienda or estate, the people were settled in villages to work the land. Missionary religious orders, mainly Franciscans and Dominicans, and later Jesuits, baptized, instructed and disciplined the people until the church was established. The missionaries desired to build a new, pure church, free from the worldliness of the church in Europe (Elizondo 1997:xiii); however, the reality was very different. The peoples of the Americas were humiliated by their military defeat, the seizure of their land and the rape of their women. In the New America they were neglected and deprived of their language and customs – a situation that could be said to continue today – and were then exploited and enslaved (Beozzo 1990). The effect of the conquest on the local population was a catastrophic population decline. Estimates of the number who died vary widely, but the figure of twenty to twenty-five million given by Bartholomé de las Casas in the sixteenth century is probably not far from the mark (Gutiérrez 1993:461–4). Warfare, brutal treatment, dislocation, malnutrition, dietary changes and lack of resistance to imported diseases are among the causes. But perhaps the greatest factor was the destruction of the Native Americans' way of life. The disruption of their society, removal from their lands and the forced separation of families and of men and women led to despair, death wishes and suicide. As well as the military conquest, there was a 'deeper violence' against their culture and religion (Elizondo 1997:xiv). As Aztec survivors said in the aftermath of the conquest, 'Well let us die, let us perish, since our gods are already dead' (Beozzo 1990:84).

The secular priests generally supported the encomienda system and were supported by it; missionaries either worked within the system to ameliorate its effects or outside it. There were often clashes between the two groups (Klaiber 1998:4). A few missionary friars and bishops tried to protect the people from the predations of the colonists and traders. The foremost example is Bartholomé de las Casas, a Spanish priest and encomienda owner, who was later briefly bishop of Chiapas in Mexico. Hearing Dominican preachers, he was persuaded that the treatment of the 'Indians' was wrong. He joined the Dominicans and campaigned for native rights both in church law and in the Spanish courts. He has been held up as the first theologian of liberation (Gutiérrez 1993:57). As a result of his efforts, some justice for Native Americans was obtained in the papal bull of 1537, and in 1542 he persuaded Charles V to enact the 'New Laws' (1542) formally ending the encomienda system. A decade later in Valladolid, Spain, Las Casas opposed the humanist philosopher Juan Ginès de Sepúlveda, laying a legal foundation for the treatment of Native Americans as human beings with 'rights'. But by then millions of the indigenous people had perished and the system had descended into slavery. In the early seventeenth century Jesuits, who were influenced by Renaissance humanism toward a more positive appreciation of human culture and nature, followed up the dream of Las Casas and persuaded the Spanish crown to allow them to use a region in central South America covering parts of present-day Argentina, Paraguay, southern Brazil and Uruguay for an alternative to the encomienda, the reducción. This was a 'Christian village' run by missionaries to protect the people, chiefly the Guarani, from the predations of other Europeans – a model which was greatly admired by subsequent generations of missionaries. Native Americans participated in leadership in the reducciónes and also joined the Jesuit order. Although some European norms were imposed, aspects of indigenous culture were preserved as well. When the Jesuit order was suppressed worldwide in the 1760s, the reducciónes were easily 'grabbed by the colonists' despite the fact that some Jesuits had been arming them (Dussel 1981:60).

The indigenous population was virtually wiped out in Brazil and most of the Caribbean Islands. But Guatemala, Bolivia, Peru and Ecuador, and large areas of Mexico and Colombia retain substantial indigenous populations, and in most other countries a large proportion of the population has some indigenous blood. The lives of the ancient peoples also live on in the landscape, the diet, local languages and customs, and in some aspects of Latin American Christianity. Although some missionaries, especially from the second generation, learnt native languages and provided almost the only documentation of local customs, few found value in these, or in the traditional religions, which they demonized (Dussel 1981:43). The collapse of indigenous culture, the imposition of the Spanish worldview and the lack of mediating figures between the old and new worlds left no opportunity for dialogue between the two (Elizondo 1997:xv). So the Native Americans were taught to worship a new god in a new way, as if all who lived before the Spanish conquest were 'children of Satan' (Hastings 1999b:342).

Despite the imperious and condescending approach, Mexicans showed great enthusiasm for the new faith. Many were prepared for the priesthood, but none were ever ordained. At the other extreme, the Incas were much less responsive. Ways were found of accommodating the pre-Columban past. For example, the Q'eqchi' of Guatemala understand the cross to be symbolic of Christ but to this day a cross erected in a field when maize is being planted symbolizes the spirit of a good harvest (Siebers 1999:268). The record of Gauman Poma de Ayala, an elderly man from what is now Peru, penned in the early seventeenth century, shows how the indigenous people tried to make sense of what had happened by fusing the past with biblical history and Christian belief. He viewed 'the Indians of old' as 'Christian' because 'although they were pagans, they observed God's commandments and the good works of compassion'. At the same time he was bewildered that there seemed to be no God in Peru anymore – but only in 'Rome and Castile' – and bemoaned the fact that the 'priests and rulers of every sort' persecuted 'the poor of Jesus Christ' (Hastings 1999b:338). Ahead of the five hundredth anniversary of the conquest in 1992, Latin American liberation theologians and Native American leaders called for redress of these injustices, in the form of resistance to the imposition of Latin culture as the definer of 'Latin' America, restitution of native lands and recognition of indigenous languages and customs (e.g. Beozzo 1990:88–9; Wagua 1990:54–5).

With the demise of the indigenous people and the growing need for work on the plantations, large numbers of Africans were imported as slaves to fill the labour shortage – a measure that Las Casas initially supported but later regretted. After the United States, Brazil and the Caribbean have the second and third largest (respectively) African diaspora populations in the world. Nearly 90 per cent of the people of the Caribbean are of African descent (Vernooij 2007). Albert Raboteau points out two differences in the experience of Africans in the Caribbean and Latin America compared to North America. First, they had much greater ongoing contact with Africa both because the high death-rate of slaves in the tropics led to a continued need to replenish them with new slaves and also because the Spanish trade continued after the British one was abolished. Second, due partly to different attitudes in Latin culture, they mixed more with other races (Raboteau 2004:92). For both these reasons, there is a much greater African influence on the culture in the Latin Caribbean and northeastern Brazil particularly. Moreover, African religions survived more than in the North perhaps, Raboteau suggests, because the gods of the African past could be accommodated under the Catholic saints, and the sacramental nature of Roman Catholic worship was more akin to African traditional religion than the plainness of North American Protestantism (87–8). African slaves were included under the umbrella of the Catholic Church but no Las Casas campaigned for their rights and there was little attempt to Christianize them, not least because this might confer rights on them that would prevent them being held as slaves. This situation allowed for the emergence of neo-African cults such as Obeah in Jamaica and Vodou in Haiti. However, when these were blamed for inciting slave uprisings, such as those in Jamaica in 1760 and Haiti in 1791, plantation owners began to see Christianization as a way of suppressing the insurrection and so greater opportunities for missionary work opened up. For moral and theological reasons as well as socio-political ones, from the eighteenth century most European missionaries shared a fear and disgust of African religions and sought to eradicate them (Stewart 2005:76–89). By this time, in addition to Catholics, Anglicans, Dutch Reformed and Moravians had arrived. Although the plantation owners in the islands under the British Crown were Scots, Irish and Welsh as well English, Anglicanism became the established form of religion there (Ward 2006:83–101).

Latin society and Roman church

Latin America today is the result of five centuries of mixing of the indigenous peoples with others from Europe, Africa and, more recently, Asia. The violence of the conquest and the later military suppression of any resistance have led to a remarkable uniformity of language and culture across twenty countries, although the unity of purpose toward a democratic society envisaged by the revolutionary leader Simón Bolívar (1783–1830) has not been achieved. However, many Latin American theologians have seen a deep divide. It is not into the many ethnic groups but a single fissure between the conquerors – or at least today's landowning elites – and 'the poor' (e.g. Ribeiro 1990:27–9).

In the immediate aftermath of the conquest, the European population grew rapidly and a network of Spanish towns grew up, together with structures of governance and social organization on the centralized feudal and militarized model of Iberia. Partly because the conquistadors did not bring their wives and families with them (Wiarda 2001:100), the European, Amerindian and African races were very soon mixed. The medieval European social hierarchy was soon modified for the new conditions, with class structure being based on a system of caste. At the top were Europeans or Creoles (American-born Europeans), followed by mestizo (white and indigenous), mulatto (white and African), castizo (white and mestizo) and so on – more than a hundred different categories in all (100). At the bottom were the Africans enslaved on the great estates and the Native Americans, who made up the rural poor. The whites together formed the ruling class and lived in the cities, where the mestizo formed urban masses.

Figure 5.1 Local believers celebrate the Real Presence of Christ in the Eucharist at the feast of Corpus Christi in the main square of the old city of Cusco, Peru, 23 June 2011. In Cusco several processions start in different parts of the city and converge on the cathedral. Image: iStock.

Especially in the Spanish colonies, the political structure under the monarchy was authoritarian and imperious. Furthermore, unlike at home, the colonies had no representative body. The social and economic order was exploitative and mercantile. Everything belonged to the crown and was expected to produce revenue for it; and on the estates the rule of the landowner was absolute. One of the main institutions imported into Latin America was the Catholic Church, which served as an arm of royal authority, and was just as absolutist (Wiarda 2001:98–9). The church acted as a bank, managed vast estates, provided education for the elite, established hierarchies and maintained social order. The Catholicism of Spain was under the monarchy and papal power was almost excluded. When unified under Ferdinand and Isabella, the crown exercised very tight control through the Inquisition. Spanish church leaders played an active role in the counter-Reformation and encouraged Christian scholarship, especially the revival of Scholasticism, bringing to the fore especially the juridical method of Thomas Aquinas and his emphasis on the natural order with its God-ordained hierarchy. This led to a tendency toward legalism at the expense of justice, or what the Latin American church historian Enrique Dussel (1981:39) has described as 'a "perfect legalism" in theory, and a shameful illegality and inadequate application of the laws in fact'. Large numbers of Creoles joined the secular clergy and 'the splendour of the baroque churches of seventeenth-century Mexico and Peru testifies to a religious culture anxious to outdo that of its mother country' (Hastings 1999b:344). But since all clerical appointments were made from Madrid, Creoles were not appointed to the highest posts, rather 'peninsulares' – Spanish and Portuguese – were brought over from Europe. Native Americans were not ordained in any numbers until the late eighteenth century and were sometimes even excluded from the Eucharist.

The colonial grip of Spain over most of Latin America lasted three centuries, and the authoritarian institutions exported from Europe stayed virtually unchanged and unchallenged until the turn of the nineteenth century (Wiarda 2001:76–8). The hold of Portugal on its American territories was looser, however, and the Portuguese were less strict about social relations. Brazilian society developed most rapidly in the eighteenth century, when the slave trade was at its height. The number of slaves imported into Brazil is estimated at more than three million, making the slave community larger than the European one. As a consequence, the culture of slavery permeated the country to a much greater extent than in Spanish territories. Despite the very large slave population in Brazil, the religious orders concentrated, as elsewhere, on evangelizing the remaining native people. The Catholic Church became quite indigenous and the anti-clericalism of the first republic (1889–1930) was in part a reaction to nineteenth-century efforts to Romanize it.

Spanish American independence was marked by a series of local wars from 1810 against what was a declining power. The Mexican war began that year with an uprising of mainly Indians and mestizos, carrying the banner of the Virgin of Guadalupe (see later) and led by a Creole priest, Miguel Hidalgo y Costilla. By 1824 the whole of Spanish America achieved its independence, and a string of new republics was created. Brazil eventually became a republic in 1889. All the new regimes were basically socially conservative. There was some commitment to modernization, but the Creole upper class kept power for itself. Independence caused a crisis for the church because it had been under control of the crown, not the papacy. There was no obvious reason why any of the people of Latin America should defend the institutional church. The church was also a landowner, and so it was both 'an instrument and beneficiary of colonialism' (Wiarda 2001:99). Furthermore, it seemed to serve few.

White males regarded themselves as Christians but 'without any existential linking of conduct and gospel' (Dussel 1981:69). They relied on the Virgin Mary and other intercessors to plead their cause but felt they had little need of bishops and other church officials (Pike 2002:438). The remainder of the population, whether devout or not, were 'second-class Catholics' (437), denied ordination to the priesthood for reasons of gender, race or illegitimacy.

In all cases, following independence, states immediately abolished the Inquisition, the bishops appointed by Spain and Portugal had to return home, and, since many new governments suppressed the religious orders as well, this led to a crisis of manpower. In the period 1820–50, the church faced a wave of assaults on its privileges, led by the new 'liberals' in Latin society, who looked to emulate the United States not only in material progress but also in the separation of church and state. Trade with Britain from the early nineteenth century was at the price of freedom for Protestant worship, initially Anglican – both Church of England and Episcopalian, although at first ministry could only be among expatriates. Following the Monroe Doctrine of 1823, US Protestant influence increased and was a source of modern ideas of knowledge, religious freedom and democracy (Martin 1990:11, 50). In the pursuit of democracy, liberals argued for state control even over the internal workings of the church, and anti-clericalism became the centrepiece of their reform programmes. As a result, the clergy became more conservative and looked to Rome for support in the crisis. They, and many other members of society, tended to see the church as the only bastion of tradition that could stabilize their nations in the precarious political conditions post-independence (Pike 2002:442–4). Its numbers were reinforced by clergy from Europe, and its Latinization contributed to the increasing isolation of the hierarchy from the people, which is a recurrent theme in Latin American theology. The church gradually worked out new relationships with different states. In several cases this was by means of civil war; for example, in Mexico in 1857–60 and again in 1910–20. In contrast, in Peru a settlement was relatively easily achieved. In general in the reordering of societies, Adrian Hastings (1999b:352) laments, the church appeared more concerned for its rights than those of the people.

The status of the church was changed by independence but the position of the aristocracy was not. By 1850 the liberals had achieved the goals of their anticlerical programme but had abandoned most of their economic and social aims. The continuing two-class nature of Latin American society provoked many uprisings and much unrest by Indians and mestizos expressing complaints about taxation and ill-treatment. Some of these included a religious motivation. On the one hand, the church sided with the state in condemning these actions of the 'ignorant, superstitious, impertinent and fanatic' (quoted in Hastings 1999b:357). Despite their differences, the elites of church and society found mutual support in maintaining their status. The clericalism of the church helped maintain the social order by reinforcing the dependent status of the other classes and of Creole women and children, and the focus on the suffering of Christ and the Virgin reminded the masses that they could expect no less in this life (cf. Pike 2002:438–9). On the other hand, the religious motivation of the poor in these struggles showed that Catholicism was not merely a colonial survival but an indigenous force and the church was forced to recognize that, but for the support of the masses, it could be 'cut out' of modern Latin America (Hastings 1999b:357).

The struggles of Catholic Church against revolutionary forces were not only in Latin America but also worldwide, but it began to revive in the late nineteenth and into the twentieth century. In 1899, realizing the importance of the continent, Pope Leo XIII convoked a plenary council of the then fifty-three Latin American bishops in Rome to define pastoral strategies to restore Catholic influence in society and culture. Catholic social teaching, which developed from this period, helped to alleviate the conditions of the poor. Through the movement Catholic Action, the church, religious and lay people worked to stabilize society by founding labour unions. In Latin America these parties demanded state intervention and a communitarian society. Alberto Hurtado Cruchaga (1901–52), a Chilean priest, was canonized by Pope Benedict XVI in 2005 for his work for social justice (becoming the second Chilean saint). Hurtado was director of the Catholic Action youth movement, and he went on to found the Chilean Trade Union Association in 1947. Later in the 1950s Catholic Action encouraged the establishment of Christian Democratic parties. Renewal of the church, aided by an influx of priests from Europe to alleviate the perennial shortage in Latin America, took place gradually over the twentieth century until in 1960 the continent could boast 35 per cent of the world's Catholics – more than in Europe (Hastings 1999b:358). In 1955 a general conference of Latin American bishops was held in Rio de Janeiro to build the capacity of the church to respond to its own problems. The Latin American Episcopal Conference (CELAM I) was the first continental gathering of its kind and became a model for others around the world.

Gender in Iberian Catholicism and indigenous religion

Although the imperial religions of both Aztecs and Incas centred on the Sun, other gods were probably more significant in people's lives, especially the goddesses, who were associated with the earth and fertility. Among them, the Aztecs worshipped the goddess Tonantzín and the Incas worshipped Pacha Mama. At dawn on the day after the feast of the Immaculate Conception (of Mary, mother of Jesus) in 1531, a native American, Cuauhtlatoatzin, baptized Juan Diego, saw a vision of 'a lady from heaven' on the hill near what is now Mexico City where the shrine of Tonantzín once stood. He understood he had seen the Virgin Mary, but he saw Mary from within his own world, with a darker skin and speaking in his native tongue. The story of his encounter is described in a later poem in the Nahuatl language, the Nican Mopohua, in which Mary is described as the one who would hear the laments of the nations and 'cure all their miseries, misfortunes, and sorrows' (see Elizondo 1997:xviii, 5–22). The miraculous imprint of the image of a dark-skinned virgin on Cuauhtlatoatzin's skirt convinced the Spanish bishop. He built a church on the site dedicated to the Virgin Mary, who in this appearance has become known as the Virgin of Guadalupe. In Juan Diego's vision, there was a fusion of the old and new worlds and the inkling of a reconciliation between them. It provided a way for the Indians to reach their heaven through the new religion, which hitherto had seemed to offer little but hardship and suffering. The vision was followed by mass conversions of Indians to Christianity, and a festival in honour of this Indian Mary. From the seventeenth century Creoles also identified with the vision.

The Spanish church, fresh from its struggle against Islam, certainly did not promote syncretism (Dussel 1981:65–6); it preferred to see the veneration of the Virgin of Guadalupe as an indigenous response to the Christian gospel. Whether this was respect or manipulation is a difficult question. From the indigenous peoples' perspective, it allowed them to some extent to worship Tonantzín disguised as Mary, and so preserve their indigenous cultures (cf. Wagua 1990:53), and it was instrumental in developing Mexican national consciousness (Lafaye 1976). From the point of view of Latin American Christianity, the event has been seen as 'revolutionary, profound, lasting, far-reaching, healing, and liberating' and comparable to Pentecost because it was the birth of an indigenous church (Elizondo 1997:xi). Its celebration has become Mexico's most popular religious event and there are many other such celebrations of the Virgin-Mother across Latin America, which include Our Lady of Copacabana (Bolivia), the Virgin of Luján (Argentina) and La Virgen de la Caridad del Cobre (Cuba). Latin America is not the only part of the world where the veneration of Mary is prominent, but it has been significant in a revival of the cult in contemporary Catholicism, especially under John Paul II, who published an encyclical *Redemptoris Mater* extolling the place of the Blessed Virgin Mary in the life of the Pilgrim Church. Guadalupe is the first-listed example of a Marian centre (RM 1987: para. 28) and in 1999 John Paul II declared Our Lady of Guadalupe the patron saint of all the Americas.

The high profile of the Virgin of Guadalupe is an example of what Frederick Pike (2002:450–1) has called the 'matriarchal' nature of popular Catholicism in Latin America, which results from a fusion of both the pre-Columbian goddess traditions and the Iberian Catholicism which was exported there. The first canonized saint of the new world was a woman, Saint Rose of Lima (1586–1617), a Creole whose extreme penance and acts of charity were very much in keeping with the intense spirituality of sixteenth-century Spain and not distinctively American (Hastings 1999b:337). Latin America has produced many other such women saints, who are understood, like the Virgin Mary, to play a mediatory role, interceding for sinners before the judgement throne of God. But in Latin America especially, the indigenous culture has encouraged the exaltation of Mary, the mother of Jesus, to such heights that she almost becomes a member of the Trinity (cf. Boff 1987[1979]). Furthermore, this 'cult of the female in the supernatural order' has had an impact on Latin American society in promoting the self-sacrificing mother–virgin and also in encouraging its opposite, the warrior–saint of special significance to upper-sector males (Pike 2002:450).

The Virgin Mary, portrayed as a manifestation of the feminine principle, requires a complementary masculine symbol (Warner 1985:335–6). Popular male saints in sixteenth-century Spain were warrior figures, especially Saint James (Santiago) of Compostela, who helped defeat the Moors. Their aggressive and assertive manliness was a role model for the conquistadors and this may partly explain the cult of machismo in Latin America today, especially among the mestizo community. This 'cult of exaggerated masculinity' involves the assertion of masculine power and control over women (and other men), manifesting virility, the repudiation of anything feminine and hostility to homosexuality (Chant 2003:14–17). This behaviour may also be related to cultural norms in the empires of pre-conquest America (15) and the behaviour of Iberian males toward their Amerindian womenfolk. Machismo is related to alienation of men from the household and is therefore not to be identified with patriarchy. It also is a compensation for a lack of masculine confidence to attain to the ideal of *macho* (or strength, courage, endurance and self-control), which results from the humiliation of Indian manliness in the conquest and subjugation of Latin America. It is perpetuated by the class/caste culture (Brusco 1995:77–91). Machismo is coupled with idealization of women and the exaggeration of femininity, which demands 'marianismo' behaviour in women of self-abnegation and submission, and an emphasis on the specifically feminine roles of motherhood and nurturance. Although marianismo is not a religious practice, the portrayal of Mary, the mother of Jesus, in Roman Catholic Marianism provided it with religious legitimation and a role model (Chant 2003:9–10). In this context where the woman is revered as a heavenly intercessor, the real woman is deemed a failure for not having lived up to the impossible ideal of being at the same time virgin and mother (Warner 1985:337).

Many problems of Latin America have been blamed on machismo, for example, the reluctance of Latin American males to offer for the (celibate) priesthood, which threatens indigenization and limits the control the church is able to exercise over local Catholic communities (e.g. Hastings 1999b:335). The promiscuity of men and their power over women is a contributing factor in the large numbers of 'street children' (Pike 2002:466), although the violence of poverty is a more important cause (Hecht 1998:192). Population growth is now slowing down, but continued opposition by the Catholic Church to most birth control methods and to abortion (ignored by many) and marianismo are often blamed for child and female mortality and poverty (e.g. Chant 2003:73–8). On the one hand, contemporary Christian feminists bemoan the culture of machismo and try to transform society, or at least work at a local level to free women from male control. For example, feminists have recovered the memory of the remarkable seventeenth century poet and scholar Sor (Sister) Juana Inés de la Cruz who, from her convent in Mexico City, challenged gender stereotypes and even blended indigenous and Christian beliefs. Julia Esquivel (1990) from Guatemala compared the suffering of Indian women at the hands of the conquistadors with those who were raped and abused by soldiers in 1980s Guatemala. She complained that the 'spirit of the conquest' is still alive today and has not yet given way to the 'discovery' of the other (75). Expatriate Cuban Ada María Isasi-Díaz (1996) developed a Mujerista theology – a Latin American women's liberation theology. Others try to rescue the biblical figure of Mary from gender stereotyping, pointing out, for example, that the exaltation of Mary is the exaltation of a poor woman (Luke 1:48; Gebara and Bingemer 1994). On the other hand, where motherhood is both privately and publicly venerated, it can be embraced and used to subvert male power (Chant 2003:9–13). In popular portrayals of the Virgin, the mother is one who submits to God's will and suffers, thus gaining a sense of spiritual superiority. An individual example of this phenomenon of the supermadre ('supermother'; Pike 2002:459) was Eva Duarte de Perón, the second wife of Juan Perón, who was president of Argentina in 1946–55. The highly popular Evita promoted and publicly revered her husband. She was seen to sacrifice herself in social work, like the female saints; she acted as a mediator between the poor and her husband; and she behaved as mother of the nation. Eva Perón founded a women's political party and ran for vice president. Idolized by the masses, her name was even put forward for canonization (Fraser and Navarro 1996). Another example of women using the sanctity of motherhood in Argentina is the group known as the 'mothers of the disappeared' or the Mothers of the Plaza de Mayo. This was the square in Buenos Aires where the women first gathered in 1977, in defiance of a ban on demonstrations, to campaign silently for justice for their children who were taken away by the military dictatorship during the 'Dirty War' and never seen again. Their motherhood did not guarantee complete immunity – one of their leaders, Azucena Villaflor, herself became one of the 'disappeared' – but other mothers were able to maintain almost the only visible political protest throughout the remaining years of the 'dirty war'.

Liberation theology and base communities

In the first part of the twentieth century, Latin American leaders reacted against the liberal positivism of the late nineteenth century and returned to the idealism which Pike sees as their more natural state. Some espoused an almost mystical form of Marxism that encouraged secularized versions of Christ's death and resurrection (Pike 2002:453–6), of which the figure of Ernesto 'Che' Guevara, the Argentinian-born Marxist guerrilla leader, was a late manifestation. Others, such as Víctor Raúl Haya de la Torre of Peru, constructed their own unorthodox religio-political movements to support their messianic status. In many cases, it was the colonial warrior–saint model that was invoked to solve the problems of society. As the century wore on, more and more nations were in the grip of an alliance between the right-wing church and military dictators. The relative prosperity that many Latin American countries had enjoyed until the mid-twentieth century ebbed away and development aspirations did not materialize.

Disillusioned with Christian democracy, and influenced by the Belgian worker priests, priests and religious joined lay Catholics in the workplace. They developed small lay communities there which were involved in social action. Latin American groups of Young Christian Workers (Jocists) had absorbed the inductive method of 'see, judge, act', which opened them to the reforms of liturgy and ecclesiology of the

Figure 5.2 A Catholic procession on Good Friday in the streets of the Old Town of Quito, Ecuador, 6 April 2012. Remembering the death of Jesus Christ Holy Week is one of the most important annual events in Ecuador. Image: iStock.

Second Vatican Council. The youth were also inspired to social justice by the Cuban Revolution of 1959. A new generation of Latin American priests, and some nuns, sought answers to the profound socio-economic problems of their continent by studying economics, sociology and political science in the Marxist-influenced atmosphere of the universities of the 1960s. They did not have strong indigenous traditions to draw on as in Asia and Africa, nor could they engage in anti-Western polemic since Latin America is culturally much akin to Europe, but Marxist analysis served instead (Freston 2001:192). It encouraged them to see the continent's problems in terms of unjust structures rather than individual failings and to view economic underdevelopment as the consequence of the inequity of the global capitalist system. In short, Latin American underdevelopment was the dark side of North American development (Bonino 1975:26–7). At a national level these church workers identified vested interests that kept the poor in poverty, and theologically they began to redefine sin as a matter of the collective failure of society and not only of personal guilt (Gutiérrez 1988:102). As a result, they came to regard revolutionary change in society as not only necessary but also justifiable.

The impact of the Second Vatican Council in Latin America

In the mid-1960s, bishops from the continent attended the Second Vatican Council. Because of the numbers of Catholics in Latin America, they constituted more than 22 per cent of the total there, although this still left Latin American Christians underrepresented. Bishop Hélder Câmara, who had founded the Brazilian branch of the relief and development agency Caritas in 1956, was particularly influential in the drafting of *Gaudium et Spes* (the constitution on the church in the modern world), but at the Council it became clear that many of the Latin American bishops' concerns differed from those of the European bishops who were dominant (Dussel 1981:139–40). However, the teaching of the Second Vatican Council with regard to social justice, empowering the laity, use of vernacular languages, encouragement of pluralism and concern for the poor offered a greater challenge to the church of Latin America than perhaps anywhere else and it also confirmed the Catholic Action in which Latin Americans were already engaged (Linden 2012:98). It produced a unique response that was to have worldwide influence. This came about in three main ways: at the second meeting of CELAM, in liberation theology and through the 'base communities' (Hastings 1999b:359–60).

CELAM II in Medellín, Colombia, in 1968 was a momentous event in the history of the Latin American church for two reasons: first it was visited by Pope Paul VI – the first time a pope had ever set foot in the 'New World'; second, the bishops took the extraordinary step of declaring the church to be a 'poor church', against injustice and for the liberation of the poor as part of evangelization, and so rejected the socio-political order that had existed in Latin America since the sixteenth century (Hastings 1999b:360; Linden 2012:114–17). The conclusions of Medellín were endorsed by all the episcopacies, and in the turbulent years of the 1970s national churches took stances on behalf of the poor and against military regimes and other injustices in several different countries (Dussel 1981:148–84). Eleven years later, the 'preferential option for the poor' was reaffirmed at CELAM III in Puebla, Mexico, despite conservative attempts to 'bury Medellín' (239). The situation of the indigenous peoples and African Americans was described as abject poverty, which represented 'institutionalized injustice' (Hennelly 1990:225–58; Dussel 1981:229–39). For many Latin American Christians, like Enrique Dussel (1981:255), these momentous events signalled a break of the Latin American church with the model of Christendom and the shift to a missionary stance. Pope John Paul II, who had been linked with the struggle against communism in Poland, was naturally worried by the use of Marxism in liberation theology but he was equally mindful of the need for solidarity with the poor. Under his leadership the 'option for the poor', but not the liberation theological method, was incorporated into Catholic social teaching in the encyclical *Centesimus Annus* (1991:para. 11).

The reverberations of the second part of the response, 'theology of liberation', are still being felt around the world today. Pike (2002:463) sees in its emergence a number of currents in the Latin American society and church: 'mystical Marxism, dependency analysis, an apocalyptic world-view extending back to pre-Columbian times, and utopianism, often verging on postmillennialism, of twentieth-century populist movements steeped in religious mythology'. Peruvian priest Gustavo Gutiérrez (1988) was the first to clearly articulate 'a theology of liberation' in 1971, which he defined as 'a critical reflection on Christian praxis in light of the word of God'. Reading the story of the exodus from Egypt, he concluded that this liberation of Israel was 'a political action' and that God's intervention in history on behalf of the oppressed is foundational to the Judaeo-Christian faith (xxix, 88). This led him, first, to interpret Christian faith from the experience of the suffering, struggle and hope of the poor; and second, to criticize society and the ideologies sustaining it, and also the activity and theology of the church, from the perspective of the poor. Gutiérrez put 'orthopraxis' alongside 'orthodoxy'; that is he made right practice, in addition to right doctrine, the test of faith (8). This revolutionary movement demanded not only a theology of liberation but also 'the liberation of theology' from being 'the erudite theology of textbooks' to 'a theology arising out of the urgent problems of real life' (Segundo 1976:4–5).

Constructively, liberation theology called for a third response: the reinvention and realignment of the church from an institution which supported and mirrored the unjust structures of society to communities with charismatic ministries appropriate to the context (Boff 1986[1977]). The creation of 'base (ecclesial) communities' was a way of involving the laity in ministry, as instructed by the Vatican Council, and utilized the encouragement given by the Council for lay people to read and interpret the Bible. Unlike celebration of the mass, reading the Bible was something the laity could do without a priest and so the communities can also be seen as a pastoral strategy to deal with the shortage of priests, as well as a response to the challenge of a growing Protestant movement. But in Recife in northeast Brazil, base communities took a new turn when, with the support of the now Archbishop Câmara, they were combined with the educational method developed by Paulo Freire. The latter involved 'conscientization' among the poor, raising their awareness of the causes of their condition and of the ideologies used to perpetuate it, to empower them to change their situation (Freire 1970). Groups of lay people were encouraged to read the Bible together (with priests participating only on an occasional basis) and to reflect on it in the light of their social condition. So, for example, they asked why the church emphasized that the people should be obedient to its teaching and yet failed to stress that Jesus challenged the religious authorities of his own day for abusing the trust placed in them and neglecting the poor. They used their conclusions as the basis for community action and then read the Bible again in the light of their experience, following the 'hermeneutic circle' explained by Segundo (1976:7–38). Perhaps as many as three million people were involved in base communities in the early 1980s, two-thirds of them in Brazil (Pike 2002:467). From this movement emerged a new way of understanding the Bible, which saw a message of social justice that could be applied directly to community life to bring about social change. As it developed, liberation theology drew also on the resources of popular Latin American religiosity to inspire a spirituality of costly identification and solidarity with the suffering and belief in the possibility of social transformation (Gutiérrez 1984). As a bishop and archbishop in Buenos Aires in the 1990s until he became Pope Francis, Jorge Bergoglio supported such local activist groups in obtaining their rights and distanced the church from the state, freely giving evidence to help those researching the church's complicity in the Dirty War (Ivereigh 2014:316–20).

Global response to the theology of liberation

Liberation theology was 'the first locally realised product' of the truly 'world Church' that Karl Rahner had hailed at the Second Vatican Council (Linden 2012:118). It encouraged a hermeneutics of suspicion that raised questions of power and vested interest in theology and had a global impact (Tombs 2002). Since it challenged church and state, liberation theology inevitably faced resistance from the authorities in Latin America and in Rome. This was particularly the case because it was easily labelled 'communist' or 'socialist'. In the 1970s and 1980s most countries in Latin America and the Caribbean were in a state of civil war between rightist and leftist forces or in the grip of military-backed governments supported by the United States to oppose communism. Because of their work on behalf of the poor and action to reduce the power of the landowning elite, Catholic priests, nuns and church workers suffered violent attack and persecution. El Salvador had the most highly charged atmosphere. Marxists opposed a military junta (backed by the United States) and so did Archbishop Óscar Romero, who had become an advocate of the poor both through his broadcasts and also through the example of his humble life. The result of his fearless response to injustice was that he was gunned down while celebrating mass in his cathedral in 1980. Even at his funeral, attended by mourners from all over the world, a bomb went off and shots were fired (Brockman 2005). Romero was beatified by Pope Francis in 2015. The violence continued to the end of the Cold War, and in the same country in 1989 six Jesuits were murdered in one incident because they were believed to be subversives.

As well as attack from political forces, liberation theologians also had to face the weight of the church hierarchy, which came to be represented by Bishop López Trujillo of Colombia, secretary of CELAM from 1972 to 1984, who tried unsuccessfully to control the base communities and to change the theological discourse. Under the prefecture of Cardinal Joseph Ratzinger, later Pope Benedict XVI, the Congregation for the Doctrine of the Faith issued two documents regarding liberation theology. The first in 1984 condemned aspects of the new theology, censuring some theologians for uncritical use of Marxist thought. Those censured included Leonardo Boff, a Brazilian priest who was a strong critic of church power structures and advocate of the base communities as a new way of being church (Boff 1986[1977]). But although Marxist social theory was used in the analysis of the question of poverty, the construction of liberation theology was mainly based on the teaching of the Second Vatican Council and on papal encyclicals on the themes of human dignity and development (Linden 2012:110–17, 148–53). It is likely that the root cause of Rome's unease was the undermining of clerical control by the 'new way of being church' in the base communities (Hastings 1999b:360–2), which led in early 1980s Nicaragua under Sandinista rule to a partial schism by the formation of the 'Church of the People' (Klaiber 1998:193–215). The second document in 1986 was more conciliatory but the repression of liberation theology continued. From the time he took office in 1978, John Paul II appointed conservative bishops to counter it and Trujillo was made a cardinal in 1983. Nevertheless, liberation theology had 'entered the bloodstream of the Church and migrated around the world' (Linden 2012:152). Since taking office in 2013, Francis I has taken quite a different tack. He has affirmed Gutiérrez, rehabilitated Boff and encouraged the restoration of diplomatic relations between the United States and Cuba. Furthermore, in his apostolic exhortation *Evangelii Gaudium* (2013), he takes up many of the themes of liberation theology: he criticizes the global capitalist system, condemns sinful structures, urges accompaniment of the poor 'on the path to liberation' and completes the action–reflection hermeneutical circle by asserting that the poor themselves are agents of evangelization.

Despite, or because of, its censure by the Vatican, liberation theology spread rapidly worldwide, first through the missionary organizations such as the Jesuits, among 'Third World theologians' through EATWOT (Ecumenical Association of Third World Theologians) and then into the wider theological community. Some Latin American Protestants also took up liberation theology. José Miguez Bonino, an Argentinian Methodist prominent in the WCC, emphasized that history is the arena in which theology must be done (Bonino 1975). Elsa Tamez (1993) from Costa Rica re-examined the doctrine of justification to show that it means God's affirmation of life for all human beings. Because of its foundations in a simple reading of the Bible, Evangelical theologians could also affirm many of liberation theology's tenets and they disseminated it worldwide through their networks. For example, Puerto Rican Baptist theologian Orlando Costas (1982) challenged Evangelicals globally to 'mission outside the [city] gate', on the periphery of society. There is no doubt that liberation theology changed the theological landscape worldwide by attempting to bring the poor and poverty – seen as integral to Jesus's ministry – into the centre of Christian concern. It raised critical questions about who has the right to do Christian theology – the powerful or the powerless? It questioned the ideological standpoint of any theology: does it support the status quo or does it represent the interests of the poor? And it encouraged Christians not to stop at charity but to raise structural questions, which influenced development agencies more generally to engage in advocacy to change the structures of society for the better. As Las Casas had understood from reflecting on the book of Ecclesiasticus, 'It is of no use 'to pretend that one believes in the God of the Bible when one "lives '. . . on the blood of the Indians" ' (Gutiérrez 1993:61). However, within Latin America, although the church gained credibility in the public eye, the structures of the church were not radically changed by liberation theology. And as far as the indigenous people are concerned, even liberation theology is 'conceived *from outside the indigenous community*' (Wagua 1990:51; italics original) and does not recognize indigenous religions or churches as such. At its height in the early 1980s, liberation theology and the base communities resembled a revival movement and some of the other messianic movements in Latin American politics, but it did not quite translate into a popular movement. One of the reasons for this was the tightened control by the hierarchy (Pike 2002:467). Many base communities continued, but their involvement was more at the level of community projects than political action (Theije 1999:116). Another reason was that the poor themselves were more interested in gaining wealth than in fighting poverty and were being attracted away from Catholicism to newer religious movements.

The Catholic Church in the restoration of democracy

Although the structures of the church remained in place, liberation theology did change the church from being the supporter of military regimes into a force for democracy and human rights (Klaiber 1998:5). The single most important factor in the installation of more democratic and centrist governments that took place across Latin America in the late 1980s and 1990s was the ending of the Cold War. But the Catholic Church played a highly important role long before 1989 and afterwards in challenging the military and promoting democracy. The church both gave the new popular democracy religious legitimation and also 'in turn received a new legitimacy from the popular classes'. The role of the church varied in each country. In some cases, the church itself was divided between a more conservative hierarchy and the liberation activists. This division was particularly acute in Nicaragua, where perhaps the most that can be said is that Christians 'braked the extremists in both camps' (6, 264). In other places in Central America the church was more constructive. Throughout the conflict in El Salvador the church acted as mediator between the two factions under the guidance of Romero's successor, Arturo Rivera y Damas. In both El Salvador and Guatemala, the church sponsored 'national dialogue' to widen participation and strengthen democracy, forcing governments and guerrillas to move more quickly toward agreement. In the Andean nations of Bolivia and Peru the church once again became an advocate of the rights of the Indians through the activities of grassroots Christians, along with peace and human-rights groups. In the Southern Cone, the church censured the dictatorship in Paraguay; it became the principal voice of opposition and supported the organizations of civil society to overthrow the regime in Brazil; and the church intervened directly in the political process to support the main opposition party in Chile. But in Argentina and Uruguay the principal voices of protest in the church were from below. Although Mexico did not experience military dictatorship, during the 1990s there was sustained oppression of the indigenous population in Chiapas. The latter was Las Casas' old diocese, yet more than four hundred years later the bishop, Samuel Ruiz, who had since 1960 revitalized Catholicism in the region, was again struggling for the rights of the Indians there who took part in the Zapatista uprisings (Hartch 2014:176–80). In most of these cases, liberal and anticlerical forces in government wished to exclude church participation but in the end the church was the only body with enough support to break the deadlock between opposing forces (Klaiber 1998).

Now that there is greater democracy in Latin America, the role of the church has changed again. Mass mobilization in the streets is not so necessary and church's efforts for a more just society are being pursued through less high-profile means. In Peru, for example, grassroots Catholic Action among the poor shifted its attention to business and the marketplace through new modes such as partnership with business corporations and encouraging microenterprise (Brooks 1999). In many cases, the public stance of the church became conservative. This was not only because of the appointment by Rome of more conservative bishops but also because contemporary political issues relating to women's rights, the family and sexuality were ones on which the hierarchy had a strong countercultural stance. So the church in Chile, for example, which stood firmly against the right-wing dictatorship of Augusto Pinochet, then became aligned with conservative political forces (Haas 1999). Another reason for the drop in political involvement was the move under John Paul II to affirm and incorporate much popular religiosity into the life of the church through the 'new evangelization'. This was a term that Latin Americans at the CELAM meeting in Puebla in 1979 were using to describe a renewed evangelization of Latin America in quite a different way from the first evangelization by conquest of nearly five hundred years before (Gorski 2015). However, the pope shifted attention from the directly socio-political to the religio-cultural. In Latin America, as elsewhere, the new evangelization became a strategy to stem the flow of people out of the church into secularism or new religious movements, of which the most threatening was seen to be Pentecostalism (Gill 1999; Norget 1999). In *Evangelii Gaudium* (2013) Pope Francis returned to a broad understanding of the term as the joyful proclamation of a renewed church through pastoral care and social action.

The rise of the Evangélicos

The Reformation bypassed Latin America, so Protestantism represents an external tradition recently introduced. Anglicanism was brought to Native Americans in the southern tip of the continent through the Patagonian (later South American) Missionary Society from 1844 (Ward 2006:103–5). Liberal leaders of newly independent nations invited Western missions for educational and other projects, especially in rural areas, among the poor and where the Catholic Church was less dominant. European immigrants brought their own forms of Protestantism with them in the nineteenth and twentieth centuries. These were mainly British and North American but also included Lithuanian Baptists who went to Brazil and Russian Mennonites who settled in Paraguay. Germans, Scandinavians, Welsh and Scots set up their own churches in Brazil, Chile, Argentina and Guatemala. More recently Korean Protestants and many others are included in the mix. But the chief Protestant influences have been from North America, which directed all kinds of missions southwards, especially after its defeat of the Spanish in 1898 and the opening of the Panama Canal in 1914 that increased US political and economic influence in the region. Protestant churches and missions have been divided about whether or not Catholics can be considered evangelized. Under pressure from Anglo-Catholics, the Protestant organizers of the World Missionary Conference in Edinburgh in 1910 decided to exclude missions in Latin America (Stanley 2009:52–5, 64–8). Nevertheless, some delegates formed the Committee for Latin American Cooperation, which strengthened mission work through the policies discussed in Scotland and nurtured Latin American leadership (Ham 2015).

Different countries showed varying patterns of Protestant growth to the mid-twentieth century according to patterns of immigration, mission activity, and political, social and religious conditions. Three examples will suffice: Protestantism gained some popularity in Brazil in the mid-nineteenth century as an ideological alternative. Presbyterians grew rapidly and became independent of their US mission in 1888 but they were overtaken in the early twentieth century by Baptists, mainly evangelized from the Southern United States (Martin 1990:62–4). In Argentina Protestantism tended to run along ethnic lines, with people of different European nations having their own churches. Methodist churches were influential in the nineteenth century but after that there was successful mission work by Plymouth Brethren, Baptists and Seventh-Day Adventists. In Chile, by contrast, there was much less migration but instead more indigenous growth of Protestantism by conversion, at first among Methodists and Baptists (74–9). However since 1960, across Latin America, it is

Figure 5.3 An Evangelical preacher expounds God's Word in Praça da Sé (Se Square) in downtown São Paulo, Brazil, 9 January 2009. He is standing beneath the statue of José de Anchieta, Spanish Jesuit missionary, saint and one of the founders of the city. Image: iStock.

Pentecostalism – in mainline and independent forms – that has become the main non-Catholic Christian movement.

In the 1980s, claims were made that Latin America was 'turning Evangelical', and since then much research has been devoted to studying the growth of Protestants, Evangelicals, Pentecostals, Independents and Marginals there. In the still overwhelmingly Catholic context of Latin America, all these non-Catholic Christians tend to be collectively labelled Evangélicos in Spanish. In 1910, there were still probably less than two million Protestants and Anglicans in the whole of Latin America. In 2009 there were estimated to be about 110 million Evangélicos of various sorts, or a little less than 20 per cent of the total population of the continent. Estimates of the proportion of Evangélicos in each country of Latin America today vary depending on what is measured. It is not possible to discuss each country in detail but only to note some prominent developments.

Various explanations have been put forward to explain the rapid growth of the Evangélicos in Latin America in general. The Evangélicos themselves saw Latin America as only superficially Catholic. They observed a lack of commitment by the people, a shortage of priests, education and services from the church and an indiscriminate mixing of Christianity with other faiths – criticisms which Catholics themselves recognized in the 1950s (Hartch 2014:13–14). So they saw Catholics turning from lostness and ignorance to a true encounter with Christ and experience of the Spirit. Sociologist David Martin (1990) sees the growth as part of a four-century-long struggle for supremacy between Anglo and Latin civilizations, dating back to the attack of the Spanish Armada on England but played out largely in the Americas, which has come in three 'waves': Puritan, Methodist and Pentecostal. This struggle is usually portrayed in the global North, and by Southern liberals, as a clash of 'freedom against authority, equality against hierarchy, individual conscience against organicism, progress against reaction, and peaceability and commerce against unproductive militarism' (5–26). Evangelical faith, Martin argues, is just one aspect of a general North Americanization of Latin America. However, Latin Americans would be some of the first to raise questions about the 'peaceable' nature of British or North American imperialism, and the negative value assumed to attach to authority structures and 'corporatism' could be strongly debated (cf. Wiarda 2001:345).

While Martin's view undoubtedly carries some truth and links in with theories of contemporary globalization, in which North America is the strongest force, Latin America may also be seen as another example of the growth of worldwide Pentecostalism, which has a significant African as well as an Anglo component. Moreover, it could be part of a wider resurgence of 'primal spirituality' (Cox 1996:161–84), or a globalization from below. It is Pentecostals and various other independent churches that have been responsible for most of the growth in Evangélicos. In the Latin American context, Protestants and Pentecostals are, by and large, two different communities. As we have said, Protestants tend to be associated with various migrations whereas Pentecostals are more indigenous. Latin American Pentecostals object to the commonly held view (also implied in a surface reading of Martin) that Pentecostalism originated in North America as 'a western attempt at domestication of the liberating power of Pentecost' (Sepúlveda 1999:113, 134). Chilean Pentecostal Juan Sepúlveda showed that the Chilean Pentecostal church is the result of an independent development that represents indigenous Chilean experience. Martin (2002:71–82) himself also insisted that Latin American Protestantism has become an indigenous movement through the rise of Latino-led Pentecostalism. A further difference is that Protestants tend to be middle-class – although they may have started poor (Martin 1990:53) – whereas Pentecostal churches in Latin America are found among the poor, which in Latin American 'pigmentocracy' implies Indian, black and mixed heritage (Freston 2001: 194). They exist in slums that the police and government agents fear to enter.

The first Pentecostal revival in Latin America was in Chile in 1909 in a Methodist church in Valparaiso, encouraged by a North American Methodist missionary who had heard of the revivals in India and Europe. It led to the founding of the Methodist Pentecostal Church (Iglesia Metodista Pentecostal). There were at least one thousand Protestant denominations in Chile by 2004. More than thirty of these were Pentecostal churches that had come out of the Methodist Pentecostal Church, and these made up 95 per cent of all the Protestants in Chile (Anderson 2004:67). Although there was a North American connection, the Methodist Pentecostal Church has never been part of North American Pentecostalism and maintains Methodist doctrine, practice and structure (Sepúlveda 1999). Pentecostal growth in Argentina (about 10 per cent) started rather later than elsewhere, when in the 1980s the evangelistic ministry of Carlos Annacondia 'converted the [existing] Evangelical community to charismatic practices' (Marostica 1999:147; Míguez 1999). Other evangelists introduced prosperity teaching, and the 'Argentine Revival' soon spread beyond Argentina itself, especially in the United States and Canada (Marostica 1999:162–5). Perhaps 18 per cent of the population of Brazil are Evangélicos, mostly Pentecostal. And since Brazil has such a large population, this means it has one of the largest populations of Pentecostals in the world. Because they are mostly practising, there are probably more Pentecostals at worship on a Sunday than there are Catholics (Anderson 2004:69). The largest denomination in Brazil is the US-based Assemblies of God (Assembléias de Deus), with as many as twenty-three million members – about eight times as large as the Assemblies of God in the United States itself. Many Pentecostal churches have been started by Brazilians. The Universal Church of the Kingdom of God (Igreja Universal do Reino de Deus; IURD) is the largest and most controversial of these. Bishop Edir Macedo, a former lottery official, encourages a 'cash-for-blessings' approach (73–4).

In addition to Martin's global culture-clash theory and Anderson's explanation in terms of global Pentecostalism, political reasons have been advanced for the growth of the Evangélicos. In the 1980s, it was suggested that Protestant evangelism in Latin

America was in conspiracy with the CIA because converts were likely to be conservative and politically quiescent, supporting the governments backed by the United States and inclined toward American culture (Martin 1990:54). The growth of the Evangélicos in Guatemala received particular attention in this regard. Hastings, a Catholic, saw this as the result of 'a huge and concerted campaign to eradicate both traditional Maya culture and Catholic influence' and 'replace both by the religious culture of the American Bible Belt'. This 'missionary offensive', in which Catholic priests and nuns were harassed and killed by government forces, was funded by US televangelists and supported by 'born-again' president Rios Montt (1982–83), a member of the highly authoritarian Pentecostal Church of the Word (El Verbo), who was simultaneously violently suppressing the Indian population (Hastings 1999:365–6).

US citizens' support of evangelism in Latin America was certainly increased by the perceived threat of communism there (Pike 2002:470); US televangelism was very effective in Central America (Brouwer, Gifford and Rose 1996:59–60); and the agenda of President Ronald Reagan to expand US influence did attract right-wing activists to join the missionary movement (Stoll 1990:xv). However, Paul Freston, an Evangelical, rejects Hasting's view by arguing that most of the circumstances were coincidental (Freston 2001:272). David Stoll (1990), who recounts the story of Guatemala in detail, argues that the Evangélicos did not all endorse American foreign policy; indeed many were critical of it and were using Evangelical religion for their own ends of raising themselves out of poverty. In the end, the need for survival pushed many of the people into the hands of those churches (Evangelical/Pentecostal) which supported the government (180–217; cf. Garrard-Burnett 2010). Freston (2001:283) adds that Catholic and left-wing accusations about American missionaries disguised the fact that Catholicism in Latin America is more 'foreign' in terms of both personnel and funding. Whatever the initial motives, Hastings (1999b:366) recognizes that the resulting Pentecostal churches are self-generating, and suggests that they result from very similar religious motives on the part of contemporary Guatemalans to those which brought their Indian ancestors into the Catholic Church three centuries before. In Chile, Pentecostals were found both supporting and actively opposing General Augusto Pinochet's regime in the 1970s and 1980s (Kamsteeg 1999). As the prominent Argentinian Methodist theologian José Míguez Bonino concluded, the growth of the Evangélicos has more to do with 'internal political and social struggles on the continent' than with external 'imperialist' forces (Bonino 1997:3).

Many structural explanations have been advanced for the growth of Pentecostal churches in Latin America. The Evangélicos are associated with modernity and also thrive in the context of urbanization. Many from traditional Catholic villages in the countryside find the new faith more available and more suited to an urban lifestyle (Wingeier-Rayo 2013). Both the democratic tendencies and the dominating tendencies of Pentecostal polity have also been suggested as reasons for its attractiveness (Gooren 2007:163). Other reasons include the need for fellowship among people displaced by industrialization and urbanization (e.g. Martin 2002:49). As Martin (1990:31–42) showed, from a phenomenological point of view there are striking parallels with the beginnings of Methodism among the poor in Europe. In the context of the integration of Latin America into the global economy, the Evangélicos contribute a work ethic; they teach and reinforce discipline in a supportive community environment and give people strength to resist the street (Martin 2002:74). Martin also saw the growth of the Evangélicos in the context of women's resistance to Latin American machismo culture. In their conservative morality, Evangelical and Pentecostal churches reform the errant male and eliminate the double standard of morality for the two genders, leading to improvements in health, work, family life and the well-being of children (Brusco 1995). The openness of women particularly to try this new form of religion may be in part because 'women prefer peaceable, stable homes to itinerant male violence' (Martin 2002:50). Ironically, therefore, conservative Evangelicalism, which has a strong patriarchal rhetoric, may actually be contributing to the undermining of machismo in Latin America (Steigenga and Smilde 1999).

But structural explanations alone do not adequately explain why, amid all the many mission endeavours in Latin America, it is Pentecostalism – in imported and indigenous forms – that has grown most. Theories which take an insider view stress that Pentecostal churches help people find ways of coping with their various problems. A recent study showed that there are a wide variety of reasons for both conversion and disaffiliation. The few common factors were a sense of crisis that precipitated conversion and a religious approach to life that led to a search for a religious solution to the problem. Social and contingency factors then determined whether the individual joined Pentecostalism or some other religion or pseudo-religion (Gooren 2007). However, this still does not explain the growth of Pentecostalism specifically – other than that it is widely available. While cultural, political, structural and individual reasons are significant, understanding growth must also have to do Pentecostalism as it 'is in itself' (Sepúlveda 1999:111, 128). From the perspective of people of the Caribbean, the turn from Catholicism to US-style Pentecostalism can be seen as a protest against, and rejection of, 'the symbolic cultural system that is the heritage of slavery and conquest' in which converts re-found their life on the written word, 'placing it in radical opposition to the image'. At the same time Pentecostalism offered a bodily experience of the Holy Spirit which mirrors many aspects of African-derived religions of the Caribbean, so that Pentecostalism subsumes the Voodoo gods (Hurbon 2001:131–4).

Commentators agree that the strength of Pentecostalism in Brazil in particular is connected with interest in the world of spirits, which is in turn related to the large proportion of the population with African ancestry and the strong presence of African-derived religions there (Anderson 2004:70; Martin 1990:68). Once suppressed by the authorities, the African-derived religions of Candomblé and Umbanda are now legal and attractive in a climate of black consciousness and where whites seek alternatives to Western rationalism (Jensen 1999). The religious culture of Brazil is such that they coexist with the others, and people who count themselves as Christians will also consult mediums and join in festivals (Prokopy and Smith 1999:11). So, one of the relevant characteristic of Pentecostalism itself is its theology of the Holy Spirit that takes seriously the world of demons and spirits which trouble the poor, whatever their ethnic background, and offers ways of dealing with their problems within this cosmology.

Taking into consideration the wider social and cultural context, Martin argues that Pentecostalism is well shaped to help people be successful in post-modernity because it energizes – through the power of the Spirit in worship, imbues confidence – because God is on your side in 'spiritual warfare', and gives hope – because God does not fail (Martin 2002:79–80). This is also the view of Sepúlveda (1999), who argues strongly that the reason Pentecostalism grew was that it had a particular appeal to the popular culture of the poor in a way that Protestantism in general did not. In particular, its healing ministry 'could be seen as a "point of contact" between primitive Christianity, revivalist Protestantism, popular Catholicism and Amerindian religiosity' (128–9).

Evangélicos in public life

The Evangélicos, most of whom now have an Evangelical belief and a Pentecostal-style faith, have taken an increasing role in the public life of Latin American nations. Edward Cleary and Hannah Stewart-Gambino (1998) and Paul Freston (2001) have produced detailed studies of Evangélicos in politics. Here we mention just a few points. First, the Evangélicos, unlike US-style Evangelicals, are generally undogmatic. They have entered politics because experience suggests practical advantages to this course, and they may withdraw also for pragmatic reasons (Cleary 1998:13). Second, unlike US Evangelicals, Latin American Evangélicos do not represent a tradition that they are trying to reinstate, so their political alignments vary considerably (Freston 2001:288); nevertheless, Brazil is the only country in Latin America with an Evangelical left wing (33). Third, compared to Evangelical and Pentecostal Christians in other parts of the Third World, in Latin America Evangélicos have been more inclined to form national political parties. These are particularly prominent in Colombia, Nicaragua and Venezuela. Many of them represent concerns for human rights and democracy but some merely seek to enlist state resources for their church (285). Fourth, in some countries the Evangélicos represent a distinct voting bloc, which has been decisive in some elections, such as the election of Alberto Fujimori in Peru in 1990. But their enthusiasm is being tempered by experience (Cleary 1998:12).

The Evangélicos have been portrayed, especially by liberation theologians and other left-leaning commentators, as other-worldly and quiescent and showing little concern for social justice (Cleary 1998:12). This impression is reinforced by the Evangelical tendency to blame the social ills of Latin America not on foreign dependency or the caste structure but on Latin Catholic social mores (Stoll 1990:180). However, within the global Evangelical movement, Latin Americans led the way from the 1970s in articulating an 'integral evangelism'. At the conference that launched the Lausanne Movement for World Evangelization in 1974, two Baptists – René Padilla from Ecuador and Samuel Escobar from Peru – who were leaders in the International Fellowship of Evangelical Students, challenged global Evangelicalism to work for justice for the poor (Stanley 2013:164–7). Nevertheless, it is true that in general Evangelicalism emphasizes personal moral transformation as a prerequisite for social change and expects a gradual leavening of society by conversion. But, as Martin and others have shown, this in itself leads to social change: it produces an improvement in the social condition of believers within existing social structures. Furthermore, Pentecostalism in particular has an orientation toward power that encourages mass movements and public demonstrations of solidarity. Pentecostal theologians even argue that Pentecostalism necessarily incorporates a practical concern and a missionary intent because the Holy Spirit is the Spirit of love (Land 1993:131–6). This may be so at a grassroot level but many of the leaders of the large Pentecostal-type mega-churches do not evidence much of this humility.

The Evangélicos are not only active in evangelism within Latin America and the Caribbean; they are also engaged in missionary work worldwide, including 'reverse mission' to the Iberian peninsula (Alvarez 2015). Brazil is reckoned to be second only to the United States in the number of missionaries sent transnationally. In 2010 it had 34,000 missionaries in the field – more than the rest of Latin America combined. Brazilian Evangélicos have been participating in world mission since the first Ibero-American Missions Congress in São Paulo in 1987, encouraged by US-based global Evangelical bodies. They serve mainly in other countries of Latin America, but also Portugal and Spain, in Africa – especially former Portuguese territories of Angola, Mozambique and Guinea Bissau, in Asia – especially East Timor, and increasingly in clandestine ways in Islamic countries where overt missionary work is forbidden. Brazilian Pentecostals, especially the aggressive IURD, have been more successful in terms of numbers of converts in many of the same countries (Hartch 2014:187–93).

Since about 1990, attention to religion in Latin America has made a rather sudden shift from Catholic liberation theology to the growth of evangelical Protestantism and Pentecostalism. This tends to ignore three other important developments: it fails to explore the significant interface between Catholicism and Pentecostalism; it neglects the bigger picture of the general pluralization of society (see later); and it ignores the Catholic response to this pluralization in general and Protestantism in particular. The overlap between Catholicism and Pentecostalism in Latin America occurs in three main areas. The first is in the charismatic spirituality that is also found in Catholicism. Since the 1970s, the worldwide Catholic Charismatic Renewal, which offers many of the same benefits as Pentecostalism such as prayer for healing, exorcism and warm fellowship, has been an established part of life in many parishes. It has often been encouraged by conservative bishops as an alternative to the base communities of liberation theology. Individuals may be members of both a base community and a charismatic group within one Catholic parish, each satisfying different spiritual needs and offering avenues of service (Theije 1999), but in most cases individual priests tend to favour one or the other; in which case, charismatically-minded Catholic lay people in a liberation theology parish may join a Pentecostal church as well as, or instead of, attending mass. The second overlap is in the common practical concern of the base communities and Evangélicos, especially indigenous Pentecostal-type churches, for the poor. Practically, as is often pointed out (e.g. Hastings 1999b:367; Martin 1990:70), both liberation theology and Pentecostal concern centre around the poor and poverty, although they appear to offer very different solutions. At the surface level, liberation theology encourages the church to take 'the option for the poor' by working with the poor in the base communities. It organizes to bring about structural change in society. In Pentecostal churches, on the other hand, the poor themselves are encouraged to pursue healing and wealth by means of prayer and personal transformation. The quip, 'when the Catholic Church opted for the poor, the poor opted for the Pentecostals' is only partly true because most of the poor remain Catholic. Digging a little deeper, the base community and Pentecostal approaches to poverty appear not so very far apart. The base communities' struggle to change social structures also results in personal transformation and spiritual growth. Conversely, joining a Pentecostal church is generally linked to upward social mobility, and many Latin American Pentecostal-type churches are deeply involved in community care and even political action. Hastings (1999b:367) feared that by undermining the base community movement, the Catholic Church in Latin America may have been 'throwing away the only instrument with which 'it could hold the Protestant advance at bay'. The third shared area is a theological interest in the Holy Spirit. Both liberation theology and Pentecostalism understand themselves as movements of the Spirit. Pike (2002:451, 463) comments that the Holy Spirit only surfaces in Latin America in 'periods of popular millennialist frenzy', of which liberation was one and Pentecostal revivals could be considered another. In the key biblical text of liberation theology, Jesus declares, '[T]he Spirit of the Lord [Holy Spirit] is upon me because he has anointed me to proclaim good news to the poor' (Luke 4:18). Pentecostalism and liberation theology may therefore be regarded as 'two manifestations of the work of the Holy Spirit for the renewal of the church' (Sepúlveda 1993). In Brazil, for example, Pentecostalism appears as 'a form of base community plus the therapeutic recourse to the Spirit found in Umbanda' (Martin 1990:60). Liberation theology also had a – largely unrealized – potential to tap into the popular religiosity of the Latin American poor (Hastings 1999b:367).

The current popularity of the Evangélicos may not be permanent. Many of the converts are only in their teens and disaffiliation may be very high – up to 68 per cent in Mexico (Gooren 2007). Protestantism, Evangelicalism and Pentecostalism are not the only alternatives to Catholicism on offer to Latin Americans these days. Christianity has further diversified with the recent arrival of Orthodox migrants from West Asia, who have introduced their ancient form of Christianity into Chile and other countries. But less superficially, in the decades since 1950, Todd Hartch (2014) finds that Latin American Christianity has been 'dramatically transformed'. He argues that, despite poor ecumenical relations, there has been 'a strange symbiosis' between Catholic and Evangélicos in Latin America that has stimulated the rebirth of Catholicism (2–3).

Christians in pluralizing societies

Although the proportion of Christians declined only slightly over the last century (from 95 to 92 per cent) there has been a further 'transformation of the religious field' in Latin America (Míguez 1999:222). Prokopy and Smith (1999) argue that 'Latin America is experiencing a genuine and profound pluralization of faith' that includes non-Christian religions. Although Catholic leaders may imply that before the arrival of Protestants Latin America was Roman Catholic, there were always other religious alternatives among the indigenous people (2). Although allegiance to indigenous religions has continued to decline overall, there are areas of revival: for example, traditional Mayan ceremonies are performed in Guatemala. In addition, there are many African-derived religions, especially in Brazil and the Caribbean. Some of these have a Roman Catholic component, including Santería in Cuba and Vodou in Haiti, and others incorporate a Protestant component, such as Baptist Shouters (Trinidad) and Kuminia (Jamaica) (Vernooij 2007; Bisnauth 1996). Migrants from South Asia brought Islam and Hinduism with them to Guyana and Suriname.. Japanese immigrants to Peru and Brazil introduced Buddhism there, and this now has several million adherents not of Japanese descent. After the Second World War, many Jews found sanctuary in Latin America and the Caribbean, and the Baha'i faith has grown rapidly as a result of missionary work. Added to this mix are other Christian-derived groups such as Mormons and Jehovah's Witnesses. Prokopy and Smith (1999) paint a picture of religious variety quite different from what is often assumed in discussion of 'the only Catholic continent'.

Caribbean case study

The most religiously diverse region is the Caribbean, together with Suriname and Guyana. In the Caribbean, not only are there African religions but also Asian religious influences through substantial Indian and Chinese communities whose presence goes back to colonial times. There are also examples of the overlapping of religious practices, such as in Trinidad, where the churches worship alongside a quarter of the population who are mostly Hindu. These 'East Indians' and the (approximately 30 per cent) Roman Catholic population, which includes a wide range of ethnicities, venerate the same shrine in Siparia. The Holy Shepherdess (La Divina Pastora), or Suparee Ke Mai (an expression of Mother Kali), is understood by both groups to grant favours, guide and protect (Boodoo 2000a). Nevertheless, 84 per cent of people in the Caribbean define themselves as Christians. African-derived religions account for about 7 per cent and the others together less than 3 per cent.

Jamaica is central to the Christian culture of the Anglophone Caribbean, or former British West Indies, and provides a case study in the evangelization of the Caribbean and its global impact. More than 90 per cent of the people of Jamaica, which was seized by Britain in 1655 and finally declared independent in 1962, are of West African descent. The island could be described as having three types of Christian church: colonial, Zion revivalist and Pentecostal (Austin-Broos 2001), each representing a different period of reception. The colonial period resulted in Catholic, Baptist, Anglican, Methodist and Seventh-Day Adventist churches but not all of these were started by the colonizers. The Baptist church originated from the work begun in 1783 by George Lisle, a freed slave from the US state of Virginia, who founded the Ethiopian Baptist Church. It incorporated aspects of African tradition and two of its leaders instigated uprisings against British rule in 1831 and 1865. The Native Baptists had their own overseas missionary society from 1842, which sent missionaries mainly to West Africa and spread the message of freedom.

The Great Revival in Jamaica in 1860–61 was stimulated by the trans-Atlantic, white-led Moody and Sankey revival but it led to the formation of independent and indigenous churches dealing with spirit possession and offering healing, such as Revival Zion. The Revivalists drew on the biblical references to Ethiopia and prophesied the end of white power. The cult of Rastafari emerged from the same poor class of Jamaican society as the Revivalists and inherited their combination of religion and African nationalism. They looked on Haile Selassi, crowned as emperor of Ethiopia (Abyssinia) in 1930, as their king (and not the British monarch) and also the black messiah, who would deliver from oppression all people of African descent. They saw Ethiopia as the promised land and regarded the black nationalist and pan-Africanist Marcus Garvey (1887–1940), who grew up in Jamaica, as a prophet (Erskine 2005). Caribbean theologians in the region and in diaspora have seen Rastafarianism as a challenge to develop a Black theology (e.g. Beckford 1998).

As British power dwindled, North American influence grew in Jamaica and by the 1950s the dominant popular religion in Jamaica was US-derived Pentecostalism. The main denominations were all US-based: the New Testament Church of God, the Church of God of Prophecy and the United Pentecostal Church (Austin-Broos 1997). The US connections did not make these churches any less Jamaican. Indeed Diane Austin-Broos (2001:157–8) argues that Jamaicans used this new form of religion to 'circumvent the colonial religious order'. Moreover, Jamaicans 'did not need "Americans" to tell them about a spirit-filled world' (149); they have their own experience of the Spirit and may be critical of aspects of the North American Pentecostal denominations to which they belong. These Pentecostal churches all now have a strong presence among the Caribbean diaspora in other parts of the world. In the case of the Church of God of Prophecy, at least, it was Jamaicans who were the primary missionaries in the expansion to Britain (150–2). Not only Pentecostal churches but also many other forms of Caribbean Christianity have spread worldwide because of extensive migration and the creation of diasporas, especially around the Atlantic (Schmidt 2008; Reid-Salmon 2008).

The Bible does not belong to any one of the Caribbean religious communities (Gossai and Murrell 2000) but Rastafarians particularly have 'made the Bible an instrument for black dignity, pride, and hope in the God of the future' (Murrell 2000:304). Post-independence there was as experiment in 'decolonizing theology' (Erskine 1981) to create a 'Caribbean theology' (Williams 1994), encouraged by EATWOT and engaged in across the former mission churches (Protestant and Catholic). As part of the development of postcolonial theory, the Bible, which had been used by the colonizers to justify their oppression, was subjected to a re-reading by the emancipated. This was an 'emancipation from below' to complement the 'emancipation from above' which freed slaves at different periods in the nineteenth century but kept populations still bound into the cultural, racial and economic systems with the former powers (Davis 1990:135–9). New sources for theological method from shared musical cultures were suggested, such as calypso and reggae (Mulrain 2004). The method that has come to the fore in Caribbean theology is not the inculturation method inspired by Garveyite pan-Africanism (there are too many cultures for coherent theological development) or the liberation theologies of Latin America (politically the Caribbean is more closely integrated with North America) but using the common denominator of the Caribbean history of slavery, colonization and forced migrations (Boodoo 2000b; Williams 1994:62–5) and developing intercultural and inter-religious dialogue (Jagessar 2007).

Catholic response to pluralism

The Catholic Church has been alarmed by its decline in membership and it has struggled to redefine its role now that 'Latin American Christians no longer recognize only one church as the font of charisma' and the Catholic Church is becoming one denomination among others (Pike 2002:472; Martin 2002:21). The church sees the rise of the Evangélicos as a regional threat. Since 1955, popes have warned about the 'mortal danger' of the advance of 'sects' – a term for all non-Catholic religious groups – in Latin America, comparing them to sheep-stealing predators (Gill 1999:19). In his exhortation to the bishops of America following the Special Assembly for America of the Synod of Bishops held in the Vatican in 1997, John Paul II urged a 'thorough study to ascertain why many Catholics leave the Church' and join 'sects' (*Ecclesia in America* 1999:para. 73). The Catholic Church responded to its new situation in two main ways: first by seeking government assistance in dealing with the 'competition' and, second, by 'institutional restructuring to become more efficient at maintaining parishioners and converting nominal Catholics into active participants in the faith' (Gill 1999:17–18).

The government assistance sought by the church included restricting the entry of foreign missionaries, limiting registration for religious groups and properties and banning groups deemed to be aggressive (Freston 2001:193–4). The church

Figure 5.4 Procession for the feast of Our Lady of Carmo (Carmel) at night in the Bela Vista neighbourhood of São Paulo, Brazil, 20 July 2014. Image: iStock.

used its historic privileges to pressure governments and lobby for financial concessions. However, with the increased numbers, the rise of democracy and therefore the political power of the 'sects', the room for tactical manoeuvre was very limited (Gill 1999:24–9). More constructively, the church increased the numbers of parishes and dioceses, continued to encourage lay participation and utilize congregational gifts, and it had considerable success at increasing clergy recruitment. Re-establishing hierarchical control over the base communities can also be seen as part of this restructuring. Alongside this the church encouraged the growth of charismatic groups and popular religiosity (Gill 1999:30–5). From the point of view of the church, what was going on was a revision of pastoral policy to offer faithful 'more personalized religious care', strengthen the 'structures of communion and mission' and 'make the most of the evangelizing possibilities of a purified popular religiosity' as part of the 'new evangelization' but sceptics saw it as encouraging the faithful away from political activities (John Paul II, *Ecclesia in America* 1999:para. 73; Gill 1999:29). The growth in the continent of Opus Dei and other conservative networks of clergy and laity also attracted the attention of commentators. Opus Dei was founded in 1928 in Spain to strengthen the faith of believers and its application to their everyday life. Many of the prelates brought in as conservatives to counter liberation theology were also members of this international organization, which emphasizes personal piety and submission to the hierarchy in matters of faith. However, Opus Dei is also part of the Catholic answer to prosperity teaching. Traditional Catholicism has focused on poverty as the context for faith, but Opus Dei appeals to the successful and to the entrepreneur; it operates mainly through courses and retreats for personal development: it replaces the 'Christian knight' with the 'godly businessman' (Pike 2002:471). Cultivating a living and personal faith in terms of both personal holiness and social service was the opening theme of John Paul II's *Ecclesia in America* (1999), which emphasized a spiritual life of conversion and guidance by the Holy Spirit alongside the traditional sacraments of Catholicism.

Despite growing involvement by Evangélicos in politics and society, it is the Catholic Church which has by far the greatest social reach. CELAM V, which took place in May 2007 at Aparecida in Brazil, expressed a series of hopes for church and society that indicate the social agenda of the church in contemporary Latin America (CELAM website). Many of these were on the agenda of all churches worldwide at the time, such as commitments to dialogue with other churches and religions, to reconciliation and to stewardship of creation. More particular to the Latin American context were commitments to 'value and respect our Indigenous and Afro-American people' and to the integration of the peoples of Latin America and the Caribbean. Equally prominent among the resolutions of CELAM V were the intention 'to impel the active participation of women in society and in the Church' and 'to strengthen with audacity' the church's ministries in support of the family and respect of life (CELAM website). The juxtaposition of these last two 'hopes', which are often seen to work against one another, shows where the main controversy in the Catholic Church lies. From an external point of view, the Catholic Church has certainly intervened politically in a way which is detrimental to feminist and sexual diversity movements, for example, in Argentina in the same-sex marriage debate in 2010 (Vaggione 2015). Many Catholics and Evangélicos take a similar stand against abortion and for traditional gender roles, sexual relations and family structures but they differ on divorce. The unacceptability of divorce for women in traditional society could explain why there is a disproportionate number of divorced women in Pentecostal churches (Mariz and Mafra 1999:207). In general, the strength of feeling aroused by these issues is because they raise fundamental questions about machismo.

Although the overwhelming majority of Latin Americans are religious, both Catholic and Protestant leaders are worried about secularization in society as faith becomes privatized – as shown by the disregard of the church's moral teaching – and individualized – as the online movement 'Catholic on my own' (*Católico a mi manera*) suggests. Part of the agenda of the new evangelization is to counteract this. CELAM V placed a strong emphasis on the Church's mission to proclaim Jesus Christ as 'the Way, the Truth and the Life' vigorously and enthusiastically with Mary the mother of Jesus as the model (CELAM V 2007:para. 362). The renewed Catholic Church is likely to continue to be very significant for all the Americas, and it may yet be that 'the religiosity of the masses' will turn back to it (Hastings 1999b:367). Latin America and the Caribbean include nearly half of the world's Catholics and have an indigenized expression of the faith that has had an impact on Catholicism worldwide, especially through liberation theology, the cult of the Virgin of Guadalupe, migration – especially to North America, and a growing world mission movement. Latin American Catholics serve in many older missionary organizations originating in Europe but increasingly they are founding their own. The first Latin American Missionary Congress (COMLA) was held in 1977 and Catholic missionaries *ad gentes* were estimated as more than four thousand by 2002 (Hartch 2014:193–205). The most well-known migrant and missionary from Latin America is the current pope. The appointment of Francis as bishop of Rome – the first pope from outside Europe in fifteen hundred years – is a sign of the strength and prestige of Latin American Catholicism and its importance for the future of the world church.

Summary

The Iberian conquistadors and the priests who supported them were mandated both to exploit and to Christianize the land and native peoples of Central and South America, Mexico and the Caribbean, Latinizing them according to the feudal, militarized pattern of churches in Spain and Portugal. While realizing their goals of wealth and faith, they crushed those of the Indians, decimated their populations and destroyed their societies; only a few defended them. Nevertheless aspects of the spirituality of the indigenous people live on in the practices of Latin American Catholicism. The Virgin of Guadalupe became a powerful symbol of indigenous faith, and in the veneration of Mary an aspect of the traditional reverence for the feminine was retained, which can be used to subvert the cult of machismo. Machismo is blamed for many of the social ills of Latin America, encourages an attitude of marianismo (which feminists challenge by rereading the biblical stories of Mary) and is also blamed for some aspects of Latin American Catholicism such as the perennial shortage of priests. In the new society in which peoples of European descent were ranked above Native Americans, and in which Africans were enslaved, the Latin Church established a close relationship with the elite. The power of the church was challenged in different countries after the weakening of the power of Spain and Portugal and political independence. New religious movements such as Protestantism, Pentecostalism and Rastafarianism were used to support emancipation and nationalist causes.

Nevertheless, in the mid-twentieth century it was still the case that the Catholic Church tended to support the powerful. This was challenged by the advent of liberation theology in the 1970s, which declared God to be on the side of the poor and held up the ideal of social justice. Brought about by a combination of the bishops' attendance at the Second Vatican Council and the priests' conscientization along with that of many grassroots Christians in 'base communities', liberation theology changed the church (although not structurally) and spread worldwide. Christians campaigned for human rights, and in most cases the church supported the people against military dictatorships. The rise during the twentieth century of the Evangélicos challenged the near religious monopoly of the Catholic Church. Evangélicos are mainly Pentecostals. Their popularity is variously explained as due to superficial evangelization, gradual Anglicization, political interference from North America or a protest against Catholicism, but it is also due to the Pentecostal experience of power over evil and the hope of a new life. The Vatican hierarchy was unsettled by the power of the base communities, the use of Marxist analysis and other aspects of the new theology, and the growth of Pentecostalism. The more conservative bishops it appointed have defended the traditional status of the church, opposed abortion and defended traditional feminine roles. There has also been some restructuring to be closer to the people and meet some of the needs indicated by the turn to Pentecostalism by encouraging popular religion under the church's umbrella. Not only is Christianity more plural, in many parts of Latin America there is growing religious plurality. There are religions derived from the African traditions of the slaves and Asian religions brought mainly by migration. The Caribbean is the most diverse. Its peoples have long exhibited a hybridity of cultures and religions. Christians there have developed distinctive churches and theological responses that use the common denominator of the Caribbean history of slavery, colonization and forced migrations.

Study questions and further readings

- Discuss the relationship of indigenous spirituality with Roman Catholicism in Latin America.
- To what extent was the Catholic Church complicit in the suffering that befell the Native Americans?
- Analyse the context that led to the rise of the liberation theology in Latin America and assess the movement's global impact.
- Assess the role the Catholic Church has played in the politics of Latin America since independence.
- Discuss the reason for the rapid growth of the *Evangélicos* and its implications for the Catholic Church in Latin America.
- What are some of the characteristics of Caribbean Christian experience, and how does Christianity there relate to churches in North America and in Europe?

Austin-Broos, D. (1997), *Jamaica Genesis*. Chicago: University of Chicago.

Freston, P. (2001), *Evangelicals and Politics in Asia, Africa and Latin America*. Cambridge: Cambridge University.

Gutiérrez, G. (1993[1992]), *Las Casas*, trans. Robert R. Barr. Maryknoll, NY: Orbis.

Hartch, T. (2014), *The Rebirth of Latin American Christianity*. Oxford: Oxford University.

Klaiber, J. (1998), *The Church, Dictatorships, and Democracy in Latin America*. Maryknoll, NY: Orbis.

Tombs, D. (2002), *Latin American Liberation Theology*. Leiden: Brill.

Wiarda, H. J. (2001), *The Soul of Latin America*. New Haven, CT: Yale Divinity.

6

North American Christianities

Chapter Outline

The majority of the population of North America, which we take as the United States of America and Canada, is descended from migrations in the past five centuries from many different parts of the world. Nevertheless, Christianity in many varied forms is the shared religion of most of them, including many Native Americans and others of non-European descent. In the United States particularly Christianity, especially the dominant Evangelicalism, has a high profile in public life. But US Christianity is highly complex, with strong Roman Catholic, African American and liberal Protestant components, which also have continuing links to their countries of origin. Christianity in North America reflects North American enterprise and experience and it draws on the many traditions that have been introduced into the continent. In terms of world Christianity, developments in the United States particularly are extremely influential because of its status as the greatest global power, its wealth, its cultural influence and its global mission movements, and so we shall concentrate our attention there, returning to Canada at the end of the chapter.

ARCTIC OCEAN
GREENLAND
ALASKA
YUKON
NORTHWEST TERRITORIES
NUNAVUT
LABRADOR
CANADA
ALBERTA
BRITISH COLUMBIA
MANITOBA
SASKATCHEWAN
QUEBEC
NEWFOUNDLAND
PRINCE EDWARD ISLAND
ONTARIO
NEW BRUNSWICK
NOVA SCOTIA
PACIFIC OCEAN
WASHINGTON
OREGON
MONTANA
NORTH DAKOTA
IDAHO
MINNESOTA
VERMONT
MAINE
NEW HAMPSHIRE
NEW YORK
MASSACHUSETTS
RHODE ISLAND
SOUTH DAKOTA
WISCONSIN
MICHIGAN
CONNECTICUT
WYOMING
NEBRASKA
IOWA
PENNSYLVANIA
NEW JERSEY
NEVADA
UTAH
ILLINOIS
OHIO
DELAWARE
CALIFORNIA
COLORADO
INDIANA
WEST VIRGINIA
MARYLAND
KANSAS
MISSOURI
KENTUCKY
VIRGINIA
ATLANTIC OCEAN
NORTH CAROLINA
UNITED STATES
TENNESSEE
ARIZONA
NEW MEXICO
OKLAHOMA
ARKANSAS
SOUTH CAROLINA
GEORGIA
MISSISSIPPI
ALABAMA
TEXAS
LOUISIANA
FLORIDA
THE BAHAMAS
NASSAU
MEXICO
HAVANA
CUBA
HAITI
PORT-AU-PRINCE
SANTO DOMINGO
JAMAICA
KINGSTON
BELIZE
GUATEMALA
HONDURAS
NICARAGUA

US Christianity: Popular and plural

At the beginning of the twenty-first century, roughly nine out of ten US Americans believed in God, six out of ten belonged to a religious organization and four out of ten were at worship on Sunday (Marty 2002:396). Classic secularization theories of religion which predicted the decline of religious adherence with modernization, on the basis that religion is a response to some form of deprivation or 'existential insecurity', have had to be revised, beginning with the US case (Berger 1970). The continued health of religion in the United States is explained in two main ways: first,

Figure 6.1 A man carries a New Testament text about salvation through the crowd celebrating Mardi Gras (Shrove Tuesday) on Bourbon Street in New Orleans, Louisiana, USA, 8 February 2013. Image: iStock.

in 'postmodern' US society the role of religion has changed from being a survival mechanism for people facing uncertainty to a means of self-expression (Norris and Inglehart 2004). This is evidenced by the growth of New Age or 'body, mind and spirit', and also by the use of therapies of 'inner healing' in Christian ministry. The second suggestion is that the increase of religious pluralism and freedom of religion in the United States leads to greater quality of religious supply and therefore higher demand for religious services (Stark and Finke 2000).

There are also demographic reasons which contribute to explaining why the religious picture in the United States is markedly different from that of Western Europe and of most other developed nations. The United States has a growing population; it is a younger nation and the proportion of (first-generation) immigrants continues to be high. Since the 1960s, more relaxed immigration controls have led to the 'browning' of the US population and of its churches. According to US Census Bureau figures from 2010, black or African Americans are 14 per cent of the population, but they are now overtaken by Hispanics (of different races; 16 per cent); the proportion of Asians (mainly East Asians) is the fastest growing, but Native Americans are less than 1 per cent of the population. A high level of immigration does not necessarily mean an increase in religious diversity; on the contrary, it may be increasing America's levels of Christian adherence because most immigrants to the United States are Christians before they arrive, or become so after arrival (Jenkins 2002:103–5). The fact that the United States is perceived as a Christian nation may be a major pull factor for migrants, and being a Christian is an advantage for integration into American society. Being a Christian may also be a push factor from countries where Christians face discrimination or persecution (Phan 2003a:230). Therefore there is less religious plurality in the United States than its racial diversity might suggest. According to the Pew Research Centre in 2015 only about 6 per cent of the population adheres to non-Christian religions, which is a smaller proportion than in Europe and in many African and Asian nations. Between 70 and 80 per cent of US Americans are Christians and many actively so.

But although there is relatively little religious plurality in the United States, Christian pluralism began there. The European development of North America was led by the conquistadors of Spain, followed by French traders, Dutch merchants and British entrepreneurs, all backed by military force. The Spanish, moving up from the Caribbean and Mexico, failed to take Florida in the sixteenth century but established towns and Franciscan missions to the 'Indians' from 1610 in what are now New Mexico, Texas and Arizona. In the eighteenth century, the Spanish began to colonize California, and under Junípero Serra in the eighteenth century a chain of Franciscan missions was established up the west coast from the tip of lower California (now part of Mexico) northwards as far as San Francisco. Like San Francisco, many Californian cities take their names from these missions, including San Diego, Santa Barbara, Santa Monica and Los Angeles. The French began to explore Newfoundland in the early sixteenth century and by the end of the seventeenth they had established small Catholic colonies in Quebec. French Jesuits, led by Jean de Brébeuf, spread out from there and attempted to reach the Hurons and Iroquois, who were fighting each other. Their work resulted in the baptism in 1676 of Kateri Tekakwitha, a young Mohawk woman whose piety resulted in her canonization by Pope Benedict in 2012 – the only native North American yet honoured in this way. The Jesuits continued their exploration and mission work, which was comparatively sympathetic to native cultures, down the Mississippi valley. Settlers followed and the town of New Orleans was established in 1718 (Gaustad and Schmidt 2002:15–29).

Not only the Catholic but also the Protestant powers felt an obligation to spread their faith to the native population. The Protestants had the added incentive to prove that the territory did not belong by papal right to Catholics and that it was rather Protestants who were called extend the faith to the Americas. Anglican clergymen Richard Hakluyt made a theological and nationalistic case to Queen Elizabeth I for England to establish settlements and towns, rather than trading posts and forts, and that these would be a more effective way to convert the 'Indians' (Gaustad and Schmidt 2002:31–6). The earliest successful settlement in North America was actually the English one at Jamestown, Virginia, founded in 1607, of which Hakluyt was named honorary rector. Little outreach to the Indians was done there but in New England John Eliot learnt native languages, translated the Bible and established towns of 'praying Indians'. The Scottish Puritan David Brainerd became the best-known missionary to the Native Americans because of his journal, which documented his work among the Lenape or Delaware Indians before his early death from tuberculosis in 1747. The Church of England became the established religion of the new state of Virginia and in the early eighteenth century clergy were sent out to pastor the colonists by the Englishman Thomas Bray's Society for the Propagation of the Gospel (SPG). John Wesley, later famous as the founder of Methodism, was an SPG missionary in the state of Georgia in the mid-1730s (O'Connor 2000).

Many of the European migrants who populated North America from the mid-sixteenth century onwards were fleeing the 'religious' wars following the Reformation. They came to the 'new world' to create new societies where they expected to be able to practise their faith as they chose. By the eighteenth century there was a patchwork of religious enclaves across the continent: the Southeastern and Southwestern parts of North America were Spanish Catholic; the centre of the continent from the Mississippi Delta to Western Canada was French Catholic; Maryland was English Catholic; Virginia and Carolina were Anglican; the New England states mostly followed the Puritan model; and the native peoples of what was later to become the state of Alaska were being evangelized by the Russian Orthodox Church (Oleksa 1992). However, Rhode Island and the 'middle colonies' of New York, New Jersey, Delaware and Pennsylvania welcomed various dissenting groups.

When the thirteen colonies rebelled against British rule and formed the United States of America in 1776, the establishment of any one national church was inconceivable and the de facto religious plurality of the new nation meant that the federal government was forced to be 'friendly but officially neutral' toward each (Williams 1990:165). Furthermore, since for many Americans the War of Independence was a struggle for freedom from the Church of England as much as from the British crown, they fiercely defended their right to worship, or not worship, without state interference. So it was agreed in the First Amendment to the Constitution that federal government would 'make no law respecting an establishment of religion, or prohibiting the free exercise thereof', and in the Sixth Amendment that no religious tests should be applied for appointment to public office. It is true that this secular constitution, which makes no invocation of God at all, was influenced by the Enlightenment reasoning of Thomas Jefferson and other political leaders of the time. But the pattern of church–state relations was also that of the dominant religious group among the settlers, the Puritans – as observed by the French political philosopher Alexis de Tocqueville. They separated the true church from the state and saw it as a community entered into by covenant rather than by birth. 'Church' referred primarily to one local congregation, whose life was free from state interference. However, each adult male member was morally responsible not only for his own conduct but also to purify society. So the church, though distinct from the state, was not separate from the society, and Puritans exercised their full voting and political rights. None of the new states retained established churches and all the churches, including the Catholic Church, had to restructure themselves as voluntary bodies by instituting synods and other bodies for decision-making.

In the creation of the United States, the toleration of a variety of Christian denominations and the separation of church and state were brought about of necessity. Nevertheless, the United States was, and remains, overwhelmingly Christian, and the primary expression of this plurality was a variety of Protestant 'denominations'. The extent and meaning of religious freedom in the United States remain a subject of debate. Conservative Christians argue that the founding fathers did not envisage America as anything other than a Protestant republic (i.e. a Christian nation without an established church) and were not advocates of religious pluralism. However, US Roman Catholics, and later Jews, challenged this perception, and in the twentieth century secularists and more liberal Christians have used the constitution to argue for full equality of treatment of all religious groups and total separation of the religions from political and civic life. The result is paradoxical. In the 1960s, corporate prayer and religious symbols were banned in public schools but they may be permissible in other public gatherings and places. On the other hand, the Christian religiosity of the overwhelming majority of Americans means that in the twenty-first century politicians of both main parties use biblical imagery and religious rhetoric to appeal for the popular vote.

Another aspect of the more-or-less level playing field created for Protestant churches in the United States was the possibility of 'both cooperation and competition' with one another (Mullin 1999:431). It is true that 'ecumenism' is not a term much used in American churches. Few of the large Evangelical denominations have joined the World Council of Churches (WCC), for example, partly because of its association in their minds with theological liberalism and dialogue with communism, which they oppose, but also because its desire for church unity is interpreted to mean the formation of a single world church and the kind of ecclesiastical imperialism against which the first US Americans fought. However, American Evangelicals have formed their own organizations to work together across denominational lines in evangelism, revival, social reform and world mission. At the same time, disestablishment coupled with a capitalist mindset created a free market of churches. While many denominations continue to draw most of their membership through their historic roots in different ethnic communities, others vie with one another for members. In a climate of religious freedom, where people are not necessarily bound to a particular faith by their birth family, community or upbringing, and which also encourages conversion, individuals are urged to make a choice about where they worship. Both in attitude and in law, churches and Christian organizations in the United States operate more as businesses than as social service organizations (as in Europe), and there is often a close relationship between business and religion, exemplified in organizations like the (Pentecostal) Full Gospel Businessmen's Fellowship and the (Catholic) Opus Dei. In this milieu, denominationalism is not seen as a failure of Christian unity, to be ashamed of, but as an opportunity for church growth. The supply-side theory that competition increases demand is in evidence where church buildings of different denominations are found on opposite corners of street blocks with competing slogans and enticing offers of services. Advertising of churches in the media is common and the successful pastor is popularly perceived as one who has a large congregation. Church growth and evangelism, in the sense of inviting and persuading people to join the faith, are recognized areas of the theological curriculum in many seminaries. Material drawn from sales and advertising, and from group dynamics, is taught to clergy in training.

Martin Marty (2002) recognizes a common 'American religion', which is chiefly preoccupied by the question of 'the one and the many'. On the one hand, the need for national unity has led, in the absence of an established religious tradition, to the creation of a single 'civil religion' or the evocation of a perceived shared Christian – or post–Second World War 'Judaeo-Christian' – tradition. On the other hand, the initial variety of denominations has continued to increase. The largest single denomination by far is the Roman Catholic Church, although this unity masks a great deal of ethnic and organizational diversity. The largest Protestant denominations are Southern Baptist, Methodist and Lutheran. Other large groupings are Congregational (Puritan, Churches of Christ), Episcopal (Anglican), Presbyterian (Reformed) and Pentecostal but these are split into smaller denominations. Orthodox churches are also represented but in many different ethnic forms. Most have organized themselves into dioceses subordinate to their original 'mother church', although during the Cold War the Russian Churches granted autocephalous status to the 'Orthodox Church of America'. This has led to a highly complex situation in which the Orthodox presence is fragmented, not much visible and seen as foreign. Orthodox bishops in the United States began to meet from the 1960s but the goal of a unified national Orthodox church is as far away as ever due to the continuing diversification of the churches, which now include Oriental as well as Eastern Orthodox (Krindatch and Erickson 2014). Another quarter or so of US Christians worship in thousands of independent local congregations, some loosely federated. This emphasis on the local congregation is a feature of the US church scene. It has been emphasized by Puritans (Congregationalists), Mennonites (Anabaptists) and especially Baptists. Mormons make up a significant marginal form of Christianity, especially concentrated in the state of Utah (Davies 2003). Jehovah's Witnesses are another significant marginal group but the Seventh-Day Adventists, who were once sectarian, are no longer so, having now joined themselves to historical Protestantism.

The Evangelical consensus

The first European settlers saw themselves as participating in a new exodus from oppression in Europe and elected to a new life in the 'promised land'. The chief challenge they encountered was not the Native American peoples, who were few and far between and relatively easily pushed westward, but the forces of nature in what appeared to be a wild landscape. The first task of the settlers was to tame the land and construct 'the architecture of civilization' (Mullin 1999:416). The Puritans proved to be the most successful and dynamic Christian force in the colonies, and as the United States extended westwards they founded new towns on the plain and simple New England model. In the 'New England Way', the church was created 'not by legislative action from above but by contractual agreement from below' as people covenanted together to form a congregation (Gaustad and Schmidt 2002:53). Their sense of personal responsibility and equality before God carried beyond the church into the society. The Bible was the Puritans' only basis of religious authority; its interpretation was the centre of worship and its study was the duty of all members not just the clergy. They considered every part of it as 'the Word of God', and relevant for instruction and guidance. From their reading of the Old Testament particularly they derived an emphasis on the sovereignty of God over all areas of life, and also a strong work ethic, which the early sociologist Max Weber (1930[1905]) argued contributed to the growth of capitalism. Puritans regarded the Christian community as the new Israel of God, with a collective mission to be a 'city set on a hill' as witness of God's kingdom to all the surrounding people. The faith, solidarity and discipline of these 'commonwealths' contributed to the survival of Puritan communities in the hostile natural environment they called, with biblical resonance, the 'wilderness'. The Puritans themselves saw their success as a sign that God had chosen them to build 'a city set on a hill', a model Christian society. Their custom of thanksgiving for God's protection and provision developed into Thanksgiving Day, a national annual holiday, and the notion of being chosen by God for the sake of the world became part of the later rhetoric of US American nationalism.

The Puritan concepts of religious conversion and revival resonate in US American Christianity today. Church membership depended on conversion, which was a personal crisis, demanding an awareness of sin, then an intense period of introspection and repentance, which would be followed by 'new birth', an experience of personal transformation manifested in a changed and moral life. This pattern of traumatic personal experience as the route to church membership, while meaningful for the first generation of settlers, proved unsustainable in the long term. Nevertheless, many hoped to revive the old way and saw a pattern in God's dealings with his people of the decline of piety followed by renewal. A 'massive religious revival' (Williams 1990:127) did indeed break out in the 1730s and 1740s that combined Puritan piety with Methodist enthusiasm in the 'Great Awakening', which 'reshaped the religious topography of Protestant North America' (Mullin 1999:423). The main catalyst for the revival was George Whitefield, the English Methodist and associate of John Wesley, whose preaching stirred the emotions and reduced his congregations to tears. Whitefield has been seen as 'America's first celebrity' (Williams 1990:130), and few of the colonists were unaware of, or unaffected by, his preaching. Jonathan Edwards, the Puritan who became the chief mover and theological interpreter of the Awakening, saw it as a 'surprising work of God' by the Holy Spirit, which he suggested was a sign that the United States had a special place in God's plan. Edwards reformulated Puritan doctrine to highlight conversion – now a more momentary experience – and bypass the process of church membership, focusing on the relationship of the individual with God. In his preaching he appealed to the emotions through sensual images, rather than to the mind, enabling the participation of a broad swath of American society, including young people, women and those who were less confident in the English language, in the revival.

The revival added Methodism to the Christian denominations in America and split the Puritans or Congregationalists, resulting in the growth of Unitarianism – a more esoteric spirituality of intellectuals seeking a more scientific faith because they were troubled by traditional doctrines of the divinity of Christ and the Trinity. Others who retained traditional doctrines nevertheless moved away from the old covenant theology towards individualism, signified by adult baptism. They swelled the ranks of the American Baptists, whose first church was founded by Roger Williams in Rhode Island in 1638. Baptist churches spread rapidly, especially in the colonial South, weakening the Anglican churches there. The Awakening unified different classes, colonies and languages in a common popular form of Christianity based on individual conversion and oriented towards mission, which broadened into a 'civil millennialism' – an expectation of the establishment of liberty and freedom in North America (Mullin 1999:425). Those touched by the Awakening gained an American identity with a sense of 'manifest destiny'. They saw themselves as independent individuals accountable only to God and his Word for their behaviour, and so resisted institutional authority – whether of state or church – in which their views were not represented. In the long term the revival may be said to have stirred anti-intellectualism (423) but its usurping of traditional society in the name of the Holy Spirit also struck at the heart of the colonial establishment (Stout 1983:128–9). The Great Awakening added a spiritual dimension to growing nationalism and led directly to the American War of Independence, which can be seen as 'a continuation of the Revival' (Williams 1990:162).

The pioneering spirit of the first settlers was continued after the War of Independence in the expansion of the United States across the North American continent as far as the Pacific Ocean, as land was purchased or ceded to the new nation. These acquisitions also introduced new populations into the United States, particularly French and Hispanic Roman Catholics. As European settlers spread out, the task of civilizing the landscape and gathering the population into churches continued in the nineteenth century. The pattern of revival Christianity also continued. What is sometimes called the 'Second Great Awakening' (1800–40) had greatest effect in the south and west beyond the Appalachian Mountains. Large numbers of settlers camped together for interdenominational meetings, where emotions ran high. Ecstatic behaviour, such as fainting, 'jerking' and 'barking', was taken as evidence that God's Spirit was at work. The revivals seemed to 'fill a cultural and psychological void' (Mullin 1999:429) and led to the precipitous growth of Methodist and Baptist churches, which rapidly overtook the Congregationalists and Anglicans as the largest US denominations. They accommodated to aspects of modernity, particularly emphasizing education and intellectual assent to faith. Their use of lay leadership, their minimal requirements for worship and their loose ecclesiology made them 'perfectly suited' to the needs of the expanding nation (Gaustad and Schmidt 2002:166). The pre-eminent figure of the Second Awakening was Charles Finney. Instead of seeing revivals as dependent on unpredictable intervention from above, Finney believed that they were the result of individual decision and that people could be induced to convert by the right techniques. Finney popularized an activist style of religious leadership which measured success in terms of numbers and employed the latest communication techniques to achieve it. This kind of pragmatic approach to evangelistic ministry, informed by sociological and psychological method and making full use of available technology, is taken for granted in the United States today and has been spread through global Evangelicalism.

Evangelical belief in a direct and contractual relationship between the individual and his/her Maker, through the atoning sacrifice of Jesus Christ, tended to separate the material and moral/spiritual worlds: the material world, including the market economy, was seen to operate according to natural laws put in place by God, whereas the moral or spiritual realm was where God intervened for the redemption of humankind (Hilton 1988:16–17). Between 1785 and 1865, mainstream Evangelicalism supported the free-market individualism that was the basis of US economic growth, and which was linked to the Puritan ethos of independence and sense of responsibility to increase and multiply in the land God had given them. The Second Awakening heightened the sense of the potential of converted humanity to do good and encouraged optimism that individuals and society could be transformed. As in Britain, US Evangelicals were concerned to effect moral change in society by engaging in new religious, social and mission movements. These were so numerous and wide-ranging that they became known as the 'benevolent empire'. They included the first American overseas missionary organizations: the American Board of Commissioners for Foreign Missions (1810) and the American Baptist Foreign Mission Society (1814) (Shenk 2004). The Awakening further spawned new movements based on a plain reading of the Bible and expectation of the imminent return of Jesus Christ such as the Seventh-Day Adventists and other millennialist groups that are today classified as 'marginal' Christians, chiefly the Jehovah's Witnesses and the Church of the Latter-Day Saints or Mormons. 'Restorationism', which attempted to recreate the primitive perfection and unity of the early church and rejected any religious practice that could not be found in the New Testament, resulted in the Churches of Christ, Disciples of Christ and other groups. Most significantly, the Second Awakening created a broad coalition of churches which shared four characteristics: conversionism, activism, Biblicism and crucicentrism (Bebbington 1989:2–17). This 'evangelical centre' effectively 'functioned as the hegemonic religious vision of the young republic' (Mullin 1999:432).

Slave religion, the Civil War and Pentecostalism

The greatest Evangelical campaign was against the system of slavery by which tens of thousands of Africans were being transported across the Atlantic each year to work in plantations in the Americas. Finney supported abolition and by the late eighteenth century most Northern Evangelicals did the same, but white Christians in the South saw it as a threat to their way of life, which depended on the slave economy, and to their security because slaves outnumbered whites on the plantations. Northerners found it difficult to mount a convincing case that slavery was against biblical teaching, and the Southerners could find scriptural texts to support it. The main Evangelical churches – Presbyterian, Methodist and Baptist – divided in the 1840s along North–South lines, anticipating the division of the nation in the Civil War two decades later. Most churches re-united in the twentieth century but the Southern Baptist denomination remains separated from its Northern counterpart.

African American churches, of course, were not divided by the issue of slavery, which was a particular problem for white Americans especially because it was 'never merely a system of labour' but also 'a system of race control' (Mullin 1999:436). Even those who opposed slavery were rarely ready to admit people of African descent to equal status in their society; that is why many white Christians favoured the founding of colonies in Africa for freed slaves to 'return' to as a solution to the problem. White Christians who were uncomfortable about slavery tended to assuage their guilt by arguing that they could save the souls of Africans by converting them to Christianity. At the same time, the conversion of slaves was contested because baptism into the Christian community might imply emancipation. So those who evangelized slaves faced the delicate 'task of ensuring that the egalitarian tendencies of Christian instruction would remain safely within the boundaries of slave management' (Raboteau 2004:171). Slaves were disadvantaged in the white churches not only by their colour but also by the literary culture and behaviour requirements of the churches. However, the new religiosity of the 'Great' and subsequent 'Awakenings' was much more accessible to African Americans because it did not require literacy or make moral demands on church membership – such as marriage – which, under the conditions of slavery, it was not possible for them to fulfil (131). Many blacks were among those who responded to the preaching of Edwards, and by the late nineteenth century, perhaps a quarter of the swelling ranks of Baptists and Methodists were black. Moreover, the revival setting, especially in the camp meetings of the Second Great Awakening, which slaves attended with their owners, was an egalitarian one in which all were sinners before God. The emotion of the meeting appealed to black as to white, and the ecstatic behaviour and congregational involvement 'were amenable to the African religious heritage of the slaves' (149).

After emancipation, it emerged that slaves had developed their own expression of church, termed by Albert Raboteau (2004) 'the invisible institution'. Although slave religion included some African traditional religion and Muslim practices, most African Americans had no awareness of this because they had been disconnected from their heritage by transportation, separated from their families and, for the bulk of the North American slave population, born in North America. Having no other religious framework and finding the biblical message of liberation compelling, many slaves adopted the Christian religion of their masters. Because many masters forbade them from learning or practising it, slaves had to 'steal away' (the title of a popular slave song) to hold secret meetings far from the house. There they invested Christianity with a distinctive content and expressed it with 'shouting', which reflected in a general way the African heritage of singing, dancing, spirit possession and magic. Raboteau (2004) describes slave religion as necessarily clandestine, led by preachers, based on the slaves' interpretation of the Bible, expressed in African-influenced music of the 'spirituals', characterized by the theology and practice of conversion and often integrated with use of 'conjure' to deal with the spirit world. 'By the eve of the Civil War, Christianity had pervaded the slave community', and it had taken on a distinctively African American form (212).

In addition to being members of white-founded denominations, most of which were segregated into black and white at a local and even national level, freed slaves had been founding their own churches since the 1750s, when black Baptist churches were started on plantations in Virginia and South Carolina. The African Methodist Episcopal (AME) Church was founded by Richard Allen who, with others, walked out of his white-dominated church in 1816 in protest at the relegation of African Christians to seats in the gallery. To achieve better treatment for blacks, the church laid considerable emphasis on what was considered proper conduct and appearance, and it stressed literacy and education. African American Baptists eventually came together nationwide to form the National Baptist Convention, the largest of several Baptist conventions, in 1895 with the goal of 'uplifting' African Americans 'independently of white involvement'. In order to bring African Americans into the mainstream of American life, some of the leaders tried to downplay the more emotional elements of worship, but this was strongly resisted by local congregations. Both the Methodists and Baptists began extensive overseas missions – to West Africa especially – and they founded institutions of higher education. By the early twenty-first century, most African American Protestants were members of one of seven denominations, which together had between twenty and twenty-five million members (Pinn and Pinn 2002:17, 77).

When they were freed after the end of the Civil War (1861–65), African Americans flocked to join churches and hundreds of black congregations sprang up in rural areas of the South, where 90 per cent of black Americans still lived in 1900. But emancipation did not bring inclusion in mainstream society, and in the Southern states particularly, the 'Jim Crow' systems of segregation were soon in place, together with more sinister forms of harassment. Hans Baer and Merrill Singer (2002) described the life of rural black churches in the late twentieth century, which they regarded as little changed, even after the civil rights movement of the 1950s and 1960s. Since there were few trained ministers, lay (usually male) leaders maintained and operated the churches in the countryside. At the main Sunday service, the prayers, hymn singing and testimony all led up to the sermon, an emotional delivery which might last over an hour, during which the congregation responded with noises of approval or conviction. African American Christianity of that era did not stress messages of judgement, as white Evangelicals tended to do, but was more inclined to celebrate God's mercy. The churches continued to be a 'center of sociability' and 'repository of the black cultural ethos', and during the 'caste-like system' of segregation and the continuing discrimination afterwards, black churches provided a 'cathartic mechanism' for coping with a hostile world (30–40).

African Americans responded positively to the post–Civil War Holiness movement (see later), to which many of them were introduced by the preaching of black woman evangelist Amanda Berry Smith. The first black Holiness congregations developed in the late nineteenth century in the rural South. Pentecostalism began in the early twentieth century as a development within these which emphasized 'spiritual gifts'. A white, former Methodist, Charles Fox Parham became the chief proponent of the doctrine that sanctification would be followed by a 'baptism in the Spirit' or 'filling with the Spirit' like the outpouring at Pentecost described in the book of Acts and that the 'initial evidence' of this would be 'speaking in tongues' or 'the gift of tongues' (glossolalia) (Acts 2:4; 1 Cor. 12:10). Parham led a revival at Topeka, Kansas, in 1900, which led to the formation of 'Pentecostal' churches. However, most scholars of Pentecostalism today, following Walter Hollenweger (1997), regard the revival at Azusa Street, Los Angeles, in 1906 as at the heart of the movement.

The Azusa Street Revival was led by African American William Seymour, who had been excluded from Parham's classroom because of his race. Seymour's revival meetings were focused around speaking in tongues but also included testimony, song (unaccompanied) and intercessory prayer and healing. The services were multiracial, including not only black and white but also the Latino and Asian residents of Los Angeles, and soon many foreign visitors (Robeck 2006). Seymour preached a clear message that, as through Pentecost Jew and Gentile were reconciled in Christ, there should be no 'color line'. Both the interracial nature of the meetings and the intimacy between the genders created scandal at the time (Hollenweger 1972:23). But the Pentecostal churches arising out of Azusa Street were not for long able to maintain the countercultural racial and gender equality of the initial revival. White members withdrew from the largest, the Church of God in Christ, in 1914 and joined others who had split from the Christian and Missionary Alliance to form the racially segregated Assemblies of God. At first the ministry of women was also prominent, including that of Jennie Moore, who later became Seymour's wife and who led the mission after his death. When the earliest Pentecostal denominations were formed women constituted a third of the ministers, but their status was always questioned and soon legally restricted (Wacker 2001:158–76). Nevertheless, Aimee Semple McPherson, a white woman who had a nationwide healing ministry in the 1920s and 1930s, founded a Pentecostal denomination – the Church of the Foursquare Gospel – and became one of the first 'televangelists'.

Although Hollenweger highlighted the countercultural nature of early Pentecostalism, Grant Wacker (2001) points out that this was also a pragmatic movement which embraced aspects of modernity and in turn had a significant impact on US American culture. Pentecostalism is an inherently missionary movement which soon produced overseas missionaries. Many of them were self-supporting and many were single women. Although some of them went with the expectation that the gift of tongues would allow them to speak other languages without going to language school, they overcame their difficulties and pioneered away from existing denominational missions in South Africa, India, Sri Lanka, China and Japan (Anderson 2007:50–65). Pentecostal origins are complex in that revivals with similar features arose in the same period in Wales in 1904–05, Pune and the Khasi Hills in India in 1905–07, Korea in 1903–07, Oslo and Sunderland in 1907, and Valparaiso, Chile, in 1909. Some of these were connected through missionaries – white and black – and through other global networks with events at Topeka or Azusa Street, but they are otherwise independent of each other and are best explained by theories of multiple origins (Sepúlveda 1999; Wilson 1999). Some revivals resulted in the establishment of independent churches but others, such as in Korea, strengthened and indigenized mission-founded churches. Pentecostal-type revivals continued to appear throughout the twentieth century in other contexts such as Lagos, Nigeria, in 1918, in China in the 1920s and 1930s, in East Africa in the 1930s and so on.

In addition to the black churches founded by freed slaves, the Azusa Street revival in 1906 led to a black-led Pentecostal movement (Yong and Alexander 2012). The largest offshoot, the Church of God in Christ, was founded by Charles Harrison Mason, an African American. Mason introduced into worship elements of African religiosity that resonated with Old Testament sacrificial traditions (Pinn and Pinn 2002:112–19). In the South, virtually all Black Holiness churches became Pentecostal (Hardesty 2003:114). Another large black Pentecostal denomination is the Pentecostal Assemblies of the World, one of the first 'Oneness' Pentecostal churches (who baptize in the name of Jesus only, not the Trinity). The Assemblies of God, which had split from the Church of God in Christ, remained segregated until 1991. In the 'miracle of Memphis' (1994), the all-white Pentecostal Fellowship of North America was dissolved to form the Pentecostal/Charismatic Churches of North America.

The social gospel, fundamentalism and the religious right

The Civil War had been traumatic for the new nation and its aftermath had contradictory effects on white American Protestants. In the places of longer-established European settlement, and among the educated middle classes, the growing post-war stability lessened the sense of crisis that had characterized the earlier conversionist faith. Evolutionary views crept in to form what became known as the 'postmillennial' view of history. In this scenario, God's kingdom is slowly but inevitably being established on earth through human activity to improve society, until the earth becomes a fit place for Christ to reign. Leading mid-nineteenth century theologian and Congregational minister Horace Bushnell, influenced by Frederick Maurice in Britain, downplayed conversion as the way of entry into Christian life and emphasized instead nurture in a Christian society. His followers were motivated to Christianize American culture. Victory in the Civil War and the achievement of emancipation gave them confidence to think it could be achieved. However, for those, particularly in the South, who had experienced the destruction of the Civil War and whose social order had been overturned by the emancipation of the slaves, the world seemed to be getting worse rather than better. They did not share the optimism of Bushnell but felt themselves to be in a battle between the forces of good and evil. White Southern Protestants perceived as threats to their way of life not only black emancipation but also the waves of new immigrants (the population of the United States increased by nearly a third between 1860 and 1890), the growth of Roman Catholicism due to migration and annexation of territory, the rapid technological changes and urbanization due to the industrial revolution (which mainly benefitted the Northern states) and social instability caused by labour disputes.

From the mid-nineteenth century, the Protestant coalition in the United States began to diverge into two different groupings often referred to as 'liberals' and 'fundamentalists'. This polarization was due partly to the differential effects of the Civil War and also due to the impact of modernity, which had been held back by the strength of the Evangelical consensus in the antebellum period and by the urgent necessities of establishing and evangelizing the nation but now struck with greater force. The divide between these two groups and its effects on present-day US Christianity has been the object of major studies in an effort to understand contemporary religious fundamentalism (Marsden 2006) and distinguish it from broader American Evangelicalism (Marsden 1991; Noll 2001).

Millennialism

In the more liberal society of New England and the old middle colonies, which was more developed and urban, there were world-class institutions of higher learning in close contact with European scholarship, where theologians engaged with German methods of biblical criticism and with the questions raised by scientific advances. But these new ideas threatened the Evangelical orthodoxy. For example, Darwin's theory of evolution implicitly questioned the sovereignty of God and the need for life-changing conversion and the methods and findings of historical criticism seemed to undermine biblical authority, another central tenet of Evangelicalism. However, the greatest crisis for the American churches in the nineteenth century came not in the realms of intellectual discussion but in pragmatic terms as questions of salvation and mission. Around the turn of the nineteenth century, and building on Bushnell's optimistic anthropology, Walter Rauschenbusch expounded Jesus's preaching of the kingdom of God, which he was sure would transcend the kingdom of evil on earth. His 'social gospel' was based more on the 'sermon on the mount' and other teachings of the historical Jesus than on doctrines of salvation and judgement, which were questioned by modernity and by the universalist views encouraged by Unitarianism. The discovery of the suffering caused by urbanization and industrial strife led to Christian criticism of capitalist society and a wave of new initiatives for social reform. In 1908, the newly inaugurated Federal Council of Churches adopted a 'social creed' to inject 'conscience and justice and love into a Christian civilization' (Gaustad and Schmidt 2002:244). Glossing over problems of human sinfulness, Rauschenbusch was confident that unity, peace and goodwill and the 'brotherhood of man' would be the corollary of the loving 'fatherhood of God'.

Those who did not share this confidence in the future were more likely to be attracted by the revivals led by Dwight L. Moody and the hymn-writer Ira D. Sankey in the last quarter of the nineteenth century. These reflected a shift in popular Evangelical piety toward 'premillennialism', in contrast to the 'postmillennialism' of Rauschenbusch. Moody placed primary emphasis on pulling drowning souls out of the sea and into the lifeboat until Jesus Christ comes again in judgement. So although he initiated many charitable activities, he did not promote long-term causes. Like the highly successful Student Volunteer Movement for Foreign

Figure 6.2 An officer of the Salvation Army collecting for the needy before Christmas in New York, USA, 19 December 2015. Image: iStock.

Missions, which was founded as a response to one of his Bible studies, he aimed for 'the evangelization of the world in this generation'. Moody's style was not sensationalist but restrained and business-like. He was able to combine an appeal to the Reformed or Calvinist emphasis on repentance from sin with the Wesleyan or Methodist expectation of a 'second blessing' after baptism by which the believer became free of sinful impulses (Williams 1990:253). His preaching encouraged the growth of 'Holiness' movements within existing churches and the establishment of new churches, like the Church of the Nazarene, the Wesleyan Church and the Church of God. The Holiness movement appealed especially to women and the focus on prayer encouraged their ministry. In the United States one of the Holiness leaders was Phoebe Palmer; she and other influential women, like the hymn-writer Fanny Crosby, encouraged a more gentle vision of Christ as the Good Shepherd. Another characteristic Holiness belief was that infirmity, sickness or disease was due to sin or Satan (not to incorrect thinking as in the Church of Christ, Scientist, founded in the same period) and that healing should be sought through prayer, laying on of hands or anointing by the elders of the church (Jas. 5:14–15). Such belief in divine healing was often combined with a rejection of modern medicine and other remedies. There were many people looking for alternative treatments in nineteenth-century America, where medical practices were unreliable and expensive and the health of the population was poor, so divine healing flourished at camp meetings and conferences (Hardesty 2003:1–4). One of the most famous healers, A. B. Simpson, working closely with his wife Margaret, founded another Holiness denomination, the Christian and Missionary Alliance. The reliance 'on faith alone' was also expressed in the new wave of missionary movements in the late nineteenth century, the 'faith missions', following the pattern developed by James Hudson Taylor's China Inland Mission (Fiedler 1994).

A difference of eschatology, and therefore in mission imperative, lay at the heart of a growing divide between modernist and conservative Evangelicals in America in the early twentieth century. Conservatives were worried that evangelism, in the narrow sense of calling for conversion, was missing from the agenda of the social gospel. Furthermore, the social gospel itself was a threat since the values of the kingdom it propounded posed a socialist challenge to the existing political and economic order. It also suggested a radically different reading of the Bible from the Evangelical norm, one they labelled 'liberal', which prioritized the incarnate life of Jesus Christ and his social teaching over the cross and doctrines of salvation, and played down sin and judgement in the light of the love of God. Those who had lost hope for society began to displace their millennial expectations from earth onto heaven. The Moody Bible Institute popularized the Scofield Study Bible (first published in 1909), which promoted 'Dispensationalism', a doctrine based on apocalyptic passages of the Bible which added to premillennialism the belief that, on Jesus's return, true believers would be 'raptured', that is, taken up from the earth to be with Christ while the tribulations of the end times were played out. After the cleansing of the earth, the believers would return with Christ to restore the nation of Israel and set up the kingdom in Jerusalem.

Anti-intellectualism

In reaction to the social gospel, conservative Evangelicals underwent a 'great reversal' and gradually withdrew from social and political involvement (Marsden 2006). While many focused their energies instead on reviving the faith through Holiness churches, others concentrated on defending traditional Evangelical doctrine against biblical criticism. In 1909 two wealthy businessmen financed a series of twelve books written by leading conservative theologians from both sides of the Atlantic that defended what were considered to be 'the Fundamentals' of Christian faith. The writings condemned higher criticism, along with liberal theology, 'Romanism', socialism and spiritualism. They argued not only for the 'infallibility' of the Bible in matters of faith and conduct but for its 'inerrancy' – that is, its historical and scientific accuracy – as well. According to this theory, the first three chapters of Genesis must be a historically and scientifically accurate record of the beginning of the world. Taking up the title of the book series, the term 'fundamentalist' was coined in 1920 as a self-designation for anti-modern Protestants in general. The perspective became dominant in many Southern denominations. The test of true faith increasingly became belief in right doctrine, rather than moral uprightness or social work. In an attempt to defend 'true doctrine', those who joined Evangelical churches and parachurch groups were expected to sign 'statements of faith' that began by affirming the inerrancy, or at least the infallibility, of the Bible, on which the rest of the edifice of Christian belief was seen to rest.

Because the fundamentalist movement challenged freedom of thought and speech, it was staunchly opposed by intellectuals and scientists and groups such as the American Civil Liberties Union. The 'monkey trial' in 1925 of a schoolteacher charged with teaching Darwinism in school, contrary to the (recently passed) law in the state of Tennessee, publically demolished the fundamentalist case. The press represented the trial as 'a clash of two worlds' – rural and urban: 'on the one side the small town, the backwoods, half-educated yokels, obscurantism, crackpot hawkers of religion . . . Opposed to these were the city, the clique of New York–Chicago lawyers, intellectuals, journalists, wits, sophisticates, modernists' (Marsden 2006:185). This compelling image of conservative religionists from the South retarding national progress, which also had echoes of the Civil War, would persist through the rest of the twentieth century. Fundamentalist Christians felt their beliefs were ridiculed by the establishment, and Evangelicalism as a whole did not emerge again into the public domain until after the Second World War. Fundamentalists did not give up, however. Still today the threat of the teaching of evolution encourages conservative

Evangelicals to home-school their children or set up Christian schools, which teach 'creationism' or the more sophisticated 'intelligent design' that seeks to redefine science to accept supernatural causation.

Social conservatism

It is important to distinguish fundamentalism from Evangelicalism as a whole, of which the former is best regarded as a militant subgroup (Marsden 2006:235). Few denominations describe themselves as 'fundamentalist' today, but many are 'fundamentalistic', displaying traits of the movement because of pressure groups within them. The largest single Protestant denomination is the Southern Baptist Convention, which since the 1980s has become more fundamentalist. The statement of faith on its website (although not binding on its member churches) begins with a declaration of belief in biblical inerrancy, and the description of 'the last things' takes a premillennialist line. This stance is out of step with other Baptists worldwide, and in 2004 it withdrew from the World Baptist Alliance citing worries about 'liberalism' and 'anti-Americanism'. The Southern Baptist Convention affirms the equality of men and women yet excludes women from leadership, arguing that God-ordained gender roles are 'distinct' and 'complementary'. Positions on this issue are one way of distinguishing fundamentalist churches from the more broadly Evangelical. Fundamentalists originally distanced themselves from Holiness groups by strongly rejecting divine healing, regarding miracles as the authentication of Jesus Christ and the apostles only. However, the influence of Pentecostal spirituality has confused this divide. The most popular 'televangelists' of the 1980s and 1990s, who offered healing and prosperity as well as eternal salvation, included both fundamentalists such as Jerry Falwell and Pat Robertson and Pentecostals such as Oral Roberts, Jimmy Swaggert and Jim Bakker. All were criticized at various times for dubious fundraising methods, financial misconduct and – in the latter two cases – sexual transgressions. But they were all Southerners, which shows how much the Christianity of the South, despised at the 'monkey trial', had become mainstream (Marsden 2006:237).

The social conservatism of fundamentalism attracts those with anti-modern tendencies, including some recent immigrant groups (Marsden 2006:194), and so fundamentalists and other Evangelicals have been co-opted into right-wing politics. In the 1950s, Evangelical preachers joined in the rhetoric against communism both because it was socialist and also because it was atheist or 'God-less'. The liberalism of the 1960s, which included assaults on traditional standards of family and sexuality and aggressive attempts to secularize American culture, together with the fallout of the battle over black civil rights, especially in the South, incensed conservative Christians and reignited 'Puritanical' moral tendencies. 'It seemed that America was a Christian nation that had forsaken its heritage' and that it was time to bring Christianity back to centre stage. The major focus of concern for Evangelicals was not now the 'Liberalism' of their fellow Christians but the 'secular humanism' of the wider society, especially with regard to family, sexuality and religion in public life. The 'custodial' control exercised over local culture by fundamentalists in the South during the first half of the twentieth century began to be applied to the whole nation in organized political movements (238–40).

Psychiatrist James Dobson's broadcasting on childcare was one example of a new genre which attempted to develop 'Christian values' and apply them to everyday life. Writer and film-maker Francis Schaeffer played an important role in convincing fundamentalists that secular humanism had replaced Christianity as the American cultural framework. In his *Left Behind* series, Tim LaHaye persuaded them that it was also a government agenda (Marsden 2006:246) and played into fears of government intrusion into people's lives that went back to the experience of the first European settlers in their search for freedom from earthly and spiritual powers. LaHaye and another popular writer Hal Lindsay revived fears of the apocalypse. Pragmatist millennialist Christians are reluctant to sit back and let the end happen but have found ways in which the end can apparently be precipitated. Quoting Matthew 24:14, some argue that world evangelization will hasten the fulfilment of prophecies of the last days.

Paradoxically, while seeking to reconstruct American society, many of the same people preach a premillennialist message that the earth will soon be destroyed (Marsden 2006:247–50). Christian fundamentalists formed an alliance with Jewish Zionists to encourage the rebuilding of the temple in Jerusalem which, based on dispensationalist theories of New Testament interpretation, they believe will trigger the return of Christ, the 'rapture' and the battle of Armageddon, in which most of the rest of the world's population will die (Chapman 2002:274–6; Sizer 2005). It is claimed that as many as one in ten Americans shares these beliefs (Halsell 2003:5). All the late-twentieth-century 'televangelists', including the more mainstream Billy Graham, were Zionists and consequently the belief is no longer limited to fundamentalists but pervades Evangelicalism. Through former presidents Jimmy Carter, Ronald Reagan and George W. Bush, Christian Zionism had a significant impact on American policy toward Israel (Marsden 2006:249–50). Christian Zionists make no attempt to understand the present conflict in the Middle East in its own terms and do not represent the views of Christians in the Middle East. Yet they take a one-sided political stance in favour of the state of Israel, and this without showing any real concern for the fate of the Jewish people (Chapman 2002:284–7).

Conservative Roman Catholic Christians, who had also been largely apolitical up to the 1970s, shared Evangelical concerns about American society to a large extent, and also had a particular grievance: 1973 permissive legislation on abortion. Influenced by films produced by Francis Schaeffer and C. Everett Koop in 1979 which argued that abortion was the culmination of secular humanist disregard for God's law, most Evangelicals were persuaded to adopt the anti-abortion agenda as part of their support for traditional family life and more traditional roles for women. In 1979 Jerry Falwell founded the 'Moral Majority' with the support of Catholic leaders, which supported Ronald Reagan's conservative Republican campaign. It was dissolved in 1989 after being succeeded by the 'Christian Coalition' supporting Pat Robertson's (unsuccessful) campaign for the Republican nomination in 1988. Pope John Paul II's encyclical *Evangelium Vitae* (1995) on the value and inviolability of human life strengthened the case for an opposition between the 'cultures' of life and death (although conservatives largely failed to see its economic message). A looser 'pro-life' coalition, termed the 'Religious Right' or 'Christian Right', was a major factor in the election of George W. Bush to president in 2000 and 2004, to the extent that the best predictor of whether a white American voted Republican was not his or her income but 'how often he or she goes to church' (Micklethwait and Wooldridge 2004:12). Today issues of sexuality pit religious conservatives against LGBT (lesbian, gay, bisexual and transgender) campaigners, who may also be church members. It is remarkable that now the deepest divide among US Christians is no longer the old Catholic–Protestant one but that between conservative Christians and those of a liberal or secular persuasion (Mullin 1999:456).

Not all American Evangelicals were satisfied with prosperity theology of the televangelists or right-wing in their politics. There was an Evangelical movement within Hippie culture of the 1960s and 1970s – the Jesus People – that encouraged communal living (Eskridge 2013). Mennonite Evangelicals, heirs of the radical Reformation, such as Ron Sider (1984) and Jon Bonk (1991), saw the problems of Christian affluence and advocated simple lifestyles. Many were embarrassed by the antics of the Religious Right. 'How did the faith of Jesus come to be known as pro-rich, pro-war, and only pro-American?' asked Jim Wallis (2005:3), a preacher and political activist. Wallis, who also has Evangelical credentials, leads Sojourners, a 'nationwide network of progressive Christians working for justice and peace'. He advocates a kind of North American liberation theology, using biblical arguments to persuade Evangelicals to be more socialist in outlook. At the same time, he is critical of 'secular fundamentalism' that has an 'allergy to spirituality' because it makes the mistake of 'throwing all people of faith into the category of right-wing conservative religion' (346).

US-led Anglophone theological developments

New theological developments in Anglophone Christianity were stimulated by some of the dramatic social and political events of the twentieth century. The Great Depression of the 1930s dented faith in American progress, and the atrocities of the Second World War and Cold War fear brought home the depth of the evil of which human beings are capable and challenged the optimistic social gospel. These insecurities provided a climate in which some of the Pietistic and Puritan doctrines of human sinfulness and need of grace could be reaffirmed (Schweitzer 1999). Among the heirs of theological liberalism and the social gospel, the brothers Reinhold and H. Richard Niebuhr, who grew up in the German Evangelical tradition, stimulated the development of theological ethics and post-liberal theology, respectively. Reinhold Niebuhr dominated Christian social thought for the first half of the twentieth century. His thought laid foundations for welfare capitalism and affected US foreign policy after the Second World War (Dorrien 1999). Influenced by the biblical realism of the German theologian Karl Barth, Niebuhr was highly critical of what he saw as the idealism of social Christianity and the sentimentality of its compassion, although he upheld its desire to restrain market forces and establish social and political democracy. Niebuhr rejected moralism, but in view of God's forgiveness he encouraged 'proximate justice', involving pragmatic solutions and necessary compromise – including 'just war' – for addressing the political issues of the age (Werpehowski 1997).

Other Christians, especially from the radical Reformation tradition, were wary of the church working with the state. It reminded them of the Constantinian settlement in Europe, which they regarded as a mistake. Stanley Hauerwas (1999) is one of the most prominent of the many theologians who continue Niebuhr's style of theological ethics and reject liberalism as a social strategy. However, he emphasizes more strongly the separation of church and state and the countercultural nature of the church, which demonstrates a new society. In the late 1960s, the exposure by the press of the horrors of the war in Vietnam broke down Christian support for US interventionism. It brought to the fore the 'peace churches': Mennonites and Quakers, who applied the pacifism of Jesus seriously to modern life. At the time their stance was expressed most clearly by the Mennonite John Howard Yoder (1972), who called Christians to follow 'the politics of Jesus' by rejecting all violence and the threat of it. In campaigning for peace they were joined by others who saw the matter from the point of view of the victims of violence: the black churches led by Martin Luther King and Catholic liberation theologians.

Cultures and evangelism

H. Richard Niebuhr (2001[1951]), professor at Yale University, was famous for his typologies of the relationship between Christ and culture, in which he stressed the work of Christ in transforming culture. He and his colleague Hans Frei laid the foundations for a post-liberal approach which shifted biblical interpretation and theological method from an Enlightenment scientific approach to a literary one that was more in keeping with the narrative tradition of Scripture. George Lindbeck added an appreciation of different forms of discourse which he thought suggested that

Christians should develop their own culture and language of faith which could not be gainsaid from within a different discourse (Placher 1997). Post-liberal theology is opposed by those who see it as withdrawal from, rather than an engagement with, the world. The stress on the countercultural nature of Christianity in the United States can also be seen as a response to the continued intellectual and scientific assault on religion, and Christianity especially, that provoked fundamentalism. Some theological movements tried to make Christian faith more credible by using the categories of philosophy and science. These include forms of 'process theology', developed from the philosophy of Alfred North Whitehead by Charles Hartshorne, which lay God open to scientific investigation by understanding God as a dynamic within evolutionary processes but at the cost of traditional Christian doctrines (Epperly 2011). Alternatively, some Anglican and Catholic theologians have attempted to preserve the integrity of traditional Christian confession in this context through 'radical orthodoxy'. Among other things, this revived the political doctrines of Aquinas and other medieval theologians to advocate instead for a much stronger role of the church in state affairs (Milbank, Pickstock and Ward 1999).

The same post-war awareness of evil encouraged the reinvigoration of the Evangelical programme of evangelism in the sense of calling for conversion. In the context of the ideologically framed wars of the twentieth-century, Evangelicals presented a Christian ideology and saw the conversion of the individual as the most effective way of solving the world's problems. In particular, communism did not simply represent a threat to the livelihoods of middle-class Christians but it was also aggressively atheistic so 'the defence of the gospel and the defence of the "Free World" . . . now became closely associated causes' (Stanley 2013:62). The National Association of Evangelicals, formed in 1942, signalled the rebuilding of an Evangelical coalition which, while sometimes displaying fundamentalistic tendencies, gradually differentiated itself from hardline fundamentalist organizations as shown particularly in the history of Fuller Theological Seminary in Pasadena, California (29–36). Today Evangelicalism can be understood as a broad coalition of diverse Protestant subgroups with a broadly similar statement of faith (Noll 2001:56–66).

The evangelist Billy Graham was the single most important figure in maintaining Evangelical unity in the second half of the twentieth century (Noll 2001:44–55). He came from a Southern fundamentalist background and preached a typical Evangelical message of the sinfulness of human beings, the necessity of conversion and the salvation offered by faith in Christ – a message which has been heard in person, as well as through the media, by millions of people. Graham's revival meetings, which began in the 1940s, had a unifying effect because they were organized at the invitation of a coalition of local churches, usually including a broad range of denominations. His organization, college at Wheaton, Illinois, and his magazine *Christianity Today* gradually became more moderate, closer to other Protestants and more academically credible. Graham defined a conservative evangelicalism over against fundamentalism on the one hand and liberalism on the other and he helped to bring Evangelicals back into the public sphere in the United States. Graham knew personally every US president from Harry Truman and was an unofficial pastor to many. Although he was outspoken against communism in the 1950s, he also publicly opposed segregation in the 1960s and was careful not to side completely with the Religious Right. Through his extensive worldwide tours and the organizations and educational networks he founded, Graham promoted this particular American brand of Christian faith globally.

Evangelicals led the rhetoric against communism and supported Cold War policies to contain and defeat it. In this they found common ground with conservatives in the Catholic Church, such as Francis Cardinal Spellman, archbishop of New York, who was active globally at a political level to oppose communist regimes. Evangelicals began their international efforts to spread the gospel as a message of freedom and an antidote to communism in war-torn Western Europe, where Youth for Christ expanded beyond US service personnel to German youth and then globally. The methods they used included literature – some of which was smuggled across communist borders, broadcasting networks such as Trans-World Radio and the Far East Broadcasting Association that breached 'the Iron Curtain', and mass rallies such as the Billy Graham 'crusades' that sent political messages as well as religious ones. Involvement with what was coming to be known as the 'Third World' also called forth compassion and the foundation of evangelical relief and development agencies such as World Vision by Bob Pierce in war-torn Korea.

Evangelical re-engagement with US society was led by the theologian Carl Henry, who tried to affirm Protestant orthodoxy linked with American revivalism and Evangelicalism. At the same time he rejected fundamentalism by a method of 'biblical theism', which aimed to make the revelation of God, verified by the Bible, rational, credible and socially constructive (Stanley 2013:131–3). His contemporary and fellow Baptist Bernard Ramm preferred to make his starting point the 'biblical realism' of Karl Barth, in whose 'neo-orthodox' Calvinist theology he found a biblical framework for an Evangelical theology (in its North American sense). Distinguishing itself from 'liberal' theology and the Europe-based Ecumenical movement which it saw as compromising with communism, US Evangelical scholarship was founded on biblical studies which wrestled with the 'difficult' passages but refused to dismiss them. During the Cold War, the Billy Graham Evangelistic Association formed networks of Evangelical theological education in Asia, Africa and Latin America that paralleled those affiliated to the WCC. It encouraged a wider, mainly Anglophone movement, supported by bodies like the 'Inter-Varsity' network, the Tyndale Fellowship and later the Langham Partnership, founded by the leading British Evangelical of the second half of the twentieth century, John Stott, to encourage biblical preaching and teaching in the non-Western world (Stanley 2013:93–120).

This said, having an activist mentality, Evangelicals tend to be less concerned with developing theology than with discovering or devising strategies to bring about conversion and the growth of the church. To the denominational missions and Faith Missions were added 'parachurch organizations', which were intended to support the work of the church but often took on a life of their own. These included youth movements such as Youth for Christ, Campus Crusade for Christ and the charismatic YWAM (Youth with a Mission). These specialized in 'personal evangelism', or one-to-one attempts to persuade another of the truth of the Christian faith (Turner 2008). This pattern, which uses techniques similar to sales and advertising, is unquestioned in the North American context, and at the heart of Evangelical mission activity, so that it is often referred to simply as 'evangelism'. So strong was this emphasis that some saw works of love and service as merely a means to bringing about conversion. Furthermore, attempts to address social issues, as earlier Evangelicals had done, were met with suspicion that they were preaching a 'social gospel' and, by implication, becoming theologically liberal (Glasser 1993). Evangelical conservatism was strengthened in the 1960s when the WCC appeared to endorse some of the revolutions of the age as a result of supporting the concerns of member churches from the Third World and also seeking to reconcile churches across the divide between the West and the communist world. In contrast, in 1966 the Billy Graham Evangelistic Association arranged a World Congress on Evangelism defiantly in West Berlin. He emphasized that it was the role of the church to proclaim the message not to be social reformers.

However, at a second such global event organized in the Swiss city of Lausanne in 1974 events took a surprising turn when leaders from Latin America and Africa criticized US-style Evangelicalism for using consumerist methods, mathematical models and an ideological approach in world evangelization and challenged the movement to show concern for the poor, fulfil the ethical demands of the gospel and distance themselves from right-wing regimes (Stanley 2013:151–79; Douglas 1975). The 'Lausanne Covenant' affirmed that 'evangelism and socio-political involvement' are both 'necessary expressions of our doctrines of God and man, our love for our neighbour and our obedience to Jesus Christ'. Although some US American leaders managed to construe the congress as a victory for continuing their methods, the event marked a turning point that showed that global Evangelicalism was not necessarily an ally of US culture and policies. At the third Lausanne congress at Cape Town in 2010, the same tensions were evident between the conversion and the social transformation agendas but these no longer ran along the lines of the US versus the global South (Dahle, Dahle and Jørgensen 2014). The international Lausanne Movement now works closely with the World Evangelical Alliance, which probably represents most Evangelicals globally and shares its broad-based approach.

With notable exceptions, Evangelical theologians have not been comfortable dealing with political questions of justice or with issues arising from religious pluralism, but they have engaged with cultural anthropology in order to communicate the gospel message more effectively. The Willowbank Report of a consultation sponsored by the Lausanne Movement in 1978 developed an appreciation of the role of culture in gospel communication, church life and also in the writing and reading of the Bible, which has been widely appreciated by other Christian bodies. However, two more controversial evangelistic methods promoted at Fuller Seminary since the 1970s that arose from the study of culture have also been extremely influential in missions worldwide. Drawing initially on studies of mass conversion movements in India, Donald McGavran and Peter Wagner (1990:163) believed that '[p]eople like to become Christians without crossing racial, linguistic, or class barriers', and argued, on biblical and sociological grounds, that the most effective way to achieve church growth was to create 'homogeneous units' within which the gospel message can therefore spread more easily and become a movement of a whole 'people group'. This orientation is maintained in world mission by 'frontier missions' (Snodderly and Moreau 2011) and initiatives such as the Joshua Project. Research into the distribution of unevangelized groups worldwide led evangelist Luis Bush in 1990 to encourage Christians to target the '10/40 window' – the region of Eurasia between latitudes 10 and 40 degrees north where most such groups are found. Other Evangelicals have strongly criticized this approach for its apparent denial of the impulses of the Christian gospel to break down barriers and unite different peoples (e.g. Bosch 2011:477–8), and because of its obsession with numbers and goal-setting (Newbigin 1995a:124–32), but it has been very popular in target-driven contexts in the United States and elsewhere.

Power and charisma

The second initiative emerging from Fuller Seminary School of World Missions was the method of 'power encounter' which was developed by some returned missionaries: Paul Hiebert, Alan Tippett and Charles Kraft, who had backgrounds in anthropology. They had all witnessed exorcism and deliverance on the 'mission field' – in India, the Pacific and West Africa (respectively) – and recognized it as part of the biblical ministry of Jesus. Instead of dismissing it as earlier generations of missionaries had done under the pressures of the Enlightenment, they argued that missionaries should practise such a ministry of confrontational prayer, and furthermore that this 'spiritual warfare' was applicable also in North America to deal with supernatural demonic powers and 'territorial spirits' (Wagner 1989). John Wimber, a California pastor, became the best-known practitioner of such 'power evangelism'. This 'signs and wonders' movement was termed the 'third wave' of the Pentecostal–charismatic movement by Peter Wagner, who believed it was effective in bringing about church growth. Despite criticism from both within (Lowe 1998) and outside (Percy 1996) the Evangelical movement, 'power encounter' was much in evidence at the second Lausanne Conference in Manila in 1989 (see Douglas 1990). A similar language of 'spiritual conflict' was developed independently by liberal theologian Walter Wink, who applied the biblical terminology of spirits, demons and angels to liberation theological concern with social and political powers and systems. However Wink (1998) emphasized that the struggle against the powers is by non-violent resistance and he deplored the 'myth of redemptive violence' which he saw as underlying cartoons and movies and many other aspects of American life. A more therapeutic method of dealing with questions of power and conflict is in evidence in the use of psychological methods in what is known as Christian or pastoral counselling, which applies the insights of psychology and the methods of psychotherapy to Christian ministry. Most North American churches offer this kind of ministry; the practitioners are usually women.

In the 1990s particularly, Evangelical theologians began to study postmodernity and to develop apologetics and methods of evangelism for a new age in which many of the old certainties against which neo-Evangelicalism defined itself seem to be breaking down and in which there is suspicion toward all 'metanarratives'. Drawing on some of the insights of the post-liberals, Richard Middleton and Brian Walsh (1995) were hopeful that Christians would rediscover resources within the biblical story which, like contemporary society, is plural and diverse. The call for a mission to Western culture and the context of postmodernity also demand new models of 'church', which tended in North America to refer to the local congregation. Two ideas emerged most clearly: 'missional church' and 'emerging church'. 'Missional church' is a response to the challenge of British missionary bishop Lesslie Newbigin's (1986:1) call for 'a genuinely missionary encounter between the gospel and [modern Western] culture'. It involves the 'continuing conversion of the church' from a static institution into an instrument of mission in its broadest sense (Guder 2000). Rather than sending missionaries elsewhere, local churches are urged to become witnesses for Christ in their own culture primarily by their attractive community life (Van Gelder 2007). 'Emerging church' encourages the creation of new types of Christian community appropriate to postmodern cultures (Gibbs and Bolger 2006).

Developments since the 1960s have confused the distinction in the United States between Evangelicals, who take the Bible as their chief source of authority, and Pentecostals, for whom the experience of the Holy Spirit is pre-eminent. The first murmurings of what came to be known as the Charismatic movement were among Episcopal (Anglican) churches in California in 1959 who learnt about 'baptism in the Holy Spirit', evidenced by speaking in tongues, from Pentecostal churches. News of 'charismatic renewal' spread through the Christian press and this encouraged further cross-over experiences between denominations. In 1967, Catholic Charismatic Renewal began from the retreat experience of students from Duquesne University in Pittsburgh who had been reading about the ministry of a Pentecostal pastor (David Wilkerson). In a related development, at the height of the 'hippie' culture, in the late 1960s and early 1970s, the Jesus Movement arose in California which offered an alternative way to 'get high' through ecstatic worship using contemporary music. Musicians included Larry Norman, Keith Green and also Andraé Crouch, who bridged the gap between the predominantly white middle-class Charismatic movement and the urban gospel music of the black churches. Many 'Jesus people' formed communes and lived alternative lifestyles as they attempted to restore the New Testament church. Campus Crusade for Christ capitalized on this youth energy when it organized Explo '72 – dubbed 'the Christian Woodstock' – in Dallas, Texas, at which they trained young people in personal evangelism. It concluded with an address by Billy Graham. The 'Explo' (Evangelism Explosion) model inspired other youth meetings globally including, reportedly, the World Youth Days instituted by Pope John Paul II in 1984. The Jesus Movement spawned informal meetings for worship and prayers that became 'fellowships', such as the Vineyard in Anaheim, California, and then global networks (Eskridge 2013). 'Baptism' or 'filling' with the Spirit were rejected by many Evangelical churches ostensibly on doctrinal grounds but also for reasons of church authority. However, all the churches were affected by the new worship styles developed through the movement, which replaced classical hymns with 'choruses' and organs with 'worship groups' (Stanley 2013:181–210).

The Charismatic movement sacralized popular culture and became a vehicle for growth in Evangelical and Catholic churches, especially when it combined with the 'signs and wonders' and prosperity movements of the 1980s. However the growth of Evangelicalism has been accompanied by a sharp decline in those denominations which maintained an older Protestant tradition and a social gospel: including Episcopal, United Methodist, American (Northern) Baptist and Presbyterian denominations. Although Evangelicalism remains a strong force in the United States, it is divided between the more hardline who would consign most of the rest of US society to hell and others who prefer to preach God's mercy and hope for the nation. There are signs that it is losing appeal to young people born and brought up in the United States. The fastest growing churches are among recent migrants. Three prominent pastors and their churches give a flavour of mainstream Evangelicalism today: Bill Hybels of Willow Creek Community Church, Chicago, has a 'seeker-friendly' approach that stresses the importance of relationships within the church and with the wider community. Rick Warren of Saddleback Church, Lake Forest, California, focuses on making disciples as the primary purpose of the church and agent of growth. Joel Osteen is pastor of Lakewood Church in Houston, Texas, which claims to be the largest Christian church in the United States and has a global broadcast network and a ministry to the poor and sick. Osteen, who is white, leads a congregation that is racially diverse and preaches a gospel of inclusivity and encouragement. Critics accuse him of ignorance of doctrinal issues and of prosperity teaching, others see a 'juvenilization' of contemporary US Christianity and caution against the 'feel-good' message, but Osteen's approach with his slogan 'You can you will!' has most in common with the self-help tradition in American life (Bergler 2012). Such mega-churches are inclusive and provide an opportunity for recent migrants to integrate into the mainstream.

Black churches, civil rights and the Africanization of Christianity

It was through religion that African Americans 'found a voice', and so black faith and politics have gone very closely together in the history of the United States (Baer and Singer 2002:xvii; Pinn and Pinn 2002:125–6). Although the black Pentecostal churches provided an alternative experience, they largely adopted a conservative Evangelical theology which did not provide tools for social critique (Yong 2005:78). However, leaders of the older black churches espoused the 'social gospel' and saw that the 'fatherhood of God' and the 'brotherhood of man' should mean that 'the destiny of our [African] race is bound up with the destiny of the world' (Ransom 2002[1905]:158). That the social gospel would lead to black civil rights was not obvious to the leaders of the original movement, but in his commitment to the social gospel in 1905, AME church leader Reverdy Ransom predicted that 'an individual life, a race or national life' which does not see its duty and destiny in terms of 'solidarity' 'will become more and more a thing to be despised' (158). Black gospel-motivated social concern issued in the civil rights movement of the 1950s and 1960s in which leading figures Martin Luther King and Ralph Abernathy were ministers of urban black churches in the South. King's theology was rooted in the biblical belief of his childhood formation that God was active in history to bring about justice through the suffering of his servants, the prophets. He was also convinced that since Jesus loved his enemies and died for them, justice could only be achieved by non-violence (Harding 1996:55). His was a social gospel influenced by reading of Rauschenbusch but tempered and shaped by his encounter with the theology of Reinhold Niebuhr, which purged him of political naïveté, helped him to distinguish between personal and institutional racism (Ling 2002:234) and also suggested the direction his leadership would take by highlighting Gandhi's satyagraha strategy (Branch 1988:73, 84–7).

Not all black Christians appreciated the theology of King, who worked toward consensus and assimilation without satisfying the anger felt by the black community at the humiliations and violence they continued to suffer despite the passing of the civil rights act in 1964. A combination of the context of slave religion, the biblical stories of the God who liberates, the civil rights and black power movements and the 'rhythm' of the liberation spirituality of poor African Americans gave rise in 1970 to 'black theology of liberation' (Hopkins 1999:15–48). James H. Cone,

Figure 6.3 Republican presidential candidate Senator John McCain (left) and Democratic candidate Senator Barack Obama (right) greet the crowd at Saddleback Church, Lake Forest, California, on 16 August 2008. They were participating in the 'Civil Forum on the Presidency' organized by the pastor Rick Warren (centre). Image: iStock.

the AME minister who first gave voice to this new approach, argued that King's Jesus was not black enough, and sought to introduce into black theology the black power ideology of Malcolm X, which affirmed black identity and the right to self-determination. Unaware at that time of the development of liberation theology in Latin America, Cone similarly refused to accept any religion which did not offer liberation. Unlike King, and like X, he was prepared to alienate white theologians. He called Christianity 'black power' because the liberation of the black poor is at the heart of the gospel, and he called white religion 'satanic' because 'God is black' (Cone 1990). Other theologians – black as well as white – found Cone's insistence that the gospel is about power dangerous and unchristian and rejected black theology as racism in reverse. A second generation of black theologians in the 1980s and 1990s developed black theology by dialoguing through the Ecumenical Association of Third World Theologians (Roberts 1987); by introducing the role of capitalism and class in black oppression (West 1979); and by relating black theology more to the music of slave religion, the language of the black poor and the traditions of Africa (e.g., Hopkins 1993).

Black Christian women like Rosa Parks and Fannie Lou Hamer stood at the forefront of the civil rights movement. Womanist – as distinguished from feminist – theology affirms black women and questions the claim of black theology that the gospel brings liberation. Delores S. Williams laid a foundation by examining the story, embedded in African American traditions, of Hagar, the 'black' (Egyptian) wife who bore Abraham his son Ishmael and then was cast out in favour of Sarah and her son Isaac. She wondered whether quality of life or mere belief in survival should be the central theme of black theology (Chopp 1997a:399). Jacquelyn Grant (1989) compared the 'white women's Christ' unfavourably with Jesus as black women understood him, as the Anointed One who suffers with them.

In the dialogue with other liberation theologians, black theologians from the United States built particularly close relationships with the political theologians of South Africa, who had been inspired by Cone's work, but found it harder to relate to the African theologians who used indigenous culture in their theologizing (Hopkins 1999:161–6). When black theology and Latin American liberation theology encountered one another, the Latin Americans, who were mainly white, were challenged to take race into account in their theology, and black theologians began to consider economic issues and employ Marxist analysis (167–72). However, black and womanist theologies are criticized for not paying much attention to issues of black poverty, solidarity with Africans in Africa and other parts of the world, or the life of the Black churches (Kee 2006:195–200; Pinn and Pinn 2002:145). Vincent Harding (1996) urges black Christians to recover the memory of the later Martin Luther King, who came increasingly under fire because, in his concern for the poor, he moved from civil rights to human rights, challenging US government policy in Vietnam and Central America and highlighting poverty at home. The election of Barack Obama in 2008 marked another milestone in the civil rights movement. Furthermore, although he was not raised in black churches, as a community activist in Chicago Obama chose to identify with and work with them. His eulogy for Rev. Clementa Pinckney following the massacre in a black church in Charlestown in 2015 showed how much of his politics has been shaped by that decision.

African American religion is increasingly diversified, especially in urban areas. Between the world wars, 'storefront churches' proliferated, catering to displaced migrants to the cities, and these sprouted new movements. More recent migrants from Africa and the Caribbean look for other forms of religious experience. Baer and Singer (2002) identify four types of African American religious sects (in a sociological sense) according to different responses by black people to their minority status. First, the established black denominations cater for those wishing to accept the cultural patterns of mainstream society. They do not have a major political role but carry out a great deal of social service. Paradoxically, perhaps, those African Americans who affiliate to white-controlled denominations (except Roman Catholicism), who are overwhelmingly middle class, tend to do more to bring about social change. Second, messianic–nationalist groups, many of them Islamic or Judaic rather than Christian in inspiration, founded by individuals who are regarded by their followers as messiahs or 'messengers of God' protest against mainstream society and seek to create a new ethnic identity. Third, conversionist sects, mainly Holiness or Pentecostal, are apolitical and mainly focused on worship. Finally, thaumaturgical groups hope to achieve the ends desired by mainstream society, such as prosperity or health, but believe they can do so by magical rituals and esoteric knowledge. Their use of the occult puts 'spiritual' (or spiritualist) churches outside the category of 'Christian', although some churches that promise healing and prosperity on the basis of Christian faith have similar patterns of worship. Some groups, such as Father Divine's Peace Mission, combine elements of all four types (273–6).

It is difficult to establish any specific characteristics of black churches in the United States that can be ascribed only to the African heritage of their members. However, it is possible to argue that African spiritual traditions of black Christians reinforced similar elements in European religion and that therefore there has been an Africanization of Christianity in North America. Raboteau (2004:59–86) points specifically to ecstatic behaviour and magical folk-belief. He suggests that the motor behaviour of jerking, shouting, clapping, antiphonal singing, hyperventilation and dancing exhibited at the camp meetings reflected the influence of slave religion on white religiosity. Similarly, African belief in the supernatural may have reinforced that dimension of white religion. A lively belief in a spirit world was (and is) prevalent across US Pentecostal churches (Wacker 2001:91–3). Walter Hollenweger (1997) described this influence as the 'black root' (among others) of Pentecostalism. He believed this explained what he saw as the distinctive behavioural characteristics of Pentecostalism and was also the reason for its growth. The adoption of Christianity by African Americans should not be seen as passive reception but as a two-way interaction in which white Americans were challenged by the Christian faith of their slaves, who later became their compatriots.

Migration and the rise of US Roman Catholicism

The focus of this chapter has been on the dominant form of religion in the United States, which is Evangelicalism, but according to Pew research, between a quarter and a third of US citizens are Roman Catholics. After California was ceded to the United States in 1848, settlers moving across from the east – Catholics and Protestants alike – were shocked to find a late-medieval Spanish Catholic presence already there around the Franciscan missions. They denounced its 'barbarities' (such as self-mortification) and the US Catholic Church took over its structures but the western and southwestern states remain predominantly Roman Catholic today. Due to immigration from Latin America, they are becoming more so. People of Hispanic descent are so prevalent that major cities like Los Angeles have majority Hispanic populations and US society is becoming bilingual.

Catholic growth and mission

As a result of French colonization, the Great Lakes region and southern Louisiana remain predominantly Catholic today. Hardship in Quebec in the nineteenth and twentieth centuries led to large migration into New England, once the Puritan stronghold, which is now predominantly Catholic. Clergy and religious exiled during and after the French Revolution strengthened the Catholic community in North America. Sulpicians fleeing the revolution in France helped the clergy by offering training. And new communities of mystical devotion – many of them founded by women – encouraged a popular Catholic spirituality that emphasized the visionary, which could hardly have contrasted more with the Puritan emphasis on the Word. While at the level of popular religion Catholicism and Protestantism seemed worlds apart, at the level of leadership Catholics were very much part of the American enterprise. The colony of Maryland was established by English Catholics. Although it later became Anglican, wealthy English Catholic families and Jesuit missionaries continued to be landowners (and slaveholders) in the South. The first Catholic bishop in the United States was John Carroll (1736–1815), descendant of a Maryland family. He was an enthusiastic supporter of democracy and of church–state separation. The first religious community, the Sisters of Charity (1809) was founded in Maryland by Elizabeth Bayley Seton, who was canonized in 1963 – the first US-born saint.

Between 1815 and 1860 the complexion of Catholicism changed drastically when two million Irish Catholics arrived in the United States, fleeing the potato famine and British oppression. From Boston and other northeastern ports they soon spread out across the country, advantaged by being English-speaking. Much of the energy of the church was spent in providing pastoral and social care for the new arrivals (Dries 1998:22–7). In 1850, the Roman Catholic Church became the single largest denomination in the United States (Gaustad and Schmidt 2002:170). The threat the new immigrants posed to the American-born poor led to widespread antagonism and anti-Catholic feeling from among the Protestant majority (Williams 1990:276–7). The inventor Samuel F. B. Morse, for example, saw massive Catholic immigration as evidence for 'a papal takeover of the American republic' (Mullin 1999:435). Catholics often set up their own community schools for reasons of language and also religious instruction. Their demands for public support for these schools sparked anti-Catholic riots in the 1840s, and in the 1850s a secret organization known as the 'Know Nothing' party was set up to oppose the election of Catholics to public office.

Figure 6.4 Pope Francis receiving an enthusiastic reception in Washington DC, USA, 23 September 2015, on his first ever visit to North America. Image: iStock.

By the end of the nineteenth century, priests of Irish descent were in a majority and dominated the leadership of the US Catholic Church. Large numbers of German Catholics were entering the United States, and many of them were wealthy enough to buy farmland, mainly in the 'German triangle' bounded by Milwaukee, St Louis and Cincinnati in the central United States, where they tried to maintain their language and religion. They and other minority Catholics, who also included Poles, Italians, Spanish and Portuguese, would be dismayed when the priest appointed by the hierarchy did not speak their language or was unfamiliar with their particular saints and customs (Williams 1990:277–82). Polish Catholics, who began to arrive from the 1870s, felt so strongly that they even founded a breakaway Polish National Catholic Church from 1897, which still exists. Some churches formed committees of lay trustees (as Protestant churches did) and tried to employ their own preferred clergy. But the Irish Americans who dominated the hierarchy until the mid-twentieth century argued for a centralized church, using English as its language medium, as the best means of defending Catholic interests. 'Liberal' Catholics wished to cooperate with American government and society as closely as possible, especially in public education, ecumenical activity and support of labour unions, but an apostolic letter in 1899 from Pope Leo XIII, who shared liberal concern for social issues, nevertheless warned against 'Americanism', by which he referred mainly to 'individualism'. As a bulwark against this, and as an alternative to 'culture-bound Protestantism' (Mullin 1999:450), some American theologians revived medieval Scholasticism.

Despite the needs in the developing nation itself, the United States has a history of Catholic overseas mission work that stretches back to the 1840s. US branches of European religious congregations took on work in the Caribbean, Latin America and Hawaii. Before long, with an eye to what Protestants were already doing, a national infrastructure for the support of missions emerged. A US arm of the Holy Childhood Association was started in 1866 and the Catholic Church Extension Society was established on a business model in 1905. In 1884, the bishops approved the establishment of the Society for the Propagation of the Faith and in 1919 the American Board of Catholic Missions. In 1908 North America ceased to be regarded as a 'mission field' by the hierarchy in Rome, and in 1909 the first American Catholic Missionary Congress was held in Chicago amid a growing US confidence and Catholic patriotism, especially since the Spanish–American War of 1898. A national organization for overseas mission, the Catholic Foreign Mission Society of America, known as the Maryknoll Fathers and Brothers, was founded in 1911 and the Maryknoll Sisters were officially recognized in 1920.

Maryknoll brothers entered China and Korea before the war, Latin America in 1942 and Africa in 1946. The sisters worked in Hong Kong from 1921 (Chu 2004). The Maryknollers developed a reputation for serving the poor and indigenous people. They promoted democracy around the world and were associated with liberation theology. Other leading sending congregations, societies and orders include: for men, the Jesuits, Franciscans, Redemptorists and Divine Word Missionaries; and for women, Marists, Medical Mission Sisters, School Sisters of Notre Dame and Sisters of Mercy. Further fields opened up along with US political influence in East Asia and sub-Saharan Africa. As American Catholics prospered, the US Catholic Church was generous in its support for missions and later for relief and development. Overseas missionary sending peaked in 1968 and has been declining since (Dries 1998). What became Catholic Relief Services – now part of Caritas International – began by resettling refugees in Europe in 1943 and then expanded to other continents. Despite its new overseas fields, the main energy of US Catholic mission has been the evangelization of immigrants to the United States, first from Europe and now from Latin America (249).

Catholics in public life

Before the Second Vatican Council (1962–65), the US Catholic Church rarely intervened in the public sphere, except to call for the protection of Catholic interests at home and overseas. Popular Catholic anti-communism was mediated by the activities of Senator Joseph McCarthy in the 1950s. However, the church took a progressive stance on economic issues. For example, leading Catholics worked with President Franklin D. Roosevelt to improve labour relations and social programmes for the urban poor, where the vast majority of Catholics were found (Mullin 1999:435). John A. Ryan's long campaign for a 'living wage' resulted in 1938 in the passing of minimum wage legislation. The Catholic Worker movement, founded by Dorothy Day and Peter Maurin in 1933, pioneered Catholic social action. From the 1960s, many individual Catholics were involved in political activism for civil rights, against war and on behalf of the poor. One of the best known is the Jesuit priest Daniel Berrigan, a radical theologian and activist, who campaigned against US foreign intervention from Vietnam to Iraq, against nuclear armaments and against abortion.

In the second half of the twentieth century, more Catholics began to enter the mainstream of American life. In part this was due to their increasing social mobility, which was symbolized in 1960 when John F. Kennedy was elected to the presidency, despite anti-Catholic attempts to derail his campaign. Although North American bishops were not prominent at the Second Vatican Council, the opening up of the Roman Catholic Church as a whole to the modern world further stimulated the vibrant intellectual life of the US Church. The American Jesuit John Courtney Murray led the Church towards a constructive engagement with US society on the grounds that the US constitution was framed in the context of an understanding of natural law ('We hold these truths to be self-evident'), it acknowledges the primacy of the spiritual ('One nation under God'), and it respects the freedom of the church through a democratic politics, which could be seen as an outworking of the freedom brought by the incarnation (Murray 1960: 175–96). At the council, Murray made a particular contribution to the Declaration on Religious Liberty, a document welcomed particularly by US American Catholics (Mullin 1999:454). However, many of the same people were horrified by the promulgation just a few years later by Pope Paul VI of the encyclical *Humanae Vitae* (1968), which prohibited almost any form of birth control.

In a rare intervention in 1983, the US bishops exercised their democratic freedom in the pastoral letter *The Challenge of Peace*, which criticized the arms race. It triggered much discussion within the church and academy on the issues of 'civil discourse' and the ways and means to engage in public life. On the whole US bishops have tended to be conservative but American Catholic theologians have been leaders in developing Catholic social theory. The moral theologian Charles E. Curran was an outspoken critic of Vatican teaching on birth control and issues of sexuality generally and was removed from his post at the Catholic University of America in 1986. Many American Catholics, however, accepted the pope's ruling, and those who supported traditional Catholic ideals of family life campaigned, with Phyllis Schlafly, against the 'equal rights amendment' to the Constitution passed in 1972 to end discrimination against women. Attempts to legislate on family life and sexuality were seen by many

Catholics, as by their Evangelical counterparts, as unwarranted interference by government in the private sphere. In the Catholic case this went against the principle of 'subsidiarity' established in Catholic social teaching.

Gender and sexuality

One result of the emphasis on the laity given by the Second Vatican Council was the opening of seminaries (although not the priesthood) to women and the emergence of a strong Christian feminist movement that was led largely by Catholic women. The first women students at Catholic seminaries were shocked by their male-centredness. Some developed a radical feminist position: Mary Daly (1973) renounced the faith altogether as irredeemably patriarchal – and therefore in her view misogynist – in favour of a 'cosmic covenant' based on pre-Christian traditions; Rosemary Radford Ruether (1983) argued that the language of theology and Christian liturgy needed to be revised for women to be able to share in it. She advocated the formation of 'feminist base communities' on a liberation theological model. Others attempted to remain true to the teaching of the church, while rethinking its traditions and authority. Elisabeth Schüssler Fiorenza (1983) re-examined the early church of the New Testament to uncover the 'memory of her' and show the extent of women's participation in the early Christian mission. Elizabeth A. Johnson (1992) recovered feminine images of God in the Bible, which she argued amounted to an alternative vision of God as 'She Who Is'. These and others support the calls for the ordination of women in the Roman Catholic Church, which have been made since 1975 when the first Women's Ordination Conference was convened in Detroit.

Other key issues for the US Catholic Church in the past decade or so have revolved around issues of sexuality. There was a sharp decline in vocations following the Second Vatican Council, which empowered the laity. The outing of homosexual practice among priests, which is condemned by the church, was a further challenge to the rule of priestly celibacy. Revelations of the sexual abuse of children, especially boys, in Catholic institutions by priests have caused shock within the Church, and without. They resulted in some dioceses filing for bankruptcy because of the size of the compensation payouts. Although it is claimed that the incidence of abuse is no higher than in the general population (Jenkins 1996) and that these problems are not unique to the Catholic Church in the United States, they have received great attention there both because of the thoroughness with which they have been investigated and also because of the size of the claims against the Church. The issues of women's ordination and homosexuality particularly highlight a divide in the US Catholic Church between conservatives and progressives. This is related by theologians to one of the key questions of the council, to which Murray made a key contribution in the affirmative: whether there could be development in theology (O'Malley 2010).

A multicultural church

Since 1900, the largest migration into the Catholic Church in the United States has been Latino. In the main this has come from Puerto Rico since it became American territory in 1898, from Cuba after Fidel Castro took power in 1959, and more recently from Mexico and Central America. The instability and relative poverty of Latin America has meant that many entered illegally, and some Catholic activists have been involved in sheltering them. The extent to which Latinos keep their own culture and language and resist integration with the wider society worries some political commentators (e.g. Huntington 2005:18) and challenges Anglo-American society, although it should not be forgotten that many Latinos are Protestants. On the one hand, Catholics from Latin America tend of be conservative morally and so they have reinforced the 'religious right' of US American politics. On the other hand, they support social policies designed to help the poor.

Latino Catholics bring with them a spirituality heavily influenced by their folk religion, which has tended to put a distance between them and other US Catholic communities (Williams 1990:378–9). However, Pope John Paul II gave encouragement to such popular religiosity, and now that the Mexican Virgin of Guadalupe is recognized as the patron saint of all the Americas, celebration of her saint-day is required in all Catholic churches. Catholic missionary organizations have been active not only in mission ad gentes but also internally, especially by incorporating migrants (Dries 1998) and dealing with sexual trafficking. Congregations which seek to help migrants may take quite different approaches to their problems: in one Latino-dominated town a Lutheran church operating in a Spanish medium encourages assimilation with 'multicultural America', while a neighbouring Catholic mission, dedicated to the Virgin of Guadalupe, helps immigrants connect with their roots and critically engages US society, challenging the identification of the United States with 'America' as a whole (Vásquez and Marquardt 2003:145–70).

Roman Catholicism is also particularly well represented among Asians in the United States, who number more than fifteen million according to census statistics, and are mainly Chinese, Filipino, Indian, Vietnamese, Korean and Japanese. Their presence further diversifies American Catholicism. Although according to canon law, parishes should be defined by territory not ethnicity, Vietnamese Catholics, for example, have several of their own parishes where their populations are most concentrated. Elsewhere they often form Vietnamese congregations using the local parish facilities. In 2003 there were approximately five hundred Vietnamese priests working both in the Vietnamese congregations and in the wider church community (Phan 2003a:230–1). The presence of migrant groups poses many questions of organization for the church, but Peter Phan, a Catholic theologian of Vietnamese descent, urges that it also presents theological opportunities for 'mutual criticism and enrichment between cultures' (238). In addition to the culture the Vietnamese bring with them, Phan argues that the experience of Vietnamese immigrants in the United States is a resource to critique the dominant culture, for example, its individualism, and suggest constructive alternatives (243). He hopes not just for an intercultural Vietnamese–American theology but also for an 'inter-multicultural theology' resulting from the encounter 'not *between* but *among*' the many different cultures represented in North America (10).

The Canadian contrast and First Nations Christians

The people of Canada are on the whole less religious than their counterparts south of the US border, but still more religious than many Western European countries. Their Christian experience provides an interesting counterfoil to that of their southern neighbours. The study of Canadian religion has tended to be a matter of Protestant–Catholic relations. Following their exploration of North America, the French government established the colony of New France (1655–1763) which eventually cut a vast swathe through the heart of the continent, from what is now Northeastern Canada through the Great Lakes to the Gulf of Mexico. Evidence of French settlement is retained in the names of cities from Quebec to Detroit and down the Mississippi to St Louis and New Orleans. French Sulpicians and Ursulines built on the work of the Jesuits to establish churches, schools, hospitals and Indian missions there. An indigenous mission, the Grey Nuns, or Sisters of Charity, of Montreal, founded by Marguerite d'Youville to work among the poor and sick was formally constituted in 1755. D'Youville was canonized in 1990 as the first Canadian-born saint.

As the British began to acquire territory in Nova Scotia, they pursued a policy of Anglicanization; however, the preservation of Roman Catholicism under British rule was assured by the Quebec Act of 1774, which created a francophone–Catholic enclave. In the face of Anglo-Protestant dominance, the Catholic Church adopted 'survivance' or maintaining the religion and the conservative ways of pre-revolutionary rural France. After the Seven Years' War between France and Britain in North America, Canada became a separate territory under the British crown and migration from France dwindled. The revival known in the United States as the Great Awakening reached Canadian Protestants, through the preaching of Henry Alline, only after the American Revolutionary War, in which the Québecois fought on the British side. In this context it was interpreted as a vindication of Canadian loyalty to the British crown, rather than

Figure 6.5 Church building in rural Canada. Image: iStock.

as an encouragement to revolution (Mullin 1999:427). Whereas in the United States, the strongest group to emerge from the Great Awakening was the Baptists, in Canada, it was the Methodist Church which grew rapidly as a result of the revival and also because of continuing working-class migration from Britain. Whereas most North-American Baptists stressed the independence of the local church, the Methodists were unified through the wider structure of the 'connexion'. Consequently, the Canadian Methodist Church, which was particularly close to the British Methodist Church, 'functioned as a culturally centripetal force', in contrast to the US pattern of independent local churches (433). Nor did the Canadian revival imbue the same sense of manifest destiny, so Canadian civil institutions were not invested with religious meaning as they are in the United States (Marty 2002:419). Even though the Anglican Church gradually came to represent a smaller proportion of Canadian Protestants, it kept its established status until 1854, when Canada was moving toward becoming a federal dominion of the British Crown, which happened in 1867.

The impulse of the Protestant churches to unity rather than competition bore fruit when in 1925 Methodists, Presbyterians and Congregationalists joined together to form the United Church of Canada. The churches in Canada were less easily split by the modernist controversies over biblical criticism and Darwinism. There was a strong Evangelical movement but it did not develop extreme fundamentalism. However, it was morally conservative. It supported a Lord's Day Act (1906) and the prohibition (of alcohol) laws in the 1920s. In 1940, Canadians were more likely than Americans to attend church, but by 1980 this statistic was reversed as Canada became a more secular society (Mullin 1999). Even in Quebec, where in the 1950s 93 per cent attended Sunday Mass, the Catholic hold over society has been strongly challenged and has diminished dramatically. Nevertheless, Canada saw a strong charismatic revival movement within the older churches from the 1970s and the emergence of new churches. Attention was drawn to it in 1994 by the controversial 'Toronto blessing', which involved 'holy laughter' (Stanley 2013:207–8). In the cities of Toronto, Vancouver and Montreal, there are many other new churches due to a more relaxed immigration policy since 1967. In Canada the most 'visible minorities' are not mainly from Africa or Latin America as in the United States but from Asia, and the new churches and congregations are most likely to be Chinese and Filipino.

Canadian churches have done more than their US counterparts to address the injustices done to the people of the 'First Nations', the Native American population. From 1876 until the late twentieth century, the denominational churches – mainly the Catholic and Anglican churches – supported the government policy of assimilation by running schools in which children were forbidden to use their native tongue and were both 'civilized' and Christianized. Some of these were boarding schools to which children were forcibly removed from their parents. They were often kept in poor conditions and sometimes sterilized and sexually abused. However, the churches were also at the forefront of addressing the issues raised by First Nations people. The Anglican, Catholic, Presbyterian and United Churches of Canada have issued apologies for their role in suppressing Native American culture and complicity with the school system. They have entered into a settlement, a truth and reconciliation process and a new covenant with the First Nations peoples (Balia and Kim 2010:109). The churches' initiatives were followed by government apologies in 2008 and 2015 and payment of compensation. The churches are further seeking to recognize the gifts and spirituality of First Nations people in their liturgical life (e.g. Carlson 1998). Christian Native Americans themselves have articulated a distinctive perspective on Christian faith. Robert Allen Warrior (1995) complained that the use of the exodus story in theologies of liberation casts his people in the role of the unfortunate Canaanites. He urged Christians to read the whole Bible and encouraged his people to look to their own resources for theologizing. George Tinker (1994) suspected that 'the way [European] immigrants pray and how they understand creation and their relationship to creation' lies at the root of the oppression his people have experienced. He argues that Western Christians should re-read the Bible to see how God's kingship is expressed not through domination but in a caring relationship to creation.

Summary

Christians – mostly Protestant – came to North America from Europe looking for freedom to practise their religion, and a place to establish a godly society. Believing God had led them to this 'promised land' they spread across the vast continent, displacing the Native Americans. The presence of groups of Christians from different ethnic groups and church traditions led to a situation of Christian pluralism, known as denominationalism. This pluralism and resistance to colonial authority encouraged the growth of independent local churches as the primary expression of the body of Christ. These were only loosely connected to the traditions of the older churches and, under the influence of the Puritans, they invested authority in the Bible as the Word of God. In Canada, where there is a different political context and there were relatively more Catholics, Christians across the country valued their connections more. In both countries the traditional European connection of church and state was severed and replaced with voluntary religion into which people 'converted' and, increasingly, a market of religious options in competition with one another. From the eighteenth century a series of revival movements further developed the independent, pragmatic faith of the settlers in the United States into the form of Christianity known there as Evangelicalism, which is conversionist, activist, biblicist and crucicentric. They developed an extensive network of charitable and missionary organizations but divided over issues of biblical authority and mission priorities. Evangelicals resist aspects of modernity they see as threatening to Christian faith and rejected the social gospel. Fundamentalism represents an extreme form of protest at the perceived loss of the Christian moral underpinnings of society. Despite predictions of secularization, most North Americans practise a private and personal form of faith in Jesus Christ, but they expect this will be respected in the public sphere and they resist legislation that impinges on areas they consider matters of religious freedom.

Africans brought as slaves to the Americas adapted European Christianity to their own needs in the 'invisible institution' of slave religion which developed, after emancipation, into black churches and denominations. It was from within this context of black Christianity that the civil rights movement was born in the United States, which was also challenged to further develop its African identity through the black theology movement. African identity also expressed itself in the most influential Pentecostal revival, at Azusa Street, which influenced other churches worldwide through the Pentecostal–charismatic movement. Many of the more recent migrants to the continent from Asia and Latin America are also Christians and have introduced still greater variety into the North American church scene, while also increasing the size and diversity of the single largest denomination, the Roman Catholic Church, which also became politically influential in the twentieth century.

Study questions and further readings

- Compare Christianity in the United States with that in Canada and account for some of the differences.
- Evaluate the contribution of Christianity to US American public life.
- Discuss the differences between Evangelicals, fundamentalists, conservatives and Pentecostals.
- In what way have African American forms of Christianity influenced the churches in the United States?
- How do you assess the contribution of Roman Catholicism to North American Christianity?
- Identify some of the twentieth-century theological developments that have arisen from the US context and influenced Anglophone Christianity.

Dries, A. (1998), *The Missionary Movement in American Catholic History*. Maryknoll, NY: Orbis.

Gausted, E. S. and L. E. Schmidt (2002), *The Religious History of America*, second edition. New York: HarperCollins.

Marsden, G. M. (2006), *Fundamentalism and American Culture*, second edition. Oxford: Oxford University.

Noll, M. A. (2001), *American Evangelical Christianity*. Oxford: Blackwell.

Pinn, A. H. and A. B. Pinn (2002), *Introduction to Black Church History*. Minneapolis, MN: Fortress.

Robeck, C. M. (2006), *The Azusa Street Mission and Revival*. Nashville, TN: Thomas Nelson.

Stanley, B. (2013), *The Global Diffusion of Evangelicalism*. Downers Grove, IL: InterVarsity.

7

Oceanic Christianities

Chapter Outline

For our purposes, Oceania comprises Australia, New Zealand, and the Pacific island groups now known as Polynesia, Melanesia and Micronesia (as a result of colonial decisions that did not always reflect island realities). The great landmass of Australia has an inhospitable 'outback', or interior, and so is settled mainly around the coast. Today's population is overwhelmingly of European descent – the indigenous population having dwindled through its suffering – but there is increasing migration from Asia. The islands of New Zealand were also colonized by Europeans but have a relatively larger indigenous (Maori) population. Most of the islands of the Pacific came under European, Japanese, United States, Australian or New Zealand control at some time in the past three centuries but in most islands (with the major exception of Hawaii) the people are predominantly indigenous. Although Oceania makes up only 1 per cent of the world's Christians, it is mostly Christian. Christian numbers in Australia and New Zealand may be declining but they continue to grow in the Pacific islands. In much of Polynesia, and in Kiribati in Micronesia, almost everyone identifies as Christian. Although its church history has much in common with other Western colonies and colonized societies, Oceania presents a unique mix of local and international agency. Furthermore, the indigenous Christians of the Pacific offer a distinctive theological perspective from their 'liquid continent', a region covering a vast area mostly composed of ocean.

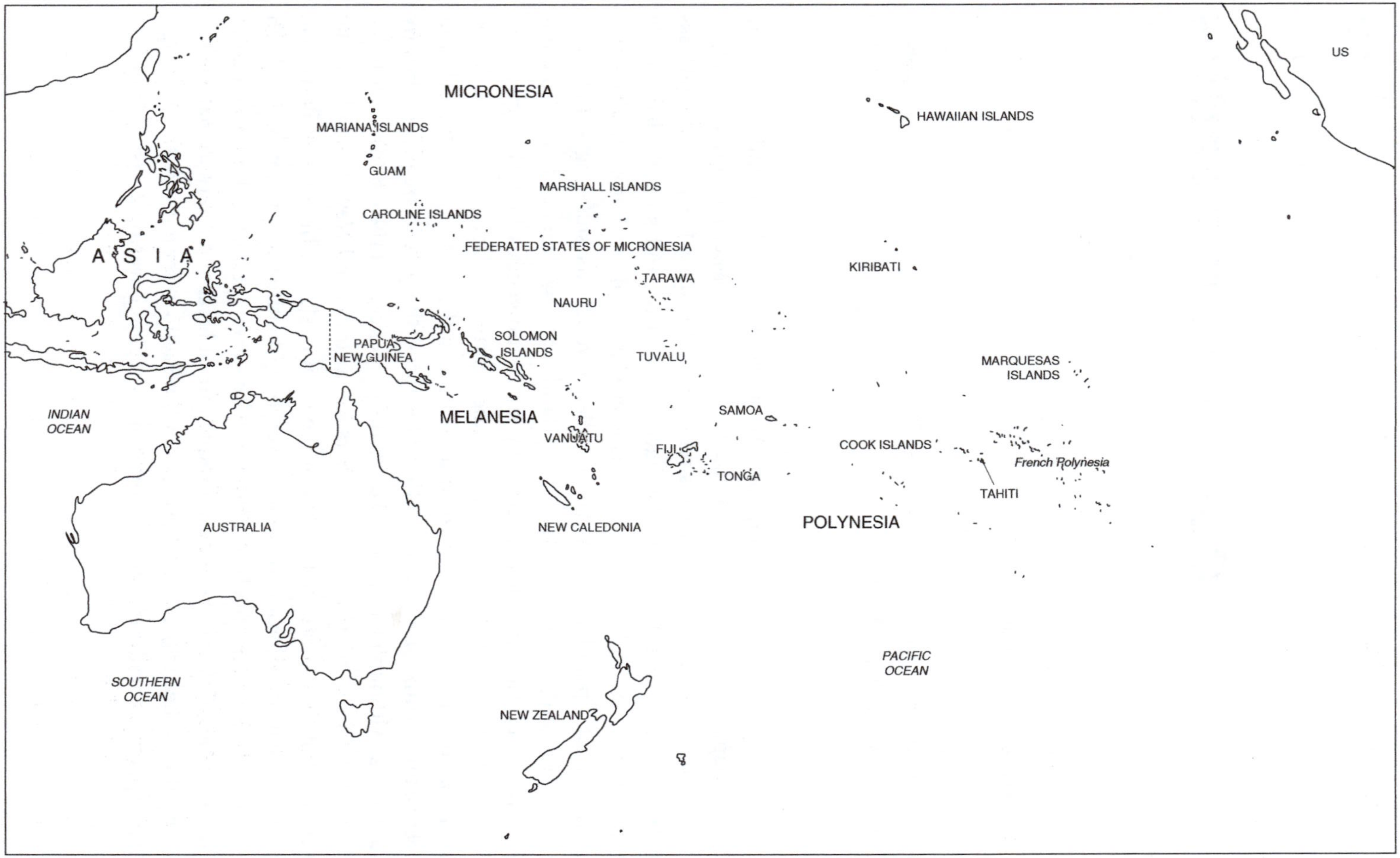

MICRONESIA
MARIANA ISLANDS
GUAM
CAROLINE ISLANDS
MARSHALL ISLANDS
FEDERATED STATES OF MICRONESIA
TARAWA
NAURU
KIRIBATI
HAWAIIAN ISLANDS
US
ASIA
PAPUA NEW GUINEA
SOLOMON ISLANDS
TUVALU
MELANESIA
VANUATU
FIJI
SAMOA
TONGA
NEW CALEDONIA
COOK ISLANDS
MARQUESAS ISLANDS
French Polynesia
TAHITI
POLYNESIA
INDIAN OCEAN
AUSTRALIA
SOUTHERN OCEAN
NEW ZEALAND
PACIFIC OCEAN

Christianity and public life in Australia

The Aboriginal peoples of Australia have been there for at least fifty thousand years. They are unlikely to have met Christians before European explorers arrived in the seventeenth century. An apostolic prefecture Terra Australis was established in 1681 but no Catholic missions were sent. The first settlers were from Britain, which established Protestant colonies there from 1788 with little regard for the existing population. The Aborigines' lack of the trappings of religion was taken to mean they had 'no organised spiritual values' and was one of the main justifications for lack of negotiation with them (Carey 1996:27–8). During European settlement, the Aborigines fought to protect their people and lands but were devastated by dispossession, inhuman treatment, disease and despair (Breward 2001:4–9). Driven further away from white settlements and with their population rapidly declining, they became largely invisible to the settler nation. Now known officially as the Aboriginal Australians and Torres Strait Islanders, only in 2013 were they recognized legally as the continent's first inhabitants.

Figure 7.1 His Holiness Pope Benedict XVI holds his final mass of World Youth Day at Randwick Racecourse in Sydney, Australia, 20 July 2008. Image: iStock.

The abolitionist William Wilberforce lobbied for an Evangelical Anglican chaplain Richard Johnson, and his wife, to accompany the first colonists of New South Wales (NSW), who were mostly male convicts transported from British gaols to the 'furthest corner' of the earth. Johnson led the first church service on Australian soil in 1788. For the next few decades, chaplains were the main ecclesial presence; they played a major role in transforming convict society and in building a stable democratic nation (Piggin and Davidson 2006:542). Many of the convicts were Irish Catholics but Catholic priests were permitted as chaplains only after the Napoleonic wars when they were deemed less of a political threat and even then the region was placed under the English Benedictines (Hilliard 1999:509–10). But after the Catholic hierarchy was established in 1842, Irish bishops became preeminent. Unlike NSW and Tasmania, the colonies of Western Australia, Victoria, South Australia and Queensland were established by dissenters and non-conformist groups (Carey 1996:1–25).

Settler Christianity in Australia stayed closely bound to Britain and Ireland until the late nineteenth century, especially as most of the clergy were supplied from there. Catholic, Anglican, Methodist and Presbyterian churches (the latter arriving in 1823) predominated until the late twentieth century. The Anglican Church had the largest number of congregations in Australia until overtaken by Catholics in the mid-1980s. The Evangelical revivals of the early nineteenth century passed Australia by but in the 1860s the preaching of Australian-born John Watsford contributed to rapid growth of Methodism. From 1836 the governor of NSW offered all the main denominations aid to build churches and establish pastoral ministry. On the one hand, this even-handed approach tended to promote sectarian rivalry, especially between Catholics and Protestants, which was exacerbated by the tensions between Britain and Ireland. On the other, denominational differences between Protestants were less strongly felt because, especially in the 'bush' or the 'backblocks', Christians were few and far between. The need to minister to remote communities led to collaborative mission initiatives involving church workers travelling on horseback, by bike and even plane. Several attempts were made at Protestant church union but they failed until in 1977 Methodists, Congregationalists and most Presbyterians came together to form a church which they described not as 'united' but 'uniting'. Open to further unions, the Uniting Church also now includes congregations of East Asian churches. To promote inclusivity, it pioneered a consensus approach to decision-making that has become a model for the World Council of Churches (WCC) and parliamentary bodies.

As new Christian denominations entered from North America in the twentieth century, a religious marketplace developed and secularization increased in keeping with global trends in Anglo-Celtic populations since the 1960s (Carey 1996:172–95). The newly optional nature of religion in the settler community contributed to a decline in the older denominations, although this lags behind Europe. However, immigration from Southern and Eastern Europe has benefitted the Catholic Church particularly and new Orthodox churches have resulted from migration since the Second World War. In keeping with global trends, and helped by migration from the Pacific Islands, Pentecostal churches are also growing. Hillsong is Australia's largest church (formerly Australian Assemblies of God). It is led by a white New Zealand couple Brian and Bobbie Houston and has planted churches in all continents, including in North America. Its music is known globally; in Australia it has even topped the charts. Migration from East Asia has brought strong Chinese, Vietnamese, Indonesian and Korean communities into urban areas. While increasingly secular white populations are exploring Asian spiritualities and constructing their own private forms of religion influenced by both (Tacey 2004:6), Asian churches are increasing the ethnic diversity of Australian Christianity.

Following the early Anglican example, the Australian churches have been exceptionally active in public life. The first Presbyterian minister, John Dunmore Lang, who arrived in 1823, promoted equality and universal suffrage in the colonies (Breward 2001:17–18). From 1841, a Catholic woman, Caroline Chisholm, promoted emigration to Australia to address problems of hunger and health in Britain and Ireland. She supported single women migrants and re-united the families of convicts and immigrants, helping anyone in need regardless of religion or nationality. Education was under the control of the main denominations until the 1880s, when a public system was introduced. However the Catholic community preferred not to participate and set up a separate system, with which Lasallians and Sisters of Mercy from Ireland, Jesuits from Austria and Marists from France assisted (Piggin and Davidson 2006:546–7). Mary MacKillop, who in 2010 became the first, and so far only, Australian-born saint, established a teacher training college in Sydney that is now part of the Australian Catholic University and a community, the Sisters of Saint Joseph of the Sacred Heart. Even after the end of transportation in 1867, the association of the church with values and morality in the public life in Australia continued. Councils of Churches were formed which used legislation to limit Sunday trading and restrain the liquor industry. On divorce, Christians were divided but the more progressive voice of Alfred Barry, Anglican bishop of Sydney, prevailed and civil divorce became law in every colony by the end of the nineteenth century. Predominantly Christian campaigns, in which Betsy Harrison Lee was a leading figure, contributed to Australian women getting the vote earlier than their American and British counterparts. However, the temperance movement suffered from a backlash from Australian men and from 'muscular Christianity' (547–9).

Despite the settler population being nearly 100 per cent Christian, partly because of sectarianism, when the Commonwealth of Australia was formed as a federation of the six colonies in 1901, its constitution was secular. It adopted both English establishment, in that it permits government support for religious institutions, and also American church-state separation by protecting against Commonwealth interference (Maddox 2012:205). Churches were active in trade unionism and for most of the twentieth century the Labor Party drew much of its support from Catholics (Thompson 2002). A disproportionate number of Australian politicians have been practising Christians. Since 1946, the Parliamentary Christian Fellowship has conducted weekly breakfasts, prayer and Bible study meetings, and from 1986, an annual National Prayer Breakfast was started both to reach out to other politicians and to bring church and state closer. The threat of communism, especially as mediated through US American Christianity, brought the churches together in 1951 to raise moral standards and evangelize the nation, but this effort dissipated with the cultural revolutions of the 1960s (Massam 2006:260). Evangelical conservativism, even fundamentalism, remains strong in Australia. Reasons for this include the exclusion of theology from universities, a strong post-war revival of Reformed theology, white supremacist views akin to those in South Africa and the United States and the influence of Irish sectarianism (Stanley 2013:57–9). Peter Jenson, archbishop of Sydney until 2013, is general secretary of the Fellowship of Confessing Anglicans, which split from the Anglican Communion due to issues of sexuality. Pentecostal and Evangelical churches have formed a religious right focused on the Family First party. Responding to such challenges, James Haire and other theologians at Charles Sturt University have led reflection on Christian involvement in public life through the Global Network for Public Theology.

From the late eighteenth century Sydney became a base for evangelical missions to the indigenous peoples of New Zealand and other islands of the Pacific, and by the late nineteenth century Australians themselves were initiating missions, especially to East Asia. The colonial authorities did not take any responsibility for the evangelization of the native peoples of Australia until Queen Victoria's reign (Carey 1996:55) but the Wesleyan Missionary Society in England sent William Walker, who arrived in 1821. Soon defeated by the challenges of the languages, peripatetic lifestyle and tribal conflict of the Aborigines and the deaths of promising youths, he turned to educational work instead. But now attention was drawn to them, the government granted land to Wesleyans, Congregationalists (London Missionary Society; LMS) and Anglicans (Church Missionary Society; CMS) for Aboriginal missions.

Although the missionaries protected Aboriginal rights by providing a physical space for them, the majority showed uncritical support for the discriminatory policies of the colonial government and the racial prejudice of the settlers. Furthermore, their preaching of the superiority of Christian faith and customs over indigenous beliefs and values hastened the collapse of native cultures (Maddox 2012:211). The more successful missions acknowledged Aboriginal cultures by teaching in the vernacular, recognizing indigenous leadership and showing a measure of insight into their spirituality. Two Moravian missions in Western Victoria established in 1858 and

1905 became independent self-governing communities. Others which emphasized self-supporting and self-governing principles in this period were run by German Lutherans, Spanish Benedictines and Anglicans.

By the twentieth century the Aboriginal population began to grow again – for which some credit may be due to the missions (Piggin and Davidson 2006:545; Carey 1996:61–5). However from 1905 till the 1970s, the Aboriginal Protection Boards took over the missions, although the churches continued to supply a religious element. Aiming to assimilate Aboriginal children the authorities forcibly removed them from their homes (Carey 1996:70–5). The remarkable growth of Christianity among the native people began with a charismatic revival that commenced in 1979 among indigenous people in Elcho Island in the Northern Territory. It spread quickly through Arnhem Land and other Aboriginal communities, especially in Western Australia. As the people experienced the Holy Spirit directly, without the mediation of missionaries, they felt empowered to raise social justice issues. This led to the birth of the Uniting Aboriginal and Islander Christian Congress. The congress is active on a range of issues such as high levels of youth suicide and restoring the elders of the community. Another activity is challenging the Australian authorities and the churches over the 'stolen generations' of children torn from their families. Many of these concerns are expressed theologically by the Rainbow Spirit Elders (2012) and by storytellers such as Denise Champion (2014). The congress is now part of the Uniting Church, which revised its constitution in 2009 to recognize that the Spirit of God was known in the land before the colonial churches arrived (cf. Porter 1990). This affirmation of Aboriginal wisdom and assertion of a continuity of Australian spirituality, despite colonization, has enabled the church to embrace both indigenous and Christian practices in its worship and processes. The Uniting Church takes a leading role in advocacy for the rights of the native people.

Contextual theology in Aotearoa New Zealand

The Maori in New Zealand are Polynesians who had been there for several hundred years before they were visited by European explorers and later traders from Britain, Australia and North America. They had highly organized tribal communities bound by rituals, belief in spirits and gods, and strong values of *mana* (authority), *tapu* (taboo; sanctity) and *uta* (reciprocity). Intrepid travellers, Maoris took opportunities to travel to the lands the Pakeha (or Europeans) came from. In Sydney some, including Ruatara, met Samuel Marsden, successor of Johnson as Anglican chaplain. With the support of the CMS, Marsden took up their invitation to lead a mission to

Figure 7.2 The altar with Maori-style carvings inside St Joseph's Church, Jerusalem, Whanganui, New Zealand. The church is part of the convent founded by Sister Mary Joseph Aubert and her Sisters of Compassion in 1892. Image: iStock.

New Zealand in 1814. In 1822, Samuel Leigh of the Wesleyan Missionary Society (Methodist) also moved to New Zealand. Both missions aimed at civilizing and Christianizing the indigenous peoples.

The Maori readily adopted the goods, technology and weaponry of the white people and took advantage of the new political situation for their own development but most were not receptive to the Christian message at first (Yates 2013). In the 1830s, there was a change in attitude that was partly due the missionaries' offer of literacy, which fascinated the Maori, and their translations of Christian literature into the Maori language. Some wives of missionaries were particularly engaged as teachers, translators and advocates for the people (Ross 2006). However, the growing weakness of the people due to war and disease was also a factor (Yates 2013:74–9). It was largely Maori initiatives that brought about a mass movement to Christianity in the 1840s (99–115). Wiremu Tamihana, for example, founded Christian communities in Te Tapiri and Peria. A gifted interpreter of the Bible, he campaigned to unite the Maori under a king (like the British) and sought peaceful relations with the colonial government, despite the fact that this was an era of cannibalism (Breward 2001:93–4, 146–8). The profound social changes in this period were not only religious but also cultural since literacy brought new power to communicate ideas and reconstruct Maori society (Piggin and Davidson 2006:551).

In 1840, the majority of Maori chiefs concluded the treaty of Waitangi with the British government which recognized Maori rights but under the British crown. Believing it offered the Maoris protection, CMS and Methodist missionaries played an important role in interpreting the treaty and garnering Maori support for it (Yates 2013:90–8). However, although Maoris set great store by Waitangi, and even invested it with the religious connotations of a covenant, the colonial government did not. Pressure from settlers led to the New Zealand Wars of the mid-nineteenth century and a breakdown of trust between some Maoris and missionaries. However, many of the Maori leaders who led the unsuccessful resistance against British troops were inspired by Christian themes and these spawned new religious movements such as Pai Marire (Breward 2001:144–54). Not all Maoris took up arms. Te Whiti and Tohu Kākahi led non-violent resistance in South Taranaki and became an inspiration to Mahatma Gandhi (Riseborough 2002). In the mid-twentieth century Maoris campaigned again for recognition of their rights under the treaty and it became the basis of a new settlement.

As more European settlers arrived, so did clergy, especially Anglican, Methodist and Presbyterian (Church of Scotland). The latter settled especially in south around Otago to create a distinctive society. Under Bishop Jean-Baptiste Pompallier, French Marist missionary priests ministered to the Catholics among them and also reached out to the Maoris from 1838 with the help of catechists, such as Hakaraia Te Hura (Yates 2013:80–9, 109–10). The bishop also brought the Irish Sisters of Mercy in the early 1860s, who made significant contributions to education and social work. Among them was a French woman, Susanne Aubert, who wrote a Maori dictionary, served the poor and founded the first New Zealand religious institute: the Daughters of our Lady of Compassion (Breward 2001:163–4).

Although Maoris were given office in the churches and from the 1840s ordained as clergy, they were in a subordinate position (Yates 2013:110). But they gained confidence through church schools and organizations such as Te Aute College Students' Association. In the early twentieth century, Maori prophets arose who preached a millennialist message that the Maori were a chosen people and they would be liberated by God's providence. Tahupotiki Ratana advocated Maori unity and a Christian healing ministry and led an independence movement that eventually established his own church in 1925. Another independent church of that period is Ringatu (Breward 2001:259–61). To recognize Maori leadership, the Anglican Church is now restructured to give Maori congregations their own structures of government (Davidson 2000). Pakeha Christians in the older churches increasingly refer to their country as Aotearoa New Zealand, using the Maori name, and incorporate aspects of Maori spirituality and language into their own liturgical life. Anglican Maoris have developed a theology through a Maori lens, *Atuatanga*, and at Catholic Institute of Theology in Auckland, Henare Tate (2013), an indigenous priest, has done similarly.

In the late twentieth century New Zealand was a centre of revival movements. The first was a charismatic renewal in 1963–4 among the Christian Brethren, a conservative group with close-knit congregations that formed an exceptionally high proportion of New Zealand Protestants. The Brethren have strong children's and youth work through global organizations such as Crusaders and Scripture Union (Stanley 2013:54–60). They also contributed to the strong Protestant overseas missions from New Zealand. This included the mission agency Servants, which specializes in serving the urban poor. It was founded in the 1980s by Viv Grigg, who took the unusual step of actually living in the slums himself. The second revival was the Maori response to a movement that swept through Australian Aboriginal and Pacific Islander communities in the late 1970s and 1980s. Various neo-Pentecostal Maori churches emerged from that. The most prominent is Destiny, founded by Brian Tamaki in 1998. Tamaki also founded a political party to defend Maori rights according to their interpretation of the treaty of Waitangi (Ross 2005:154–57) but the movement is becoming increasingly sectarian (Lineham 2013). Christian adherence is declining in New Zealand among the Pakeha population especially, who are increasingly secularized. But at the same time the faith is being invigorated by immigrants from Samoa, Tonga and the Cook Islands, who bring new forms of worship with them.

Peacemaking in the Pacific

In the Pacific, generally 'the Bible came before the flag', since the islands were of relatively little interest to governments, and 'Protestants preceded Catholics' – except in the case of the Marianas (Davidson 2004:142). Furthermore, in many cases it was Pacific people themselves who spread the gospel to other islands. Protestant missions to the Pacific Islands did not start with those closest to European settlement. The Melanesians were known to be war-torn and inclined to cannibalism but the Polynesians and Micronesians had drawn the attention of Western Romantics for their remoteness and apparently innocent charm (Foreman 1982:4). Among the motivations of the missionaries was a desire to protect the people from the predations of traders in goods and slaves and from sexual exploitation by sailors and whalers. However, this approach tended to degenerate into missionary paternalism.

Polynesia

The LMS sent its first missionaries to Tahiti, Tonga and the Marquesas in 1797, and eventually in 1812 King Pomare II took baptism and started a Christian movement (Breward 2001:24–9). Although an indigenous messianic movement called Mamaia arose, which rejected missionary sexual morality and celebrated power and the acquisition of Western goods, the mission church prevailed. Wesleyans began

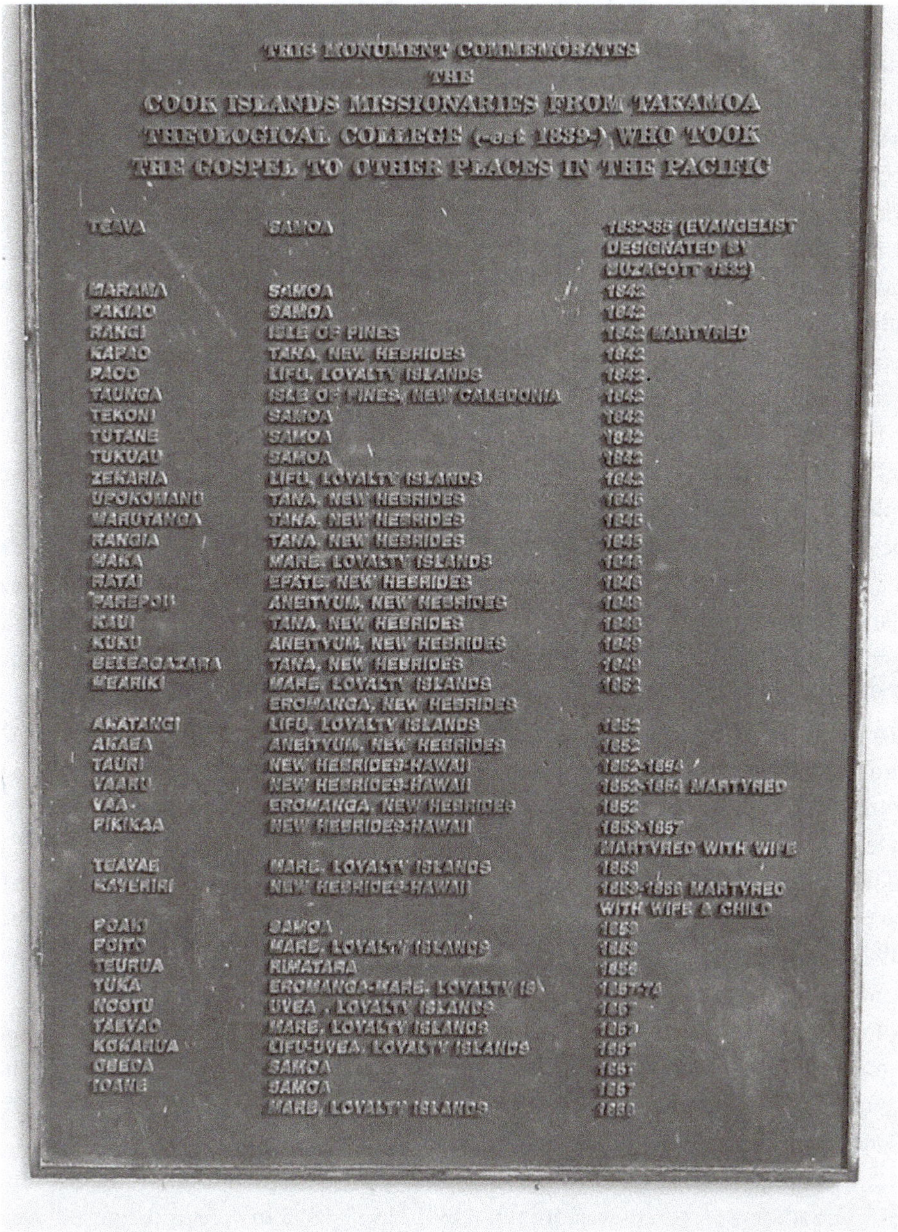

Figure 7.3 Plaque listing nineteenth-century Cook Island missionaries sent out from Takamoa Theological College, Rarotonga (founded by the London Missionary Society in 1839). They took the gospel to other places in the Pacific and several of them were martyred.

work on Tonga in 1822 and a church was established there with the support of chief Taufa'ahau (George) of Ha'apai who, in 1850, set up a Christian kingdom (Swain and Trompf 1995:198–205). In the contest with the powers of the native priests, which often centred on illness and death, the God of the new religion (with the aid of modern medicine) proved more powerful. Polynesians were especially in awe of the Bible and literacy and keen to learn to read. They burnt fetishes and, although traditional beliefs in a spirit-world persisted, largely abandoned their traditional rituals. They were also prepared to forego social customs condemned by missionaries, such as drinking, tattooing and dancing (which were also associated with sexual excesses), and the chiefs adopted Western clothing. The differences between Western and Polynesian cultures were so great that the churches still tend to stress behaviour more than belief, and church discipline on matters such as smoking, drinking, adultery, divorce and second marriage is often severe (Breward 2001:31–41, 51–64).

In Polynesia, the relative homogeneity of culture, language and social structure facilitated the acceptance of Christianity. However the tales of missionary success belie the fact that the initiative was largely with the islanders themselves. In these societies based on birth and rank, the success or otherwise of the mission depended to a large extent on whether the local chief supported it or not. When he did, whole island populations joined the church. Rulers gave the missionaries status but they also used Christianity to enhance their political power (Breward 2001:26). Furthermore, in many cases it was Christian islanders who evangelized other islands. With LMS encouragement, Tahitian evangelists spread the message to their close kin in the Cook Islands and across language barriers to Samoa, Tonga, Fiji and Hawaii (29–31). From 1832 Cook Islanders were commissioned by the LMS to work in Samoa, New Caledonia and the today's Solomon Islands. Several of them were martyred, such as Pikika'a and Keveriri in 1857, who were killed and eaten along with their families by the people in what is now Vanuatu for fear that they had brought disease (Liua'ana 1996:68). From 1838, King George sent Tongan evangelists to spread Methodism to Samoa and Fiji.

In most cases the islands still reflect the patchwork of the first Protestant denominations, which agreed among themselves to concentrate on different island groups, and the churches still tend to be national churches (Piggin and Davidson 2006:551–2). However, the Samoans, who were particularly confident, accepted both Congregationalism and Methodism and also sheltered a Marist mission from 1845. A Samoan pastorate was ordained by LMS in 1875 to spread the gospel westward (Liua'ana 1996:41–4). Since the local workers needed training and resources, LMS started a printing press and a missionary training college on Raratonga (Cook Islands) in the 1830s. Another LMS college was founded in Samoa in 1844 and a Wesleyan college in Tonga in 1866. These provided opportunities for lively debates about the adoption of elements of local culture in worship and education, which continue today. Already by the 1830s the Protestant churches in the Pacific had emerged as self-supporting communities with indigenous leadership, missionary movements and indigenized versions of Christian faith, which depended both on the islanders' previous religion and on the particular theology of the missionaries (Swain and Trompf 1995:206).

Christianity 'provided an alternative language for religious aspirations' and a 'new construction of religious and political community' (Breward 2001:23). Foreign pastors and local chiefs shared ecclesial and political authority (65). The traditions of the missionary period became deeply rooted and can be seen in Sunday clothes, church buildings and services. In the Cook Islands, the LMS introduced the Western calendar and set Sunday on the basis of the days they had counted since their departure from Australia. However, after the International Date Line became established, it transpired that they were worshipping on a Saturday. This circumstance contributed to the early success of Seventh-day Adventist churches in the islands in the late nineteenth century. But the LMS church (now the Cook Islands Christian Church) decided to change its Lord's Day to the new calendar in 1900 by adding an extra Christmas day in 1899. Although they had earlier worshipped together, after this was done, Adventists were penalized because the rigid Sabbath-keeping of the established church was enforced by the island police. Nevertheless, the persistence of the Adventists broke the LMS monopoly and paved the way for the introduction of other new denominations, mainly from the United States. The Church of the Latter-Day Saints (Mormons) has been active in the region since the 1840s when missionary work began in Hawaii. Mormons have a special interest in the Polynesians because they believe they are descendants of Israel.

Since revivals in the 1980s, Pentecostal churches of both indigenous and foreign origin have grown rapidly. Pentecostal-charismatic worship has both an affinity with traditional religiosity and also a modern and prosperous image. The charismatic Youth With A Mission in particular, with local leadership, has contributed to reshaping youth identity in a way that connects with global trends. Pentecostal-charismatic Christianity evokes a popular response in the islands and its appeal is also because the mission churches have become inflexible (Davidson 2004). Their reluctance to change is partly because of their faithfulness to the received tradition but this is also bound up with nationalist impulses. The use of local languages and styles of worship in Protestant worship has protected Polynesians against the dominance of English and French. However, in the globalized Pacific of today, church elders struggle to maintain the traditions of the mission when exposure to Western culture among the youth is so high.

French colonial expansion in the Pacific caused rivalry between Catholic and Protestant missions but also in some cases allowed local leaders to gain a measure of autonomy and advantage. Catholic missions arrived in Polynesia with the Picpus fathers in the Gambier Islands in 1834 and Tahiti in 1836 and Marists, led by Bishop Pompallier, in Tonga in 1842 and in Samoa in 1845. When Tahiti came under French Polynesia, the LMS work was handed over to the (Protestant) Paris Evangelical Mission (in 1863). Several Catholic missionaries – like Louis Elloy in Samoa – gained a deep understanding of Polynesian culture but it was largely excluded from the liturgy until after the Second Vatican Council. Then conscious 'inculturation' included the use of flowers in baptism in the Eucharist and incorporation of dances, chants and local songs. The development of the permanent diaconate following the Council improved local representation in church leadership by allowing married men to minister but the number of local priests is still low (Hezel 2012:236–8).

Micronesia

While British missions evangelized the Pacific from east to west, the American Board of Commissioners for Foreign Missions (Congregational) worked from north to south, beginning in Hawaii from 1820. Such was the indigenous response that in 1865, they declared it Christianized and withdrew the mission, giving responsibility to Hawaiian leaders, although in practice US missionaries remained in charge. Hawaiians continued the evangelization efforts in Eastern Micronesia, where they established a mission training school, and in Kiribati until French missionaries of the Sacred Heart with superior resources gained the support of the population in the first few years of the twentieth century (Foreman 1982).

Western Micronesia had been reached in the seventeenth century by Jesuits from the Philippines, together with Spanish troops, who occupied Guam and the Mariana Islands from 1668 until it was ceded to the United States following the Spanish–American War of 1898. Catholic evangelization did not proceed to the rest of Micronesia until, following the award of the Caroline Islands to Spain in 1885, Capuchin missionaries and locals evangelized most island groups. When Germany acquired the Spanish islands in 1899, the Spanish Capuchins were replaced with German ones and the situation was reversed in the early twentieth century. The year after their arrival, the Jesuits on Guam established the first school in the Pacific. It was for boys but soon afterwards they opened another for girls. A network of elementary schools was developed and three centuries later, after the Second World War, American Jesuits established leading high schools. Mission education developed literacy, improved the standard of living and trained future leaders for the whole region until government schools were established more recently. Healthcare has been another area in which Catholic missions made significant improvement to the lives the people. It follows the example of Jacopo Chavarri, a Jesuit brother, who worked in Marianas from 1693 for 50 years as a pharmacist treating the people as they succumbed to Western illnesses. The missions also functioned as mediators between the islanders and the wider world, advocating for the rights and welfare of the people. Guam and the Marianas remain strongly Catholic societies in which Church and community are closely linked as shown by the enthusiasm with which Church festivals are celebrated (Hezel 2012).

Melanesia

Although it is closest to Australia, Melanesia was the last region of the Pacific to be evangelized. Reasons for this include islander hostility to missionaries and inter-tribal conflict in a region which has much greater diversity of peoples and languages. Furthermore, because these islands are nearer the equator, tropical diseases presented problems for Europeans and other islanders. The Melanesians were so impressed with the personal possessions and technologies of Europeans that some of them believed the goods were the product of divine spirits and developed 'cargo cults', which were later replaced by money cults (Swain and Trompf 1995:167–81).

Tongan Methodists had made a start in Fiji in 1835 and, after the warrior and cannibal Varani was converted, there was a popular revival. Eventually Chief Cakobau took baptism in 1857 and his killing stone was turned into a baptismal font. Tongan missionary Joeli Bulu helped establish a Fijian style of Christianity by utilizing local chants for the creed, incorporating fables in sermons and praying in a way which resembled traditional invocations (Breward 2001:31–41, 51–64, 157–8; Swain and Trompf 1995:198–205). Polynesians taught Melanesians improved house-building, cultivation, fishing, crafts and feasting (Latukefu 1996:31–6). The energetic Anglican bishop of New Zealand, George Selwyn, took seriously his additional charge to reach out to the Pacific Islands, especially because of a growing slave trade in the region, and in 1854 an Anglican diocese of Melanesia was created. From the late nineteenth century Australian and New Zealand organizations gradually took over much of the European mission work in the Pacific. In the Solomon Islands, the South Seas Evangelical Mission developed out of an indigenous Australian mission to plantation workers in Queensland from 1886. Catholic missions established a strong presence in the region in the late nineteenth century (Piggin and Davidson 2006:553–4).

Being closer to Asia as well as Australia, Papua, the largest landmass of Melanesia – today divided into Indonesian (West) Papua and the independent nation of Papua New Guinea (PNG) – attracted various missions. These included in the 1870s the Polynesian Wesleyan mission with dedicated Fijians (Latukefu 1996:25–6) and Catholics such as the Society of the Divine Word, Franciscans, Capuchins and Passionists. Along with German colonization came Lutherans from 1886, whose most famous missionary, Christian Keysser, proposed the evangelization of tribes, rather than individuals, through the concept known as *Volkskirche* (or people's church). So successfully did the people spread the faith that the Evangelical

Lutheran Church of Papua New Guinea is still the dominant Protestant church there. It was only in the 1930s that it was discovered that there were hundreds of tribal groups living isolated – even from each other – in the inaccessible Papuan highlands. After the Second World War there was an influx of evangelical denominational and interdenominational missions aiming to reach them, including the Unevangelized Fields Mission (now Crossworld). Wycliffe Bible Translators and the Summer Institute of Linguistics worked to translate the scriptures into the most viable of the hundreds of mutually unintelligible languages. Christian agencies also provide many of the social services of PNG, whose people are among the poorest people in Asia. The Charismatic revivals that swept across Melanesia in the 1970s and 1980s affected many of the groups in Papua deeply. Christian faith both unsettled traditional morality and also provided an eschatological hope for people transitioning to modernity (Robbins 2004).

In a region with such a heterogeneous population and a long history of intertribal warfare, although there were a few instances of tensions between rival denominations, Christian faith (in various forms) was used by kings and states to unify the people. Warriors who turned to Christ by and large understood that they should give up fighting except perhaps in the sense of warfare against evil spirits. In the 1960s, Canadian Don Richardson of the Regions Beyond Missionary Union famously used the custom of the Sawi tribes in PNG, who offered a child to one another as a peace offering, to introduce Jesus as the final 'peace child' (Richardson 1974). Others also worked for reconciliation between warring groups, such as Amos Tozaka, a Methodist in the Solomon Islands, who made two dangerous trips into the territory of chief Liliboe to offer peace in 1919 (Foreman 1982:106). The Melanesian Brotherhood, the largest male religious community in the Anglican Communion, was founded by Ini Kopuria, a Solomon Islander, in 1925 to win converts in the pattern of Jesus's disciples and Saint Francis. Lay brothers went out to communities, accepting their hospitality and offering practical help with fishing, house-building and other tasks, as well as sharing Christian teaching. Many responded to the message when they saw that the brothers were unafraid of devils and ancestral spirits (Carter 1998). More recently, during civil unrest in the Solomon Islands in 2003, seven members of the brotherhood were killed after one of them, Nathaniel Sado, tried to make peace with Harold Keke, a rebel leader.

The Pacific War (1941–5) brought intense suffering to Pacific Islanders as a result of Japanese invasions and American and Australian counter-attacks. There was also large-scale displacement due to atomic testing programmes by the United States, Britain and France. During the war, while missionaries and church leaders were interned by the Japanese, new syncretistic movements developed in churches declaring independence from the missions. The churches had laid the social foundations for independence and in most cases Protestant churches became self-governing before their respective nations. Christians were active in national independence movements as well (Foreman 1982). Except for Tonga, which had never been colonized, independence began in 1962 with Western Samoa. In the post-independence period regional interchurch coordinating bodies have helped to keep the peace and challenge governments over corruption and governance issues.

With the growth of air transportation, the islands have become both integrated into global society and also diversified through migrations from different parts of Asia. After Hawaii, in which the native population has now declined to less than a tenth, the island most affected is Fiji where the British brought large numbers of North Indians to work on the sugar plantations. The Indian population, which exceeds a third, is mostly Hindu but the churches include Indians, especially the Methodist Church, which is by far the largest. They have been interceding in clashes between the Indians and the native Fijians, who are mostly Christian. Many Pacific families are divided across islands or have members settled in New Zealand, Australia and other parts of the world in order to find work, receive education, improve their livelihood and escape environmental problems. Networks of diaspora churches are an important way in which Pacific communities are held together.

Mining, prospecting and weapons-testing have wreaked havoc on the natural environment of the Pacific and made some islands uninhabitable. Volcanic activity and tsunamis pose a constant danger, and rising sea levels due to global warming threaten the existence of these low-lying islands. In the late twentieth century writer Epeli Hau'ofa (1993:7), who was born of Tongan missionary parents working in Papua New Guinea, explained that the universe of the peoples of the Pacific 'comprised not only land surfaces, but the surrounding ocean', 'the underworld with its fire-controlling and earth-shaking denizens, and the heavens above . . . that people could count on to guide their ways across the seas'. So environmental degradation not only has physical but also spiritual effects. Since the end of the Second World War, the Pacific Conference of Churches and the Catholic Bishops' Conference of the Pacific have been raising these issues in international forums and church networks, such as the Justice, Peace and the Integrity of Creation programme of the WCC (Boseto 1995:183). Pacific theologians have been rising to the challenge of doing theology in this 'liquid continent', especially at the Pacific Theological College in Fiji (Pearson 2010). The 'father' of Pacific theology, Tongan theologian Sione 'Amanaki Havea, first chairman of the Pacific Council of Churches, described his reflections as 'coconut theology' (Havea 1987:14–15). In the 2004 Otin Taai (Sunrise) declaration, Pacific churches together committed themselves 'to care for the earth as our response to God's love for creation'. They affirmed an affinity between biblical teaching on creation and traditional Pacific Island stories of the interrelatedness of the whole earth. Reflecting on the story of Noah, they concluded that God's rainbow promise was not a guarantee against flooding in the future but an invitation to respond by reducing the human causes of climate change.

Summary

Oceania has a diverse Christian history which includes the evangelization of European and other settlers, especially in Australia and New Zealand, as well as of indigenous peoples. In the settler communities in Australia, the churches helped to create a law-abiding and just society and continue to play a significant role in education and public life. However, most Christians were not attentive to the rights of Aboriginal Australians and Torres Strait Islanders, and it is only now that some churches are addressing past injustices and campaigning on their behalf. In New Zealand, nineteenth-century missionaries facilitated a settlement with the Maori people and, although the colonial government did not honour this, the churches today are increasingly forming partnership relations with Maori churches. Revival movements since the 1970s have contributed to the growth of Christianity among the Aborigines and Maoris and the establishment of indigenous churches. The settler Christian populations of Australia and New Zealand are influenced both by the asceticism of East Asian religions and also by the holistic spirituality of the Pacific Islanders, which is mediated also through the spirituality of their migrant churches. Combined with secularization and North American cultural influence, this has led to experimentation with new and alternative forms of religion and a decline in Christian adherence.

Despite the large cultural gulf between the Pacific Islands and European missionaries, many of the peoples of the Pacific Islands embraced the Christian gospel and its moral codes with enthusiasm, partly because it seemed to offer material benefits and also because they were fascinated by the power of literacy. Generally after a chief was baptized, a people movement followed and in many cases the islands are more than 90 per cent Christian. European missions supported native initiatives to spread the gospel to other islands. Christians belong to a variety of churches; denominational differences generally correspond to people groups and have been linked to ethnic nationalism. Despite this, churches were an integral part of the reconfiguration and modernization of Pacific society in the twentieth century and, on the whole, a unifying factor. Today many are raising the concerns of the Pacific nations, particularly about the environmental degradation of the ocean and its habitats, in international Christian forums. Especially during and since the Second World War, local leadership, new religious movements, late-twentieth-century Pentecostal-charismatic revivals and church policies of inculturation have all contributed to the indigenization of the churches. At the same time, forces of globalization have internationalized youth culture and spread the Pacific churches across Oceania.

Study questions and further readings

- In what ways is the experience of Christians in the Pacific distinct from other Christians, and how is this reflected in the ways faith is expressed?
- Compare the relations of settlers in Australia and New Zealand with the respective indigenous peoples. Analyse the religious factors involved.
- Assess the contribution of the churches to the shaping of Australia.
- Identify and comment on the relationship of the churches in Oceania with Europe, North America and Asia.

Breward, I. (2001), *A History of the Churches in Australasia*. Oxford: Oxford University.

Carey, H. M. (1996), *Believing in Australia*. St Leonards, NSW: Allen and Unwin.

Robbins, J. (2004), *Becoming Sinners*. Berkeley: University of California.

Swain, T. and G. Trompf (1995), *The Religions of Oceania*. London: Routledge.

Yates, T. (2013), *The Conversion of the Maori*. Grand Rapids, MI: Eerdmans.

8

The Significance of World Christianity

Chapter Outline

Our survey of Christianity continent by continent has considered Christianity as a world religion primarily because it is present across the globe in countless local expressions which are linked by crisscrossing networks. We have seen that the expansion of Christianity globally results from its missional and inclusive theology and from trade and migration as well as intentional missionary activity. Christianity is spread primarily by indigenous believers and developed by them in local ways. Having considered various Christianities within regional contexts, in this chapter we will draw some conclusions about world Christianity as a whole and discuss the implications for religious studies, theological education (Werner et al. 2010; Bevans et al. 2015) and the development of theology. We shall do this under the four perspectives we have used to examine Christianity in each region: first, the history of the spread and reception of Christianity; second, forms of worship, church and theology; third, interreligious relations; and fourth, interaction with society, politics and economics.

Polycentric histories of Christian spread and reception

The issues raised by Christianity as a world religion for the study of Christian history include how to deal with its polycentric nature, the legacy of Christendom and issues of agency in mission and evangelization.

Multiple histories

First, Christianity is polycentric in every respect. So, for example, it is not possible to identify a geographical centre of the Christian faith. Jerusalem and Bethlehem continue to have special meaning because of their associations with the historical Jesus and, for some Christians, the expectation that they will play a special role in the end times. But access to them has been difficult over the centuries because of hostility and instability in the region; they do not function as organizational centres and most Christians do not feel any obligation to visit them. The Roman Catholic Church has a clear centre in Rome, but this allegiance is not necessarily shared by other Christians. The Orthodox churches have always been multicentric, and each of the many Protestant denominations has its own historical centre and organizational headquarters. Pentecostalism is polycentric by definition and in its origins and organization.

Christianity's polycentric nature is the source of its linguistic and ethnic diversity. It is written into the New Testament and subsequent Christian theology. So the historiography of Christianity is complex because it is not the history of one people group, one organization or one movement but an interweaving of many of them. Books on Christianity that treat it historically run the risk of giving the impression that there is one linear history. Many histories are told from the perspective of a particular contemporary Christian confession in order to explain its tradition but largely ignore the other churches. So, for example, Paul Kollman (2010) takes issue with several studies of African Christianity for giving the impression that it consists only of African Independent and Pentecostal churches and begins in the nineteenth century. Or they are told from the history of a particular people. Until recently most books in English on Christian history gave the impression that Christianity began in the Middle East and took a line westward. It was refined by the Greeks and came of age in Europe. Many maps of early Christian history continue to reinforce this by cutting off the early spread into Africa at the bottom and Asia at the right.

Books that attempt to deal with the whole of Christianity can be divided into those that treat the topic chronologically and others which approach it geographically, like this one. There are a few recent histories of Christianity that confine themselves to

Christianity in the West, and perhaps also the Orthodox East. However, most contemporary historians of Christianity find that from the twentieth century at least they cannot avoid being 'all over the map' because histories 'differ from continent to continent, country to country, tradition to tradition, and even neighbourhood to neighbourhood' (Bednarowski 2008:6). Historians may view world Christianity as a recent stage in the development of Christianity linked with modernity (e.g. Woodhead 2004). This may be seen as the result of world missions from the West (e.g. Dowley 2013) or more generally of globalization during the period of European empires and US hegemony which spread Western culture, including Christianity, worldwide (McManners 2002). Other historians see the relationship as more dialectical: part of Christianity's 'ambivalent relationship to European and American power' (McLeod 2006:6). Still others treat Christianity as a world religion from its origins. This may be done positively, drawing attention to the continuously polycentric and plural character of 'the world Christian movement' (Irvin and Sunquist 2001; 2012), or negatively, lamenting the demise of some of the earliest forms of Christianity under the oppression of imperial forms (e.g. Jenkins 2008).

The recognition of Christian plurality has prompted the use of the plural 'Christianities' (Gilley and Stanley 2006; McLeod 2006; Phan 2011) and encouraged a regional approach, combining history with ecclesial, geopolitical and intercultural approaches (e.g. Davies and Conway 2008; Farhadian 2012; Jacobsen 2011). These vary in the extent to which they integrate the treatment of different regions and analyse the relationship of Christianity to global affairs more generally. But it is noteworthy that few discuss the theoretical framework for doing history in a polycentric way. It poses a major challenge to Western historiographical method, which has assumed a linear historical development. Hans Küng (1995) put forward Thomas Kuhn's paradigm theory – developed in the history of science – as a way of explaining how different Christian theologies arose in different historico-cultural periods and coexist today (cf. Bosch (2011[1991]). However, this approach sees each paradigm as developing out of the previous one and so does not entirely escape the linear historical model. Others have found Michael Foucault's 'archaeology of knowledge' and 'concepts of discursive fields' fruitful for a history of Christianity in space as well as time (e.g. Stringer 2005:10–14). Further research is urgently needed on this question.

Beyond Christendom

Second, the world Christianity approach signals the end of the Christendom concept and the decentring of Europe in Christian studies. The decision of the European Union not to claim a Christian foundation for Europe shows that it no longer sees itself as a bloc of Christian kingdoms. Furthermore, whereas the World Missionary Conference in Edinburgh in 1910 attempted (with some difficulty) to divide the world into two territorially: Christian and non-Christian (Stanley 2009:49–72), a century later the *Atlas of Global Christianity* (Johnson and Todd 2009) emphasized Christianity's worldwide distribution. For the formerly colonized and others on the receiving end of aggressive Western mission, the end of Christendom may be welcomed as liberation from the dominance of the European mission churches or centralized control from Rome (e.g. Erskine 1981; Segundo 1976). Protestants descended from the radical Reformation and from newer independent traditions see the end of Christendom as the end of the error of the Constantinian settlement of 313 AD that compromised the Christian faith by tying it to worldly powers (e.g. Hauerwas 1999). However, not surprisingly, some Europeans suspect that 'world Christianity' reflects a US perspective on the world which is anti-European. Seeing themselves through others' eyes may be a painful experience for Europeans (Becker and Stanley 2014) but any treatment of world Christianity should recognize the achievements of European Christianity as well as the criticisms. As we have seen, in many cases in the modern period, people of other cultures are attracted to Christianity because they see in Europe and European peoples a realization of its social teaching.

Figure 8.1 The closing ceremony of the conference of Edinburgh 2010, the centenary project of the World Missionary Conference held in the Assembly Hall of the Church of Scotland, Edinburgh, 6 June 2010. The choir in the foreground is from the Scottish Council of African Churches and the sermon was delivered by the Archbishop of York, Dr John Sentamu, originally from Uganda. Photograph by World Council of Churches.

For some scholars of world Christianity, the decentring of Europe provides a way to focus on the Christian faith as it is expressed in other parts of the world (Hanciles 2008). While this is true, in our view, the strength of world Christianity is that it provides an integrated understanding of global Christian dynamics from which the West cannot be excized. It draws attention to the currents of Christianity globally, its transnational ties and movements (Kalu and Low 2008). Our study suggests that the destinies of the Christianities of North and West and the South and East are linked in very many respects: through historical and institutional ties, through mission activity and migration and through common Christian interest, especially in view of the global rise of militant Islam, aggressive secularism and other challenges to Christian faith.

Others worry that the fact of world Christianity may mean the creation of a new Christendom that is every bit as aggressive and exclusive as the old. In *The Next Christendom*, Philip Jenkins (2002) presented a future scenario of North–South confrontation between two Christianities: the one liberal, rational and socially progressive, and the other traditional on social issues, conservative in beliefs and moral issues and interested in the supernatural and in personal salvation rather than radical politics (161–2). We agree with Jenkins in so far as there is a sector of traditional Western Christianity that finds it very difficult to engage with the Christianity of 'the South' and, as the current situation in the Anglican Communion demonstrates, a hardline view in 'the South' which regards 'the North' as apostate. But we do not see this estrangement as a problem for the whole of Christianity since, as we have shown there are many theological voices and there are conservatives and supernaturalists in the North also, as the recent formation of the Fellowship of Confessing Anglicans shows. Even if 'Southern Christianity' is taken together, it is difficult to conceive of it as a world-dominating group. Despite the 'success' stories of church growth in Africa, Latin America and some countries in Asia, there are vast numbers of small and struggling churches that can hardly be described as constituting 'the next Christendom'. It is these weak groups which exhibit a more accurate picture of Christianity in Africa, Asia, Latin America and other regions outside the North and West. Global Christian interaction is much more complex and multidirectional than the binary of the North–South movement of the Cold War, which has in any case been superseded by the rise of the East and the globalized world of today. Christendom was never a geographical fact or a political reality – only an ideological construct. In this sense of mindset, granted, Christendoms will persist unless challenged by constructive encounter with other Christians.

Recognizing indigenous agency

Third, as Dana Robert (2009) points out, Christianity became a world religion through processes of mission. However, the study of mission history tends to focus on the activities of Western missionaries in the colonial period rather than encompassing the varied processes of evangelization that stretch back to the early church and the missional initiatives from other continents today. Work is being done to recover the history of non-Western missions (especially Irvin and Sunquist 2001; 2012) and this presents an ongoing challenge. Contemporary mission research reveals that, even within the churches that were planted by foreign mission activity, it was local believers – such as black evangelists and Bible women – who spread the good news and built up the church. This native agency is shown by many cases in which it was the local people who invited the missionaries, negotiated their entry, supported and facilitated their work. Although those who brought the gospel were often reluctant to transfer leadership even to candidates they had trained, the present diversity of world Christianity is testimony to the indigenous nature of the churches. In addition, countless new churches and denominations have been founded in parts of the globe once considered by Europeans 'mission fields' which are entirely locally staffed and funded and even have their own world missions.

A full understanding of the spread of Christianity is also hampered in two other ways: first, by undue attention to intentional missionary activity rather than the wider category of 'Christian witness', which includes the unconscious and spontaneous way in which ordinary Christians share their faith. Second, it is hindered by a divide between church history and mission history. This is a hangover from the Christendom era in which both Catholic and Protestant mission activity was directed only *ad gentes*, or abroad, and separated from the pastoral care of those who had been members of the church for generations. In the Catholic Church since the Second Vatican Council the Congregation for the Evangelization of Peoples has encompassed both, since the Church itself needs ongoing evangelization, but in practice missionary congregations are not integrated with parish life or with decision-making structures. The study of spread of world Christianity must include not only the history of mission but also the reception of the faith in varied contexts and the local history of the church and its evangelizing activity.

Lamin Sanneh (2003) attempts to make a distinction between 'world Christianity' as 'the movement of Christianity as it takes form and shape in societies that previously were not Christian' and 'global Christianity', which he takes to refer to 'the faithful replication of Christian forms and patterns developed in Europe'. In this model, 'world Christianity' represents a grassroots movement, while 'global Christianity' is seen as the result of a more intentional, political attempt to spread particular institutions across the world (23). World Christianity is a 'globalization from below' as opposed to 'an imposition from the world's great powers' (Carpenter 2005:vii). In practical terms, this is an impossible distinction because 'global Christianity' often gives rise to 'world Christianity' as local churches become independent of foreign control, and what was brought from Europe (or elsewhere) becomes 'contextualized'. And syntactically, the term 'world Christianity' is also not free from connotations of being monolithic or culturally uniform. But conceptually it is helpful to realize the dual dimensions of both terms.

Church and mission are further integrated by the realization that it is not only missionaries who cross borders and travel globally but ordinary Christians, and even whole churches in migration. The spread of early Christianity and Christianity in Asia in the first millennium was closely linked to trade. In the middle ages, pilgrimages and crusades were boundary-crossing activities. Peter Phan and Elaine Padilla (2014) have shown how migration is a fundamental religious way of being and pointed up the challenges this discovery poses for Christian theology (Phan and Padilla 2013). In all eras, migrating and colonizing communities have taken their faith with them. Their arrival has also impacted the faith and practice of the existing populations and raises questions for Christian theology about reception and hospitality (Spencer 2008; Frederiks 2015). Therefore migration and diaspora studies are closely related to world Christianity as many recent studies have shown (Hanciles 2008; Im and Yong 2014; Wild-Wood 2008). The Pentecostal–charismatic movement demonstrates this globalization from below most clearly. Its growth could be regarded as US-Americanization (Martin 1990:280), but it could equally be seen as an Africanization, a Latinization or even a Shamanization of world Christianity. Pentecostalism is essentially missionary (Anderson 2007), yet it is a movement with virtually no 'visible means of support' such as 'the force of a great leader', 'a captivating theology' a 'national or social class impatient for expression' (Wilson 1999:105), a political ideology (Martin 2002:167) or the sponsorship of wealthy individuals. Nevertheless, it is among the largest and most widespread movements on the planet (Wilson 1999:105).

Diversity in Christian belief and practice

As we have seen the common allegiance to Jesus Christ of the world's Christians is expressed in a myriad of different ways so that it may not always be obvious to an outsider that different churches are part of the same religion. Nevertheless there are shared Christian symbols across cultures: the ubiquitous Christian rituals of baptism and Eucharist; biblical images in Christian art like the cross, Madonna and child, and the dove for the Holy Spirit; narrative themes in Christian literature like annunciation, redemption and the betrayal of the last supper; and moral codes like the Ten Commandments and the Golden Rule. From the first centuries there has been debate among the churches about what can be authentically traced to the apostolic tradition, what is orthodox and catholic, and what is heterodox or heretical. This discussion about Christian diversity applies to patterns of worship, church structures and theological thought, among other matters.

Patterns of worship

Worship is central to the life of Christian communities as an expression of their corporate identity. Arguably, it is prior to questions of belief and doctrine. As we have seen, the strands of world Christianity can be distinguished according to the focus of their worship: Sacrament, Bible or Spirit. Although at some time or other all the denominations have claimed that their style of worship goes back to the first church, historical studies suggest a 'hermeneutical suspicion' about this (Bradshaw 2009). They show, first, that it is not possible to establish with much certainty how the first Christians worshipped, and second, that there was significant diversity in the early period. Although it is the most centralized, even the Catholic Church recognizes a number of historic minority rites. In the twentieth century, significant ecumenical liturgical reform in the Western churches was brought about by such factors as Western discovery of Syriac documents from the Middle East, the theological movement to go back to earliest sources to renew the church today (ressourcement) and the influence of mystical and Pentecostal–charismatic Christianity.

Among the historic churches which maintain traditional worship patterns, liturgical studies has become a developed field (e.g. White 2000). Its most impressive achievement has been the *Baptism, Eucharist and Ministry* document (1982), for which, in an unprecedented way, Orthodox, Protestant and Roman Catholic leaders worked together through the Faith and Order Commission of the World Council of Churches (WCC). 'Once unthinkable consensus' was reached on justification by faith, the two natures of Christ and other key areas of doctrinal debate (Kinnamon 2004:51) and an unofficial liturgy (the 'Lima liturgy') was developed from these discussions which has been widely distributed and used. Since 1982, however, progress toward common worship has stalled. One of the main sticking points is the question of ministry, particularly the ordination of women and practising homosexuals in many of the historic Protestant churches. Although real issues for many mainline churches, which threaten their global unity, other Christians who are not steeped in the tradition, or who do not share the same cultural background, may not understand what the problem is about.

In addition to movements for liturgical unity, anthropological and sociological insights on the polycentric development of worship, which broaden the study beyond textual analysis, give grounds for greater diversity. Liturgical change is sometimes intentional and the result of careful deliberation or it may come about spontaneously and piecemeal as local people respond to the good news in ways they find most appropriate (Farhadian 2007). Since the Second Vatican Council, the Catholic Church has officially encouraged inculturation of liturgy. In fact little local innovation in its public worship has been officially approved but the Church cannot police everything that happens on the ground (Phan 2003b). Since Christianity is essentially polycentric and multi-traditional, the greater the indigeneity the more diversity we would expect to see. Perhaps the core of Christian commonality is shared values rather than words or actions (Stringer 2005).

Church structures

This study of world Christianity has revealed the plurality of churches and diversity of church structures today. This fact requires a rethinking of the meaning of church unity and necessitates both a regionalization and an internationalization of older Christian churches. When the WCC was planned in the interwar years, it seemed logical that bringing unity to the churches in Europe would be a step towards world peace since, because of alliances and colonies, events in Europe influenced the rest of the world. The inclusion in the post-war WCC of Orthodox Churches helped to bridge the Cold War divide in Europe and Catholic involvement after the Second Vatican Council further aided the unification of the continent. At the same time, a number of developments intervened to prevent the WCC bringing a wider Christian unity. First, independence movements and decolonization required a reconception of the relationship between 'older' and 'younger' churches as a partnership and many resisted unity according to European models. Nevertheless, significant progress was made in the context of strong centripetal forces in international affairs. Furthermore, local church unions were achieved by denominations of a similar heritage and even in a few cases (like India) across the divide between episcopal and non-episcopal churches. Second, from the 1960s, Evangelicalism set itself in opposition to the Ecumenical movement and established alternative instruments of unity through the World Evangelical Alliance and the Lausanne Movement. Third, churches which were independent of European denominations and new Pentecostal–charismatic movements became the majority in Africa and parts of Asia and they tended not necessarily to see themselves as part of the ecumenical movement because of its colonial background. Pentecostals and charismatics are connected globally through several different bodies such as the Pentecostal World Fellowship and International Catholic Charismatic Renewal and these cut across traditional denominational lines. Many locally initiated churches are outside the Renewal networks as well, but as long as they call themselves Christian, they will tend to seek a connection with world Christianity. Fourth, in the later twentieth century global forces became centrifugal, encouraging fragmentation and insistence on diversity (Marty 2004). The final reason why European hopes of global ecumenism were not realized was that, over time, the 'global church families' of Protestant Christians formed by the colonial denominations came under strain and denominational distinctions became confused. For example, organizationally, Methodists in Korea follow the Presbyterian pattern of church leaders with 'elders'; Pentecostal churches in Africa adopt Anglican models of hierarchy; Catholic and Orthodox congregations in the United States have to fit their organizations within the same legal structures as Protestants, which means the adoption of some form of democratic decision-making. Such developments, schisms within churches and the growth of transdenominational movements such as Evangelicalism and Pentecostalism, weakened these bodies. As the goal of visible and organic unity receded, even within denominations, in the 1980s the WCC shifted its emphasis towards 'fellowship' (*koinonia*) as a way of bringing together a wider constituency, and also of encouraging bilateral dialogues, for example, between Pentecostals and Roman Catholics, Anglicans and Orthodox. More recently it has simply facilitated a more open space in which Christians of all kinds can come together in the shape of the Global Christian Forum, which held its first meeting in Nairobi in 2007 (van Beek 2009). In the wake of setbacks to the ecumenical agenda of visible and structural unity in the late twentieth century, the world Christianity paradigm presents an alternative approach to ecumenism of mutual recognition and collaboration in mission.

In all the attention to Pentecostalism in recent scholarship in world Christianity, the study of the Catholic Church, which shapes the lives of more than half of all Christians and is the major ecclesial player in world affairs, has been neglected. From a Catholic and Orthodox perspective, the denominational model with which Protestant churches work appears itself to be a contextual ecclesiology (Collins and Ensign-George 2011). This drives home the necessity for Christianity to be studied

Figure 8.2 A meeting of the Commission for World Mission and Evangelism at the World Council of Churches headquarters in Geneva, Switzerland, 24 April 2007. Photograph by Jacques Matthey.

from an ecumenical or world perspective rather than through the lens of any particular church or confession. During and after the Second Vatican Council, the Catholic Church reached out to other Christians. Its excommunication of the Orthodox was annulled and Protestants were welcomed as 'separated brethren'. In 1999 the Catholic Church and the Lutheran World Federation declared that the Reformation debate about justification was over because they had reached agreement on its meaning. Although the prospect of unity between Catholic and Protestant churches is far off, considerable progress has been made in Catholic–Evangelical and Catholic–WCC relations towards 'common witness', which continues today (Gibaut and Jørgensen 2014).

Despite its centralized structure, the Catholic Church has its own internal challenges of growing diversity and pressure for more local autonomy. It not only includes multiple religious orders and lay movements such as Foculare and Opus Dei but also diverse regional and ethnic churches. Although the Second Vatican Council was dominated by European theologians and was mainly European in its concerns, the leading theologian Karl Rahner (1979) later reflected that the Council glimpsed a truly 'world church' and the council's ecclesiology celebrated the universal church as a communion of local churches, each bringing varied gifts (Gaillardetz 2008:291). Paradoxically, the council both increased centralization and also encouraged internationalization of the curia and the formation of local bishops' conferences to guide local affairs, although their canonical status was not clarified (Haynes 2012:48–9). In preparation for the year 2000, John Paul II initiated regional synods. However, these were controlled by Rome and concerned especially for evangelization. They did not satisfy those looking for greater devolution or assure them that the Vatican was committed to listening to regional voices (Phan 2002). The election in 2013 of the first pope from outside Europe for 1500 years, Francis I, was a symbolic step toward internationalization and recognition that more than half of all Catholics live in the Americas. Moreover, in *Evangelii Gaudium* (2013), the pope embraced the internationalization agenda by self-limiting his jurisdiction, encouraging the regional bishops' conferences to decide on non-theological matters, giving them greater authority through citing their documents and promising structural change.

Roman Catholicism, Protestantism and Evangelicalism all arose in the North and West; however, for demographic reasons, the strength of all of these movements arguably now lies outside their continents of origin. Strong new movements are spreading globally from the South and East fuelled by migration. The large-scale emigration of Orthodox Christians from their homelands especially poses challenges to their polity as ethnically defined churches are flung together in diaspora (Clapsis 2004). As we have seen, the Anglican Communion and other church families face similar jurisdictional issues. The increasing voluntarism of religion and marketplace of churches threatens the traditional systems of parishes of the (former) state churches of Europe even in their own homelands. New media offer opportunities for initiatives of cooperation and unity, while also making more obvious Christian diversity. As the territorial and denominational models weaken, global movements such as Evangelicalism and Pentecostalism unify Christians from below through means of networks while from above the Catholic Church becomes more 'networked' (Linden 2012). Robert Schreiter (1997) argues for a 'new catholicity', not in the sense of the Catholic Church to which only part of the Christian community belongs, but in the sense of the 'Church catholic'. This catholicity will be 'marked by a wholeness of inclusion and fullness of faith in a pattern of intercultural exchange and communication' (122, 132). Such catholicity would not be expressed by a single global institution but in terms of conversation – perhaps leading to communion – between and among both global and local expressions of Christian faith. When Christians anywhere are baptized, they join the 'one, holy, catholic and apostolic' church. Today the global nature of this belonging is becoming more apparent, even at a grassroots level, but it is not always reflected in works of ecclesiology.

Theological thought

World Christianity demands new methods of biblical interpretation and doing theology. The diversity of Christianity encourages the use of the Bible as the starting for theology. The Orthodox churches may quote the Church Fathers and Roman Catholics from scholastic theologians, but public church documents increasingly cite biblical references because the Bible (in various languages and with minor differences) is a source of authority for virtually all Christians. The Bible is in origin an Asian book, although until recently Christians of European descent claimed a virtual monopoly on its interpretation. Today not only Bibles but also commentaries are also found in Chinese, Tamil and many other languages. There is a growth in cross-cultural or intercultural reading of the Bible and theologizing. Literature that brings together readings from different cultural perspectives reveals the extent to which earlier interpretations were conditioned by colonial perspectives (Oduyoye and Vroom 2003; Sugirtharajah 1995). For example, during the colonial period, European scholars were virtually unanimous that when Jesus answered the question posed to him, he meant that taxes should be paid to Caesar. Only in the later colonial period did scholars in countries struggling for independence begin to question this interpretation of Jesus's wise answer (Rayan 1985). Liberation theology and the Pentecostal–charismatic movement further opened up socio-political hermeneutics and narrative readings, respectively. Differences in biblical hermeneutic are a major source of tension, not only between Christians in North and South (Jenkins 2006), but between churches in the same region and within churches of the same confession. It is important therefore that greater attention is given to how decisions are made about what interpretation(s) are right (e.g. Broggi 2015).

The growth of world Christianity means that, as in the early church theology was a matter for ecumenical (i.e. whole world) discussion between representatives of different parts of the world church, so now doing theology is again recognized to be a 'world endeavour' (Vanhoozer 2006:115). But there are difficulties in the way of it being a mutual endeavour. The vast majority of seminaries and theology departments of universities and colleges (including in non-Western countries) cover subjects, topics and theologians that are mostly Western. Theology for most of these institutions is understood as an appendage of traditional Western Christianity. Even in the Catholic Church, it is possible to complete the whole of one's theological education without reading any theologians from outside the West (Gaillardetz 2008). Theologians in other countries are therefore generally familiar with Western theology; it is Christians in the West who are challenged to get to know their Christian brothers and sisters in other continents. Kenyan theologian John Mbiti (1976:17) asked Western Christians forty years ago how there can be mutuality and reciprocity 'if only one side knows the other fairly well, while the other side either does not know or does not want to know the first side'.

Lack of knowledge of other ways of thinking is not just a problem for churches but for Western society in general. It requires an educational approach that helps people enter one another's world views and see through another's eyes (cf. Pobee and Ositelu 1998:2–3). It also depends on a prior recognition that, whereas there is a body of documents that all Christians share, all theologies are developed contextually. Although in one sense Christian theology in Europe has been done in a global context for several hundred years (Schwarz 2005), this is not the same as accepting that it is a local theology, which is the approach required by world Christianity (Schreiter 1985). Hearing from one another will help Western Christians to recognize that their churches are inculturated and contextual in the same way that African, Asian and Latin American churches are (Meneses 2006; Ramachandra 2006:229). Freedom from European dominance in the study of theology and church history allows for a variety of ways for theologies to be developed in relation to different cultures, religions and philosophies (e.g. Bevans 2002; Tennent 2007; Cartledge and Cheetham 2011). The aim is not one global theology but the internationalization of Christian theology (e.g. Kärkkäinen 2013) and a truly global and respectful conversation among Christian scholars from different parts of the world.

There have been attempts to bring Christian theologies from other parts of the world to the attention of Western theologians since the 1960s. In English this has been mainly through Orbis Books, the publishing arm of the Maryknoll Fathers in the United States, by SPCK and Regnum Books in the United Kingdom, and by WCC Publications in Geneva. Western theologies tend to interact with philosophical quests for understanding and articulate systems of doctrines for sustainable and consistent conduct of Christian life. These theologies reflect the churches' historic position of majority, authority and financial stability. Asian, African, Latin American, Caribbean and Oceanian theologies, and theologies from the 'Fourth World' within the West, have been more interested in the sociological and political dimensions of Christian praxis from a position of marginalization in a given society.

Two influential new movements in theology have emerged from outside the West in recent decades. The first is various theologies of liberation and identity, including Latin American liberation theology, Dalit theology from India and minjung theology from Korea. Latin American liberation theology was spread globally through the Catholic missionary communities and through SEDOS, the Service of Documentation and Study on Global Mission. Protestant theologies were disseminated through EATWOT, which brings together Third World theologians and church, mission and academic networks. A second area of theology that has developed especially from non-Western sources is pneumatology, or theology of the Holy Spirit. Growing interest in pneumatology in the West after years of neglect was sparked by rediscovery of the Fathers, dialogue with the Orthodox and engagement of theology with the mystical traditions, especially with the Syriac tradition of a feminine Spirit (e.g. Moltmann 1992; Rogers 2005). Pentecostal–charismatic theologians have added to its systematic development (Yong with Anderson 2014). Experience of the Spirit in other continents as liberator, empowerer, life-giver, medium of dialogue and one among a world of many spirits has deepened understanding (K. Kim 2007). Its broad appeal is shown by the recent WCC statement on mission and evangelism, *Together towards Life*, which is framed pneumatologically.

Plurality in Christian interreligious relations

World Christianity provides a way of studying Christianity within departments of religious studies. Hitherto Christianity has usually been studied as theology or divinity. These disciplines have engaged in the study of its scriptures, doctrine, institutions and ministries using mainly historical and philosophical methods. Because of the existence of theology as a discipline, departments of religious studies, which have emerged more recently, have tended to redress a balance and focus on other world religions to the neglect of Christianity and theological methods. World Christianity, however, legitimizes the application of sociological and anthropological methods to the study of that religion. It is hoped that the study of world Christianity will also include, as here, the historical and theological analysis that enables scholars to understand its inner dynamics more fully and so predict its likely trajectory better. Studying Christianity in the context of other religions (and philosophies) helps to clarify its distinctives as well as its commonality with other faiths (cf. Ward 1998). It also allows Christians to see themselves from outside, to clarify the nature and the ground of any exclusive claims and consider the manner in which they may be made (cf. Griffiths 1990). In addition to the study of Christianity alongside other world religions, such as Islam and Hinduism, the locally rooted nature of Christianity also encourages attention to relevant indigenous religions and new movements.

Interreligious studies has been neglected or suppressed in Western theology until recently due to Christianity's dominant status in Western society and also its exclusive claims over other religious traditions. For Christians in Asia and Africa particularly, living with the people of other faiths has always been a part and parcel of their religious lives. Their theologies and praxes of living together (*convivence*) are one of their most significant contributions to Christian theology globally (Sundermeier 1992). However, Western theologians have not always taken account of the varied views among non-Western theologians. We have seen how India has been the preferred Western 'laboratory' for interreligious relations (Knitter 1995:157). Commentators on John Hick's theology of pluralism (Hick and Knitter 1987) – both those who supported his approach and those who challenged it (D'Costa 1990) – saw parallels between his views and advaitic (non-dualist) philosophical approaches to religious difference. However, within India, advaitic philosophy was already rejected by many other theologians as intellectually elitist and neglectful of Dalit and tribal criticism of brahminical traditions as oppressive (Rayan 1989). Furthermore, as we saw in chapter 2, in the case of inter-religious relations, the contours of debate vary in different Asian contexts and according to the religion. This example shows the dangers of Western theologians hearing only elite or selected views from another region.

Although a model of dialogue between religions is enjoined by both the Catholic Church and the WCC, it is balanced by proclamation, evangelism and even prophetic condemnation of corrupt religious practices. Dialogue with Islam may be possible in the context of the West, but we have seen how Christians in Islamic contexts have been marginalized and silenced. Western Christians have not always heard the hardships of Christians in Islamic lands that are now becoming so acute. The depletion of Christian communities in West Asia and other tensions between Muslims and Christians call into question claims of the infinite 'translatability' (Sanneh 1989) of Christianity and its nature as a religion capable of taking root in multiple cultures. The flow of refugees from the region suggests that there is a destructive 'clash of civilizations' between Christianity and Islam (Huntington 2011) and even that religions are inherently sources of conflict. Furthermore, there are apparently intractable differences between the two faiths theologically: Islamic theology includes a refutation of the Christian doctrines of the Trinity and Christology and a suspicion of the veracity of the Christian scriptures; while Islam was accused by Benedict XVI at Regensburg in 2006 of a tendency to irrationality and violence. The study of world Christianity raises the need for a much more complex approach to religious plurality than Hick's.

Varied patterns of Christian engagement with public life

Christian faith is exercised at many different social levels. It is both a personal faith and a public confession. It is practised in homes and in public buildings. It is the faith of both the poor and the wealthy. The profile of a church in any particular society depends on its particular theology and also on the attitude of the state: churches may be established institutions in Europe or underground groups in China, mutually supportive communities in Africa or protest groups in Latin America, businesses in North America or caste groups in India. Most churches encourage their members' self-improvement and develop as communities, generating social capital. They are committed to charitable, social and development work.

A distinction is often made between 'church' and 'sect' or 'mainline' and 'fringe'; between those churches which seek credibility and a voice in the public sphere and those that have a more personal and domestic agenda. As we have seen, it is not possible to make this distinction along the lines of particular denominations. Given the opportunity and a cause, any kind of church may decide to participate in public life. Once Evangelical and Pentecostal–charismatic Christians were fitted entirely into the latter category, but in Africa, Asia and the Americas the terms 'mainline' and 'mainstream' to refer to the historic churches of Europe is no longer appropriate in many cases. From the perspective of this study, it might be better to see a distinction between those churches concerned to interact at a philosophical level with other world religions and ideologies, and others who are relating to popular belief systems, which include local or tribal religions, 'primal religiosity' and the culture of 'post-modernity'. There are strong movements of the latter type within the older denominations, but the hierarchies tend to be nervous of them because of the dangers enthusiasm poses to social harmony; they tend to distinguish between rational and irrational approaches. From the other side, the restrictions imposed by some of the older denominations are often represented as resisting the 'supernatural' dimensions of faith. But it is not only Pentecostal–charismatics and fundamentalists who are in danger of syncretizing the Christian faith. History is full of compromises churches have made and often these are for political reasons. The 'German Christians' under the Nazis furnishes the most infamous example.

The church's relation to the state has always been controversial and will probably remain so. Even within churches, a minority of Christians may oppose the church hierarchy on grounds of conscience or social justice. We have seen a number of different patterns of church–state relations: at one extreme, the church dominates the state, as in the case of medieval Western Europe, or at the other extreme, the church withdraws from involvement in political life, as Evangelicals did in the 'great reversal'. The church may be oppressed by the state, as under communism, or it may collude with the state as the Dutch Reformed Church did in South Africa in the apartheid years. The church may become part of the state power, as in many countries of Latin America under military juntas, or it may form the main opposition to state power, as in Uganda under Idi Amin.

Whatever the context, followers of the one who preached the kingdom of God will be involved socially in advocating for the needy and challenging injustice. We have seen many different political theologies such as theologies of liberation and development and postcolonial theologies. In the current situation in which most of the world lives under democratic governments that permit churches to play a role in public life, we have seen the rise of public theologies: 'Christians in public conversation contributing to the formation of personal decisions and collective policy-making in economic, political, religious and social realms' (Kim 2011:3). Although the term was not in use then, the 'benevolent empire' of Evangelicalism, the social gospel movement and Catholic social teaching can be seen as examples of public theology. At the heart of it is the idea that Christians participate in public life not only to protect Christian interests but also for the common good. This is a key principle of Catholic social teaching, based on the dignity of all human beings as made in the image of God (Curran 2002). It holds that, in order to promote this dignity, any democratic state should provide mechanisms for equality and freedom of individuals and create community for the maximum consensus. Foundational to this approach is that no one party determines what the common good is for a particular group, wider society or nation; rather, determining the common good is an ongoing process of seeking the good for the majority while also protecting minorities. Together with the other key concepts of subsidiarity and solidarity, the theology of the common good challenges majoritarianism and provides alternatives between the poles of liberal democracy and social democracy.

More broadly, public theologians challenge monopoly of the public space in any form, whether it is by the state, the market, the media, the academy, civil society or a particular religion, and promote universal access and critical debate. Public theology aims to bridge between secular and sacred understandings of contemporary issues, inspired by the wisdom tradition of the Hebrew Bible. It uses advocacy, campaigns and public debate (Kim 2011). On a global scale, the churches have worked with the United Nations, which they helped to found, for the common good in several ways: eradicating poverty (Taylor 2011), promoting liberal democracy (Woodberry 2012) and working for reconciliation (Schreiter and Jørgensen 2013). We predict that churches will continue to play an active role in national and international affairs, not limited to the religious domain but, for example, dealing with issues of ecology, economic justice and social equality. In most cases they will do so from a minority status but in solidarity with Christians in other parts of the world through the global bodies and networks of world Christianity.

Conclusion

When Protestant (and Anglo-Catholic) mission and church leaders from Europe and North America met at the watershed World Missionary Conference in Edinburgh in 1910 to discuss the state of the project of world evangelization, they rejoiced at the growth of churches around the world but few foresaw how this would accelerate or its implications for the nature and shape of Christianity just a century later (Stanley 2009). Whereas in 1910 about 70 per cent of Christians were in Europe, today that figure is reversed. It is no longer true to say, if it ever was, that Christianity is a European religion; indeed it is hard to say to whom it belongs (Sanneh 2003; Daughrity 2015). If present church growth and population trends continue, by 2050 Africa will be the continent with the most Christians – one billion. It will be followed in order by Latin America (and the Caribbean), Asia, Europe (with only half as many – five hundred thousand), North America and then Oceania.

In 2010 there was a centenary gathering in Edinburgh and many others in different parts of the world. Then the growth of Christianity as a world religion was a matter for celebration (Kim and Anderson 2011) but there was also sober and critical reflection (Balia and Kim 2010) on the history of mission and inter-church history and consideration of the unjust power relations between different churches and Christian movements (Longkumer, Sorenson and Biehl 2016). The challenge we wish to bring in this book is not merely that Christianity is a non-Western religion because historically its origins are in Asia; nor just that non-Western Christianities should be taken more seriously by theologians and scholars of Christianity because Christianity's numerical strength now lies in the global South. What we argue is that all aspects of Christian studies, including church history, theology, inter-religious and societal relations, must be reshaped and revised in light of the nature of Christianity as a world religion. A vast amount of scholarship has been dedicated to the study of Western Christianity and Western missions, but now there is need for a conscious effort to research the Christian history, theology, interreligious and social engagement and missionary activities of Asia, Africa, Latin America, the Caribbean, Oceania, and Eastern Europe. The existence and varied nature of Christianity in each part of the world and the transnational movements of Christian migration, mission and relationships between them should not only be acknowledged but integrated into all study and teaching of Christianity.

Study questions and further readings

- In what ways should the world Christianity paradigm impact the study of Christian history?
- To what extent is the diversity of Christianity reflected in theology?
- Assess the importance of a world Christianity perspective for interfaith relations and/or Christian involvement in public life.
- How do you see the future of world Christianity?
- Redesign a theology course, taking into account the fact that Christianity is a world religion.

Gaillardetz, R. R. (2008), *Ecclesiology for a Global Church*. Maryknoll, NY: Orbis.
Hanciles, J. J. (2008), *Beyond Christendom*. Maryknoll, NY: Orbis.
Linden, I. (2012), *Global Catholicism*, second edition. London: Hurst.
Sanneh, L. (2008), *Disciples of All Nations*. Oxford: Oxford University.
Tennent, T. C. (2007), *Theology in the Context of World Christianity*. Grand Rapids, MI: Zondervan.

Bibliography

Adamo, D. T. (2000), 'The Use of Psalms in African Indigenous Churches in Nigeria', in G. West and M. Dube (eds), *The Bible in Africa*. Leiden: Brill, 336–49.

Adeyemo, T., ed. (2006), *Africa Bible Commentary*. Grand Rapids, MI: Zondervan.

Adogame A. (1999), *Celestial Church of Christ*. Frankfurt: Peter Lang.

Adogame A. (2013), *The African Diaspora*. London: Bloomsbury.

Ajayi, J. F. A. (2001), *A Patriot to the Core*. Ibadan: Spectrum.

Allen, R. (1956[1912]), *Missionary Methods: St Paul's or Ours?* London: World Dominion.

Alvarez, M., ed. (2015), *Latin American Mission*. Oxford: Regnum.

Amjad-Ali, C. (2012), 'Pakistan', in R. E. Hedlund (ed.), *The Oxford Encyclopaedia of South Asian Christianity*. Delhi: Oxford University, 516–25.

Anderson, A. H. (2000), *Zion and Pentecost*. Pretoria: UNISA.

Anderson, A. H. (2001), *African Reformation*. Trenton, NJ: Africa World.

Anderson, A. H. (2004), *An Introduction to Pentecostalism*. Cambridge: Cambridge University.

Anderson, A. H. (2007), *Spreading Fires*. London: SCM.

Anderson, W. B. and O. U. Kalu (2007), 'Christianity in Sudan and Ethiopia', in O. U. Kalu (ed.), *African Christianity*. Trenton, NJ: Africa World, 75–116.

Armour, R. (2002), *Islam, Christianity, and the West*. Maryknoll, NY: Orbis.

Asamoah-Gyadu, J. K. (2005), *African Charismatics*. Leiden: Brill.

Asamoah-Gyadu, J. K. (2013), *Contemporary Pentecostal Christianity*. Oxford: Regnum.

Ault, J. (2013), *African Christianity Rising* [DVD]. Northampton, MA: James Ault Productions.

Austin-Broos, D. (1997), *Jamaica Genesis*. Chicago: University of Chicago.

Austin-Broos, D. (2001), 'Jamaican Pentecostalism', in A. Corten and R. Marshall-Fratani (eds), *Between Babel and Pentecost*. Bloomington: Indiana University, 142–62.

Ayegboyin, D. and S. A. Ishola (1997), *African Indigenous Churches*. Lagos: Greater Heights.

Azumah, J. A. (2001), *The Legacy of Arab-Islam in Africa*. London: Oneworld.

Baawobr, R. (2015), 'The Journey of the Young Churches', in P. Grogan and K. Kim (eds), *The New Evangelization*. London: T&T Clark, 165–78.

Baer, H. A. and M. Singer (2002), *African American Religion*, second edition. Knoxville: University of Tennessee.

Baker, D. (2008), *Korean Spirituality*. Honolulu: University of Hawai'i Press.

Balia, D. and K. Kim (2010), *Edinburgh 2010: Witnessing to Christ Today*. Oxford: Regnum.

Ballhatchet, K. and H. (2002), 'Asia', in J. McManners (ed.), *The Oxford History of Christianity*. Oxford: Oxford University, 508–38.

Barrett, D. B. (1982), *World Christian Encyclopedia*, first edition, Nairobi: Oxford University Press.

Barrett, D. B., G. T. Kurian and T. M. Johnson (2001), *World Christian Encyclopedia*, second edition, 2 vols. Oxford: Oxford University Press.

Bauman, C. M. (2015), *Pentecostals, Proselytization, and Anti-Christian Violence in Contemporary India*. Oxford: Oxford University.

Bays, D. H. (2012), *A New History of Christianity in China*. Chichester: Wiley-Blackwell.

Bebbington, D. W. (1989), *Evangelicalism in Modern Britain*. London: Unwin Hyman.

Bechtloff, D. (2002), 'Madagascar's Christians and the Beginning of National Identity', in K. Koschorke (ed.), *Transcontinental Links in the History of Non-Western Christianity*. Wiesbaden: Harrassowitz, 329–42.

Becker, J. and B. Stanley, eds (2014), *Europe as the Other*. Göttingen: Vandenhoeck & Ruprecht.

Beckford, R. (1998), *Jesus Is Dread*. London: Darton, Longman and Todd.

Bediako, K. (1992), *Theology and Identity*. Oxford: Regnum.

Bediako, K. (1997), 'African Theology', in D. F. Ford (ed.), *The Modern Theologians*, second edition. Oxford: Blackwell, 426–44.

Bednarowski, M. F. (2008), 'Multiplicity and Ambiguity', in M. F. Bednarowski (ed.), *Twentieth-Century Global Christianity*. Minneapolis, MN: Fortress, 1–31.

Behera, M. N., ed. (2011), *Interfaith Relations after One Hundred Years*. Oxford: Regnum.

Behera, M. N. and M. Biehl, eds (2015), *Witnessing to Christ in North East India*. Oxford: Regnum.

Belshaw, D., R. Calderisi and C. Sugden, eds (2001), *Faith in Development*. Oxford: Regnum.

Beozzo, J. O. (1990), 'Humiliated and Exploited Natives', in L. Boff and V. Elizondo (eds), *1492–1992: The Voice of the Victims*. London: SCM, 78–89.

Berger, P. L. (1970), *A Rumour of Angels*. London: Penguin.

Berger, P. L. (1996), *Twisted Cross*. Chapel Hill, NC: University of North Carolina.

Berger, P. L. and S. P. Huntington (2002), *Many Globalizations*. Oxford: Oxford University.

Bergler, T. E. (2012), *The Juvenilization of American Christianity*. Grand Rapids, MI: Eerdmans.

Bergunder, M. (2008), *The South Indian Pentecostal Movement in the Twentieth Century*. Grand Rapids, MI: Eerdmans.

Bevans, S. B. (2002), *Models of Contextual Theology*, second edition. Maryknoll, NY: Orbis.

Bevans, S. B., ed. (2013), *A Century of Catholic Mission*. Oxford: Regnum.

Bevans, S. B., T. Chai, N. Jennings, K. Jørgensen and D. Werner, eds (2015), *Reflecting on and Equipping for Christian Mission*. Oxford: Regnum.

Bevans, S. B. and R. P. Schroeder (2004), *Constants in Context*. Maryknoll, NY: Orbis.

Beyer, P. (1994), *Religion and Globalization*. London: SAGE.

Bisnauth, D. A. (1996), *A History of Religions in the Caribbean*. Trenton, NJ: Africa World.

Blicke, P. (2007), 'Communal Reformation', in R. P. Hsia (ed.), *Reform and Expansion 1500–1660*. Cambridge: Cambridge University, 75–89.

Boesak, A. A. (1977), *Farewell to Innocence*. Maryknoll, NY: Orbis.

Boff, Leonardo (1986[1977]), *Ecclesiogenesis*, trans. R. R. Barr. London: Collins.

Boff, Leonardo (1987[1979]), *The Maternal Face of God*, trans. R. R. Barr. Maryknoll, NY: Orbis.

Bonino, J. M. (1975), *Doing Theology in a Revolutionary Situation*. Philadelphia: Fortress.

Bonino, J. M. (1997), *Faces of Latin American Protestantism*, trans. E. L. Stockwell. Grand Rapids, MI: Eerdmans.

Bonk, J. J. (1991), *Missions and Money*. Maryknoll, NY: Orbis.

Boodoo, G. (2000a), 'The Faith of the People', in H. Gossai and N. S. Murrell (eds), *Religion, Culture, and Tradition in the Caribbean*. London: Macmillan, 65–72.

Boodoo, G. (2000b), 'Christologies, Caribbean', in V. Fabella and R. S. Sugirtharajah (eds), *Dictionary of Third World Theologies*. Maryknoll, NY: Orbis, 52–3.

Bosch, D. J. (2011[1991]), *Transforming Mission*, second edition. Maryknoll, NY: Orbis.

Boseto, L. (1995), 'The Gospel of Economy from a Solomon Islands Perspective', in R. S. Sugirtharajah (ed.), *Voices from the Margin*, second edition. London: SPCK, 179–84.

Boyd, R. H. S. (2014), *Beyond Captivity*. Bangalore: Centre for Contemporary Christianity.

Bradshaw, P. F. (2009), *Reconstructing Early Christian Worship*. London: SPCK.

Branch, T. (1988), *Parting the Waters*. London: Macmillan.

Breward, I. (2001), *A History of the Churches in Australasia*. Oxford: Oxford University.

Brock, S. (2010a), 'The Syrian Church in the Modern Middle East', in A. O'Mahony and E. Loosley (eds), *Eastern Christianity in the Modern Middle East*. London: Routledge, 13–24.

Brock, S. (2010b), 'Syriac Churches of the Middle East and Dialogue with the Catholic Church', in A. O'Mahony and J. Flannery (eds), *The Catholic Church in the Contemporary Middle East*. London: Melisende, 107–18.

Brockman, J. R. (2005), *Romero*, second edition. Maryknoll, NY: Orbis.

Broggi, J. D. (2015), *Diversity in the Structure of Christian Reasoning*. Leiden: Brill.

Brookes, A. (2007), *The Alpha Phenomenon*. London: CTBI.

Brooks, S. (1999), 'Catholic Activism in the1990s', in C. Smith and J. Pokopy (eds), *Latin American Religion in Motion*. New York: Routledge, 67–89.

Brouwer, S., P. Gifford and S. D. Rose (1996), *Exporting the American Gospel*. New York: Routledge.

Brown, C. G. (2001), *The Death of Christian Britain*. London: Routledge.

Brown, J. M. (2003), 'Who Is an Indian?', in B. Stanley (ed.), *Missions, Nationalism, and the End of Empire*. Grand Rapids, MI: Eerdmans, 111–31.

Brown, P. (1997), *The Rise of Western Christendom*. Oxford: Blackwell.

Brown, T. (2006), 'Introduction', in T. Brown (ed.), *Other Voices, Other Worlds*. London: Darton, Longman and Todd, 1–4.
Bruce, S. (1995), *Religion in Modern Britain*. Oxford: Oxford University.
Brusco, E. (1995), *The Reformation of Machismo*. Austin: University of Texas.
Buchenau, K. (2010), 'The Serbian Orthodox Church', in L. N. Leustean (ed.), *Eastern Christianity and the Cold War, 1945–91*. Abingdon: Routledge, 60–78.
Bulangalire, M. (2006), 'The Consequences of the Enlightenment', *International Review of Mission* 95(378–9), 293–6.
Burgess, R. (2008), *Nigeria's Christian Revolution*. Oxford: Regnum.
Burrows, W. R. (1993), *Redemption and Dialogue*. Maryknoll, NY: Orbis.
Burrows, W. R. (1996), 'A Seventh Paradigm?', in W. Saayman and K. Kritzinger (eds), *Mission in Bold Humility*. Maryknoll, NY: Orbis, 121–38.
Buthelezi, M. (1976), 'Daring to Live for Christ', in G. H. Anderson and T. F. Stransky (eds), *Third World Theologies*. New York: Paulist, 176–80.
Buthelezi, M. (1997[1972]), 'Salvation as Wholeness', in J. Parratt (ed.), *A Reader in African Christian Theology*, second edition. London: SPCK, 85–90.
Carey, H. M. (1996), *Believing in Australia*. St Leonards, NSW: Allen and Unwin.
Carlson, J. (1998), 'First Nations Spirituality and the Anglican Church in Canada', in A. Wingate, K. Ward, C. Pemberton and W. Sitshebo (eds), *Anglicanism*. London: Mowbray, 40–5.
Carpenter, J. A. (2005), 'Preface', in L. Sanneh and J. A. Carpenter (eds), *The Changing Face of Christianity*. Oxford: Oxford University, vii–ix.
Carter, R. A. (1998), 'Where God Still Walks in the Garden', in A. Wingate, K. Ward, C. Pemberton and W. Sitshebo (eds), *Anglicanism*. London: Mowbray, 45–51.
Cartledge, M. J. and D. Cheetham (2011), *Intercultural Theology*. London: SCM.
Casson, J. (2000), 'Missionaries, Mau Mau and the Christian Frontier', in P. N. Holtrop and H. McLeod (eds), *Missions and Missionaries*. Woodbridge, UK: Boydell, 200–15.
Catto, R. (2013), 'The Church Mission Society and Reverse Mission', in A. Adogame and S. Shankar (eds), *Religion on the Move!* Leiden: Brill, 81–95.
Chadwick, H. (2002), 'The Early Christian Community', in J. McManners (ed.), *The Oxford History of Christianity*. Oxford: Oxford University, 21–69.
Chadwick, O. (2002), 'Great Britain and Europe', in J. McManners (ed.), *The Oxford History of Christianity*. Oxford: Oxford University, 349–95.
Chaillot, C. (1998), *The Syrian Orthodox Church of Antioch and All the East*. Geneva: World Council of Churches.
Chaillot, C. (2002), *The Ethiopian Orthodox Tewahedo Church Tradition*. Paris: Inter-Orthodox Dialogue.
Champion, D. with R. Dewerse (2014), *Yarta Wandatha*. Adelaide: Denise Champion.
Chan, K.-K. (2015), 'Religious Freedom and Christian Mission', in H. A. Gravaas et al. (eds), *Freedom of Belief and Christian Mission*. Oxford: Regnum, 283–4.
Chant, S. with N. Craske (2003), *Gender in Latin America*. New Brunswick, NJ: Rutgers University.
Chapman, C. (2002), *Whose Promised Land?* Oxford: Lion.

Chia, E. K. (2011), 'Malaysia and Singapore', in P. C. Phan (ed.), *Christianities in Asia*. Chichester: Wiley-Blackwell, 77–94.

Chidester, D. (2000), *Christianity*. London: Penguin

Choi, H. A. (2005), *Korean Women and God*. Maryknoll,, NY: Orbis.

Choi, H.-W. (2009), *Gender and Mission Encounters in Korea*. Berkeley: University of California.

Choong, C. P. (2008), 'Studying Christianity and Doing Theology *Extra Ecclesiam* in China', in Sebastian C. H. Kim (ed.), *Christian Theology in Asia*. Cambridge: Cambridge University, 89–108.

Chopp, R. S. (1997a), 'Feminist and Womanist Theologies', in D. F. Ford (ed.), *The Modern Theologians*, second edition. Oxford: Blackwell, 389–404.

Chopp, R. S. (1997b), 'Latin American Liberation Theology', in D. F. Ford (ed.), *The Modern Theologians*. Oxford: Blackwell, 409–25.

Christian Conference of Asia, ed. (1981), *Minjung Theology*. London: Zed.

Chu, C. Y. (2004), *The Maryknoll Sisters in Hong Kong, 1921–1969*. New York: Palgrave Macmillan.

Clapsis, E., ed. (2004), *The Orthodox Churches in a Pluralistic World*. Geneva: World Council of Churches.

Cleary, E. L. (1998), 'Introduction', in E. L. Cleary and H. W. Stewart-Gambino (eds), *Power, Politics and Pentecostals in Latin America*. Boulder, CO: Westview, 1–24.

Cleary, E. L. and H. W. Stewart-Gambino, eds (1998), *Power, Politics and Pentecostals in Latin America*. Boulder, CO: Westview.

Coe, S. (1976), 'Contextualizing Theology', in G. H. Anderson and T. F. Stransky (eds), *Third World Theologies*. New York: Paulist, 19–24.

Cohn-Sherbok, D. (2006), *The Politics of Apocalypse*. London: Oneworld.

Collins, P. M. and B. Ensign-George (2011). *Denomination*. London: T&T Clark.

Cone, J. H. (1990[1970]), *A Black Theology of Liberation*, third edition. Maryknoll, NY: Orbis.

Conradie, E. M. (2015), *The Earth in God's Economy*. Berlin: Lit Verlag.

Cortright, D. (2008), *Peace*. Cambridge: Cambridge University.

Costas, O. (1982), *Christ Outside the Gate*. Maryknoll, NY: Orbis.

Cousins, B. (2004), 'The Russian Orthodox Church, Tatar Christians and Islam', in A. O'Mahony (ed.), *Eastern Christianity*. London: Melisende, 338–71.

Cox, H. (1996), *Fire from Heaven*. London: Cassell.

Cragg, K. (1992), *The Arab Christian*. London: Mowbray.

Cragg, K. (2000), 'Being Made Disciples', in K. Ward and B. Stanley (eds), *The Church Mission Society and World Christianity, 1799–1999*. Grand Rapids, MI: Eerdmans, 120–43.

Cray, G. (2004), *Mission-Shaped Church*. London: Church House.

Cunningham, L. S. (2009), *An Introduction to Catholicism*. Cambridge: Cambridge University.

Curran, C. E. (2002), *Catholic Social Teaching, 1891–Present*. Washington, DC: Georgetown University.

D'Costa, G., ed. (1990), *Christian Uniqueness Reconsidered*. Maryknoll, NY: Orbis.

Dahle, M. S., L. Dahle and K. Jørgensen, eds (2014), *The Lausanne Movement*. Oxford: Regnum.

Daly, M. (1973), *Beyond God the Father*. Boston, MA: Beacon.

Daughrity, D. B. (2015) *To Whom Does Christianity Belong?* Minneapolis, MN: Fortress.

Davidson, A. K. (2000), 'Culture and Ecclesiology', in K. Ward and B. Stanley (eds), *The Church Mission Society and World Christianity, 1799–1999*. Grand Rapids, MI: Eerdmans, 198–227.

Davidson, A. K. (2004), 'The Pacific Is No Longer a Mission Field?', in D. M. Lewis (ed.), *Christianity Reborn*. Grand Rapids, MI: Eerdmans, 133–53.

Davie, G. (1994), *Religion in Britain since 1945*. Oxford: Blackwell.

Davie, G. (2000), *Religion in Modern Europe*. Oxford: Oxford University.

Davie, G. (2002), *Europe: The Exceptional Case*. London: Darton, Longman and Todd.

Davies, D. J. (2003), *An Introduction to Mormonism*. Cambridge: Cambridge University.

Davies, Noel and M. Conway (2008), *World Christianity in the Twentieth Century*. London: SCM.

Davies, Norman (1996), *Europe: A History*. New York: HarperCollins.

Davis, K. (1990), *Emancipation Still Comin'*. Maryknoll, NY: Orbis.

Daye, R. (2004), *Political Forgiveness*. Maryknoll, NY: Orbis.

De Gruchy, J. W. (1995), *Christianity and Democracy*. Cape Town: David Philip.

De Gruchy, J. W. with S. de Gruchy (2004), *The Church Struggle in South Africa*, third edition. London: SCM.

Deberri, E. P. and J. E. Hug (2003), *Catholic Social Teaching*, fourth edition. Maryknoll, NY: Orbis.

Dempster, M. W., B. D. Klaus and D. Petersen (1999), *The Globalization of Pentecostalism*. Oxford: Regnum.

Devanandan, P. D. (1964), *Preparation for Dialogue*. Bangalore: CISRS.

Devasahayam, V., ed. (1997), *Frontiers of Dalit Theology*. Delhi: ISPCK.

Dorrien, G. (1999), 'The Golden Years of Welfare Capitalism', in Gregory Baum (ed.), *The Twentieth Century*. Maryknoll, NY: Orbis, 91–103.

Douglas, J. D., ed. (1975), *Let the Earth Hear His Voice*. Minneapolis, MN: World Wide.

—, ed. (1990), *Proclaim Christ Until He Comes*. Minneapolis, MN: World Wide.

Dowley, T., ed. (2013), *The History of Christianity*, second edition. Oxford: Lion Hudson.

Draper, J. A. (2011), *Eye of the Storm*. London: T&T Clark.

Dries, A. (1998). *The Missionary Movement in American Catholic History*. Maryknoll, NY: Orbis.

Dube, M. W. (2001a), 'Fifty Years of Bleeding', in M. W. Dube (ed.), *Other Ways of Reading*. Atlanta, GA: Society of Biblical Literature, 50–60.

Dube, M. W. (2001b), 'Divining Ruth for International Relations', in Musa W. Dube (ed.), *Other Ways of Reading*. Atlanta, GA: Society of Biblical Literature, 179–95.

Dunn, J. D. G. (2006), *Unity and Diversity in the New Testament*, third edition. London: SCM.

Dupuis, B. (1999), 'After the Bolshevik Revolution', in G. Baum (ed.), *The Twentieth Century*. Maryknoll, NY: Orbis, 27–34.

Dupuis, J. (1997), *Toward a Christian Theology of Religious Pluralism*. Maryknoll, NY: Orbis.

Dussel, E. (1981), *A History of the Church in Latin America*, trans. A. Neely. Grand Rapids, MI: Eerdmans.

Dussel, E. (1990), 'The Real Motives for the Conquest', in L. Boff and V. Elizondo (eds), *1492–1992: The Voice of the Victims*. London: SCM, 30–46.

Ela, J.-M. (1988), *My Faith as an African*. Maryknoll, NY: Orbis.

Elizondo, V. (1997), *Guadalupe, Mother of a New Creation*. Maryknoll, NY: Orbis.

Engelsviken, T., E. Lundeby and D. Solheim, eds (2011), *The Church Going Glocal*. Oxford: Regnum.

England, J. (1996), *The Hidden History of Christianity in Asia*. Delhi: ISPCK.

Epperly, B. G. (2011), *Process Theology*. London: T&T Clark.

Erskine, N. L. (1981), *Decolonizing Theology*. Maryknoll, NY: Orbis.

Erskine, N. L. (2005), *From Garvey to Marley*. Gainesville: University of Florida.

Eshete, T. (2009), *The Evangelical Movement in Ethiopia*. Waco, TX: Baylor University.

Eskridge, L. (2013), *God's Forever Family*. Oxford: Oxford University.

Esquivel, J. (1990), 'Conquered and Violated Women', in L. Boff and V. Elizondo (eds), *1492–1992: The Voice of the Victims*. London: SCM, 68–77.

Farhadian, C. E., ed. (2007), *Christian Worship Worldwide*. Grand Rapids, MI: Eerdmans.

Farhadian, C. E., ed. (2012), *Introducing World Christianity*. Chichester: Wiley-Blackwell.

Fernandes, E. S. (1994), *Toward a Theology of Struggle*. Maryknoll, NY: Orbis.

Fiedler, K. (1994), *The Story of Faith Missions*. Oxford: Regnum.

Fiorenza, E. S. (1983), *In Memory of Her*. London: SCM.

Flynn, G. and P. D. Murray, eds (2012), *Ressourcement*. Oxford: Oxford University.

Foreman, C. W. (1982), *The Island Churches of the South Pacific*. Maryknoll, NY: Orbis.

Francisco, J. M. C. (2011), 'The Philippines', in P. C. Phan (ed.), *Christianities in Asia*. Chichester: Wiley-Blackwell, 96–127.

Fraser, N. and M. Navarro (1996), *Evita*. London: André Deutsch.

Frederiks. M. (2015), 'Religion, Migration and Identity', *Mission Studies* 32(2): 181–202.

Freeman, D. (2015), 'Pentecostalism and Economic Development in Sub-Saharan Africa', in E. Tomalin (ed.), *Handbook of Religions and Global Development*. London: Routledge, 114–26.

Freire, P. (1970[1968]), *Pedagogy of the Oppressed*, trans. M. B. Ramos. New York: Seabury.

Freston, P. (2001), *Evangelicals and Politics in Asia, Africa and Latin America*. Cambridge: Cambridge University.

Frykenberg, R. E. (2008), *Christianity in India*. Oxford: Oxford University.

Gaillardetz, R. R. (2008), *Ecclesiology for a Global Church*. Maryknoll, NY: Orbis.

Gallagher, R. L. (2008), 'The Integration of Mission Theology and Practice', *Mission Studies* 25:185–210

Garnett, J., M. Grimley, A. Harris, W. Whyte and S. Williams, eds (2006), *Redefining Christian Britain*. London: SCM.

Garrard-Burnett, V. (2010), *Terror in the Land of the Holy Spirit*. Oxford: Oxford University.

Garrison, D. (2014), *A Wind in the House of Islam*. Monument, CO: Wigtake.

Gaustad, E. S. and L. E. Schmidt (2002), *The Religious History of America*, second edition. New York: HarperCollins.

Gebara, I. and M. C. Bingemer (1994), 'Mary – Mother of God, Mother of the Poor', in U. King (ed.), *Feminist Theology from the Third World*. London: SPCK, 275–81.

Getui, M. N. (2003), 'Material Things in Contemporary African Society', in J. N. K. Mugambi and A. Nasimiyu-Wasike (eds), *Moral and Ethical Issues in African Christianity*. Nairobi: Acton, 59–72.

Gibaut, J. and K. Jørgensen, eds (2014), *Called to Unity for the Sake of Mission*. Oxford: Regnum.

Gibbs, E. and R. K. Bolger (2006), *Emerging Churches*. Grand Rapids, MI: Baker Academic.

Gifford, P. (1998), *African Christianity*. London: Hurst and Co.

Gifford, P. (2005), 'A View of Ghana's New Christianity', in L. Sanneh and J. A. Carpenter (eds), *The Changing Face of Christianity*. Oxford: Oxford University, 81–96.

Gill, A. (1999), 'The Struggle to be Soul Provider', in Christian Smith and Joshua Pokopy (eds), *Latin American Religion in Motion*. New York: Routledge, 17–42.

Gill, R. (2003), *The 'Empty' Church Revisited*. Aldershot: Ashgate.

Gilley, S. and B. Stanley, eds (2006), *World Christianities c.1815–c.1914*. Cambridge: Cambridge University.

Gilroy, P. (1993), *The Black Atlantic*. London: Verso.

Gispert-Sauch, G. (1997), 'Asian Theology', in D. F. Ford (ed.), *The Modern Theologians*, second edition. Oxford: Blackwell, 455–76.

Gitari, D. (1996), *In Season and Out of Season*. Oxford: Regnum.

Glasser, A. F. (1993), 'Evangelical Missions', in J. M. Phillips and R. T. Coote (eds), *Toward the Twenty-First Century in Christian Mission*. Grand Rapids, MI: Eerdmans, 9–29.

Gonzales, J. L. (2001), *Acts*. Maryknoll, NY: Orbis.

Gooren, H. (2007), 'Pentecostal Conversion Careers in Latin America', in Frans Wijsen and Robert Schreiter (eds), *Global Christianity*. Amsterdam: Rodopi, 157–75.

Gorski, J. F. (2015), 'From "Mission" to "Evangelization"', in P. Grogan and K. Kim (eds), *The New Evangelization*. London: T&T Clark, 31–44.

Gossai, H. and N. S. Murrell, eds (2000), *Religion, Culture, and Tradition in the Caribbean*. London: Macmillan.

Grant, J. (1989), *White Women's Christ and Black Women's Jesus*. Atlanta: Scholars.

Greengrass, M. (2007), 'The Theology and Liturgy of Reformed Christianity', in R. P. Hsia (ed.), *Reform and Expansion 1500–1660*. Cambridge: Cambridge University, 104–24.

Griffiths, P. J., ed. (1990), *Christianity through Non-Christian Eyes*. Maryknoll, NY: Orbis.

Grim, B. J., T. M. Johnson, V. Skirbekk and G. A. Zurlo (2014), *Yearbook of International Religious Demography 2014*. Leiden: Brill, 2014.
Grogan, P. and K. Kim (2015), *The New Evangelization*. London: T&T Clark.
Guder, D. L. (2000), *The Continuing Conversion of the Church*. Grand Rapids, MI: Eerdmans.
Gutiérrez, G. (1984[1983]), *We Drink from Our Own Wells*. Maryknoll, NY: Orbis.
Gutiérrez, G. (1988[1971]), *A Theology of Liberation*, second edition, trans. C. Inda and J. Eagleson. London: SCM.
Gutiérrez, G. (1990), 'Towards the Fifth Centenary', in L. Boff and V. Elizondo (eds), *1492–1992: The Voice of the Victims*. London: SCM, 1–10.
Gutiérrez, G. (1993[1992]), *Las Casas*, trans. Robert R. Barr. Maryknoll, NY: Orbis.
Haas, L. (1999), 'The Catholic Church in Chile', in C. Smith and J. Pokopy (eds), *Latin American Religion in Motion*. New York: Routledge, 43–66.
Hackel, S. (2002), 'The Orthodox Churches of Eastern Europe', in J. McManners (ed.), *The Oxford History of Christianity*. Oxford: Oxford University Press, 539–67.
Halsell, G. (2003), *Forcing God's Hand*. Brentwood, MD: Amana.
Ham, C. E. (2015), 'Emerging Contemporary Contexts of Mission', in M. Alvarez (ed.), *Latin American Mission*. Oxford: Regnum, 235–47.
Hanciles, J. J. (2008), *Beyond Christendom*. Maryknoll, NY: Orbis.
Hanciles, J. J. (2014), 'The Black Atlantic and the Shaping of African Christianity, 1820–1920', in K. Koschorke and A. Herman (eds), *Polycentric Structures in the History of World Christianity*. Wiesbaden: Harrassowitz, 29–50.
Hardesty, N. (2003), *Faith Cure*. Peabody, MA: Hendrickson.
Harding, V. (1996), *Martin Luther King*. Maryknoll, NY: Orbis.
Harrison, H. (2013), *The Missionary's Curse and Other Tales from a Chinese Catholic Village*. Berkeley, CA: University of California.
Hartch, T. (2014), *The Rebirth of Latin American Christianity*. Oxford: Oxford University.
Hastings, A. (1967), *Church and Mission in Modern Africa*. London: Burns and Oates.
Hastings, A. (1976), *African Christianity*. London: Geoffrey Chapman.
Hastings, A. (1979), *A History of African Christianity, 1950–1975*. Cambridge: Cambridge University.
Hastings, A. (1994), *The Church in Africa, 1450–1950*. Oxford: Clarendon.
Hastings, A., ed. (1999a), *A World History of Christianity*. London: Cassell.
Hastings, A. (1999b), 'Latin America', in Adrian Hastings (ed.), *A World History of Christianity*. London: Cassell, 328–68.
Hau'ofa, E. (1993), 'Our Sea of Islands', in E. Waddell, V. Naidu and E. Hau'ofa (eds), *A New Oceania*. Suva, Fiji: The University of the South Pacific, 2–16.
Hauerwas, S. (1999), *After Christendom*. Nashville, TN: Abingdon.
Haustein, J. (2011). *Writing Religious History*. Wiesbaden: Harrassowitz Verlag.
Havea, S. A. (1987), 'Christianity in the Pacific Context', in *South Pacific Theology*. Oxford: Regnum, 11–15.
Haynes, J. (2012), *Religious Transnational Actors and Soft Power*. Aldershot: Ashgate.

Healey, J. (2010), 'The Church across the Border', in A. O'Mahony and E. Loosley (eds), *Eastern Christianity in the Modern Middle East*. London: Routledge, 41–55.
Healey, J. and D. Sybertz (1996), *Towards an African Narrative Theology*. Maryknoll, NY: Orbis.
Hecht, T. (1998), *At Home in the Street*. Cambridge: Cambridge University.
Hedlund, R. E., ed. (2004), *Christianity Is Indian*. Delhi: ISPCK.
Hedlund, R. E., S. Kim and R. B. Johnson (2011), *Indian and Christian*. Delhi: ISPCK.
Heelas, P. and L. Woodhead (2004), *The Spiritual Revolution*. Oxford: Blackwell.
Heimann, M. (1999), 'Christianity in Western Europe from the Enlightenment', in Adrian Hastings (ed.), *A World History of Christianity*. London: Cassell, 458–507.
Heimann, M. (2006), 'Catholic Revivalism in Worship and Devotion', in S. Gilley and B. Stanley (eds), *World Christianities c.1815–c.1914*. Cambridge: Cambridge University, 70–83.
Hempton, D. (2005), *Methodism*. New Haven, CT: Yale University.
Hennelly, A. T., ed. (1990), *Liberation Theology*. Maryknoll, NY: Orbis.
Hezel, F. X. (2012), 'Christianity in Micronesia', in C. E. Farhadian (ed.), *Introducing World Christianity*. Chichester: Wiley-Blackwell, 230–43.
Hick, J. and P. F. Knitter, eds (1987), *The Myth of Christian Uniqueness*. Maryknoll, NY: Orbis.
Hilliard, D. (1999), 'Australasia and the Pacific', in Adrian Hastings (ed.), *A World History of Christianity*. London: Cassell, 508–35.
Hilton, A. J. B. (1988), *The Age of Atonement*. Oxford: Clarendon.
Hinchliff, P. (2002), 'Africa', in John McManners (ed.), *The Oxford History of Christianity*. Oxford: Oxford University, 474–507.
Hofmeyr, J. W. and G. J. Pillay, eds (1994), *A History of Christianity in South Africa, Vol. 1*. Pretoria: Haum Tertiary.
Hollenweger, W. J. (1972), *The Pentecostals*, trans. R. A. Wilson. London: SCM.
Hollenweger, W. J. (1997), *Pentecostalism*. Peabody, MA: Hendrickson.
Holter, K. (2000), 'Africa in the Old Testament', in G. West and M. Dube (eds), *The Bible in Africa*. Leiden: Brill, 569–81.
Hopkins, D. N. (1993), *Shoes That Fit Our Feet*. Maryknoll, NY: Orbis.
Hopkins, D. N. (1999), *Introducing Black Theology of Liberation*. Maryknoll, NY: Orbis.
Hopkins, D. N. (2001), 'The Religion of Globalization', in D. N. Hopkins, L. A. Lorentzen, E. Mendieta and D. Batstone (eds), *Religions/Globalizations*. Durham, NC: Duke University, 7–32.
Horton, R. (1971), 'African Conversion', *Africa*, 41(2):85–108.
Huang, H. (2015), 'Approaching Civil Society under Construction', in P. Z. Huang (ed.), *Yearbook of Chinese Theology 2015*. Leiden: Brill, 215–48.
Hudson, D. D. (2000), *Protestant Origins in India*. Grand Rapids, MI: Eerdmans.
Hulsman, C. and R. Attallah (2015), 'Egypt – the Church under Pressure', in H. A. Gravaas, et al. (eds), *Freedom of Belief and Christian Mission*. Oxford: Regnum, 167–80.
Huntington, S. P. (2005), *Who Are We?*. London: The Free.

Huntington, S. P. (2011), *The Clash of Civilizations and the Remaking of World Order*, third edition. New York: Simon & Schuster.
Hurbon, L. (1990), 'The Slave Trade and Black Slavery in America', in L. Boff and V. Elizondo (eds), *1492–1992: The Voice of the Victims*. London: SCM, 90–100.
Hurbon, L. (2001), 'Pentecostalism and Transnationalisation in the Caribbean', in A. Corten and R. Marshall-Fratani (eds), *Between Babel and Pentecost*. Bloomington: Indiana University, 124–41.
Hwa, Y. (1997), *Mangoes or Bananas?* Oxford: Regnum.
Iliffe, J. (2007), *Africans*, second edition. Cambridge: Cambridge University.
Im, C. H. and A. Yong, eds (2014), *Global Diasporas and Christian Mission*. Oxford: Regnum.
Imo, C. (2008), 'Evangelicals, Muslims, and Democracy', in T. O. Ranger (ed.), *Evangelical Christianity and Democracy in Africa*. Oxford: Oxford University, 37–66.
Ingleby, J. (2010), *Beyond Empire*. Milton Keynes, UK: Author House.
Irvin, D. T. and S. W. Sunquist (2001), *History of the World Christian Movement. Vol I*. Maryknoll, NY: Orbis.
Irvin, D. T. and S. W. Sunquist (2012), *History of the World Christian Movement. Vol II*. Maryknoll, NY: Orbis.
Isasi-Díaz, A. M. (1996), *Mujerista Theology*. Maryknoll, NY: Orbis.
Isichei, E. (1995), *A History of Christianity in Africa*. Grand Rapids, MI: Eerdmans.
Ivereigh, A. (2014), *The Great Reformer*. New York: Henry Holt.
Jacob, A. (2001), 'Jacobite Syrian Orthodox Church, India', in S. W. Sunquist (ed.), *A Dictionary of Asian Christianity*. Grand Rapids, MI: Eerdmans, 405–7.
Jacobsen, D. (2011), *The World's Christians*. Chichester: Wiley-Blackwell.
Jagessar, M. (2007), *Full Life for All*. Zoetermeer: Boekencentrum, 2007.
Jenkins, P. (1996), *Pedophiles and Priests*. Oxford: Oxford University.
Jenkins, P. (2002), *The Next Christendom*. Oxford: Oxford University.
Jenkins, P. (2006), *The New Faces of Christianity*. Oxford: Oxford University.
Jenkins, P. (2007), *God's Continent*. Oxford: Oxford University.
Jenkins, P. (2008), *The Lost History of Christianity*. Oxford: Lion.
Jensen, T. G. (1999), 'Discourses on Afro-Brazilian Religion', in C. Smith and J. Pokopy (eds), *Latin American Religion in Motion*. New York: Routledge, 275–94.
Jin, Z. and Yonghui Qui, eds (2011), *The Blue Book of Religions*. Beijing: Social Sciences Academic.
Johns, J. (2002), 'Christianity and Islam', in John McManners, *The Oxford History of Christianity*. Oxford: Oxford University, 167–204.
Johnson, E. A. (1992), *She Who Is*. New York: Crossroad.
Johnson, T. M. and K. R. Ross, eds (2009), *Atlas of Global Christianity*. Edinburgh: Edinburgh University Press.
Josua, H. (2015), 'The Middle East', in H. A. Gravaas et al. (eds), *Freedom of Belief and Christian Mission*. Oxford: Regnum, 190–213.
Juergensmeyer, M. (2000), *Terror in the Mind of God*. Berkeley: University of California.
Juergensmeyer, M., ed. (2003), *Global Religions*. Oxford: Oxford University.

Kahindi, L. W. (2003), 'The Role of African Churches in Democratization', in G. Wamue and M. M. Theuri (eds), *Quests for Integrity in Africa*. Nairobi: Acton, 125–38.

Kalu, O. U. (2006a), 'Ethiopianism and the Roots of Modern African Christianity', in S. Gilley and B. Stanley (eds), *World Christianities c.1815–c.1914*. Cambridge: Cambridge University, 576–92.

Kalu, O. U. (2006b), 'African Christianity', in Hugh McLeod (ed.), *World Christianities c.1914–c.2000*. Cambridge: Cambridge University, 197–218.

Kalu, O. U. (2008), *African Pentecostalism*. Oxford: Oxford University.

Kalu, O. U. and Alaine Low, eds (2008), *Interpreting Contemporary Christianity*. Grand Rapids, MI: Eerdmans.

Kamsteeg, F. (1999), 'Pentecostalism and Political Awakening in Pinochet's Chile and Beyond', in C. Smith and J. Pokopy (eds), *Latin American Religion in Motion*. New York: Routledge, 187–204.

Kanyoro, M. R. A. (2001), 'Cultural Hermeneutics', in M. W. Dube (ed.), *Other Ways of Reading*. Atlanta, GA: Society of Biblical Literature, 101–13.

Kaoma, K. J. (2015), *Creation Care in Christian Mission*. Oxford: Regnum.

Kärkkäinen, V.-M. (2013), *Christ and Reconciliation*. Grand Rapids, MI: Eerdmans.

Kasibante, A. (1998), 'Beyond Revival', in A. Wingate, K. Ward, C. Pemberton and W. Sitshebo (eds), *Anglicanism*. London: Mowbray, 363–8.

Katoppo, M. (1979), *Compassionate and Free*. Geneva: World Council of Churches.

Kaye, B. (2008), *An Introduction to World Anglicanism*. Cambridge: Cambridge University.

Kee, A. (2006), *The Rise and Demise of Black Theology*. Aldershot: Ashgate.

Kerr, D. A. and K. R. Ross, eds (2009), *Edinburgh 2010: Mission Then and Now*. Oxford: Regnum.

Kim, I.-J. (2003), *History and Theology of Korean Pentecostalism*. Zoetermeer: Boekencentrum.

Kim, K. (2007), *The Holy Spirit in the World*. Maryknoll, NY: Orbis.

Kim, K. (2015), 'Critical Perspectives on Religions – Especially Christianity – in the Development of South Korea Post-1945', in E. Tomalin (ed.), *The Routledge Handbook on Religions and Global Development*. New York: Routledge, 250–65.

Kim, K. and A. Anderson (2011), *Edinburgh 2010: Mission Today and Tomorrow*. Oxford: Regnum.

Kim, R. Y. (2015), *The Spirit Moves West*. Oxford: Oxford University.

Kim, S. C. (2015), 'Vatican II, Culture, and Society', in W. Ma and K. S. Ahn (eds), *Korean Church, God's Mission, Global Christianity*. Oxford, Regnum, 148–59.

Kim, S. C. H. (2003), *In Search of Identity*. Oxford: Oxford University.

Kim, S. C. H. (2011), *Theology in the Public Sphere*. London: SCM.

Kim, S. C. H. and K. Kim (2015), *A History of Korean Christianity*. Cambridge: Cambridge University.

Kim, S. H. and W. Ma, eds (2011), *Korean Diaspora and Christian Mission*. Oxford: Regnum.

King, R. (1999), *Orientalism and Religion*. London: Routledge.

Kinnamon, M. (2004), 'Assessing the Ecumenical Movement', in J. Briggs, M. A. Oduyoye and G. Tsetsis (eds), *A History of the Ecumenical Movement, 1968–2000*. Geneva: World Council of Churches, 51–81.

Kinoti, H. W. (2003), 'The Integrity of Creation', in G. Wamue and M. M. Theuri (eds), *Quests for Integrity in Africa*. Nairobi: Acton, 1–16.

Kirk, J. A. and K. J. Vanhoozer, eds (1999), *To Stake a Claim*. Maryknoll, NY: Orbis.

Kitamori, K. (1965), *Theology of the Pain of God*, fifth edition. Richmond, VA: John Knox.

Klaiber, J. (1998), *The Church, Dictatorships, and Democracy in Latin America*. Maryknoll, NY: Orbis.

Knitter, P. F. (1995), *One Earth Many Religions*. Maryknoll, NY: Orbis.

Knox, Z. and A. Mitrofanova (2014), 'The Russian Orthodox Church', in Lucian N. Leustean (ed.), *Eastern Christianity and Politics in the Twenty-First Century*. Abingdon: Routledge, 38–66.

Kollman, Paul (2010), 'Classifying African Christianities', *Journal of Religion in Africa* 40:3–32.

Komonchak, J. A. (1999), 'Returning from Exile', in Gregory Baum (ed.), *The Twentieth Century*. Maryknoll, NY: Orbis, 35–48.

Kotila, H. (2006), 'Contemporary Worship as an Expression of Post-modern Spirituality', in K. Tirri (ed.), *Religion, Spirituality and Identity*. Bern: Peter Lang, 65–83.

Koyama, K. (1974), *Water Buffalo Theology*. London: SCM.

Kozhuharov, V. (2015), 'Freedom of Religion and Christian Mission in Russia before and after the Era of the Soviet Union', in H. A. Gravaas et al. (eds), *Freedom of Belief and Christian Mission*. Oxford: Regnum, 370–81.

Krindatch, A. D. and J. H. Erickson (2014), 'Orthodox Churches in America', in L. N. Leustean (ed.), *Eastern Christianity and Politics in the Twenty-First Century*. Abingdon: Routledge, 251–79.

Kumari, P., ed. (1993), *A Reader in Feminist Theology*. Madras: Christian Literature Society.

Küng, H. (1995), *Christianity*. London: SCM.

Kung, L. Y. (2005), 'Reconciliation as Trust-Building', in K. Kim (ed.), *Reconciling Mission*. Delhi: ISPCK, 176–200.

Kwok, P.-L. (1992), *Chinese Women and Christianity, 1860–1927*. Atlanta, GA: Scholars.

Kwok, P.-L. (2000), *Introducing Asian Feminist Theology*. Sheffield: Sheffield Academic.

Kyomo, A. A. (2003), 'Faith and Healing in the African Context', in M. Vähäkangas and A. A. Kyomo (eds), *Charismatic Renewal in Africa*. Nairobi: Acton, 145–56.

Lafaye, J. (1976), *Quetzalcoatl and Guadalupe*. Chicago, IL: University of Chicago.

Laksana, A. B. (2014), 'Multiple Religious Belonging or Complex Identity', in F. Wilfred (ed.), *Christianity in Asia*. Oxford: Oxford University, 493–509.

Land, S. J. (1993) *Pentecostal Spirituality*. Sheffield: Sheffield Academic.

Latourette, K. S. (1971 [1945]), *A History of the Expansion of Christianity, Vol. 7*. London: Eyre and Spottiswoode.

Latukefu, S. (1996), 'Pacific Islander Missionaries', in D. Munro and A. Thornley (eds), *The Covenant Makers*. Suva, Fiji: Pacific Theological College, 17–40.

Lawrence, C. H. (2001), *Medieval Monasticism*, third edition. London: Routledge.

Ledyard, G. (2006), 'Kollumba Kang Wansuk, an Early Catholic Activist and Martyr', in R. E. Buswell and T. S. Lee (eds), *Christianity in Korea*. Honolulu: University of Hawai'i, 38–71.

Lee, M. (1999), 'Experience of Religious Plurality in Korea', *International Review of Mission*, 88(351):399–413.

Lee, T. S. (2010), *Born Again*. Honolulu: University of Hawai'i.

Leung, K.-L. (2001), 'China', in S. W. Sunquist (ed.), *A Dictionary of Asian Christianity*. Grand Rapids, MI: Eerdmans, 139–46.

Leustean, L. N. (2010a), 'Eastern Christianity and the Cold War', in L. N. Leustean (ed.), *Eastern Christianity and the Cold War, 1945–91*. Abingdon: Routledge, 1–15.

Leustean, L. N. (2010b), 'The Romanian Orthodox Church', in L. N. Leustean (ed.), *Eastern Christianity and the Cold War, 1945–91*. Abingdon: Routledge, 40–59.

Leustean, L. N. (2014), 'Eastern Christianity and Politics in the Twenty-First Century', in L. N. Leustean (ed.), *Eastern Christianity and Politics in the Twenty-First Century*. Abingdon: Routledge, 1–20.

Liechty, J. and C. Clegg (2001), *Moving beyond Sectarianism*. Blackrock: Columba.

Linden, I. (2012), *Global Catholicism*, second edition. London: Hurst.

Lineham, P. (2013), *Destiny*. Auckland: Penguin.

Ling, P. J. (2002), *Martin Luther King, Jr*. London: Routledge.

Lipner, J. (1999), *Brahmabandhab Upadhyay*. New Delhi: Oxford University.

Liua'ana, F. (1996), 'Erand of Mercy', in D. Munro and A. Thornley (eds), *The Covenant Makers*. Suva, Fiji: Pacific Theological. College, 41–79.

Lo, L.-K. (2011), 'Taiwan, Hong Kong, Macau', in P. C. Phan (ed.), *Christianities in Asia*. Chichester: Wiley-Blackwell, 172–95.

Longkumer, A., J. S. Sorenson and M. Biehl, eds (2016), *Mission and Power*. Oxford: Regnum.

Lowe, C. (1998), *Territorial Spirits and World Evangelisation?* Sevenoaks: OMF.

Ludwig, F. (2002), 'African Independent Churches in West Africa around 1900', in K. Koschorke (ed.), *Transcontinental Links in the History of Non-Western Christianity*. Wiesbaden: Harrassowitz, 259–72.

Lupunin, N. (2010), 'The Russian Orthodox Church', in L. N. Leustean (ed.), *Eastern Christianity and the Cold War, 1945–91*. Abingdon: Routledge, 19–39.

Ma, J. C. (2001). *When the Spirit Meets the Spirits*, second edition. Frankfurt: Peter Lang.

Ma, W. (2011), 'Asian (Classical) Pentecostal Theology in Context', in A. Anderson and E. Tang (eds), *Asian and Pentecostal*. Oxford: Regnum, 49–76.

MacCulloch, D. (2009), *A History of Christianity*. London: Allen Lane.

Maddox, M. (2012), 'Christianity in Australia and New Zealand', in C. E. Farhadian (ed.), *Introducing World Christianity*. Chichester: Wiley-Blackwell, 203–17.

Mafico, T. L. J. (2000), 'The Biblical God of the Fathers and the African Ancestors', in G. West and M. Dube (eds), *The Bible in Africa*. Leiden: Brill, 481–9.

Magesa, L. (2003), 'Charismatic Movements as "Communities of Affliction"', in M. Vähäkangas and A. A. Kyomo (eds), *Charismatic Renewal in Africa*. Nairobi: Acton, 27–44.

Makrides, V. N. (2010), 'The Orthodox Church of Greece', in L. N. Leustean (ed.), *Eastern Christianity and the Cold War, 1945-91*. Abingdon: Routledge, 253–70.

Maluleke, T. S. (1999), 'The South African Truth and Reconciliation Discourse', in L. Magesa and Z. Nthamburi (eds), *Democracy and Reconciliation*. Nairobi: Acton, 215–41.

Mandryk, J. (2010), *Operation World*, seventh edition. Colorado Springs, CO: Biblica.

Manorama, R. (1992), 'Dalit Women', in T. D. Francis and F. J. Balasundaram (eds), *Asian Expressions of Christian Commitment*. Madras: Christian Literature Society, 194–8.

Mariz, C. and C. Mafra (1999), 'Family and Reproduction among Protestants in Rio de Janeiro', in C. Smith and J. Pokopy (eds), *Latin American Religion in Motion*. New York: Routledge, 205–19.

Marostica, M. (1999), 'The Defeat of Denominational Culture in the Argentine Evangelical Movement', in C. Smith and J. Pokopy (eds), *Latin American Religion in Motion*. New York: Routledge, 147–72.

Marsden, G. M. (1991), *Understanding Fundamentalism and Evangelicalism*. Grand Rapids, MI: Eerdmans.

Marsden, G. M. (2006), *Fundamentalism and American Culture*, second edition. Oxford: Oxford University.

Martin, D. (1990), *Tongues of Fire*. Oxford: Blackwell.

Martin, D. (2002), *Pentecostalism*. Oxford: Blackwell.

Martin, M.-L. (1976), *Kimbangu*, trans. D. M. Moore. Grand Rapids, MI: Eerdmans.

Marty, M. and S. Appleby (1992). *The Glory and the Power*. Boston: Beacon.

Marty, M. E. (2002), 'North America', in John McManners (ed.), *The Oxford History of Christianity*. Oxford: Oxford University, 396–436.

Marty, M. E. (2004), 'The Global Context of Ecumenism 1968–2000', in J. Briggs, M. A. Oduyoye and G. Tsetsis (eds), *A History of the Ecumenical Movement, 1968-2000*. Geneva: World Council of Churches, 3–22.

Massam, K. (2006), 'Christian Churches in Australia, New Zealand and the Pacific, 1914–1970', in Hugh McLeod (ed.), *World Christianities c.1914–c.2000*. Cambridge: Cambridge University, 252–61.

Masuzawa, T. (2005), *The Invention of World Religions*. Chicago: Chicago University.

May, M. A. (2004), 'The Unity We Share, the Unity We Seek', in J. Briggs, M. A. Oduyoye and G. Tsetsis (eds), *A History of the Ecumenical Movement, 1968-2000*. Geneva: World Council of Churches, 83–102.

Mayr-Harting, H. (2002), 'The West', in John McManners (ed.), *The Oxford History of Christianity*. Oxford: Oxford University, 101–29.

Mbiti, J. (1969), *African Religions and Philosophy*. London: Heinemann.

Mbiti, J. (1971), *New Testament Eschatology in an African Background*. London: Oxford University.

Mbiti, J. (1976), 'Theological Impotence and the Universality of the Church', in G. H. Anderson and T. F. Stransky (eds), *Third World Theologies*. New York: Paulist, 6–18.
Mbiti, J. (1986), *Bible and Theology in African Christianity*. Nairobi: Oxford University.
McCallum, F. (2010), 'The Maronites in Lebanon', in A. O'Mahony and E. Loosley (eds), *Eastern Christianity in the Modern Middle East*. London: Routledge, 25–40.
McCullum, H. (2004), *The Angels Have Left Us*. Geneva: World Council of Churches.
McDonnell, K. (1975), *The Holy Spirit and Power*. Garden City, NY: Doubleday.
McGavran, D. A. and C. P. Wagner (1990), *Understanding Church Growth*, third edition. Grand Rapids, MI: Eerdmans.
McGuckin, J. A. (2008), *The Orthodox Church*. Oxford: Blackwell.
McLaughlin, R. E. (2007), 'The Radical Reformation', in R. P. Hsia (ed.), *Reform and Expansion 1500–1660*. Cambridge: Cambridge University, 37–55.
McLeod, H. (1997), *Religion and the People of Western Europe, 1789–1989*, second edition. Oxford: Oxford University.
McLeod, H. (2006), 'Introduction', in Hugh McLeod (ed.), *World Christianities c.1914–c.2000*. Cambridge: Cambridge University, 1–14.
McManners, J. (2002), *The Oxford History of Christianity*. Oxford: Oxford University.
Mekonnen, D. R. and K. Tronville (2015), 'Freedom of Belief and the Church in Eritrea', in H. A. Gravaas et al. (eds), *Freedom of Belief and Christian Mission*. Oxford: Regnum, 259–69.
Meneses, E. H. (2006), 'Bearing Witness in Rome with Theology from the Whole Church', in C. Ott and H. Netland (eds), *Globalizing Theology*. Grand Rapids, MI: Baker Academic, 231–49.
Meredith, M. (2006), *The State of Africa*, second edition. London: The Free.
Meyer, B. (1999), *Translating the Devil*. Edinburgh: Edinburgh University.
Micklethwait, J. and A. Wooldridge (2004), *The Right Nation*. London: Penguin.
Middleton, J. R. and B. J. Walsh (1995), *Truth Is Stranger Than It Used to Be*. Downers Grove, IL: InterVarsity.
Míguez, D. (1999), 'Exploring the Argentinian Case', in C. Smith and J. Pokopy (eds), *Latin American Religion in Motion*. New York: Routledge, 221–34.
Milbank, J., C. Pickstock and G. Ward, eds (1999), *Radical Orthodoxy*. London: Routledge.
Miller, D. A. (2015), 'Power, Personalities and Politics', *Mission Studies* 32(1), 66–86.
Min, K.-B. (2004), 'National Identity in the History of the Korean Church', in C.-S. Yu (ed.), *Korea and Christianity*. Fremont, CA: Asian Humanities, 121–43.
Miyahira, N. (2008), 'Christian Theology under Feudalism, Nationalism and Democracy in Japan', in S. C. H. Kim (ed.), *Christian Theology in Asia*. Cambridge: Cambridge University, 109–28.
Miyamoto, Y. (2011), *Beyond the Mushroom Cloud*. New York: Fordham University.
Moffett, S. H. (1998), *A History of Christianity in Asia, Vol. I*, second edition. Maryknoll, NY: Orbis.
Moffett, S. H. (2005), *A History of Christianity in Asia, Vol. II*. Maryknoll, NY: Orbis.

Moltmann, J. (1973), *The Crucified God*, trans. R. A. Wilson and J. Bowden. London: SCM.
Moltmann, J. (1992), *The Spirit of Life*, trans. M. Kohl. London: SCM.
Mombo, E. (2006), 'Kenya Reflections', in T. Brown (ed.), *Other Voices, Other Worlds*. London: Darton, Longman and Todd, 142–53.
Morris, C. (2002), 'Christian Civilization', in John McManners (ed.), *The Oxford History of Christianity*. Oxford: Oxford University, 205–42.
Moyo, A. (2003), 'Material Things in African Society', in J. N. K. Mugambi and A. Nasimiyu-Wasike (eds), *Moral and Ethical Issues in African Christianity*. Nairobi: Acton, 49–57.
Mugambi, J. N. K. (2002), *Christianity and African Culture*. Nairobi: Acton.
Mugambi, J. N. K. and A. Nasimiyu-Wasike, eds (2003), *Moral and Ethical Issues in African Christianity*. Nairobi: Acton.
Mullin, R. B. (1999), 'North America', in Adrian Hastings (ed.), *A World History of Christianity*. London: Cassell, 416–57.
Mullins, M. R. (1998), *Christianity Made in Japan*. Honolulu: University of Hawai'i.
Mullins, M. R. (2014), 'Kagawa Toyohiko (1888–1960) and the Japanese Impact on American Society', in A. L. Park and D. K. Yoo (eds), *Encountering Modernity*. Honolulu: University of Hawai'i, 162–93.
Mulrain, G. M. (2004), 'The Caribbean', in J. Parratt (ed.), *An Introduction to Third World Theologies*. Cambridge: Cambridge University, 163–81.
Murray, J. C. (1960), *We Hold These Truths*. Kansas City, MO: Sheed and Ward.
Murre-van den Berg, H. (2006), 'The Middle East: Western Missions and Eastern Churches, Islam and Judaism', in S. Gilley and B. Stanley (eds), *World Christianities c.1815–c.1914*. Cambridge: Cambridge University, 458–72.
Murrell, N. S. (2000), 'Blackman's Bible and Garveyite Ethiopianist Epic with Commentary', in H. Gossai and N. S. Murrell (eds), *Religion, Culture, and Tradition in the Caribbean*. London: Macmillan, 271–306.
Mwamba, M. T. S. (2000), 'The Evolving Role of the Church', in D. O'Connor and others (eds), *Three Centuries of Mission*. London: Continuum, 395–408.
Mwaura, P. N. (2003), 'African Instituted Churches and Socio-economic Development', in G. Wamue and M. M. Theuri (eds), *Quests for Integrity in Africa*. Nairobi: Acton, 75–94.
Nazir-Ali, M. (1991), *From Everywhere to Everywhere*. London: Collins.
Ndung'u, N. W. (2000), 'The Role of the Bible in the Rise of African Instituted Churches', in Gerald West and Musa Dube (eds), *The Bible in Africa*. Leiden: Brill, 36–47.
Neill, S. (1964), *A History of Christian Missions*. London: Penguin.
Newbigin, L. (1986), *Foolishness to the Greeks*. Grand Rapids, MI: W.B. Eerdmans.
Newbigin, L. (1995a), *The Open Secret*, second editon. Grand Rapids, MI: Eerdmans.
Newbigin, L. (1995b), *Proper Confidence*. Grand Rapids, MI: Eerdmans.
Niebuhr, H. R. (2001[1951]), *Christ and Culture*, second edition. New York: HarperCollins.

Nirmal, A. P. (1988), 'Towards a Christian Dalit Theology', in A. P. Nirmal (ed.), *A Reader in Dalit Theology*. Madras: Christian Literature Society, 53–70.

Noble, I., K. Bauerová, T. Noble and P. Parushev (2015), *The Ways of Orthodox Theology in the West in the Twentieth Century*. Yonkers, NY: St Vladimir's Seminary.

Nolde, O. F. (1993), 'Ecumenical Action in International Affairs', in H. E. Fey (ed.), *The Ecumenical Advance*. Geneva: World Council of Churches, 261–85.

Noll, M. A. (1994), *The Scandal of the Evangelical Mind*. Grand Rapids, MI: Eerdmans.

Noll, M. A. (2001), *American Evangelical Christianity*. Oxford: Blackwell.

Norget, K. (1999), 'Progressive Theology and Popular Religiosity in Oaxaca, Mexico', in C. Smith and J. Pokopy (eds), *Latin American Religion in Motion*. New York: Routledge, 91–110.

Norris, P. and R. Inglehart (2004), *Sacred and Secular*. Cambridge: Cambridge University.

O'Connor, D., ed. (2000), *Three Centuries of Mission*. London: Continuum.

O'Mahony, A. (2010a), 'Introduction', in A. O'Mahony and J. Flannery (eds), *The Catholic Church in the Contemporary Middle East*. London: Melisende, 7–18.

O'Mahony, A. (2010b), 'The Coptic Church in Modern Egypt', in A. O'Mahony and E. Loosley (eds), *Eastern Christianity in the Modern Middle East*. London: Routledge, 56–77.

O'Mahony, A. and J. Flannery, eds (2010), *The Catholic Church in the Contemporary Middle East*. London: Melisende.

O'Mahony, A. and E. Loosley, eds (2010), *Eastern Christianity in the Modern Middle East*. London: Routledge.

O'Malley, J. W. (2010), *What Happened at Vatican II?* Cambridge, MA: Belknap.

Oborji, F. A. (2006), *Concepts of Mission*. Maryknoll, NY: Orbis.

Ochs, P. (1997), 'Judaism and Christian Theology', in D. F. Ford (ed.), *The Modern Theologians*, second edition. Oxford: Blackwell, 607–25.

Oden, T. C. (2007), *How Africa Shaped the Christian Mind*. Downers Grove, IL: InterVarsity.

Oduyoye, M. A. (1986), *Hearing and Knowing*. Maryknoll, NY: Orbis.

Oduyoye, M. A. (2008), 'African Women Theologians', in M. F. Bednarowski (ed.), *Twentieth-Century Global Christianity*. Minneapolis, MN: Fortress, 83–106.

Oduyoye, M. A. and H. M. Vroom, eds (2003), *One Gospel – Many Cultures*. Amsterdam: Rodopi.

Oleksa, M. (1992). *Orthodox Alaska*. Crestwood, NY: St. Vladimir's Seminary

Oliver, E. (1999), 'Response', in A. H. Anderson and W. J. Hollenweger (eds), *Pentecostals after a Century*. Sheffield: Sheffield Academic, 45–7.

Omenyo, C. N. (2003), 'Charismatization of the Mainline Churches in Ghana', in M. Vähäkangas and A. A. Kyomo (eds), *Charismatic Renewal in Africa*. Nairobi: Acton, 5–26.

Ong, E. (1998), 'Anglicanism in West Malaysia', in A. Wingate, K. Ward, C. Pemberton and W. Sitshebo (eds), *Anglicanism*. London: Mowbray, 172–8.

Orevillo-Montenegro, M. (2006), *The Jesus of Asian Women*. Maryknoll, NY: Orbis.

Orobator, A. E., ed. (2011), *Reconciliation, Justice and Peace*. Maryknoll, NY: Orbis.

Paas, S. (2015), 'Americans, Africans, and Australians Coming to Amsterdam', *Mission Studies* 32(1):4–31.

Panikkar, R. (1981), *The Unknown Christ of Hinduism*. London: Darton, Longman and Todd.

Pano, N. (2014), 'The Albanian Autochephalous Church of Albania', in L. N. Leustean (ed.), *Eastern Christianity and Politics in the Twenty-First Century*. Abingdon: Routledge, 231–9.

Park, C.-W. (2011), *Cultural Blending*. London: Continuum.

Parratt, J. (1995), *Reinventing Christianity*. Grand Rapids, MI: Eerdmans.

Parratt, J., ed. (1997), *A Reader in African Christian Theology*, second edition. London: SPCK.

Pearson, C. (2010), 'The Purpose and Practice of a Public Theology in a Time of Climate Change', *International Journal of Public Theology* 4(3):356–72.

Percy, M. (1996), *Words, Wonders and Power*. London: SPCK.

Persoon, J. (2004), 'Between Ancient Axum and Revolutionary Moscow', in A. O'Mahony (ed.), *Eastern Christianity*. London: Melisende, 160–214.

Peyrouse, S. (2014), 'Christian Minorities on the Central Asian Silk Roads', in F. Wilfred (ed.), *Christianity in Asia*. Oxford: Oxford University, 51–64.

Phan, P. C., ed. (2002), *The Asian Synod*. Maryknoll, NY: Orbis.

Phan, P. C., ed. (2003a), *Christianity with an Asian Face*. Maryknoll, NY: Orbis.

Phan, P. C., ed. (2003b), *In Our Own Tongues*. Maryknoll, NY: Orbis.

Phan, P. C., ed. (2011), 'Vietnam, Cambodia, Laos, Thailand', in P. C. Phan (ed.), *Christianities in Asia*. Chichester: Wiley-Blackwell, 128–47.

Phan, P. C. and E. Padilla, eds (2013), *Contemporary Issues of Migration and Theology*. New York: Palgrave Macmillan.

Phan, P. C. and E. Padilla, eds (2014), *Theology of Migration in the Abrahamic Religions*. New York: Palgrave Macmillan.

Phillips, J. M. (1981), *From the Rising of the Sun*. Maryknoll, NY: Orbis.

Phillips, P. T. (1996) *A Kingdom on Earth*. University Park: Pennsylvania State University.

Phiri, I. A. (2008), 'President Frederick Chiluba and Zambia', in T. O. Ranger (ed.), *Evangelical Christianity and Democracy in Africa*. Oxford: Oxford University, 95–129.

Pieris, A. (1988), *An Asian Theology of Liberation*. Maryknoll, NY: Orbis.

Piggin, S. and A. Davidson (2006), 'Christianity in Australasia and the Pacific', in S. Gilley and B. Stanley (eds), *World Christianities, c.1815–c.1914*. Cambridge: Cambridge University.

Pike, F. B. (2002), 'Latin America', in J. McManners (ed.), *The Oxford History of Christianity*. Oxford: Oxford University, 437–73.

Pillay, G. J. (1994), *Religion at the Limits?* Pretoria: University of South Africa.

Pinn, A. H. and A. B. Pinn (2002), *Introduction to Black Church History*. Minneapolis, MN: Fortress.

Pirouet, L. (1978), *Black Evangelists*. London: Collings.

Pirouet, L. (1989), *Christianity Worldwide*. SPCK Church History 4: AD 1800 onwards. London: SPCK.

Placher, W. C. (1997), 'Postliberal theology', in D. F. Ford (ed.), *The Modern Theologians*, second edition. Oxford: Blackwell, 343–56.

Pobee, J. S. and G. Ositelu II (1998), *African Initiatives in Christianity*. Geneva: World Council of Churches.

Podmore, C. (1998), *The Moravian Church in England, 1728–1760*. Oxford: Clarendon.

Pokrovsky, G. (2003), *The Way of a Pilgrim*. London: Darton Longman and Todd.

Porter, A. (2004), *Religion versus Empire*. Manchester: Manchester University.

Porter, M. (1990), *Land of the Spirit?* Geneva: World Council of Churches.

Prior, J. (2011), 'Indonesia', in P. C. Phan (ed.), *Christianities in Asia*. Chichester: Wiley-Blackwell, 60–75.

Prokopy, J. and C. Smith (1999), 'Introduction', in C. Smith and J. Pokopy (eds), *Latin American Religion in Motion*. New York: Routledge, 1–16.

Raboteau, A. J. (2004), *Slave Religion*, second edition. Oxford: Oxford University.

Rack, H. D. (2002), *Reasonable Enthusiast*, third edition. London: Epworth.

Rahner, Karl (1979), 'Towards a Fundamental Theological Interpretation of Vatican II', *Theological Studies* 40(4):716–27.

Rainbow Spirit Elders (2012), *Rainbow Spirit Theology*, second edition. Hindmarsh, South Australia: ATF.

Rajkumar, P. J., J. P. Dayan and I.P. Asheervadham (2014), *Mission at and from the Margins*. Oxford: Regnum.

Rakodi, C. (2015), 'Development, Religion and Modernity', in E. Tomalin (ed.), *Handbook of Religions and Global Development*. London: Routledge, 17–35.

Ramachandra, V. (1996), *The Recovery of Mission*. Carlisle: MARC.

Ramachandra, V. (2006), 'Globalization, Nationalism, and Religious Resurgence', in C. Ott and H. Netland (eds), *Globalizing Theology*. Grand Rapids, MI: Baker Academic, 213–30.

Ransom, R. C. (2002[1905]), 'Duty and Destiny', in A. H. Pinn and A. B. Pinn (eds), *Introduction to Black Church History*. Minneapolis, MN: Fortress, 153–8.

Rassam, S. (2010), 'Iraqi Christians: The Present Situation', in A. O'Mahony and J. Flannery (eds), *The Catholic Church in the Contemporary Middle East*. London: Melisende, 185–207.

Rayan, S. (1985), 'Caesar versus God', in S. Kappen (ed.), *Jesus Today*. Madras: AICUF, 88–97.

Rayan, S. (1989), 'Spirituality for Inter-Faith Social Action', in X. Irudayaraj (ed.), *Liberation and Dialogue*. Bangalore: Claretian Publications, 64–73.

Reid-Salmon, D. A. (2014), *Home Away from Home*, second edition. Abingdon: Routledge.

Reimer, A. J. (1999), 'Theologians in Nazi Germany', in G. Baum (ed.), *The Twentieth Century*. Maryknoll, NY: Orbis, 61–75.

Ribeiro, D. (1990), 'The Latin American People', in L. Boff and V. Elizondo (eds), *1492–1992: The Voice of the Victims*. London: SCM, 13–29.

Richard, P. (1990), '1492: The Violence of God and the Future of Christianity', in L. Boff and V. Elizondo (eds), *1492–1992: The Voice of the Victims*. London: SCM, 59–67.

Richardson, D. (1974), *Peace Child*. Glendale, CA: Regal.

Riseborough, H. (2002), *Days of Darkness*, second edition. Auckland: Penguin.
Robbins, J. (2004), *Becoming Sinners*. Berkeley: University of California.
Robeck, C. M. (2006), *The Azusa Street Mission and Revival*. Nashville, TN: Thomas Nelson.
Robert, D. L. (2000), 'Shifting Southward: Global Christianity since 1945', *International Bulletin of Missionary Research* 24(2):50–8.
Robert, D. L. (2008), 'The First Globalization', in O. U. Kalu and Alaine Low (eds), *Interpreting Contemporary Christianity*. Grand Rapids, MI: Eerdmans, 93–130.
Robert, D. L. (2009), *Christian Mission*. Chichester: Wiley-Blackwell.
Robert, D. L. and M. L. Daneel (2007), 'Worship among Apostles and Zionists in Southern Africa', in C. E. Farhadian (ed.), *Christian Worship Worldwide*. Grand Rapids, MI: Eerdmans, 43–70.
Roberts, J. D. (1987), *Black Theology in Dialogue*. Philadelphia, PA: Westminster.
Robertson, R. (1992), *Globalization*. London: SAGE.
Robinson, D. (2004), *Muslim Societies in African History*. Cambridge: Cambridge University.
Robinson, R. (2003), *Christians of India*. New Delhi: Sage.
Rogers, E. F. (2005), *After the Spirit*. Grand Rapids, MI: Eeerdmans.
Rookes, P. and J. Rookes (2012), *Commitment, Conscience or Compromise*. N.p.: Lap Lambert.
Ross, C. (2005), 'Reflections from "Far Away" Islands', in T. Yates (ed.), *Mission and the Next Christendom*. Sheffield: Cliff College, 147–61.
Ross, C. (2006), *Women with a Mission*. Auckland: Penguin.
Rudolph, S. H. (1997), 'Introduction', in S. H. Rudolph and J. Piscatori (eds), *Transnational Religion and Fading States*. Oxford: HarperCollins, 1–24.
Ruether, R. R. (1983), *Sexism and God-Talk*. London: SCM.
Saayman, W. (1991), *Christian Mission in South Africa*. Pretoria: University of South Africa.
Salinas, M. (1990), 'The Voices of Those Who Spoke Up for the Victims', in L. Boff and V. Elizondo (eds), *1492–1992: The Voice of the Victims*. London: SCM, 101–9.
Samartha, S. (1979), *Guidelines on Dialogue*. Geneva: World Council of Churches.
Samartha, S. (1991), *One Christ – Many Religions*. Maryknoll, NY: Orbis.
Sanneh, L. (1983), *West African Christianity*. London: C. Hurst.
Sanneh, L. (1989), *Translating the Message*. Maryknoll, NY: Orbis.
Sanneh, L. (2003), *Whose Religion Is Christianity?* Grand Rapids, MI: Eerdmans.
Sanneh, L. (2008), *Disciples of All Nations*. Oxford: Oxford University.
Sauer, G. (2008), 'What Does Common Identity Cost', in S. C. H. Kim, P. Kollontai and G. Hoyland, *Peace and Reconciliation*. Aldershot: Ashgate, 21–34.
Schmidt, B. (2008), *Caribbean Diaspora in the USA*. Aldershot: Ashgate.
Schnelle, U. (2005), *Apostle Paul*, trans. by M. E. Boring. Grand Rapids, MI: Baker Academic.
Schreiter, R. J. (1985), *Constructing Local Theologies*. Maryknoll, NY: Orbis.
Schreiter, R. J. (1997), *The New Catholicity*. Maryknoll, NY: Orbis.
Schreiter, R. J. (1998), *The Ministry of Reconciliation*. Maryknoll, NY: Orbis.

Schreiter, R. J. and K. Jørgensen (2013), *Mission as Ministry of Reconciliation*. Oxford: Regnum.

Schröter, S., ed. (2010), *Christianity in Indonesia*. Berlin: Lit Verlag.

Schwarz, H. (2005), *Theology in a Global Context*. Grand Rapids, MI: Eerdmans.

Schweitzer, D. (1999), 'The Great Depression', in G. Baum (ed.), *The Twentieth Century*. Maryknoll, NY: Orbis, 49–60.

Segundo, J. L. (1976), *The Liberation of Theology*, trans. J. Drury. Maryknoll, NY: Orbis.

Selvanayagam, I. (2012), *Being Evangelical and Dialogical*. Delhi: ISPCK.

Sepúlveda, J. (1990), 'Pentecostalism and Liberation Theology', in H. D. Hunter and P. D. Hocken (eds), *All Together in One Place*. Sheffield: Sheffield Academic, 51–64.

Sepúlveda, J. (1999), 'Indigenous Pentecostalism and the Chilean experience', in A. H. Anderson and W. J. Hollenweger (eds), *Pentecostals after a Century*. Sheffield: Sheffield Academic, 111–34.

Sered, D. and Y. Ben-David (2015), in H. A. Gravaas et al. (eds), *Freedom of Belief and Christian Mission*. Oxford: Regnum, 214–26.

Shenk, W., ed. (2004), *North American Foreign Missions, 1810–1914*. Grand Rapids, MI: Eerdmans.

Shorter, A. (1999), 'Inculturation', in J. A. Scherer and S. B. Bevans (eds), *Faith and Culture*. Maryknoll, NY: Orbis, 54–67.

Shorter, A. (2006), *Cross and Flag in Africa*. Maryknoll, NY: Orbis.

Siddiqui, A. (1997), *Christian–Muslim Dialogue in the Twentieth Century*. Basingstoke: Macmillan.

Sider, R. J. (1984), *Rich Christians in an Age of Hunger*, second edition. Downers Grove, IL: InterVarsity.

Siebers, H. (1999), 'Globalization and Religious Creolization among the Q'eqchi'es of Guatemala', in C. Smith and J. Pokopy (eds), *Latin American Religion in Motion*. New York: Routledge, 261–73.

Sizer, S. (2005), *Christian Zionism*. Leicester: IVP.

Skreslet, S. H. (2012), *Comprehending Mission*. Maryknoll, NY: Orbis.

Schmidt-Leukel, P., ed. (2005), *Buddhism and Christianity in Dialogue*. London: SCM.

Smythe, P. A. (2004), *The Heaviest Blow*. Münster: Lit Verlag.

Snodderly. B. and A. S. Moreau (2011), *Evangelical and Frontier Mission*. Oxford: Regnum.

Somaratna, G. P. V. (2012), 'Sri Lanka', in R. E. Hedlund (ed.), *The Oxford Encyclopaedia of South Asian Christianity*. Delhi: Oxford University, 647–50.

Song, C.-S. (1988), *Theology from the Womb of Asia*. London: SCM.

Spencer, S., ed. (2008), *Mission and Migration*. Sheffield: Cliff College.

Spencer, S., ed. (2010), *Anglicanism*. London: SCM.

Stamoolis, J. J. (2001), *Eastern Orthodox Mission Theology Today*. Eugene, OR: Wipf and Stock.

Stanley, B. (1990), *The Bible and the Flag*. Leicester: Apollos.

Stanley, B. (1992), *The History of the Baptist Missionary Society, 1792–1992*. Edinburgh: T. and T. Clark.

Stanley, B. (2009), *The World Missionary Conference, Edinburgh 1910*. Grand Rapids, MI: Eerdmans.
Stanley, B. (2013), *The Global Diffusion of Evangelicalism*. Downers Grove, IL: InterVarsity.
Stark, R. and R. Finke (2000), *Acts of Faith*. Berkeley: University of California.
Steenbrink, K. (2010), 'The Power of Money', in S. Schröter (ed.), *Christianity in Indonesia*. Berlin: Lit Verlag, 105–36.
Steigenga, T. J. and D. A. Smilde (1999), 'Wrapped in the Holy Shawl', in C. Smith and J. Pokopy (eds), *Latin American Religion in Motion*. New York: Routledge, 173–86.
Stern, David H. (1991), *Messianic Jewish Manifesto*, second edition. Clarksville, MD: Jewish New Testament.
Stewart, D. M. (2005), *Three Eyes for the Journey*. Oxford: Oxford University.
Stinton, D. (2004), *Jesus of Africa*. Maryknoll, NY: Orbis.
Stoll, D. (1990), *Is Latin America Turning Protestant?* Berkeley: University of California.
Storaker, K. (2015), 'Mission and Persecution', in H. A. Gravaas et al., *Freedom of Belief and Christian Mission*. Oxford: Regnum, 331–43.
Stout, H. S. (1983), 'The Transforming Effects of the Great Awakening', in M. A. Noll, N. O. Hatch, G. M. Marsden, D. F. Wells and J. D. Woodbridge (eds), *Christianity in America*. Grand Rapids, MI: Eerdmans, 127–30.
Stringer, M. (2005), *A Sociological History of Christian Worship*. Cambridge: Cambridge University.
Sugirtharajah, R. S., ed. (1995), *Voices from the Margin*. Maryknoll, NY: Orbis.
Sugirtharajah, R. S., ed. (2001), *The Bible and the Third World*. Cambridge: Cambridge University.
Sundermeier, T. (1992), 'Convivence', *Scriptura* 10:68–80.
Sunquist, S. W., ed. (2001), *A Dictionary of Asian Christianity*. Grand Rapids, MI: Eerdmans.
Swain, T. and G. Trompf (1995), *The Religions of Oceania*. London: Routledge.
Tacey D. (2004), *The Spirituality Revolution*. New York: Brunner-Routledge.
Tackett, T. (2006), 'The French Revolution and Religion to 1794', in S. J. Brown and T. Tacket (eds), *Enlightenment, Reawakening and Revolution 1660–1815*. Cambridge: Cambridge University, 536–55.
Tamez, E. (1993), *The Amnesty of Grace*, trans. S. H. Ringe. Nashville, TN: Abingdon.
Tang, E. (2011), '"Yellers" and Healers', in A. Anderson and E. Tang (eds), *Asian and Pentecostal*. Oxford: Regnum, 394–410.
Tanner, N. E. (2001), *The Councils of the Church*. New York: Crossroad.
Tanner, N. E. (2002), *Is the Church Too Asian?* Rome: Chavara Institute.
Tate, H. (2013), *He Puna Iti i te Ao Marama*. N.p.: Libro International.
Taylor, M. (2011), *Not Angels But Agencies*. Peterborough: Hymns Ancient & Modern.
Tennent, T. C. (2007), *Theology in the Context of World Christianity*. Grand Rapids, MI: Zondervan.
Ter Haar, G. (1992), *Spirit of Africa*. Trenton, NJ: Africa World.
Ter Haar, G. (1998), *Halfway to Paradise*. Cardiff: Academic.

Theije, M. de (1999), 'CEBs and Catholic Charismatics in Brazil', in C. Smith and J. Pokopy (eds), *Latin American Religion in Motion*. New York: Routledge, 111–24.
Theissen, G. (2003), *The New Testament*. London: T&T Clark.
Thomas, M. M. (1966), *The Christian Response to the Asian Revolution*. London: SCM.
Thomas, M. M. (1997), 'Indian Theology', in K. Müller, T. Sundermeier, S. B. Bevans and R. H. Bliese (eds), *Dictionary of Mission*. Maryknoll, NY: Orbis, 202–12.
Thomas, S. M. (2005), *The Global Resurgence of Religion and the Transformation of International Relations*. New York: Palgrave Macmillan.
Thompson, R. C. (2002), *Religion in Australia*. Oxford: Oxford University.
Thornton, J. K. (2002), 'Rural People, the Church in Kongo and the Afroamerican Diaspora', K. Koschorke (ed.), *Transcontinental Links in the History of Non-Western Christianity*. Wiesbaden: Harrassowitz, 33–44.
Tiedemann, R. G. (1999), 'China and Its Neighbours', in A. Hastings (ed.), *A World History of Christianity*. London: Cassell, 369–415.
Tiénu, T. (2006), 'Christian Theology in an Era of World Christianity', in C. Ott and H. Netland (eds), *Globalizing Theology*. Grand Rapids, MI: Baker Academic, 37–51.
Tinker, G. E. (1994), 'Spirituality and Native American Personhood', in K. C. Abraham and B. Mbuy-Beya (eds), *Spirituality of the Third World*. Maryknoll, NY: Orbis, 119–32.
Tira, S. J. and E. Wan (2014), 'Filipino Diaspora Kingdom Workers', in A. Adogame, J. McLean and A. Jeremiah (eds), *Engaging the World*. Oxford: Regnum, 125–52.
Titaley, J. A. (2008), 'From Abandonment to Blessing', in S. C. H. Kim (ed.), *Christian Theology in Asia*. Cambridge: Cambridge University, 71–88.
Tombs, D. (2002), *Latin American Liberation Theology*. Leiden: Brill.
Trevett, C. (2002), *Montanism*. Cambridge: Cambridge University.
Tsetsis, G. (2004), 'The Significance of Regional Ecumenism', in J. Briggs, M. A. Oduyoye and G. Tsetsis (eds), *A History of the Ecumenical Movement, 1968–2000*. Geneva: World Council of Churches, 461–8.
Turaki, Y. (2006), 'Homosexuality', in T. Adeyemo (ed.), *Africa Bible Commentary*. Grand Rapids, MI: Zondervan, 1355.
Turner, J. G. (2008), *Bill Bright and Campus Crusade for Christ*. Chapel Hill, NC: University of North Carolina.
Ugeux, B. (2006), 'Questions Which New Spiritualities Pose to Evangelization in Europe', *International Review of Mission* 95(378–9): 324–8.
Vaggione, J. M. (2015), 'The Catholic Church, Contemporary Sexual Politics and Development in Latin America', in E. Tomalin (ed.), *Handbook of Religions and Global Development*. London: Routledge, 167–79.
Van Beek, H., ed. (2009), *Revisoning Christian Unity*. Oxford: Regnum.
Van den End, T. (2001), 'Indonesia', in Scott W. Sunquist (ed.), *A Dictionary of Asian Christianity*. Grand Rapids, MI: Eerdmans, 374–80.
Van der Merwe, H. (2003), 'The Role of the Church in Promoting Reconciliation in Post-TRC South Africa', in A. R. Chapman and B. Spong (eds), *Religion and Reconciliation in South Africa*. Philadelphia, PA: Templeton Foundation, 269–81.

Van Elderen, M. (2001), *Introducing the World Council of Churches*. Geneva: World Council of Churches.

Van Gelder, C. (2007), *The Ministry of the Missional Church*. Grand Rapids, MI: Baker.

Van Klinken, A. and E. Chitando (2015), 'Masculinities, HIV and Religion in Africa', in E. Tomalin (ed.), *Handbook of Religions and Global Development*. London: Routledge, 127–37.

Vandana (Mataji) (1991), *Find Your Roots and Take Wing*. Bangalore: ATC.

Vanden Berg, T. M. (2005), 'Culture, Christianity, and Witchcraft in a West African Context', in L. Sanneh and J. A. Carpenter (eds), *The Changing Face of Christianity*. Oxford: Oxford University, 45–62.

Vanhoozer, Kevin J. (2006), 'One Rule to Rule Them All?', in C. Ott and H. Netland (eds), *Globalizing Theology*. Grand Rapids, MI: Baker Academic, 85–126.

Vásquez, M. A. and M. F. Marquardt (2003), *Globalizing the Sacred*. New Brunswick, NJ: Rutgers University Press.

Vassiliadis, P., ed. (2013), *Orthodox Perspectives on Mission*. Oxford: Regnum.

Vernooij, J. (2007), 'Religion in the Caribbean', in F. Wijsen and R. Schreiter (eds), *Global Christianity*. Amsterdam: Rodopi, 147–56.

Vischer, L. (2004), 'Major Trends in the Life of the Churches', in J. Briggs, M. A. Oduyoye and G. Tsetsis (eds), *A History of the Ecumenical Movement, 1968–2000*, 23–50.

Visser 't Hooft, W. A. (1993), 'The Genesis of the World Council of Churches', in R. Rouse and S. C. Neill (eds), *A History of the Ecumenical Movement, 1517–1948*, fourth edition. Geneva: World Council of Churches, 697–724.

Volf, M. (1996), *Exclusion and Embrace*. Nashville, TN: Abingdon.

Vysotskaya, A. (2015), 'Is the Silk Road Still Open?', in H. A. Gravaas et al. (eds), *Freedom of Belief and Christian Mission*. Oxford: Regnum, 309–19.

Wacker, G. (2001), *Heaven Below*. Cambridge, MA: Harvard University.

Währisch-Oblau, C. (2012), *The Missionary Self-Perception of Pentecostal/Charismatic Church Leaders from the Global South in Europe*. Leiden Brill.

Währisch-Oblau, C. and F. Mwombeki, eds (2010), *Mission Continues*. Oxford: Regnum.

Wagner, P. C. (1989), 'Territorial Spirits and World Missions', *Evangelical Missions Quarterly* 25(3):278–88.

Wagner, P. C., ed. (1986), *Church Growth*. Wheaton, IL: Tyndale House.

Wagua, A. (1990), 'Present Consequences of the European Invasion of America', in L. Boff and V. Elizondo (eds), *1492–1992: The Voice of the Victims*. London: SCM, 47–56.

Wall, A. F. (1996), *The Missionary Movement in Christian History*. Maryknoll, NY: Orbis.

Wallis, J. (2005), *God's Politics*. New York: HarperCollins.

Walls, A. F. (2002a), *The Cross-Cultural Process in Christian History*. Maryknoll, NY: Orbis.

Walls, A. F. (2002b), 'Sierra Leone, African American Remigration and the Beginnings of Protestantism in West Africa', in K. Koschorke (ed.), *Transcontinental Links in the History of Non-western Christianity*. Wiesbaden: Harrassowitz, 45–56.

Walls, A.F. and C. Ross, eds (2008), *Mission in the 21st Century*. London: Darton, Longman and Todd.
Walters, A. S. (2002), *We Believe in One God?* Delhi: ISPCK.
Walters, P. (1999), 'Eastern Europe since the fifteenth century', in Adrian Hastings (ed.), *A World History of Christianity*. London: Cassell, 282–327.
Walters, P. (2006), 'The Revolutions in Eastern Europe and the Beginnings of the Post-Communist Era', in Hugh McLeod (ed.), *World Christianities c.1914–c.2000*. Cambridge: Cambridge University, 348–65.
Ward, B. and G. R. Evans (1999), 'The Medieval West', in Adrian Hastings (ed.), *A World History of Christianity*. London: Cassell, 110–46.
Ward, H. N. (2012), 'Naitō Julia and Women Catechists in the Jesuit Mission in Japan and the Philippines', in C. Liennemann-Perrin, A. Longkumer and A. S. Joye (eds), *Putting Names with Faces*. Nashville, TN: Abingdon, 247–58.
Ward, Keith (1998), *Concepts of God*. London: OneWorld.
Ward, Kevin (1999), 'Africa', in A. Hastings (ed.), *A World History of Christianity*. London: Cassell, 192–237.
Ward, Kevin (2006), *A History of Global Anglicanism*. Cambridge: Cambridge University.
Ward, K. and B. Stanley, eds (2000), *The Church Mission Society, 1799–1999*. Grand Rapids, MI: Eerdmans.
Ward, K. and E. Wild-Wood, eds (2012), *The East African Revival*. Farnham, UK: Ashgate.
Ware, T. (1993), *The Orthodox Church*, second edition. London: Penguin Books.
Warner, M. (1985), *Alone of All Her Sex*. London: Picador.
Warrior, R. A. (1995), 'A Native American Perspective', in R. S. Sugirtharajah (ed.), *Voices from the Margin*, second edition. London: SPCK, 277–85.
Weber, M. (1930[1905]), *The Protestant Ethic and the Spirit of Capitalism*. London: George Allen and Unwin.
Wedderburn, A. J. M. (2004), *A History of the First Christians*. London: T&T Clark.
Wells, K. M. (1990), *New God, New Nation*. Honolulu: University of Hawai'i.
Werner, D., D. Esterline, N. Kang and J. Raja, eds (2010), *Handbook of Theological Education in World Christianity*. Oxford: Regnum.
Werpehowski, W. (1997), 'Theological Ethics', in D. F. Ford (ed.), *The Modern Theologians*, second edition. Oxford: Blackwell, 311–26.
Wessels, A. (1994), *Europe, Was It Ever Really Christian?* London: SCM.
Wessels, A. (1995), *Arab and Christian?* Kampen: Kok Pharos.
Wessels, A. (2006), *Muslims and the West*, trans. John Bowden. Leuven: Peeters.
West, C. (1979), 'Black Theology and Marxist Thought', in G. S. Wilmore and J. H. Cone, *Black Theology*. Maryknoll, NY: Orbis, 552–67.
White, J. F. (2001), *Introduction to Christian Worship*, third edition. Nashville, TN: Abingdon.
Wiarda, H. J. (2001), *The Soul of Latin America*. New Haven, CT: Yale Divinity.
Wickeri, P. L. (1988), *Seeking the Common Ground*. Maryknoll, NY: Orbis.
Wickeri, P. L. (2007), *Reconstructing Christianity in China*. Maryknoll, NY: Orbis.
Wild-Wood, E. (2008), *Migration and Christian Identity in Congo*. Leiden: Brill.

Wilfred, F. (2014), 'South Asian Christianity in Context', in F. Wilfred (ed.), *Christianity in Asia*. Oxford: Oxford University, 31–50.

Williams, L. L. (1994), *Caribbean Theology*. Frankfurt: Peter Lang.

Williams, P. (1990), *America's Religions*. New York: Macmillan.

Wilson, E. A. (1999), 'They Crossed the Red Sea, Didn't They?', in M. W. Dempster, B. D. Klaus and D. Petersen (eds), *The Globalization of Pentecostalism*. Oxford: Regnum, 85–115.

Wingeier-Rayo, P. (2013), 'Migration and the Growth of Evangelical Christianity', in A. Adogame and S. Shankar (eds), *Religion on the Move!* Leiden: Brill, 385–94.

Wink, W. (1998), *The Powers That Be*. New York: Doubleday.

Woodberry, R. D. (2012), 'The Missionary Roots of Liberal Democracy', *American Political Science Review* 106(2):244–74.

Woodhead, L. (2004), *Christianity*. Oxford: Oxford University.

Woodhead, L. and R. Catto, eds (2012), *Religion and Change in Modern Britain*. London: Routledge.

Xi, Lian (2010), *Redeemed by Fire*. New Haven, CT: Yale University.

Yates, T. (1994), *Christian Mission in the Twentieth Century*. Cambridge: Cambridge University.

Yates, T. (2013), *The Conversion of the Maori*. Grand Rapids, MI: Eerdmans.

Yang, F. (2012), *Religion in China*. Oxford: Oxford University.

Ying, F.-T. (2011), 'Mainland China', in P. C. Phan (ed.), *Christianities in Asia*. Chichester: Wiley-Blackwell, 148–70.

Yoder, J. H. (1972), *The Politics of Jesus*. Grand Rapids, MI: Eerdmans.

Yong, A. (2005), *The Spirit Poured Out on All Flesh*. Grand Rapids, MI: Baker Academic.

Yong, A. and E. Y. Alexander, eds (2012), *Afro-Pentecostalism*. New York: New York University.

Yong, A. with J. A. Anderson (2014), *Renewing Christian Theology*. Waco, TX: Baylor University.

Yu, C.-S., ed. (1996), *The Founding of Catholic Tradition in Korea*. Mississauga, Ontario: Korea and Related Studies.

Wilfred, F. [illegible] Asia, 'The [illegible]', in F. Wilfred (ed.) [illegible]
[illegible] (2014), [illegible]
Williams, [illegible] Handbook [illegible]
Williams, [illegible] Religion, New York: [illegible]
Wilson, [illegible] (2017) 'They Crossed the Red Sea, Didn't They?' in M. [illegible]
[illegible] and [illegible] Research Guide, [illegible]
Oxford: [illegible]
Wingate, [illegible] and the Growth of [illegible]
[illegible] 1 [illegible] Religion [illegible]
Wittgenstein, [illegible]
[illegible] Contemporary [illegible]
[illegible]
[illegible]
Woodhead, [illegible] Religion [illegible]
[illegible]
[illegible] Dharma [illegible]
Wright, [illegible] Teaching [illegible], Cambridge: Cambridge
[illegible]
Young, [illegible]
[illegible]
[illegible]
[illegible] Blackwell [illegible]
[illegible]
[illegible] (2004), [illegible]
[illegible] (2013), [illegible], New York: [illegible]
[illegible]
[illegible] (2017), [illegible]
[illegible]
[illegible] (1996), The Founding of [illegible]
[illegible] and Related Studies.

Index